D1171745

The Causes and Cures of Criminality

PERSPECTIVES ON INDIVIDUAL DIFFERENCES

CECIL R. REYNOLDS, *Texas A&M University, College Station*
ROBERT T. BROWN, *University of North Carolina, Wilmington*

Recent volumes in the series

THE CAUSES AND CURES OF CRIMINALITY
Hans J. Eysenck and Gisli H. Gudjonsson

HANDBOOK OF MULTIVARIATE EXPERIMENTAL PSYCHOLOGY
Second Edition
Edited by John R. Nesselroade and Raymond B. Cattell

HISTORICAL FOUNDATIONS OF EDUCATIONAL PSYCHOLOGY
Edited by John A. Glover and Royce R. Ronning

THE INDIVIDUAL SUBJECT AND SCIENTIFIC PSYCHOLOGY
Edited by Jaan Valsiner

LEARNING STRATEGIES AND LEARNING STYLES
Edited by Ronald R. Schmeck

METHODOLOGICAL AND STATISTICAL ADVANCES IN THE STUDY OF INDIVIDUAL DIFFERENCES
Edited by Cecil R. Reynolds and Victor L. Willson

THE NEUROPSYCHOLOGY OF INDIVIDUAL DIFFERENCES
A Developmental Perspective
Edited by Lawrence C. Hartlage and Cathy F. Telzrow

PERSONALITY DIMENSIONS AND AROUSAL
Edited by Jan Strelau and Hans J. Eysenck

THEORETICAL FOUNDATIONS OF BEHAVIOR THERAPY
Edited by Hans J. Eysenck and Irene Martin

A Continuation Order Plan is available for this series. A continuation order will bring delivery of each new volume immediately upon publication. Volumes are billed only upon actual shipment. For further information please contact the publisher.

The Causes and Cures of Criminality

Hans J. Eysenck and Gisli H. Gudjonsson
Institute of Psychiatry
University of London
London, England

Plenum Press • New York and London

Library of Congress Cataloging in Publication Data

Eysenck, H. J. (Hans Jurgen), 1916–
The causes and cures of criminality.

(Perspectives on individual differences)
Bibliography: p.
Includes index.
1. Criminal psychology. 2. Crime prevention. 3. Rehabilitation of criminals. I. Gudjonsson, Gisli H. II. Title. III. Series.
HV6080.E89 1988 364.3′01′9 88-28898
ISBN 0-306-42968-3

First Printing – February 1989
Second Printing – March 1991

A Division of Plenum Publishing Corporation
233 Spring Street, New York, N.Y. 10013

Printed in the United States of America

Sedulo curavi humanas actiones non ridere,
non lugere, neque detestari, sed intelligere.
SPINOZA

(I have made a ceaseless effort not to ridicule, not to bewail,
nor to scorn human actions, but to understand them.)

Foreword

The title that the authors have chosen for this book, *The Causes and Cures of Criminality*, suggests that it may be just another book speculating on the sociological evils that need to be put right for "everything in the garden to be lovely." If this is the expectation, the reader could not be more mistaken.

The recurrent theme, in fact, is a strong accent on psychological experiments. Both authors have tackled the theoretical and practical side of crime through an exhaustive literature review of past experimental work. Hans J. Eysenck has concentrated on the constitutional and biological theory of criminality, whereas Gisli Gudjonsson has concerned himself more with a review of ongoing research into therapy and possible prevention of antisocial behavior.

Part I goes into considerable detail on the causes of criminality, stressing much of the strangely neglected area of individual differences in personality. Research studies point to a very heavy involvement of heredity in the causation of criminality, but the authors are careful to acknowledge that much can be done environmentally to discourage a life of crime once those persons who are at risk have been identified.

Probably one of the most common pronouncements currently made in criminology is that "nothing works," i.e., nothing will deter antisocial behavior, whatever you do. Hence it is cheering to meet the following comment in this book: "The notion that 'nothing works' is erroneous and misleading. What is important is identifying factors that can differentiate between successful and unsuccessful intervention outcome."

In Part II, sentencing effectiveness and prevention and treatment of illegal behavior are discussed by Gudjonsson, who, as Senior Lecturer in Forensic Psychology, has had much court experience. Here, too, it is refreshing to detect an optimistic confidence in "cure," provided psychological theories and individual differences are taken into account—particularly because sentencers, at all levels, are often told by criminologists (especially those who rely heavily on sociological arguments) that it really does not matter what they do, crime will increase anyhow.

My own personal view, as a magistrate, is that our society intervenes far too late in the process of antisocial behavior as this develops in children. It is much easier, and more viable, to make strict rules in the home and at school and *enforce* these, than to try weird and wonderful rehabilitation programs on adults whose lives have been ruined by society's permissive unwillingness to get involved until it is too late for the life habit of crime to be reversed. This is, perhaps, why the judiciary feels that it is too late by the time offenders come to court after years of "wrongdoing," i.e., antisocial habits have been so leniently dealt with as to suggest reinforcement rather than deterrence.

The Causes and Cures of Criminality explains the psychological and biological mechanisms behind the formation of criminality in certain people who are at risk to develop this sort of inevitably self-defeating behavior. Furthermore, it sets out possible early interventions to discourage this tendency before antisocial behavior becomes an accepted life-style. It is hoped that readers of this book will be convinced of the need to take the psychological component into account, in both the causes and the cures of criminality.

Sybil B. G. Eysenck
Institute of Psychiatry
University of London
London, England

Preface

This is not a textbook of criminology. It is a book about psychological problems and issues related to crime, and because crimes are committed by people, we believe that psychology is a fundamental discipline which underlies any advances we may make in the prevention of crime, and the treatment of criminals. Among the questions to be discussed, therefore, are such important issues as the existence and nature of the crime-prone personality, the relative influence of genetic and environmental factors on criminality, the way in which different types of punishment determine the future conduct of criminals, and the like. These are all important issues, and we have tried to adduce as much factual evidence as is available at the moment, and to come to some provisional conclusions on these points.

Our main concern has been with the individual, his intelligence, his personality, and other similar factors which largely decide whether he will drift into crime, remain a criminal, or pursue a socially less undesirable career. There has been a distinct change in the academic climate, where after a period of unqualified belief in the insight and predictive possibility of clinical judgements of psychiatrists and psychologists the actual failure of mental health experts in the field had led to a very negative approach. Thus in 1974, a task force of the American Psychological Association concluded that "the state of the art regarding predictions of violence is very unsatisfactory. The ability of psychiatrists or any other professionals to reliably predict future violence is unproved" (p. 30). Several years later, in 1978, a task force of the American Psychological Association concluded in an even more categorical fashion that "the validity of psychological predictions of dangerous behavior . . . is extremely poor, so poor that one could oppose their use on the strictly empirical ground that psychologists are not professionally competent to make such judgements" (p. 10). In addition, the failure of standardized psychometric tests, such as the MMPI, in predictive studies had led to the conclusion that it was neither possible nor wise to predict dangerous or violent behavior (Monahan, 1981).

In recent years, following the demonstration by Paul Meehl (1954) that statistical prediction is more relevant than clinical prediction, this situation has changed very greatly. As Duckitt (1988) has shown, such actuarial predictions in the case of criminal conduct and violence, based on actual conduct-related items, have been extremely successful. Consider just as an example the work of Fischer (1983, 1984), working in the State of Iowa prison system. His formula uses six base predictor scores derived from the offender's current offenses, subsequent abuse involvement, history of violence, escapes, and prior offenses, which are combined additively and interactively to classify offenders into five empirically derived risk categories. One study looked at the percentage of individuals committing new violent offenses three years after being released: 64% of those scored "very poor risks" were arrested for new violent offenses, and 43% of those scored "poor risks." However, only 13% of those scored "fair risks," 7% scored "good risks," and 2% scored "excellent risks" received new violent charges. This gives an overall accuracy rate for very poor risk as opposed to fair, good, and excellent of 81%. When a more inclusive criterion is used, the predictive accuracy accounted for 87.5% of the total new violence in the entire sample.

In the face of such figures, it should hardly be necessary to argue the case for a wider use of psychological expertise in the prison system. There have been similar changes in the general climate with respect to the importance of genetic factors, which are now widely admitted to be important and which contribute well over half of the total variance as far as criminal behavior is concerned. There has been a recognition that personality factors are of very great importance, and even the doctrine of "stigmata," although in a very revised form, has made a successful return. These are some of the themes which are treated in this book, and we hope to persuade the reader that a new wind is blowing through these fields, driving away many miasmas of ideological preconceptions and theoretical biases.

Throughout we have laid stress on one particular point, namely the importance of factual, empirical, and, if possible, experimental evidence. As David Hume wrote, so many years ago: "If we take in our hand any volume, let us ask, Does it contain any abstract reasoning concerning quantity or number? No. Does it contain any experimental reasoning concerning matter of fact and existence? No. Commit it then to the flames; for it can contain nothing but sophistry and delusion." We have tried to avoid sophistry and delusion by concentrating on empirical fact. Clearly the evidence is not all in on any of the topics discussed, but there is now sufficient evidence to give us a clear indication of what are viable, and what are defunct directions of research. Gradually criminology is becoming a science, rather than being a football kicked about by ideological partisans of one persuasion or another. Our aim has been to accelerate this process, and we hope to persuade the reader of the value of the material collected together.

REFERENCES

American Psychiatric Association. *Clinical aspects of the violent individual.* Washington, D.C.: American Psychiatric Association,

American Psychological Association. Report of the task force on the role of psychology in the criminal justice system. *American Psychologist*, 1978, *33*, 1099–1113.

Duckitt, J.H. The prediction of violence. *South African Journal of Psychology*, 1988, *18*, 10–18.

Fischer, D.R. The impact of objective parole criteria on parole release rates and public protection. Des Moines, Iowa: Iowa Office for Planning and Programing, 1983.

Fischer, D.R. Prediction and incapacitation: Issues and answers. Paper presented at the annual meeting of the American Society of Criminology, 1984. Quoted by Duckitt, 1988.

Meehl, P. *Clinical versus statistical prediction: A theoretical analysis and review of the evidence.* Minneapolis: University of Minnesota Press, 1954.

Monahan, J. *Predicting violent behavior: An assessment of clinical techniques.* Beverly Hills, California: Sage, 1981.

Contents

PART TWO: SENTENCING, PUNISHMENT, AND REHABILITATION

CHAPTER ONE

Introduction to Personality and Individual Differences

In this book we attempt to give a factual account of the causes of criminality, a term we understand to mean the entire social behavior of people who violate the laws of their country. This is not a book on crime, which would have to be much more inclusive, taking into account sociological, economic, judicial, political, and other factors. We have concentrated on psychological causes of crime, not only because as psychologists we are more competent to deal with these factors, but also because we believe that they have been relatively neglected in recent years and require explicit statement and justification. This we have tried to provide. It should be noted that our concentration on psychological causes should not be interpreted to mean that other factors are not important, or do not require study.

We should also note, however, that in many ways we disagree with various sociological theories that have become widely popular since World War II but which, we believe, are fundamentally erroneous and counter to fact. Let us first of all consider the definition of crime itself, because here we find ourselves in opposition to many sociological theories that would seem to deny the objective nature of any definition of crime that has been given, or can be given. Taking (rather arbitrarily) *The New Criminology* by Taylor, Walton, and Young (1973) as an example of modern sociological writing, we find there an argument that "crime" is essentially defined by political *fiat* by the power of the state, in a rather arbitrary fashion, dependent on the particular economic and social interests of those in power at the moment as representatives of a given social class. The authors argue quite consciously "for a political economy of criminal action, and of the reaction it excites, and for a politically-informed social psychology of these on-going social dynamics" (p. 279). According to this view, there is no objective definition of crime, and the frequent changes in actions defined as criminal or not would seem to lend substance to their case.

It seems difficult to accept this view in light of the fact that the same types of antisocial activities (e.g., theft, burglary, physical attacks, murder, rape) have from the beginning of time been outlawed in practically all those societies of which we have knowledge. In other words, there is a large body of behavior that is universally condemned as "criminal" irrespective of the social system involved. Ancient Rome and Greece, feudal England and France, Third World nations as well as capitalist or communist modern countries, equally outlaw these practices; this universality may be regarded as sufficient evidence to justify our view that an objective definition of crime is possible.

The notion of subjectivity is given apparent support by a failure to discriminate between two very different types of "crime," which may be labeled victimless and victimful—terms that are inelegant but necessary in this connection (Ellis, 1988)! Victimful crimes are those committed against specified persons, leading to definite loss or injury to the victim. It is this class of crimes, generally understood by the average person as constituting the vast majority of what he or she considers crimes and what are considered crimes by the state, which constitutes the objective core of our conception of "crime," and it is to a clarification of the psychological factors involved in committing such crimes that this book is dedicated.

In contrast, victimless crimes are subjectively defined by religious and other persons who wish to use the power of the state in order to enforce behavior consonant with their own religious, moral, or ethical views. As these views change, so does the definition of these activities as criminal or noncriminal. Examples are easy to find. Prostitution is one obvious example; women selling their favors for money, or men buying such favors, are not committing a crime in the sense that they are directly injuring anyone. Attitudes have varied from the requirements of temple prostitution, forcing all adolescent girls to prostitute themselves at least once, through the relatively liberal legal permission of prostitution in Germany and England, to the illiberal prohibition of prostitution in the United States to the insane cruelties of the Middle Ages when prostitutes were publicly whipped, had their heads shaven, tar poured upon them, and were sometimes even executed (Bargon, 1982).

It is particularly in relation to sex where the law is often invoked to enforce prevailing systems of morality and to act as a preventive agent to "sin"; homosexuality as well as prostitution and adultery (which is still illegal in New York!) are the prime examples, but even quite specific sexual acts may be the subject of legal action. Thus in Georgia oral and anal sex are legally prohibited, even between married partners!

Victimless "crimes" of this kind are so defined in different ways by different societies and are subject to differing moral and ethical value systems.

It is not only sexual behavior that has been made the subject of victimless criminalization. The Volstead Act made the selling and consumption of alcoholic drinks illegal during Prohibition in the United States, and in Muhammadan countries even the possession of beer or a bottle of wine may lead to extreme penalties. Smoking has often been legally prohibited, with penalties of flogging, ear slitting, and the like. It is indeed difficult to think of any pleasure-giving activity that has not at some time or other, in some place or other, been condemned as immoral and made punishable by law.

It is perhaps oversimplifying things to present the difference between victimful and victimless crimes as an absolute. We are probably dealing with a continuum, the respective ends of which are clearly marked, but where there is some gray area between the extremes. Traffic offenses, such as drunken driving or illegal parking, are difficult to classify. If the drunken driver hits a pedestrian or another vehicle, there is indeed a victim; but if he or she does not, it is still possible to argue that the driver's activity is socially harmful to others—at least potentially—and should therefore be punished. Pretending to love a woman in order to have sex with her is certainly a victimful type of behavior, but is not usually reckoned to be subject to criminal prosecution. There are many acts along the continuum from altruistic behavior through normal conduct to victimless but possibly antisocial behavior to victimful behavior in criminality. We are here concerned only with the victimful end and the objectivity of its definition. It seems likely that much of what we have to say about victimful criminality will also be true, in a somewhat muted fashion, of victimless behavior judged by most people to be antisocial, but we will not stress this point. Sociologists usually cite the vagaries of judicial procedures with respect to victimless crime as evidence of subjectivity, but such examples do not alter the fact that victimful crimes are practically universally condemned in all societies and hence deserve to be considered as an objectively definable class of actions.

Let us next turn to a class of theories of crime that has been very popular in recent years and that contrasts powerfully with the psychological theories we will be dealing with in this book. These are sociological theories, often derived from Marxian writings, which are essentially *situational*. There has been a good deal of controversy in psychology generally about the respective contribution of situational and personality factors to specific types of activity, leading to the commonsense conclusion that both, and their interaction, have to be studied in order to

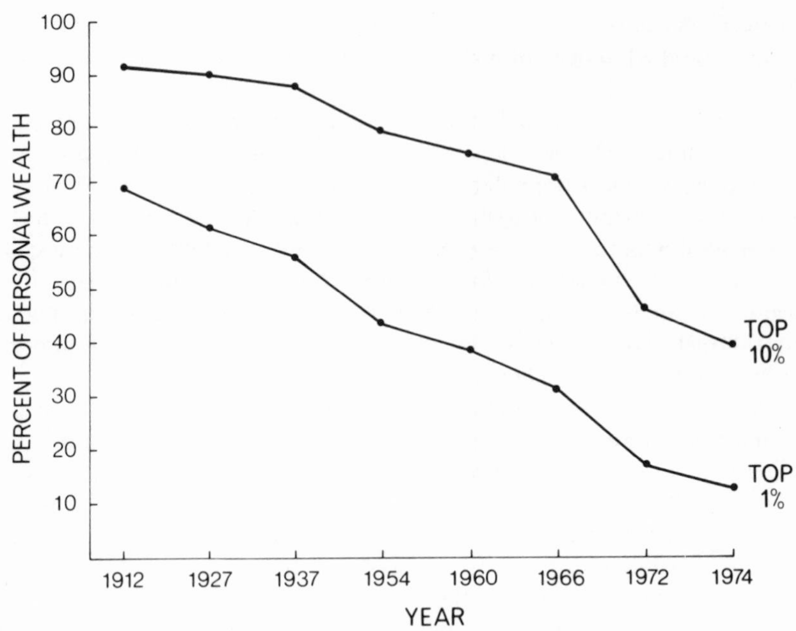

FIGURE 1. Percent of personal wealth owned by top 10% and top 1% of the population, from 1912 to 1974, in Great Britain.

come to any meaningful conclusions (M. W. Eysenck & H. J. Eysenck, 1980, 1985). Both situational and personality-oriented theories have to be studied empirically in order to see to what extent they make a contribution to the explanation of specific types of conduct and to what extent they interact.

Many—if not most—sociological theories boil down to what might be called *economic* theories, i.e., crime as the result of poverty, whether relative or absolute, deprivation, and similar economic causes. Although such theories have always had an intuitive appeal, they do not accord with the facts. Consider Figure 1, which looks at relative poverty. During the period examined, the share of personal wealth of the top 10% of the population in Great Britain fell from over 90% to just about 40% and that of the top 1% from almost 70% to something like 13%. Yet during the latter part of this period, crimes certainly rose rather than fell. It is difficult to know very much about the earlier part of the curve because records were kept in a different way at that time.

How about absolute poverty? Consider the years from 1979 to 1987, during which there was a particularly steep rise in crime. At the beginning of this period, only half of the population owned their own homes; at the end the figure was two thirds. At the beginning of the period, only 7% of the voters owned shares of stock but at the end over 20% of the electorate were shareholders. Car ownership increased from 54% to over 66%, and 81% of families by 1987 had telephones, compared with 67% in 1979. In 1979, just over 30% of the country had the sort of jobs, income, and life-style to make them "middle class"; today the term "middle class" could apply to at least 40% of the population. Union membership, a good index of deprivation and class conflict, dropped from 13.3 million to 9.7 million. Altogether there has been what Marx might nowadays describe as the "bourgeoization of the proletariat," which according to sociological and economic theories of crime should have led to a marked decrease, but what we have observed is a considerable increase. Thus the facts go counter to the theory. These figures are for England, but similar ones apply in the United States.

This improvement in living conditions should have led to a *decline* in crime, according to sociological and economic theories, but instead we have had a continuous *increase*. Figure 2 shows data for England, Fig-

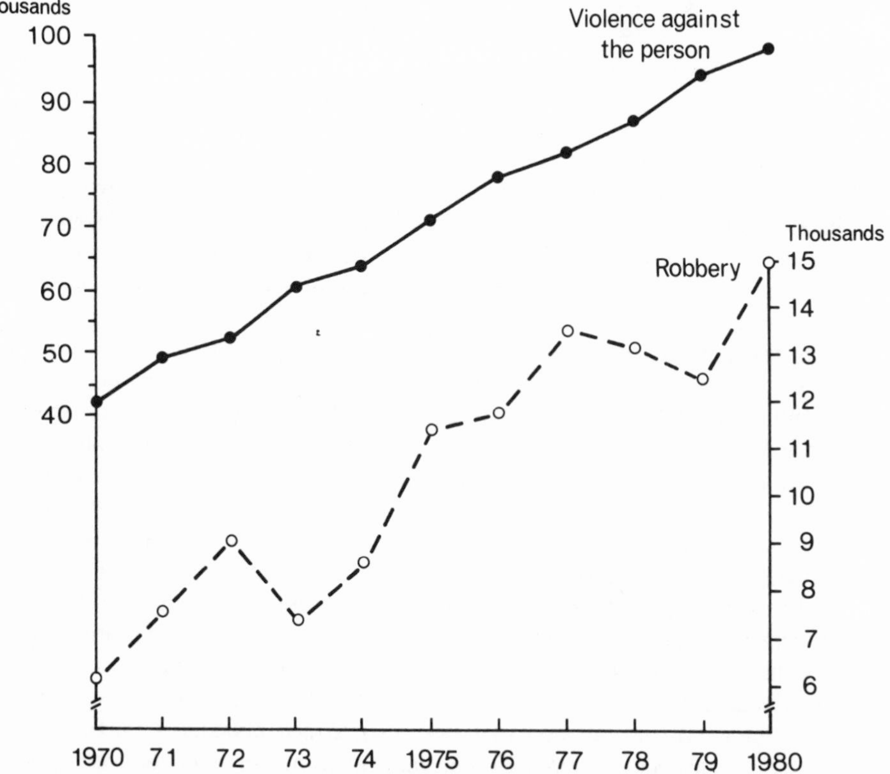

FIGURE 2. Increase in violence against the person, and in number of robberies, from 1970 to 1980, in Great Britain.

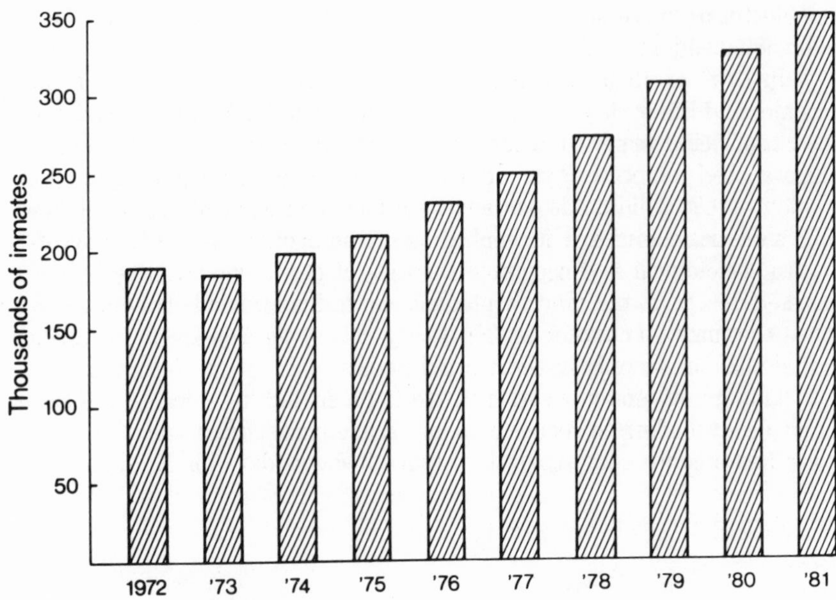

FIGURE 3. Increase in U.S. prison population, from 1971 to 1981.

ure 3 for the United States. Other documentation will be presented in the book. But these official government data, however careful we must be in analyzing them, leave little doubt about the facts—the expected decline has not happened! It is important to keep this failure of the prediction in mind when assessing the value of sociological theories.

Unemployment, admittedly, has risen, but here again if we compare the amount of criminality in England or the United States today with that in Germany during the years of the inflation and after, when unemployment was very much higher in Germany than in England now (over 30%!), criminality was conspicuously *lower* in Germany than in England. Many such comparisons can be made, but they seldom give much support to sociological theories. Even if we could grant them some degree of validity, these theories would nevertheless still have to operate through the minds of the individuals concerned, leading to essentially psychological interpretations. Whether individuals are absolutely or relatively poor and deprived is less relevant to their actions than whether they *feel* themselves to be poor and deprived, and in any case such feelings may lead to radically different actions according to whether one is or is not a religious Christian, a confirmed Marxist, or a Fascist. Whatever external reality may be, value systems are vital in predicting what kind of action an individual will undertake in any given set of circumstances, and equally important are personality and other psychological variables.

Psychological factors in criminality relate to genetic and constitutional causes and to personality and other sources of individual differences. Such factors have often been misunderstood, and even more frequently misinterpreted, in the context of crime and crime prevention. To say, as we shall do as a result of a very extensive body of evidence, that genetic factors are powerfully involved in criminal activity, is not the equivalent of saying that "crime is destiny" and that for a given person such behavior may be predestined and inevitable. It is not crime itself or criminality that is innate; it is certain peculiarities of the central or the autonomic nervous system that react with the environment, with upbringing, and many other environmental factors to increase the probability that a given person would act in a certain antisocial manner. No social determinism is involved in such estimates of probability, and the evidence is now conclusive that some such interactionist view is more in line with the evidence than a purely environmentalistic (or a purely genetic) one.

Similarly, to find that certain traits of personality—such as impulsivity, anxiety, sociability, or whatever—are correlated with antisocial behavior is not to say that they *inevitably* produce such behavior. As we shall note, they might also produce success in certain types of sport or praiseworthy behavior on the battlefield. The infinite complexity of human behavior in modern society allows only *probabilistic* estimates, but these can be powerful instruments in understanding behavior and providing us with a better theoretical insight into criminality than other relevant factors. Indeed, it is only by acquiring such an understanding that we shall be able to undertake the task of reforming the criminal and altering the criminal's patterns of behavior for the better.

In the chapters on sentencing and therapy or treatment, we look at the consequences of our psychological analysis for the socially so very important questions of what can be done to get the criminal to alter his or her behavior and become a responsible and respectable member of society. The task is not an easy one, as shown by the fact that all known societies have essentially failed to eradicate criminality. Even the Soviet Union has now given up the vain attempt at pretense and has admitted the existence of widespread criminality, after almost three quarters of a century of Communist indoctrination. There are many claims for one system or another, but few of these claims have been found to be justified on an empirical basis; we seem to be able as little now as two or three thousand years ago to change the behavior of our criminals or to prevent our youngsters from entering the underworld of crime. That alone is a good and powerful reason for surveying the evidence and attempting to come to some conclusions about our present state of knowledge in this field.

Here again, what we have said previously about sociological and economic theories bears repetition. Whatever is done by situational management—that is, by changing laws, by introducing penalties not involving incarceration, by changing methods of parole, by criminalizing or decriminalizing certain activities, or by changing our whole system from capitalism to communism, or vice versa—all these activities *can only influence conduct along psychological pathways and are hence subject to psychological analysis.* Whatever we do, we are dealing with *people* whose reactions to social changes are difficult to predict and are usually different from person to person depending on personality, temperament, mood, and the like. *No system of criminology has any meaning that disregards this central feature of all criminology: the individual person whom we are trying to influence.* Hence we believe that psychology stands right at the center of all the different disciplines that are involved here—from anthropology and sociology to economics and law. The failure to take psychological knowledge into account has been the prime reason for the inefficiency of our attempts to reduce crime.

One of the reasons for the present unsatisfactory state of affairs is that most people consider judges, magistrates, prison governors, parole board members, and others who are concerned with the administration of the law as experts in the field whose opinions deserve attention. Clearly, this is not so. Judges, magistrates, and others sentence criminals, but they have no way of knowing what the *effect* of the sentence has been on the future career of the criminal. Thus they are completely blind, ignorant of the most important information they need in order to test their views of sentencing against reality. If we were to judge a shooting contest, we would not rest content with shooters' opinions of how well they had done; we would want to look at the consequences of their shooting, that is, the actual *scores!* Yet that is precisely what is not forthcoming in our judicial proceedings; hardly ever will the judge, the magistrate, or anyone else concerned with sentencing know how the criminal reacted, whether he or she gave up crime altogether, or whether he or she became a habitual criminal! Hence the views of the "experts" are no better informed than those of any other lay person; perhaps they are worse, if anything, because such people have little personal acquaintance with the criminal milieu.

Only systematic follow-up studies, on a large scale, can tell us what precisely were the effects of different sentences—strict, lenient, suspended, concurrent, parole, bail, or what not. There is no substitute for proper scientific study; vague impressions largely biased by preconceived notions will not do. The frequent occasions where murderers and rapists indulge in their favorite pastimes while on parole, or bail, or after short sentences, suggest that all is not well and that judges need feedback as much as any other individuals who wish to improve their scoring rates. Psychology teaches us that *knowledge of results* is an indispensable element in learning; without it there is no improvement of any kind. Our present system guarantees lack of such knowledge, and hence absence of learning and improvement; this is not a recommendation!

We may end this introduction with a heartfelt plea. Until recently, criminology and the enactment and enforcement of laws has been the plaything of powerful figures who were able to impress their views on society and introduce changes that might or might not have the desired effect on crime and criminality. Thus punishments could be made stricter or more lenient, the death penalty might be introduced or abolished, special centers for juveniles might be set up, special prisons introduced for neurotic or psychotic offenders, laws might be changed to protect the criminal or leave the criminal less protected, rules covering parole or probation, or simultaneous sentencing, etc., might be introduced or revoked—all in a relatively haphazard fashion without any fundamental rhyme or reason. Powerful emotions were more active in all this than thought and reason—the beating and hanging brigade finds its equally appalling image at the other end in the "do-gooding" groups. Both act in line with preconceptions having no scientific validity and wish to impose their views regardless of consequences.

Our plea is a very simple one. We would argue that *whenever changes are made in the criminal system, the consequences of these changes should be monitored and scientific studies done to demonstrate empirically just what the effects of these changes are*. Hitherto we have been working in the dark. Wholesale changes are made, but at the end no one knows whether the effects of these changes have been positive or negative, beneficial or detrimental. It is often assumed, for instance, that the consequences of "doing good," that is, giving the prisoner the benefit of the doubt, treating the prisoner leniently, appealing to the prisoner's better nature, and so on, must be good, but this is to confound the *intention* of doing good with the *reality*. Parole or probation given too easily to murderers and rapists has often led in the past to avoidable repeated crimes of a similar nature, which could have been prevented by a less benign attitude and a realization of some of the facts about genetics and personality contained in this book.

However that may be, we have found a general tendency among people concerned with the administration of the law, including probation officers and members of parole boards, to dislike the application of scientific methods to an evaluation of their activities. Similarly, lawyers in the United States were very hostile to an investigation of the jury system and the psychological study of what actually goes on when a jury is deliberating. There are many myths in this field, and those actively working in the field are reluctant to see these myths destroyed, as they very well might be by scientific investigations. This attitude, however, is not conducive to our learning anything worthwhile about the process of punishment and its effects. Monitoring the effectiveness of any given method is a minimum requirement; better still would be the carrying out of actual experiments to test specific theories. Thus if there are two possible types of punishment for a given offense, criminals might be assigned at random to one or the other and then followed up to see whether a differential decrease of recidivism was recorded for these different types of punishment. We cite one such example in the book, which found very marked differences; such knowledge is invaluable if we wish to prevent the recurrence of crime.

In the field of rehabilitation, empirical studies are more frequent than experimental ones, but they require great care if erroneous interpretations are to be avoided. Consider a study, reviewed in more detail in a later chapter, in which a comparison was made between criminals who had committed similar crimes but who received long as opposed to relatively short sentences. Their later criminal careers were similar, and it was concluded that short sentences are as effective as long sentences in preventing future crimes. Such a conclusion is of course quite unwarranted, because such a study does not contain any element of *randomness*, which alone justifies statistical analyses. In sentencing, judges take into account a criminal's previous career; more serious criminals are given longer sentences than first-time offenders. Thus the comparison made is between serious offenders and first timers, and it is well known that serious offenders are much more likely to offend again than first timers. If, therefore, the future careers of offenders given long and short sentences show little difference, this suggests that the longer sentences were very effective in reducing the criminality of the *confirmed* criminal. In a proper experimental situation, criminals would have been assigned on a random basis to receive long and short sentences respectively, and this element of randomness would eliminate subjective interpretations of the results.

It may seem to many readers that no serious investigators would make such obvious errors of interpretation, but unfortunately we have found that the literature on criminality is full of such naive studies and interpretations. To some readers this may recall the old saying about "lies, damned lies, and statistics," but note that it is easy to lie without statistics and that the use of statistics is unlikely to fool anyone familiar with psychometrics, biometrics, or mathematical statistics—or just possessing common sense! The faulty design and conclusions in the experiment mentioned above may fool the layman but not the statistician. Lying successfully with statistics is an art that requires a high degree of sophistication, knowledge, and dedication; even then it is unlikely to be successful.

The use of the experimental method in this connection does of course run into serious ethical and judicial problems. Can we justify giving different sentences to offenders on the basis of a random selection scheme? Most people would probably reply in the negative, asserting that justice requires that each case be considered on its merits and an appropriate sentence pronounced by the judge. Such a view, however, gives an unduly idealistic picture of reality. It is well known that different judges may hand out quite different penalties for what seem similar or identical crimes, so that chance does play a large part in the prisoner's fate. Chance depending on the judge's whim, however, does not enable us to investigate the actual *consequences* of the penalties imposed, as far as rehabilitation is concerned; chance within the framework of the scientific experiment does. It gives us a unique opportunity to obtain objective knowledge on which to base future action.

How important is the possession of such knowledge? Let us consider for a moment the death penalty. It has often been asserted, and equally frequently denied, that the death penalty constitutes a genuine deterrent. This is an important question, although it must be acknowledged that for some people religious and other considerations play a greater part than does the empirical question of the effectiveness of the death penalty as a deterrent. As we shall see later on, the most extensive and well-controlled statistical investigation has suggested that the execution of one murderer may prevent eight innocent people from being killed. This is not the place to describe the very convoluted and difficult statistical argument; nor do we wish to assert that the conclusion is necessarily correct and that the true number of lives saved may not be greater, or smaller, or even reduced to nil. It seems clearly important to us that we should know the true answer, and that is only possible ultimately through a properly planned experiment.

Here again it will be argued that introducing a random element into such a study would be a violation of justice. However, there is such a random element already in the fact that in some states in the United States the death penalty is admitted whereas in others it is not. Thus chance does play a part in what happens to the criminal, depending on which state his or her crime was committed in, but we do not reap the benefit of certain knowledge. We realize that for most people this will be a novel idea, and perhaps an unwelcome one, but criminology will never emerge from its hesitant state of uncertainty on vital matters of this kind without adopting the experimental method as the only appropriate answer to its questions, in particular as far as sentencing and rehabilitation are concerned.

These, then, are some of the themes that run through our book. It is perhaps unique in concentrating on certain areas that for a long time have been neglected and consigned to the historical dustbin, but that nevertheless have given rise to a good deal of empirical study recently, with positive results. The "new criminology" of Taylor *et al.* (1973) assumes a rather old-fashioned look in the face of this new evidence; if there is a "new look," it lies in the field of personality and individual differences, constitutional factors and genetics as predisposing factors to antisocial and criminal behavior. This revival of ancient ideas, on a much stronger factual basis, may lead to a reconsideration of many views that have been taken for granted over the past 30 years or so but that certainly need to be looked at again. We do not claim to know all the answers, but we think we know some of the truly important questions that need to be asked in order to understand the causes of crime.

A recognition of the simple fact that the human being is a *biosocial* animal is the beginning of wisdom in this process (H. J. Eysenck, 1980a, 1980b). Purely environmentalistic theories of criminality are as unacceptable as purely genetic ones; social factors are equally important as biological ones, and of particular interest must be their interaction (Mednick, Moffitt, & Stack, 1987). That these truths, so obvious even to the uninitiated, should require reestablishment is a sad commentary on the influence of ideological prejudices regarding what should be factual judgments. No progress is possible without recognition of our dual nature—driven by the biological factors of our evolutionary development, socialized by environmental factors of many kinds, uncertainly trying to reconcile our selfish genes with the social needs of altruism. We need whatever help science can give us in attempting to reach a higher level of development.

It is sometimes said that appeals to genetic causes in fact support the status quo and are hence politically conservative. This is not so. It is a fundamental axiom in philosophy that *what should be* cannot be derived from *what is*, and facts do not determine values. Where biology points in one direction, society in another, we have a choice that cannot be usurped by *a priori* assumptions. Because nature is "red in tooth and claw" does not mean that civilized society is impossible. Political choices must take factual knowledge into account, but ultimately such choices are *value judgments* and not preempted by biological considerations.

In any case, it is quite wrong to think that the political Left is identified with environmental theories, the political Right with genetic ones (H. J. Eysenck, 1982). Marx and Lenin made this quite clear when they *explicitly* stated that socialism was concerned with *social* equality and "not at all with the equality of physical and mental abilities of individual persons" (Lenin, 1965, p. 140). Many other quotations show that socialist thinking in this respect does not differ from capitalist thinking as far as the facts are concerned; any differences that emerge relate to *values* and *conclusions* drawn from these facts (H. J. Eysenck, 1982).

One last point may be apposite. The title of this book is provocative; it suggests that it is possible to discover the causes of crime and criminality and that it may even by possible to discover cures for such conducts. It would be naive in the extreme to imagine that anything of the kind had already been accomplished; clearly, we are only at the beginning of a long road toward such a desirable conclusion. However, a number of facts have been established and are already known, and these may at least point us in the right direction. If these facts are out of line with modern theories about criminality, as they often are, then so much the worse for these theories. We will evaluate such factors throughout the course of the book and try to indicate in our last chapter just what we believe the present situation to be in the light of these facts. How much light these facts actually throw on the causes and cures of criminality, it must of course be left for the reader to decide. We are cautiously optimistic that a new paradigm is developing in this field and that it may be useful in directing further research. More than that we would not claim for it.

PART ONE

PERSONALITY AND INDIVIDUAL DIFFERENCES

CHAPTER TWO

The Constitutional Theory of Criminality

INTRODUCTION: STIGMATA

The term *constitution* has several different meanings, although there is of course some general underlying consensus about its provenance. It is defined in the *Encyclopaedia of Psychology* (H. J. Eysenck, Arnold, & Meili, 1972) as

> "human reactive potential and reaction style (form and performance). It is grounded on heredity and *Anlagen* or fundamental dispositions, and those acquired in early childhood, or more rarely at a later date, and can be determined as a type or an individual constitution." (p. 213)

Constitutional types are defined as

> theoretical groupings or psychophysical (occasionally exclusively physical: the "biotype") characteristics which are assembled either by statistical frequency method or by arbitrary selection." (p. 214)

The Encyclopaedic Handbook of Medical Psychology (Krauss, 1976) defined *constitution* as

> The sum total of a person's physical, physiological and biochemical characteristics determined mainly by genetic factors and partly by environmental influences. . . . Human physique in its manifold aspects provides the most readily measurable aspect of constitution." (p. 102)

Last, the *Dictionary of Behavioral Science* (Wolman, 1973), in an even more all-embracing manner, defines *constitution* as "The total hereditary and acquired characteristics which determine an individual."

In relation to criminality, the term *constitutional* refers largely to the major physical characteristics of a person, such as his or her physique or body build, certain characteristic bodily features or "stigmata," or more rarely to biochemical and hormonal characteristics underlying his or her behavior (e.g., Buikhuisen, 1987; Nachsham & Denno, 1987; Rubin, 1987; Schalling, 1987; and Volavka, 1987). Constitutional theories of criminality have their origin in antiquity, but they owe their modern emergence into popular consciousness to the Italian psychiatrist Cesare Lombroso (1876, 1917), who was the originator of the theory of a special criminal type, *homo delinquens (il reo nato)*, resembling primitive man, whom Lombroso regarded as a prototype of the born criminal. The child was also considered as a little savage who, as a result of heredity and development, shows many of the characteristics of the born criminal.

Criminal man was thought to be not only predisposed but *predestined* to crime, and was stigmatized by a series of physical characteristics such as small cranial capacity; low, receding forehead; facial protuberance; strongly developed jaws and cheekbones; low brain weight; atypical formations in the gyri; anomalies of the ears, eyes, lips, teeth, or palate; tufted, curly hair; extra fingers or nipples, abnormalities of the genitals; femininity in men and masculinity in women; infantilism; stammering; and left-handedness. At least five of these or similar "degenerative symptoms" had to be present before a person would be classified as *homo delinquens*.

On the psychological side, the criminal was identified as a moral imbecile, without remorse, conscience, or pity; cynical, treacherous, conceited, impulsive, cruel, and lazy. The criminal normally lacks feelings for the sufferings of others, a lack of feeling that was supposed to be the result of reduced sensitivity to pain. Originally, Lombroso considered practically all offenders to be born criminals, but he gradually reduced the proportion to about one third. A good account of Lombroso's theory is given by Hurwitz and Christiansen (1983).

Lombroso's specific theory of stigmata was disproved by a British investigator, C. B. Goring (1913) who conducted comparative studies of criminals and noncriminals and showed that an anatomical–constitutional criminal type did not exist. He based his conclusion on a detailed study of 3,000 English criminals, using measurements and descriptions of 96 different physical and psychological peculiarities. It is to be noted that Goring was in complete agreement with Lombroso about the dominating influence of biological factors, but he rejected Lombroso's theory of the "born criminal" and introduced instead the concept of criminal diathesis, an early precursor of what would now be called the "threshold model." This posits a constitutional proclivity, which may be either mental, moral, or physical, and which is present to some degree in all individuals, but varying from weak through middling to strong. The probability of becoming criminal increases as the diathesis increases, but never completely determines the fate of a given person. Figure 4 shows in diagrammatic form the threshold model of criminality.

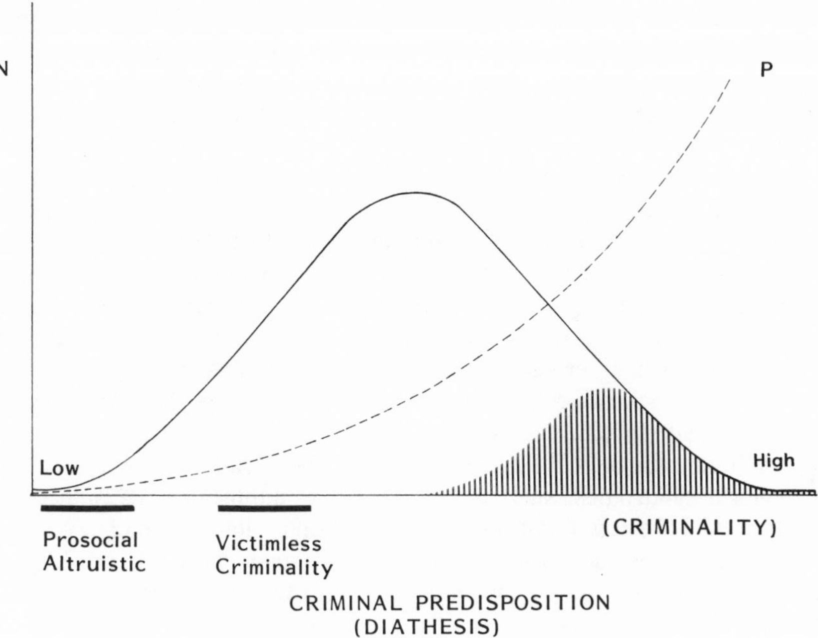

FIGURE 4. Threshold model of criminality.

In this figure the baseline shows the criminal diathesis, probably a mixture of physical, psychological, and social characteristics. The large Gaussian distribution indicates how this diathesis is distributed in the population, and the shaded distribution in the right-hand corner indicates the members of the actual criminal group. P indicates the increase in *probability* of criminal conduct as the criminal diathesis increases. The "threshold" at which diathesis is turned into actual criminal conduct is determined by various social and environmental factors, such as unemployment, severity of laws, and rigor of enforcement. This is the theory that will form the basis of our treatment of the constitutional type.

Most of the modern work on constitutional factors has been concerned with types of physique or body build, but there has been an interesting development in recent years reviving the notion of "stigmata" and showing that in actual fact there was some very real significance in these physical characteristics, now labeled "minor physical anomalies", or MPAs.

Interest in these MPAs goes back to Down's (1866) finding that the type of mental retardation he called "Mongolism" was associated with physical anomalies, such as cleft palate and attached earlobes. Still (1902) reported a high incidence of anomalies in hyperactive children, a cognitively not abnormal group, predictive of antisocial conduct (Satterfield, 1987). Goldfarb and Batstein (1956) found a higher rate of such minor anomalies in behaviorally disordered children compared with a normal sample.

General interest in MPAs was reawakened when Waldrop and Halverson (1971) standardized a test comprising 17 nonobvious but measurable minor physical anomalies characteristic of the face, hands, and feet. The actual MPAs in this list are asymmetrical ears, soft and pliable ears, malformed ears, attached earlobes, hypertelorism (widely spaced eyes), low-seated ears, multiple hair whorls, atypical head circumference, single palmar creases, webbed toes, large one-two toe gap, furrowed tongue, smooth-rough tongue, epicanthus, curved fifth finger, long third toe, and steepled palate.

A high rate of MPAs in children has been linked to a variety of behavioral syndromes, such as Down's syndrome (Smith, 1970), schizophrenia (Goldfarb & Batstein, 1956; Campbell, Geller, Small, Petti, & Ferris, 1978), learning disabilities (Steg & Rapaport, 1975), and hyperactivity (Firestone, Levy, & Douglas, 1976; Quinn & Rapaport, 1974; Rapaport & Quinn, 1975).

These are all clinical or subclinical behaviors, but in normal children, too, correlations have been found between MPAs and personality variables characteristic of antisocial behavior. In particular, high correlations have been found between MPAs and active, aggressive, and impulsive behavior in preschool boys (Bell & Waldrop, 1982; Firestone, Peters, Rivier, & Knights, 1978; Halverson & Victor, 1976; O'Donnell, O'Neill, & Staley, 1979; O'Donnell & van Tuinan, 1979; Waldrop, Bell, MacLaughlin, & Halverson, 1978; Waldrop & Goering, 1971; Waldrop & Halverson, 1971; Waldrop, Pederson, & Bell, 1968). With girls, correlations are lower and less consistent, indicating a relationship between MPAs and withdrawn, inhibited, and fearful behavior (Burg, Hart, Quinn, & Rapaport, 1978; Rapaport & Quinn, 1975; Waldrop, Bell, & Goering, 1976). In addition, a link has been found between MPAs and clumsiness in both sexes.

In adults, a study by Paulhus and Martin (1986), using rather small numbers of males and females, found results very similar to those reported for children. The total number of MPAs was correlated significantly with physical activity in males, with aggression and misbehavior in males, with aggression and misbehavior in the combined samples of males and females, and with clumsiness in males only. Significant correlations were also found with emotionality (primarily in males), activity (in a combined sample), sociability (in males only), and extraversion (in males only). In addition, on an even smaller subsample, dominance was positively correlated, and nurturance negatively, with MPAs in males;

in females correlations were along the same lines, but smaller and insignificant.

No studies seem to have been done comparing criminals with noncriminals with respect to MPAs, but it is interesting that the correlations with behavior and personality are all in the direction one would have expected from the known relationships between personality and antisocial conduct (see Chapter 3). Thus criminals are characterized by a high degree of psychoticism, hyperactivity, aggression, impulsivity and activity, emotionality–neuroticism, and sociability. These correlations will be discussed in much greater detail in a later chapter.

It might appear at first that the relation between MPAs and temperament could be accounted for by the self-fulfilling nature of social reactions to unusual features, but this is not so. MPAs are usually not noticed by people who possess them, nor by others; only trained observers on the lookout for them are likely to discover MPAs. In normal populations, individuals with many MPAs are not found any less physically attractive than those with none (Rapaport & Quinn, 1975; Rosenberg & Weller, 1973).

MPAs are usually evident at birth and show considerable stability through childhood (Quinn & Rapaport, 1974); they are unlikely to change through the life span, although no studies are available as yet to demonstrate this. This suggests strongly that genetic factors are predominant, although it has also been suggested that factors operating during the first trimester of pregnancy may influence the occurrence of MPAs and also affect the development of the nervous system and thus in turn a person's temperament (D. W. Smith, 1970; Steg & Rapaport, 1975). Clearly, MPAs are *constitutional* factors of considerable interest, demonstrating that Lombroso's original theories, however exaggerated, may have had a kernel of truth.

Even stronger support for what one might call the "Lombroso theory" comes from two plastic surgeons who inspected over 11,000 photographs of criminals comparing them with over 7,000 photos of noncriminals (Masters & Greaves, 1967). They give overall figures of 60% of deformation, defined as surgically correctable facial defects, among criminals, as compared with 20% in noncriminals. Among males, the percentage was 57%, among females 68%. Although the definition of facial deformity used by Masters and Greaves is different from that used by Lombroso in defining his stigmata, the general idea underlying both approaches shows definite similarities. The major points of deformity mentioned by Masters and Greaves are protruding ears, nasal deformity, receding chin, acne scars, scars on face, and eye deformity. Protruding ears account for about half the deformities among males, nasal deformities similarly for females.

Masters and Greaves also looked at comparative results for five different categories of crime—suicide, homicide, rape, prostitution, and sexual deviation. Homicides had the lowest percentage of deformities (44%). Prostitutes rather unexpectedly had a high degree of clear-cut facial disfigurement of both congenital and acquired origin (69%). The figures are striking, but it is not known whether similar figures would be obtained in countries other than the United States.

Wolfgang (1960) has summarized Lombroso's contribution in a more balanced manner than is usual:

> These ill-defined measurements, unwarranted deductions and inadequate control groups constitute serious deficiencies of his research. But he also manifested imaginative insight, good, intuitive judgement, intellectual honesty, awareness of some of his limitations, attempted to use control groups, and desired to have the theory tested impartially. Many researchers today fare little better than this. (p. 317)

It would certainly go counter to the known facts to suggest that constitutional factors of the kind envisaged by Lombroso were uncorrelated with criminality, or more particularly the type of personality associated with antisocial conduct.

PHYSIQUE: THE KRETSCHMER-SHELDON SYSTEM

The study of stigmata or MPAs has since Goring (1913) had much less influence on criminology than the study of *physique*. This is a complex subject, with many different typologies and methods of measurement, reviewed in detail by H. J. Eysenck (1970) and Rees (1973). Contrary to the psychometric and factor analytic evidence, which suggests the existence of two major factors (height and width, respectively), most investigators have accepted the Kretschmer-Sheldon three-type theory illustrated in Figure 5 (Kretschmer, 1948; Sheldon & Stevens, 1940). The work of Kretschmer preceded that of Sheldon by some twenty years; Kretschmer's book went through a whole series of revised editions each reporting additional material. Figure 5 is taken from Martiny (1948), representing the French tradition, which, although strong, is often neglected in Anglo-American work.

The three-type theory dates back essentially to the French writer Rostan (1828), who postulated a *digestive* type (thickset, round), which Kretschmer called *pyknic;* a *cerebral–respiratory* type (thin, elongated), which Kretschmer called *asthenic* or *leptosomatic;* and an intermediate *muscular* type (broad, muscular), which Kretschmer called the *athletic*. Kretschmer also added another concept, that of the *dysplastic* type of body build, which essentially denotes the incompatible mixture of different types in different parts of the body.

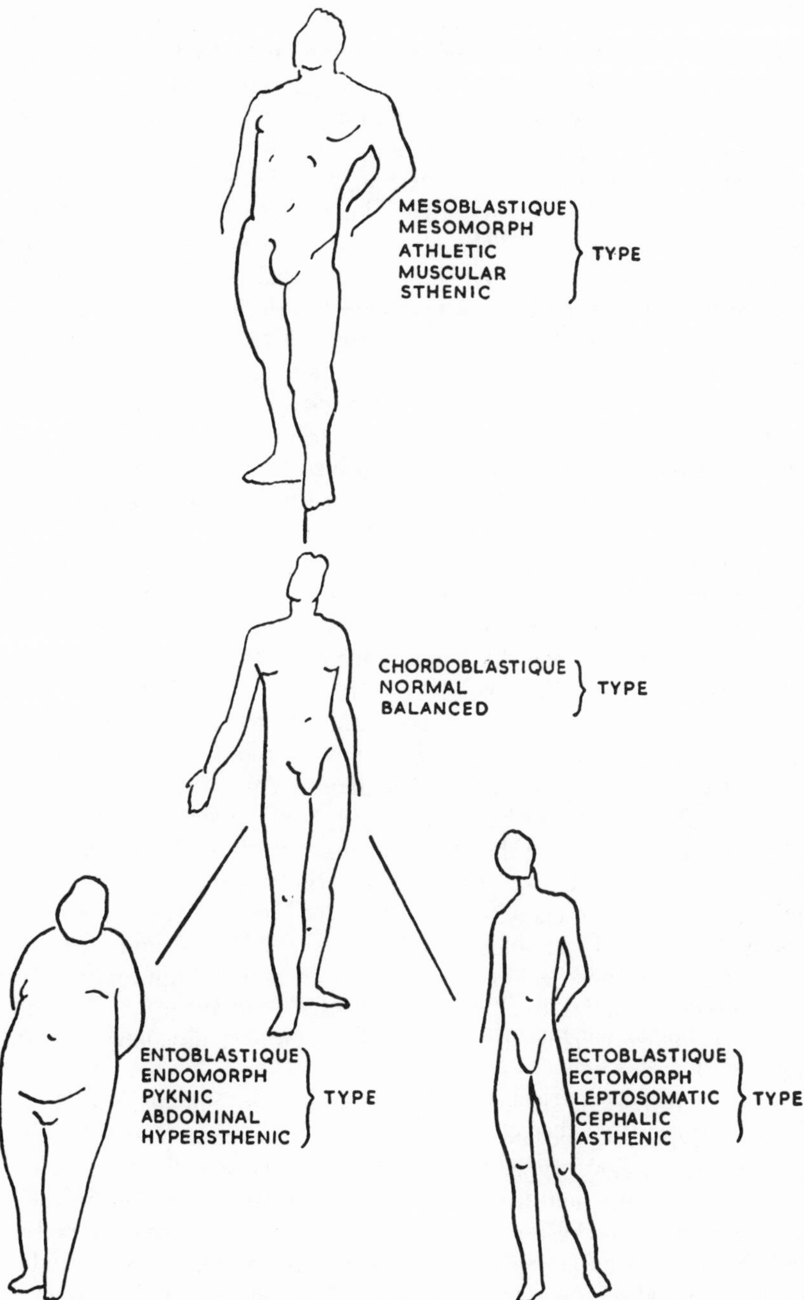

FIGURE 5. Martiny's model of the three-factor theory of body build (Martiny, 1948).

To this essentially threefold division on the physical side, Kretschmer added an essentially threefold division on the mental side. In the first editions of his book, the temperamental typology was a twofold one based on the two main groups of functional psychoses, the schizophrenias and the manic–depressive disorders, respectively. Schizophrenics were believed to be largely *leptosomatic* in body build, manic-depressives largely *pyknic*. In later years, Kretschmer came more and more to regard (on the physical side) the athletic type as not being intermediate between the other two but as being quite separate from them in many ways. Similarly, on the level of personality description, he took the epileptic as a prototype, postulating a special set of traits as characteristic of the epileptic personality and linking this type with athletic and dysplastic body build. Kretschmer did not regard schizophrenia and manic–depressive illness as categorically different from normal personality types, but rather as exaggerated forms of a schizoid (introverted) and cycloid (extraverted) personality, respectively; in the normal field also he postulated a correlation with body build.

The outline of Kretschmer's system was very closely followed by Sheldon and Stevens (1940), who have also incorporated a number of ideas from other writers and has used various novel techniques. The first of the general ideas that characterize Sheldon's scheme is derived from such writers as Bessonet-Favre (1910), Bauer (1923), and Castellino (1927), who tried to link up the different types of body build with the germinal layers in the embryo. As is well known, there are three of these—the ectoderm, endoderm, and mesoderm, to which should perhaps be added the mesenchyme (Hertwig, 1881), which acts as a kind of "packing tissue" between the other germinal layers and gives rise to the connective tissues, the myocardium, and the visceral musculature, the endocardium, and the endothelium of the blood vessels, the lymph glands, lymph vessels, and the spleen. Body types resulting from *overdevelopment* of any of these components would correspond approximately to Kretschmer's pyknics (endoderm), athletics (mesoderm), and leptosomatics (ectoderm). This, at least, is the argument developed by Sheldon.

In his inspection of some 4,000 male bodies. Sheldon found three extreme types of variants, one of which corresponded closely to Kretschmer's pyknic type. Sheldon found that "the digestive viscera, especially the gut, held a more or less predominant position in the organic economy. In these people the most manifest external characteristic is a conspicuous laying on of fat, which is an indication of predominance of the absorptive functions—the functions of the gut—over the energy-expanding functions." Sheldon (1940) goes on to say that

> The functional elements of the digestive system are derived embryologically almost entirely from the endoderm, the innermost of the original three em-

> bryonic layers. We can quite naturally therefore refer to the extremes of type one as those exhibiting a condition of endomorphy. (p. 85)

In a similar way, bones, muscles, connective tissue, and the heart and blood vessels were seen to predominate overwhelmingly in the variants of type two, which correspond to Kretschmer's athletics. This type Sheldon therefore called the *mesomorph*, as these functions are derived predominantly from the mesoderm, the second embryonic layer. As regards the third type, Kretschmer's leptosomatic or asthenic type,

> The principal derivatives from the embryonic ectodermal layer are the skin itself, hair and nails, sense organs (exteroceptors), and the nervous system, including the brain. Relative to total bodily mass, all three organs are conspicuous in the bodily economy of the extreme variants of type three. . . . Hence, we have named them ectomorphs, or persons exhibiting ectomorphy. (p. 93)

Having thus adopted the Continental ideas of embryological determination of body type, Sheldon introduced another idea borrowed from Plattner (1938), namely that of considering these three genetic "factors" as components of total body build, each having a certain determinable influence. This influence is rated by Sheldon on a 7-point scale so that each body type may be represented by a set of three numbers denoting respectively the influence of each of the three common components. Thus, 1-1-7 would be a person characterized by an almost complete lack of endomorphy and mesomorphy and a complete dominance of the ectomorphy component. All other combinations are similarly described in terms of three numbers. There are 343 theoretical possibilities of deriving different somatotypes from these three components, but of all these Sheldon reports that only 76 have been encountered by him in actual practice.

Several additional scales are used by Sheldon. One of these, taken over from Kretschmer, is dysplasia. "This variable is defined as any inconsistent or uneven mixing of the primary components in different regions of the body" (p. 102). This Sheldon refers to as the "d" index. It is derived in the following way. The whole body is split up into five regions, the first dealing with the head, the second with the trunk (breadth), the third with the arms, the fourth with the trunk (thickness), and the fifth with the legs. Somatotype ratings are made of each of these five regions, and the sum of the disagreements constitutes the "d" index.

Another index, the "g" index, is concerned with gynandromorphy, that is, the extent to which a physique presents traits ordinarily associated with the opposite sex. Last, yet another index, the "t" index, relates to textural variations among persons ranging from coarse to fine. The description of this index in Sheldon's work is not at all clear, but Sheldon reports a rerating reliability on 1,000 cases of .93.

The only really novel contribution that Sheldon has made to this field is his technique of anthropometric measurement. He makes use of a photographic technique in which each subject is photographed identically posed from three different angles; all measures and ratings are then taken from these standard photographs. There are obvious advantages in this method, although one would like to know a good deal more about repeat reliabilities and correlations of measures so obtained with those derived from more orthodox procedures.

Many criticisms have been made of this scheme, apart from the fact that practically all its crucial aspects are derivative. The evidence suggests that a two-dimensional rather than a three-dimensional system is indicated by the data; even on Sheldon's own showing, quite considerable correlations going into the 60s and 70s are found between the three components that are clearly not independent (Ekman, 1951a; Humphreys, 1957; Sills, 1950). Evidence relating to the notion of an embryological determination of body type is either absent or discouraging. Hunt (1949), to take but one example, has convincingly pointed out the lack of agreement between somatic characteristics and the degree of development of the endodermal, mesodermal, and ectodermal derivatives. Neither is the stability of somatotypes over time as perfect as Sheldon suggested; Zuck (1958) found correlations from ages 17 to 33 averaging in the 70s, with one being as low as .24.

It should be noted that the study of physique and delinquency has been carried but almost exclusively in males. This is largely due to the fact that males are much more frequently represented among delinquents, in a ratio of about 10 to 1; it is also due to the fact that the study of female body build is rather more complex than that of male body build, demanding more complex formuli (H. J. Eysenck, 1970; Rees, 1973; Rees & H. J. Eysenck, 1945). The fact that crimes committed by women tend to be different from those committed by males (e.g., prostitution and other sex-related crimes, essentially of the victimless variety) make it impossible to extrapolate from findings among male delinquents to what might be found among female delinquents (Ellis, 1988).

PHYSIQUE AND PERSONALITY

We must now turn to the relationship between physique and personality (Sheldon & Stevens, 1942). Sheldon began by collecting a list of 650 traits of temperament, most of which were supposedly related to introversion or extroversion. After several revisions and a thorough study of some 30 students by means of a series of analytic interviews, the number of traits used was considerably reduced to 22, which appeared to fall into three main clusters. Traits in each of these clusters showed consistently positive intercorrelations among themselves and consistently negative correlations with the traits of each of the other clusters. Further traits were added to these clusters, until finally each cluster was made up of 20 traits altogether. These clusters were labeled "viscerotonia," "somatotonia," and "cerebrotonia" respectively, as they seemed to deal respectively with the functional predominance of the digestive viscera, the functional and anatomical predominance of the somatic structures, and the prepotency of the higher centers of the nervous system.

Sheldon's prescription for the use of his scale is somewhat unusual.

> The procedure recommended for using the scale for temperament is as follows: Observe the subject closely for at least a year in as many different situations as possible. Conduct a series of not less than twenty analytic interviews with him in a manner best suited to the situation and to the temperaments and interests of the two principals. (p. 22)

Each trait is to be rated on a 7-point scale in such a way that for each person a formula is given containing the numbers, each measuring strength of one of the three components. Thus, 1-1-7 would be a person almost entirely lacking in viscerotonia and somatotonia, with cerebrotonia completely dominant. Table 1 shows the traits constituting Sheldon's three components.

TABLE 1. Sheldon's System of Personality Description: The Scale for Temperament[a]

I Viscerotonia	II Somatotonia	III Cerebrotonia
( ) 1. Relaxation in posture and movement	( ) 1. Assertiveness of posture and movement	( ) 1. Restraint in posture and movement, tightness
( ) 2. Love of physical comfort	( ) 2. Love of physical adventure	— 2. Physiological over-response
( ) 3. Slow reaction	( ) 3. The energetic characteristics	( ) 3. Overly fast reactions
— 4. Love of eating	( ) 4. Need of enjoyment and exercise	( ) 4. Love of privacy
— 5. Socialization of eating	— 5. Love of dominating, lust for power	( ) 5. Mental overintensity, hyperattentionality, apprehensiveness

(continued)

Table 1. (*continued*)

I Viscerotonia	II Somatotonia	III Cerebrotonia
— 6. Pleasure in digestion	( ) 6. Love of risk and chance	( ) 6. Secretiveness of feeling, emotional restraint
( ) 7. Love of polite ceremony	( ) 7. Bold directness of manner	( ) 7. Self-conscious motility of the eyes and face
( ) 8. Sociophilia	( ) 8. Physical courage for combat	( ) 8. Sociophobia
— 9. Indiscriminate amiability	( ) 9. Competitive aggressiveness	( ) 9. Inhibited social address
— 10. Greed for affection and approval	— 10. Psychological callousness	— 10. Resistance to habit, and poor routinizing
— 11. Orientation to people	— 11. Claustrophobia	— 11. Agoraphobia
( ) 12. Evenness of emotional flow	— 12. Ruthlessness, freedom from squeamishness	— 12. Unpredictability
( ) 13. Tolerance	( ) 13. The unrestrained voice	( ) 13. Vocal restraint, and general restraint of noise
( ) 14. Complacency	— 14. Spartan indifference to pain	— 14. Hypersensitivity to pain
— 15. Deep sleep	— 15. General noisiness	— 15. Poor sleep habits, chronic fatigue
( ) 16. The untempered characteristic	( ) 16. Overmaturity of appearance	( ) 16. Youthful intentness of manner
( ) 17. Smooth, easy communication of feeling, extraversion of viscerotonia	— 17. Horizontal mental cleavage, extraversion of somatotonia	— 17. Vertical mental cleavage, introversion
— 18. Relaxation and sociophilia under alcohol	— 18. Assertiveness and aggression and alcohol	— 18. Resistance to alcohol, and to other depressant drugs
— 19. Need of people when troubled	— 19. Need of action when troubled	— 19. Need of solitude when troubled
— 20. Orientation toward childhood and family relationships	— 20. Orientation toward goals and activities of youth	— 20. Orientation toward the later periods of life

[a]The 30 traits with parentheses constitute collectively the short form of the scale.

Note. From *The Varieties of Temperament* by W. H. Sheldon and S. S. Stevens, New York: Harper, 1942.

The final list of 60 traits is claimed by Sheldon to have been selected on the basis of intercorrelations among the ratings on 78 traits for a series of 100 male subjects. These correlations are given in his book; they are considerably higher than correlations between trait ratings usually are. Apart from his inspection cluster analysis, Sheldon has not carried out any factorial study. Adcock (1948) has attempted such a study of Sheldon's figures, but despite several attempts found that he was faced each time with the problem of finding the root of a negative number. He remarks: "Obviously there is something peculiar about these intercorrelations" (p. 315) and goes on to attempt a rather complex interpretation.

Lubin (1950), who has made a statistical investigation of these intercorrelations, remarks that "the peculiarity is so great that one is forced to ask whether it may not be outside the bounds of mathematical possibility?" (p. 188). He goes on to show that several of Sheldon's product moment correlations could not be simultaneously obtained from any actual set of measurements because they violate the well-known conditions for consistency. He concludes: "It follows that some at least of his figures must contain errors of arithmetical calculation." We may deduce from these observations that Sheldon's edifice is based on a somewhat insecure foundation, and any conclusions drawn from these figures should be regarded with great caution.

The three components isolated by Sheldon are not independent: viscerotonia correlates −.34 with somatotonia and −.37 with cerebrotonia; somatotonia and cerebrotonia intercorrelate −.62. It is clear that a much more parsimonious description of the 60 traits rated would be possible in terms of two orthogonal factors rather than three correlated components. This has been demonstrated on Sheldon's own material by Ekman (1951b).

More recently, Sheldon, Hartl, and McDermott (1949), with the help of Wittman, extended this work to abnormal mental states. Considering the psychotic syndrome in each case to be merely an exaggeration of the neurotic, they posit three main components of abnormality, which are again rated on a 7-point scale where the numbers are prefaced by a Greek letter. The three psychiatric components in each case signify the *absence* or *lack* of one of the three normal components. Thus, cerebropenia (the suffix *penia* denotes lack of, or an abnormally low degree of, the component named) signifies the absence of cerebrotonia; visceropenia signifies the absence of viscerotonia; and somatopenia signifies the absence of somatotonia. Corresponding to these three "penias" we have three great neurotic and psychotic syndromes. Cerebropenia at the neurotic level leads to hysteria, at the psychotic level to manic-depressive psychosis. Visceropenia at the neurotic level leads to psychasthenia, at the psychotic level to paranoid schizophrenia. Somatopenia at the neurotic level leads to neurasthenia, and at the psychotic level to hebephrenic schizophrenia.

We are now ready to consider correlations between body type, as rated by Sheldon, and Stevens (1942), and temperamental types, as rated by him also. A total of 200 young students constituted the sample, as will be remembered from our discussion of Sheldon's rating experiments. The correlations between endomorphy and viscerotonia was .79, between mesomorphy and somatotonia .72, and between ectomorphy and cerebrotonia .83.

> These are higher correlations than we expected to find, and they raise some questions of great interest. If we were to regard the product moment correlations as a measure of the degree to which two variables are made up of common elements, correlations of the order of .8 would suggest that morphology and temperament as we measure them may constitute expressions at their respective levels of essentially common components.

(Strictly speaking, it is, of course, the *square* of the correlation coefficient that is indicative of the number of common elements, i.e., 62%, 52%, and 69%.) Correlations are also given by Sheldon between the three temperamental components and several other bodily indices. Thus, the "t" index (textural component) correlates .36 with cerebrotonia, but only insignificantly with the other two components. IQ and sexuality also correlate positively with cerebrotonia but hardly at all with the other two components. One might expect from these correlations that the "t" component would correlate with IQ, which it does (.39), and with esthetic intelligence (.58) and sexuality (.40).

These findings are not easy to believe. We have noted previously the serious statistical errors apparent in Sheldon's work. We must now note here the even more important experimental error of having the same observer rate personality and body build in his subjects, when it is almost certain that his hypotheses will influence his ratings. The correlations actually found are much higher than those reported by any other investigators (when corrected for attenuation, on the assumption of any reasonable reliability for ratings, they very closely approach unity). Such results obviously have to be checked and repeated before very much credence can be given to them.

One major independent study of Sheldon's claims is that by Fiske (1944). The number of significant findings in his study of adolescent boys is not conspicuously greater than chance expectancy. The use of Sheldon's improved procedure for classifying physique yielded the same paucity of significant relationships to physique that has been found in earlier studies. This conclusion deserves particular emphasis because the somatotyping of the subjects in this study was done by Sheldon himself and a considerable variety of procedures were used for the purpose of personality measurement. In addition, the statistical procedure employed (analysis of variance) was superior to any employed in Sheldon's own studies.

Some support for Sheldon's scheme is given in a comparatively objective study by Child (1950), who used 414 Yale students, who had been somatotyped by Sheldon himself, as subjects. A special questionnaire was constructed for this study based on Sheldon's description of the various personality correlates of his somatotypes and chi-squared analyses made of tables relating body type to questionnaire items. Altogether, 96 predictions were made, based on Sheldon's views. Of the relations empirically observed, 74 (77%) were in the predicted direction, 20 reached significance at the 5% level, and 10 at the 1% level. Of the 21 correlations contrary to prediction, only 1 was significant at the 5% level and none at the 1% level. The three dimensions of physique differed in the confirmation of predictions. The measured difference is that many fewer predictions are confirmed at acceptable levels of statistical significance for endomorphy than for the other two dimensions of physique.

Child also made an attempt to study the magnitude of relationships between physique and self-rated behavior by constructing scales of viscerotonia, somatotonia, and cerebrotonia, from the most significant items, i.e., those showing the highest correlation with body build. These scales were derived from half of the population and applied to the other half. The resulting correlations are quite low. The correlations between viscerotonia and endomorphy (.38) and cerebrotonia and ectomorphy (.27) are in the predicted direction, but are about as low as correlations between body type and temperament have usually been found to be. It is thus possible but not certain that appropriate measures based on ratings, such as were used here, have quite a sizable relationship with dimensions of physique. It is reasonably certain that this relationship does not at all approach the magnitude of the relationships reported by Sheldon between dimensions of physique and his measures of temperament.

Scattered investigations by other workers substantiate this conclusion. Thus, Davidson, McInnes, and Parnell (1957), investigating body build and temperament in a group of 100 seven-year-old children, found symptoms of anxiety and emotional unrest associated with ectomorphy. They also found a relationship between ectomorphy and meticulous, fussy, and conscientious traits of personality. In general, the correlations between somatotype and psychological attributes were of a low order. Parnell (1957) compared somatotype distributions in 405 healthy students with a group of some 200 students who had sought psychiatric care. Ectomorphy was six times more common in the patient group, mesomorphy five times more common in the healthy group. D. W. Smith (1957) studied somatotypes in relation to MMPI scales in a group of 181 students. Many of his correlations are significant and most of them are in the direction predicted from Sheldon's system. Nevertheless, the modal level of his correlation is only between .3 and .4, thus falling very short of Sheldon's claims.

It will be remembered that Sheldon extended his scheme of temperament analysis to include psychotic and neurotic manifestations. Here we are concerned with the relationship between the morphological components and psychiatric diagnosis, as based on the work of Wittman (1948) in which 155 psychotic male patients constituted the experimental group and were somatotyped by Sheldon himself. Wittman made a rating for these patients on the traits from her checklist, thus obtaining an average rating for each of the primary psychiatric components. This rating procedure apparently had a good deal of reliability, as correlations of Wittman's ratings with those of an independent rater averaged .86. Correlations were then run between these ratings and the morphological components. The first psychiatric component (manic–depressive) correlated .54 with endomorphy, .41 with mesomorphy, and −.59 with ectomorphy. The second psychiatric component (paranoid) correlated −.04 with endomorphy, .57 with mesomorphy, and −.34 with ectomorphy. The third psychiatric component (hebephrenic) correlated −.25 with endomorphy, −.68 with mesomorphy, and .64 with ectomorphy. These correlations are rather high, and as the two parts of the study (psychiatric ratings and morphology ratings) were apparently kept separate, they are of considerable interest.

In summary, it may be said that Sheldon's results, wherever they are comparable with the work of his predecessors, agree fairly well with their conclusions. Sheldon's studies suffer from methodological and statistical weakness that make it difficult to accept some of his claims, particularly insofar as they relate to the size of correlations observed between somatotype and temperament. Correlations with objective tests (Fiske, 1942; Janoff, Beck, & Child, 1950; H. C. Smith, 1949) are rather low, even where they are in the expected direction. In spite of their messianic ring, Sheldon's contributions cannot be dismissed, but neither can they be accepted at face value. They probably contain sufficient truth and insight to be worthy of proper scientific investigation.

Broadly speaking, the work of Kretschmer and Sheldon agrees well enough with a large number of other studies of physique and temperament not linked with their particular systems (H. J. Eysenck, 1970; Rees, 1973), which demonstrate that there exists a correlation of between .3 and .4 between extroversion and broad body build, as opposed to introversion and lean, thin body build. In Sheldon's system this dimension would go from extreme ectomorphy to a point intermediate between endomorphy and mesomorphy (ectopenia). Using terms to be explained in a later chapter on personality, endomorphy is probably more closely related to the *sociability* aspect of extraversion, mesomorphy to the *activity and assertiveness* aspect of extraversion. Our interest in Sheldon's system is motivated very largely by the relationship observed between his types of physique and criminal and antisocial behaviour. Before we turn to this, it will be useful to look at some earlier research.

EARLY STUDIES OF CRIMINALITY AND PHYSIQUE

Among the earliest pioneers was Goring (1913), whose failure to find evidence for Lombroso's stigmata has already been mentioned. Goring found a significant defect in general intelligence in his criminal group; he also found "a generally defective physique." This might, of course, have been due to defective diet, and in any case East (1942) was able to demonstrate that Goring's results did not apply to his sample of 4,000 English young offenders.

The work of E. A. Hooton (1939a, 1939b) was considerably more specific, being based on measurements and statistical analyses of a comprehensive sample of American offenders. From his study of thieves, murderers, sexual offenders, and other typical criminals, he concluded that the main cause of crime was *biological inferiority*. This was defined as inferiority in body weight, small stature, less shoulder breadth, chest depth and breadth, and head capacity. Hooton found facial height significantly smaller, the nose lower and wider, the ears shorter and broader in proportion to their length, and the face short in proportion to its width. The morphological observations were claimed to support the Italian view that criminals more often have low and backward sloping foreheads and either thicker or thinner tips of their noses than normal. Further than this, Hooton claimed to be able to demonstrate the occurrence of anthropologically abnormal body types for various categories of crime, different from one to the other.

Hooton's research has been much criticized. His control groups were too small and generally inadequate; his definition of criminality was loose, and his statistical techniques open to criticism. His findings have been difficult to replicate, and though it may be true that at the time certain criminal groups did show "inferiority" to the normal population in weight and stature, this might just as well be evidence for malnutrition in childhood as support for a genetic hypothesis.

Hooton had little theoretical background for his work, but Kretschmer's theory gave rise to a number of studies, mainly in Germany, which were summarized by Exner (1939). Of the 565 criminals investigated *in toto*, 50% were athletics, and there was a severe deficiency in pyknics! Some authors maintained that the athletic type of body build was shown particularly by criminals guilty of violence, robbery, and homicide, the characteristic crime of leptosomes being simple larceny. Thus Bohmer (1939) found in his study of 100 prisoners that all robbers and thieves were athletic, and of these 20% had previous convictions for acts of brutality, as opposed to pyknics who had none. Altogether, pyknics seem to have been underrepresented among criminals; Schwab (1983) found leptosomes most frequently represented, with pyknics trailing behind. He also found a large number of mixed types, which seems a more likely result than Exner's failure to find any. It is necessary to be somewhat critical of all this work, if only because it was mostly carried out during the Hitler period, when ideological preconceptions took precedence over factual accuracy. However, there is nothing in Nazi ideology to suggest that the athletic type should be particularly prone to criminal acts or that pyknics should be more law abiding; hence these conclusions may not have been influenced by political considerations.

CRIMINALITY AND THE SHELDON SYSTEM

We must now turn to the relationship between criminality and the Sheldon indices of body build. Sheldon, Hartl, and McDermott (1949) carried out a study of 200 delinquent youths who were somatotyped according to his system and were compared with 4,000 college students. It was found that the sample of delinquents differed sharply from the college somatotype distribution, having a distinct and heavier massing in the endomorphic–mesomorphic sector. Ectomorphs were rare, as were ectomorphic mesomorphs in comparison with endomorphic mesomorphs. As a generalization, they concluded that the 200 delinquent youths were decidedly mesomorphic and decidedly lacking in ectomorphy, but that there appeared to be no strongly defined tendency, either way, with regard to endomorphy.

Sheldon has suggested a way of representing the three-dimensional nature of his system in two dimensions and has published a distribution of somatotypes for a male college population of 4,000, in which each black dot represents 20 cases (Figure 6). For comparison, he also gives a distribution of somatotypes for his 200 delinquents (Figure 7). It is quite obvious that the dots are distributed almost at random for the normal sample, with perhaps the majority in a circle around the center, whereas for the delinquents the majority are in the endomorphic–mesomorph part, with hardly any in the ectomorphic third of the dia-

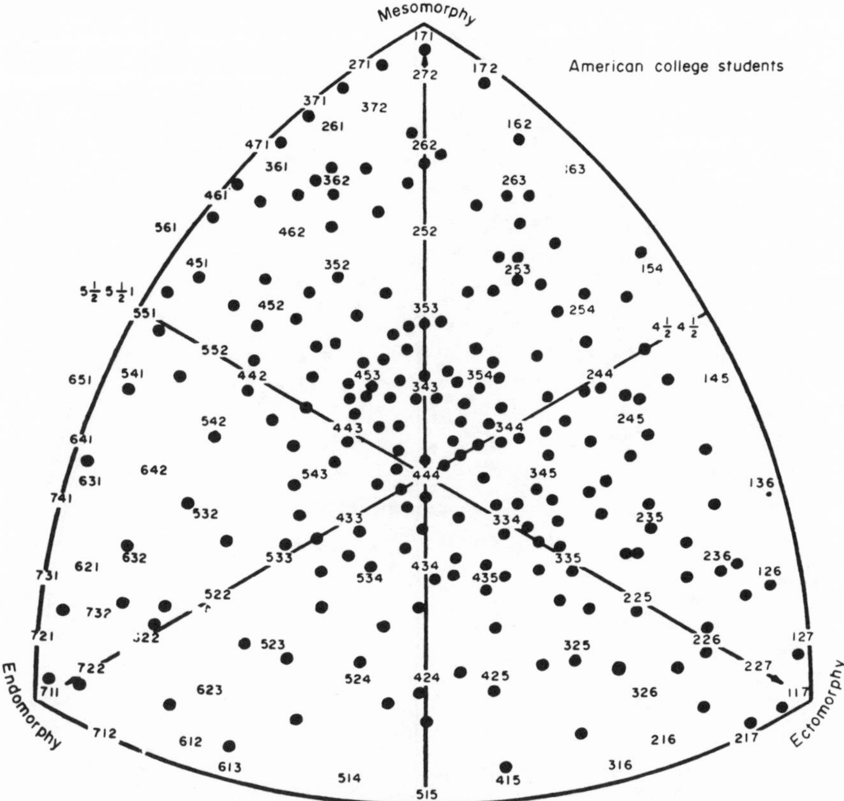

FIGURE 6. Distribution of 4,000 male college students according Sheldon's system. Each dot represents 20 cases (Sheldon, Hartl, & McDermott, 1949).

gram. This is a good *ad oculos* demonstration of the relationship between endomorphic mesomorphy and delinquency.

It should not be necessary, but may be useful nevertheless because of frequent misapprehensions on this point, to emphasize that the existence of a moderate correlation between body build and delinquency in several studies does *not* mean a kind of predestination of mesomorphs, particularly endomorphic mesomorphs, for a life of crime! The nonsensical nature of such belief can be illustrated best by looking at the inversion of the statement, to the effect that mesomorphs are most likely to indulge in crime. This would be implied by the doctrine of predestination, but is clearly not a logical deduction from the observed correlation. Figure 8 shows the distribution of somatotypes of 114 Loughborough Training College students, that is, budding athletes and teachers of

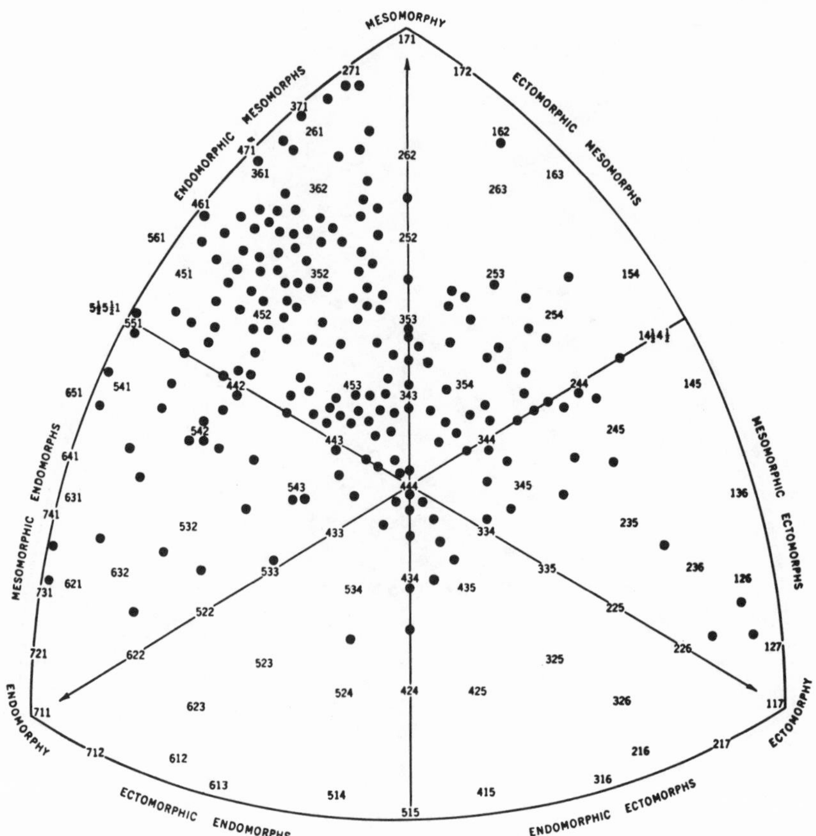

FIGURE 7. Distribution of 200 male delinquents according to Sheldon's system (Sheldon, Hartl, & McDermott, 1949).

athletics; the distribution is very similar to that of the criminals, and quite unlike that of the normal students! Yet there are very few if any delinquents in this group.

Much the same might be said of the distribution of somatotypes among Olympic weightlifters or Olympic wrestlers (H. J. Eysenck, Nias, & Cox, 1982; Tanner, 1964). Olympic track and field athletes, on the other hand, are far more frequently found in the ectomorphic–mesomorphic and ectomorphic part of the diagram (Tanner, 1964). Unpublished studies also indicate that members of commando and parachute regiments in the army are almost entirely to be found in the mesomorphic and the endomorphic–mesomorphic group, without showing any undue delinquency. And to anticipate, H. J. Eysenck, Nias, and Cox

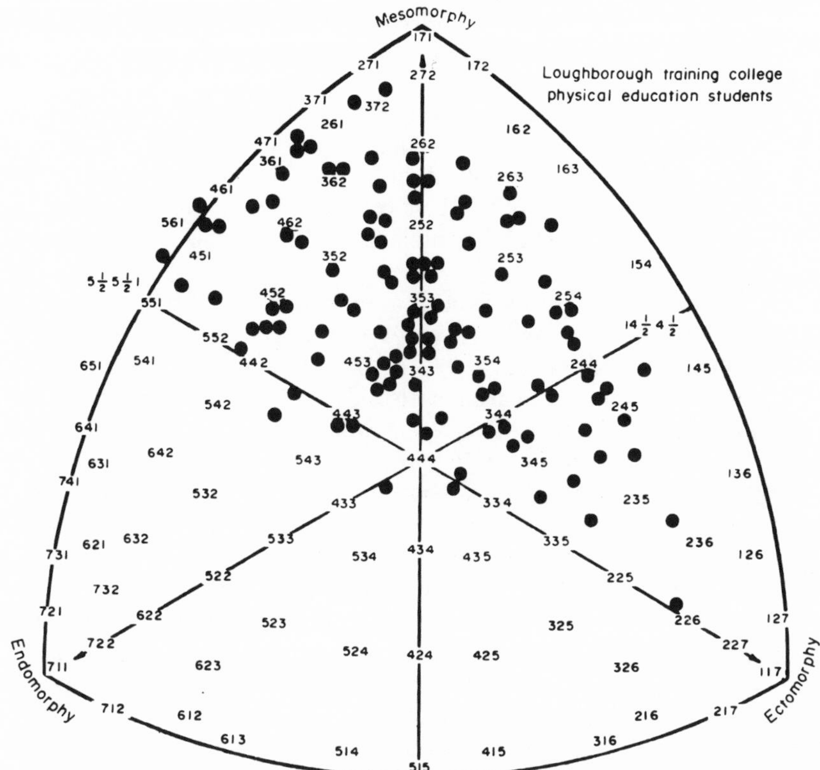

FIGURE 8. Distribution of 114 Loughborough (Athletic) Training College students according to Sheldon's system (Tanner, 1964).

(1982) have shown that sportsmen generally show similar personality traits to delinquents, without any such taint. As will be explained later on, personality and its associated body build creates certain needs and motivations that *may* manifest themselves in crime, in sports, in service with the army or the police, or in other ways; the direction of the expression of these needs and motives depends crucially on environmental factors, as well as on genetic ones.

Hartl, Monnelli, and Elderken (1982) carried out a 30-year follow-up of Sheldon's work, in which they characterized the now grown-up youths in terms of their future careers. Some of the youths had become criminals, some had turned into quite normal individuals, others still had psychosocial problems of one kind or another. The most important differentiation between normals and criminals in this sample was with respect to *mesomorphy;* future criminals were very significantly more mesomorph than normals, even in this already excessively mesomorph group. Thus mesomorphy is a predictive characteristic, related to future conduct.

It is interesting to note that a psychiatric rating made 30 years before the follow-up proved quite highly predictive also; it related to "affective exaggeration," i.e., what we would now call *neuroticism.* This is important confirmation of the general finding that there is a relationship between neuroticism and criminality, which in this case was shown to be predictive.

A well-known study by Glueck and Glueck (1956) involved 500 juvenile delinquent boys and 500 carefully matched nondelinquent controls. The Gluecks found that 60% of their delinquents were predominantly mesomorphic, compared with only 31% of the nondelinquents. This was a major difference between the groups in addition to a lower ectomorphic component in the delinquent group.

Gibbens (1963) carried out a study in which 58 young offenders were somatotyped according to Sheldon's rules; he found 29 men, i.e., exactly 50%, predominantly mesomorphic in physique, but only 11 predominantly endomorphic or ectomorphic; 12 had balanced physiques.

Epps and Parnell (1952), working as Gibbens did in England, studied a group of 177 young women, between the ages of 16 and 21, undergoing Borstal training. Anthropometric measurements were carried out on the delinquent group and compared with those of a group of 123 university women. It was found that delinquents were heavier in body build and more muscular and fat; in other words, they showed a predominance of mesomorphy and endomorphic mesomorphy. In temperament, they showed a predominance of somatotonia and viscertonia, that is, high psychoticism and high extraversion, to use terms to be explained in detail later.

Cortes and Galtti (1972) also verified the predominance of mesomorphic physique in young delinquents. Using 100 delinquents and 100 matched controls, they found that 57 of the delinquents but only 19 of the controls were predominantly mesomorphic. The delinquent group also contained fewer endomorphs (14% versus 37%) and fewer ectomorphs (16% versus 33%) as compared with the nondelinquent groups.

One of the most compelling studies in this field is that by Seltzer (1950, 1951), who used many different types of anthropometric measurements to compare subjects in two juvenile groups of 496 delinquents and 486 nondelinquents. Seltzer found delinquents to be

> absolutely and relatively more mesomorphic than the non-delinquents. The delinquents are also decidedly weaker in ectomorphy than the juveniles in the control group. The situation with regard to endomorphy, on the other hand, presents a more complicated picture. The data indicate that instances

> of extreme endomorphs are more common among the non-delinquent, but apart from these cases the relative endomorphic strength of the delinquents is by and large greater than that of the non-delinquents. Statistically significant differences in somatotype categories revealed the delinquents, relative to the non-delinquents, manifesting an excess of extreme mesomorphs, of mesomorphs, and endomorphic mesomorphs and a deficiency of extreme ectomorphs, of extreme andromorphs, of ectomorphs, and of mesomorphic ectomorphs. (p. 350)

In these data, is there any evidence of the physical inferiority suggested by Hooton and Goring? As Seltzer (1951) points out, if we define physical inferiority as representing smaller growth size, more fragile skeletal structure, weaker musculature, and less masculinity, then, from his own data, there is no evidence that the delinquents are physically inferior to the nondelinquents; indeed, there is a tendency for the reverse to be true. Of the 16 growth measurement he considered, the delinquents display *larger* mean dimensions in eleven instances. In body weight, for example, the delinquents are on the average almost 3 pounds heavier than the nondelinquents. However, the differences are on the whole quite small and certainly do not reflect any substantial superiority in growth size on the part of the delinquents. On the other hand, in skeletal structure and muscularities, the delinquent series displays considerably more ruggedness, massiveness, and hardness than the nondelinquent growth. Thus the most impressive extensive work really contradicts the assertions of the early workers in this field.

> Our data give no support to those who characterise juvenile delinquents as stunted, underdeveloped, defective, and constitutionally inferior biological organisms. (p. 364)

Seltzer uses his discovery that body disproportions are significantly less evident in the delinquent than in the nondelinquents, and from a previous study of the correlation between body disproportions and personality traits (Seltzer, 1946), he concludes that

> it would appear that the delinquents have a relatively greater frequency of those traits indicating vitality, directness, relative insensibility to fine external influences, the pragmatic trait, and sociability. The members of the nondelinquent group, because of the more disproportionate nature of their physiques, should be characterised by relatively greater frequency of those traits indicative of sensitivity and complexity of the personality, and a lesser capacity for making easy social adjustments at the personal level. They also have a strong sense of responsibility, and have difficulty in freeing themselves from the early moral attitudes. They are highly aware of their own thoughts and subjective feelings and tend to pay more attention to what is going on within themselves than do more natural and outgoing boys.

Altogether, it is clear from Seltzer's description that his findings argue for a greater degree of extraversion among delinquents and introversion among nondelinquents. Because his work on the relationship between physique and personality was done on normals, there is no direct evidence here about the personality patterns characteristic of delinquents, but as we shall see in a later chapter his conclusions are borne out by more direct studies.

It should be noted that in the Sheldon system there are other ratable characteristics of body build that have also been found relevant. The most important of these are *andromorphy* and *gynemorphy*, that is, the expression of masculine and feminine characteristics throughout the body. Sheldon, Hartl and McDermott (1949) and Hartl *et al.* (1982) found that high andromorphy was another constitutional element highly correlated with criminality. They report a study of 283 inmates of the Duerl State Penitentiary in California, where ratings were made of somatotypes and the andric-gynic components of body build. They present tables of the various components and conclude that "these data corroborate the association between criminality and the physique of high mesomorphy, low ectomorphy, and high andromorphy" (p. 535).

The fact that criminals tend to have a *male* type of body build is not surprising in view of the fact that crime is largely a male preoccupation. When women commit crimes, these are often of a sexual nature (e.g., prostitution), and these sexual crimes are of the victimless type we have agreed to be outside our definition of criminality. The fact that there is a considerable relationship between male physique and male psychology has been demonstrated by Schlegel (1983), who investigated pelvis shape. The andromorph pelvis is funnel shaped, the gynemorph pelvis is tube shaped, but both varieties (and intermediate forms, of course) can be found in both sexes. Measuring the diameter of the pelvic outlet by means of the distance between the ischimic tuberosities, Schlegel found quite high correlations between this measure and personality traits typically associated with male behavior, both in the social and the sexual field. Similar results with respect to more general features of physique have been reported by Seltzer (1945).

Physique is certainly a constitutional factor, and heredity undoubtedly plays a large part in determining it. Dahlberg (1926) compared the variability of anthropometric measurements in identical and nonidentical twins, with results showing that heredity accounted for 90% of the variability of body length measurements and slightly less for the variability of body breadth, head, and face dimensions. This finding is similar to a later one by Newman, Freeman, and Holzinger (1937). It would, of course, be nonsensical to exclude the influence of environmental factors, such as malnutrition and activity. In extreme cases, these can be very strong, but heredity plays a much more important part than environment in the ordinary run of European and American groups who formed the subjects of the studies here reviewed. It is important to note that genetic influences need not, and in the case of body shape do not, complete their work right from the beginning. As in the case of puberty, genetic influences may determine changes in rate of growth at various stages of development. A good survey of these changes has been made by Rees (1973).

CONCLUSION

The exaggerated claims for the importance of physique and stigmata by early writers like Lombroso have been shown to have little basis in fact. Minor physical anomalies, carefully measured on a quantitative basis, have been shown to be associated in both children and adults with types of behavior and personality that are more frequently found in criminals than in noncriminal groups, but there is no *direct* evidence of association with criminality. Physique, on the other hand, has been found in many different studies to be associated with criminality, and these studies gain in importance by the fact that different methods of measurement have been used, as well as different theoretical systems; furthermore, the work has been carried out by different investigators in different countries. There seems little doubt that mesomorph physique and high andromorphy are positively correlated with delinquency, and that ectomorphy is negatively correlated with delinquency. There is a strong genetic component to the development of different types of physique, although environmental factors also play a somewhat minor part, and this suggests that personality features associated with physique will also be found to differentiate criminals and noncriminals, perhaps on a partly genetic basis. These conclusions may not apply to types of delinquency not studied by the various authors mentioned. It is perfectly possible that those who commit computer crimes are more ectomorph than the muggers, robbers, and thieves who form the bulk of the criminal samples.

It is unfortunate that little work has been done on differentiating criminals of different kinds with respect to body build, but the reason may be that the number of crooks using computers to enrich themselves is vanishingly small, and it would be very difficult to obtain a reasonable sample. This may in part be due to the unwillingness of companies to prosecute former employees guilty of misconduct in this field. However, the point should always be remembered that the criminals studied by Sheldon, Seltzer, the Gluecks, and others may not be typical of *all criminals*, although they undoubtedly constitute a very large proportion of all criminals.

It is important not to misinterpret the conclusion that genetic factors play a part, through the physical developments of the person and the associated temperamental variables, in the determination of antisocial conduct. Seltzer (1951) has put it very well.

> The conclusion, that there are inherent biological factors which are in part responsible for delinquent behaviour, must not be taken to imply inherent criminality in individuals or the existence of fixed criminal anthropological types. But rather that the biological differences of delinquents reflect their possession of certain complexes of *normal* basic personality traits which under certain circumstances make them more readily activated towards the commission of anti-social acts. These personality traits or their combination are by no means the exclusive property of delinquents, but they are to be found *in greater frequency* in the delinquent population than in the non-delinquents (p. 73).

This is the essence of the threshold model illustrated in Figure 4.

CHAPTER THREE

Crime and Personality

THE DESCRIPTIVE VARIABLES: PERSONALITY RESEARCH

Implicit in our discussion of genetic factors in crime and the relationship between constitution and criminality has been the theory that criminality is closely related to personality. Such a relationship has been posited quite explicitly by H. J. Eysenck (1964) in his book *Crime and Personality*, the latest edition of which appeared in 1977 (H. J. Eysenck, 1977). The term *personality* is used in so many different ways that it may be useful to establish the particular definition of it that will be used in this book. Factors related to personality may be divided into those normally subsumed under the term *ability* and those normally subsumed under the term *temperament*. Of the former, the most important, and the most widely researched, is general intelligence, or Spearman's *g*. Temperamental variables are more numerous but, as Royce and Powell (1983) have shown in a large-scale survey of the existing correlational and factor analytic literature, there are three major higher order factors, which they call *emotional stability*, *emotional independence*, and *introversion–extraversion*. The hierarchical structure of the affective system deduced by them from the existing literature is similar to that suggested by H. J. Eysenck and S. B. G. Eysenck (1976).

These major dimensions of personality, or higher order factors, are built up from the observed correlations between primary (lower order) traits and constitute Eysenck's (H. J. Eysenck, 1970; H. J. Eysenck, 1981; H. J. Eysenck & M. W. Eysenck, 1985) system of personality. The terms used in this system are somewhat different from those suggested by Royce and Powell, and will be used in preference throughout this chapter. Introversion–extraversion remains as such and is referred to by the letter E. Emotional stability is looked at from the opposite end of instability or neuroticism and is referred to by the letter N. Emotional independence is labeled psychoticism or P, for reasons given elsewhere (H. J. Eysenck & S. B. J. Eysenck, 1976).

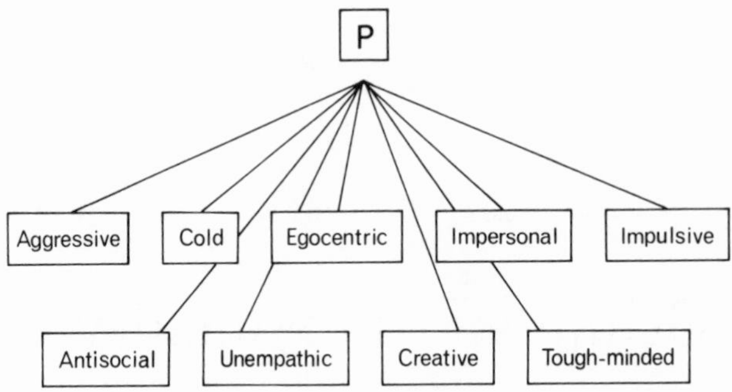

FIGURE 9. Psychoticism as a dimension of personality.

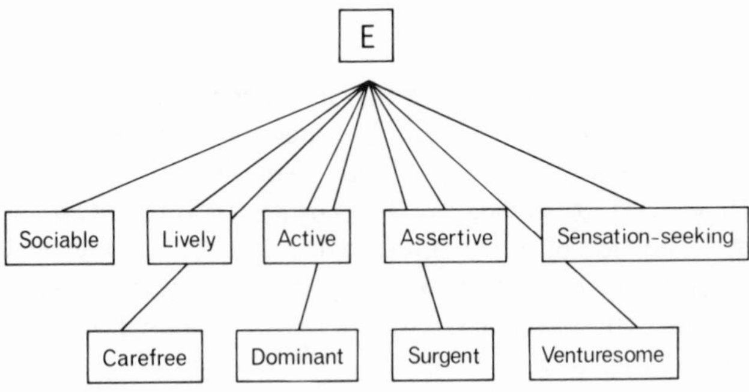

FIGURE 10. Extraversion as a dimension of personality.

It will be useful to list their traits that by their intercorrelation make up these higher order factors. The constitution of psychoticism is shown in Figure 9; it should be noted that males have much higher P scores than females. The traits listed are those characterizing the high P individual; low P individuals are empathic, unselfish, altruistic, warm, peaceful, and generally more pleasant, although possibly less socially decisive individuals.

The concept of extraversion is well known and does not require much discussion; Figure 10 shows the major traits that make up by their intercorrelations the trait of extraversion. Introverts, of course, show the opposite set of traits, but it should be noted that many individuals are not *either* extraverted *or* introverted. In all three personality dimensions we are dealing with a continuum, with a majority of people at neither extreme, but rather in the middle.

Neuroticism or instability is made up of a number of traits listed in Figure 11 below. Stability, its opposite, is, or course, shown by the

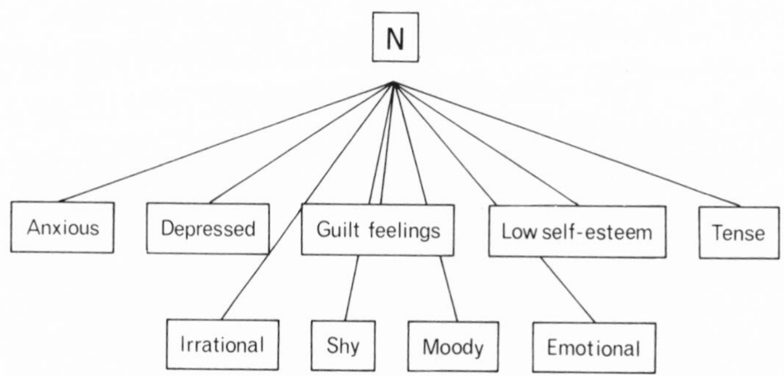

FIGURE 11. Neuroticism as a dimension of personality.

absence of these various traits, and again most people will be found at neither extreme but in the middle. There is a distinct tendency for women to have higher N scores than males. All three factors (P, E, and N) show a decline with age (H. J. Eysenck, in press a).

In laying emphasis on the *major* dimensions of personality, we do not intend to play down the contribution made by the primary ability and temperament factors (traits); undoubtedly, these may play an important part under special circumstances and contribute variance additional to that contributed by the higher order factors. Nevertheless, there is strong evidence to indicate that far more of the contributions to the prediction of everyday life behavior comes from the higher order factors than from the primaries (H. J. Eysenck & M. W. Eysenck, 1985), and furthermore far more is known about *g*, P, E, and N than about the primaries. In addition, these are more difficult to pin down, and different measures only correlate moderately with each other, although they are meant to measure the same factor. Correlations between different measures of impulsivity, or of sensation-seeking behavior, are only around 0.3; in other words, they share only less than 10% of the variance! It certainly seems advisable to place the emphasis on the higher order factors rather than on the primaries, but without denying their existence and possible importance under certain circumstances.

Before looking at the relationship between these four major personality factors (intelligence, psychoticism, extraversion, and neuroticism) with criminality, it will be useful to summarize some of the evidence relating to a number of characteristics they share in common. These can be only briefly stated here; detailed evidence on all these points will be found elsewhere (H. J. Eysenck, 1982; H. J. Eysenck & M. W. Eysenck, 1985).

In the first place, factors similar to or identical with intelligence, psychoticism, extraversion, and neuroticism appear in practically all the different testing and measuring instruments that have been constructed. In intelligence measurement, the universality of positive correlations between cognitive tasks of any kind ("positive manifold") is universally acknowledged, and the centrality of a concept of general intelligence *(g)* is no longer in question (see Snow, Kyllonen, & Marshalek, 1984, using multidimensional scaling methods, and Gustafsson, 1984, using confirmatory factor analysis. See also H. J. Eysenck, 1982). For personality, the studies of Royce and Powell (1983) and of H. J. Eysenck and M. W. Eysenck (1985) already cited contain ample evidence on this point in relation to temperament.

In the second place, these dimensions are not confined to European and North American populations, or their descendants (e.g., in Australia). Evidence for a general intelligence factor has been found among blacks, Japanese-Chinese, as well as for many other groups (Jensen, 1980), and for personality by H. J. Eysenck and S. B. G. Eysenck (1983, and Barrett & S. B. G. Eysenck, 1984). In the studies by Barrett and Eysenck, the Eysenck Personality Questionnaire (H. J. Eysenck & S. B. G. Eysenck, 1975) was given in translation to 25 different national and racial groups, chosen from the most diverse backgrounds all over the world, and the items were then correlated and factor analyzed for groups of about 500 males and 500 females in each country. Indices of factor comparison averaged around .98; that is, the factors in these different countries were as similar as those obtained from males and females within a given country! Thus the major dimensions of personality are *universal* as far as different national, racial, and cultural groups have been studied, to an extent that is truly surprising.

The results suggest that there must be a biological, genetic underpinning for these four major dimensions of personality, and the evidence seems to suggest that this is indeed so (H. J. Eysenck, 1981, 1982; H. J. Eysenck & M. W. Eysenck, 1985). Some of the evidence will be reviewed in Chapter 4 on genetic factors, and it will be shown that when corrections are made for errors of measurement, well over 50% of the total variance for IQ, psychoticism, extraversion, and neuroticism is genetic in nature. The environmental variance is largely *between families* for IQ and *within families* for temperamental variables. Errors of measurement are, of course, larger for temperament than for ability, and the corrections to be made in the raw heritability figures are larger. However, on the major issues, there can be no doubt any longer that genetic factors are more important than environmental ones in the determination of differences in ability and temperament, at least in those countries where such investigations have been carried out (which now include the USSR) (Krilov, Kulakova, Kantonistova, & Chamaganova, 1986).

It would be expected, from what has been said before, that scores on IQ and temperament tests would be *consistent* over the years, that is, that people would preserve their rank on all the factors in question, even over long periods of time. This is indeed so, as Conley (1984, 1985) has demonstrated. When corrections are made for differences in reliability of measurement, it is found that consistency is almost as high for temperamental variables as it is for ability variables, and over periods of 40 years or so there is relatively little change in the ranks occupied by different people on these various dimensions. This is an important fact when predictions are to be made from early personality to later conduct such as antisocial and criminal behavior.

It seems to be implicit in what has been said that there must be strong biological determinants of behavior, both in the sphere of abilities and temperaments, and although research is still being pursued very actively in these various areas, it may already be said that testable theories have been worked out in all these fields and that a good deal of evidence is available to support some of these theories. Evidence for the abilities side has been reviewed by H. J. Eysenck and Barrett (1985) in detail and by H. J. Eysenck and M. W. Eysenck (1985) in connection with temperament. More will be said on this point later on.

It has been suggested that the system of personality here sketched so briefly constitutes a paradigm in personality research (H. J. Eysenck, 1983) and that it brings together the major findings from many different areas of work, many different investigators, and many different countries. Clearly, this paradigm is based on the concept of *traits*, and at first sight the opposition to trait theory sparked in the 1960s by Michel and others would seem to make acceptance of such a claim doubtful. However, as M. W. Eysenck and H. J. Eysenck (1980) have pointed out, the evidence against Michel's views and in favor of trait theory is now overwhelming, and the pendulum has been swinging back from an antitrait position toward one that, like that advocated above, posits an interaction between traits as dispositional characteristics and situations relevant to response styles following these dispositions.

An important demand on any viable system of personality description and causal analysis must be that it can be integrated with important social behaviors, such as sexual behavior (H. J. Eysenck, 1976), neurosis (H. J. Eysenck, 1973), and criminality (H. J. Eysenck, 1977). It is the purpose of this chapter to document the relationship between personality and criminality, or antisocial behavior, and to demonstrate that strong relationships of this kind do exist, thus supporting the general theory.

Before turning to a consideration of the evidence, a word must be said about psychopathic, sociopathic, or "personality disorder" behavior. There are many different definitions and descriptions of this type of antisocial behavior, usually incorporating traits like unreliability, untruthfulness, insincerity, lack of remorse or shame, inadequate motivation for social behavior, poor judgment, and failure to learn from experience; pathological egocentricity and incapability for love; general poverty of major affective reactions; specific loss of insight and unresponsiveness in general interpersonal relations; impersonal sex life, trivial, and poorly integrated; and a failure to follow any life plan. In spite of these symptoms, psychopaths often present with a convincing mask of sanity (Cleckley, 1976; Hare & Cox, 1978; Robins, 1966). Psychopathy and criminality are not to be identified, although both are characterized by antisocial behavior; psychopaths are not necessarily criminals in the legal sense, and criminals may not be psychopathic in their behavior. Nevertheless, both share the trait of antisocial behavior, and it seems likely that they will also share personality traits related to this type of behavior (H. J. Eysenck, 1980; H. J. Eysenck & S. B. G. Eysenck, 1978).

H. J. Eysenck (1977) has suggested, on a theoretical basis, that antisocial behavior is related to psychoticism, extraversion, and neuroticism, and H. J. Eysenck and S. B. G. Eysenck (1978) have suggested that psychopathy is similarly related to these three dimensions of personality. This concept finds an echo in DSM–III (see H. J. Eysenck, Wakefield, & Friedman, 1983). Here personality disorders are grouped into three clusters. These clusters, as it happens, resemble quite closely the psychological personality dimensions of P, E, and N. The first cluster includes paranoid, schizoid, and schizotypal personality disorders; individuals with these disorders often appear "odd" or eccentric. This clearly is the essence of the *psychoticism* factor. The second cluster includes histrionic, narcissistic, antisocial, and borderline antisocial personality disorders, and it is stated that individuals with these disorders often appear dramatic, emotional, or erratic. These traits are characteristic of *extraversion*. The third class includes avoident, dependent, compulsive, and passive–aggressive personality disorders, and it is stated that individuals with these disorders often appear anxious or fearful. This description clearly resembles our *neuroticism* factor. (DSM–III also has a residual category, which is labeled "a typical mix of other personality disorders"; this is used for other conditions that do not qualify as personality disorders described in the manual. Clearly, this is a waste paper category of no particular interest.)

It will be clear that on the descriptive side there is a good deal of agreement between DSM–III and the system of personality description elaborated by psychologists, the only point of argument really being whether a categorical (psychiatric) or a dimensional (psychological) system is better suited to the description of personality disorders. H. J.

Eysenck (1987a) has presented evidence to show that a categorical system is effectively ruled out by the evidence and a dimensional system is more likely to do justice to the facts. Let us here merely note that there are considerable points of similarity between the psychiatric and the psychological descriptions of psychopaths and "personality disorders" and that these also show considerable similarities with antisocial and criminal subjects. It is the latter with whom we will mainly be concerned, but the large literature on psychopathy will also be considered when relevant.

INTELLIGENCE AND CRIMINALITY

Is intelligence a factor in the causation of criminal behavior? The question is an old one, and there is now a great deal of evidence regarding a statistical correlation (negative) between intelligence and antisocial and criminal behaviour. One likely explanation might be that those whose intelligence is low enough to prove a handicap for educational success will find it difficult to earn a satisfactory living along orthodox lines and may therefore turn to crime. This argument does not dispose of the possibility that within the criminal community indulging in theft, robbery, burglary, aggression, and so on, those with higher IQs might be less likely to be caught than those with lower IQs. When it is remembered that less than 20% of crimes of this type are cleared up by the police, the argument assumes an additional plausibility. However, it is easy to see that this plausibility is only apparent and not real. We are not talking about criminals who commit only one theft, burglary, or felonious assault in the course of their lives; we are dealing with criminals who indulge in hundreds of crimes in the course of a year or two; hence we must multiply the probabilities of getting caught by the frequency, and a simple statistical calculation along these lines suggests that very few will remain free for the duration of their lives! It will be remembered that most criminals have a long list of crimes they wish to have "taken into account" when they are caught and when sentence is about to be passed. These crimes were unsolved at the time, but the criminal nevertheless has finally been caught.

Another complication is that intelligence is not uncorrelated with personality. Thus psychoticism shows a *negative* correlation with intelligence (H. J. Eysenck & S. B. G. Eysenck, 1976), and as we shall see, psychoticism is one of the major determinants of antisocial behavior. If that is so, it is difficult to know which is the more important variable, intelligence or psychoticism. Is a correlation between intelligence and criminality due to the fact that both are correlated with psychoticism?

No single study has attacked this problem, and hence the question cannot be answered. However, correlations between criminality and psychoticism tend to be higher, as we shall see, than those between criminality and intelligence (about .20); it is therefore arguable that psychoticism is the more important variable, although the correlation with intelligence is not high enough, when partialed out, to eliminate intelligence completely from the equation.

Altogether, it makes good sense to implicate low intelligence in criminality. People with high IQs have a better chance to succeed in their educational endeavors, to achieve middle-class status, and to enter professions and jobs carrying social approval and reasonably high rates of financial reward. People with low IQ often have little alternative, if they want to achieve a reasonable degree of affluence, to entering a career of crime or prostitution. Clearly, mugging, larceny, burglary, and other similar activities do not require as high an IQ as does medicine, or jurisprudence, or a successful academic career. Business, too, requires a reasonably high IQ in order to be successful, although other factors, of course, also play an important part, including personality, luck, and health. We may conclude that intelligence is a factor in the causation of criminality, but that its contribution is probably smaller than one might have thought at first.

Summaries and large-scale studies by Sutherland (1931), Naar (1965), West (1967), Woodward (1955), and Brown and Courtless (1967) are generally in agreement that although more offenders have an IQ below average than above, the mean IQ of offenders is within the average range, that is, 90 to 109 IQ, with a mean probably around 92. Less than 10% of convicted criminals have an IQ below 70. Reichel (1987) gives a good summary of the evidence. In addition, Matarazzo (1972, pp. 433–439) has found that on the Wechsler scales, criminals have a relatively lower verbal IQ than performance IQ. Earlier research, as Franks (1956) has pointed out, does not show any particular *pattern* of IQ scores, for example, contrasting verbal and nonverbal intelligence.

Although the correlation between delinquency and low IQ is undisputed, it is often argued that IQ is a spurious variable in the relationship between socioeconomic states (SES) and delinquency, a lower rearing-class status reflecting intellectual and emotional deprivation that motivates later illegal activity. Others have argued that intelligence, regardless of rearing status, is a chief determinant of criminal behaviour. A classic review of the evidence concerning the intelligence of delinquents and criminal offenders has made a strong case that IQ has an effect on criminal behavior *independent* of social class and race (Hirschi & Hindelang, 1977).

Clearly, only large-scale follow-up studies can settle this question, and the recent work of McGarvey, Gabrielli, Bentler, and Mednick (1981) and Moffitt, Gabrielli, Mednick, and Schulsinger (1981) appears to have decided the matter. These investigators found that the negative correlation between IQ and level of delinquent involvement *remains* after SES effects are partialed out. They also found that rearing social class does relate to criminal behavior, but indirectly. The model tested and supported in their research was that rearing-class status predicts educational performance, which in turn precedes the development of criminal activity. They posit that low IQ children may be likely to engage in delinquent behavior because their poor verbal abilities limit their opportunities to obtain rewards in the school environment.

An important question still remains to be answered, namely whether prison inmates differ psychometrically from the general population mainly on the *g* factor or whether there are different psychometric patterns (such as the verbal versus performance difference already mentioned) that produce the overall difference. Jensen and Faulstich (in press) have looked into this problem, using the revised Wechsler adult scales on white and black delinquents and comparing their results with age-standardized scores based on a national probability sample. They found that the main source of the differences between criminal and noncriminal groups was predominantly produced by differences in *g;* they also found that the higher performance versus verbal subscores typically found in criminal offenders constituted a relatively weak effect when *g* was removed.

It should be added that all the data obtained refer, of course, to offenders and criminals who have been caught, and the possibility exists that more intelligent criminals, possibly engaging in white-collar crimes such as offenses involving computers, may not be caught in equal proportions. There is probably some effect along these lines, but it should not be exaggerated. The number of white-collar offenders, particularly those involved with computers, is probably quite small compared with the large number of delinquents involved in stealing, burglaries, muggings, and assaults, so that their inclusion would not materially affect the issue. Schmid (1980) gives some data to show that white-collar criminals, even the most successful ones, do not in fact have high IQs. However, it is worthwhile to remember that the published figures deal largely with only some kinds of criminal activity, although that activity is probably the most widespread of all.

If correlations between IQ and criminality are usually between −.2 and −.3, that is, contributing between 4% and 9% of the variance, it must be remembered that the determination of criminality is far from perfect and that any reasonable correction for attenuation would probably bring these values up to something like 12 to 16%. However, the main interest of the IQ dimension in relation to criminality lies in rather a different direction, namely the explanatory value it has for the very frequently observed racial differences in criminality between whites and blacks. This differentiation contrasts with that between white and oriental races, with whites usually having higher prevalence rates for delinquency. Ellis (in press) has summarized 49 studies pertaining primarily to serious victimful offenses, and in this meta-analysis found an unusually high probability of criminal behavior for blacks when compared with whites, and especially when compared with orientals. He concludes that there are consistent tendencies for blacks to have the highest rates of criminal behavior, orientals to have the lowest rates, and whites to have intermediate rates. "The results are less clear for fairly minor and/or victimless offenses." Note that these studies come from at least five different countries, showing that the relationship is not confined to the United States or Great Britain, but is fairly universal.

Gordon (1986a, 1986b, in press) has, on the basis of large-scale data from the United States, suggested that the *only* cause for the differential prevalence of delinquency between blacks and whites is the difference in IQ and that the many putative causes of delinquency must be subsumed by IQ parameters because they would no longer add anything to IQ for explaining differences in prevalence between the races. His argument is a powerful one, and the data are on such a scale that they would be difficult to fault. Gordon begins his argument by pointing out that black–white differences in the United States, on tests of general intelligence, amount to almost 1.1 white standard deviations in every period studied (Coleman *et al.*, 1966; Department of Defense, 1982; Department of Health, Education and Welfare, 1976; Jensen & Reynolds, 1982; Kaufman & Doppelt, 1976; Shuey, 1966). The differences average around 16 points of IQ, but, of course, this difference varies from northern to southern states and is merely a global average. The black standard deviation is about .80 as large as the white standard deviation.

There is, of course, no necessary relation linking the strength of causes within groups to their strength as explanations of differences between groups. Gordon was led to working out his models by bringing together four different areas of knowledge. The first of these was the existence of sex- and race-specific estimates of a statistic called *lifetime prevalence* of delinquency (Gordon, 1973; Gordon & Gleser, 1974). This referred to the proportion of individuals born in the same year who qualified in some way as delinquent at 18.0 years. *Prevalence* is an *offender* rate rather than an *offense* rate, and each person is counted only once, unlike the case with some incidence rates. When calculated for entire communities or nations, prevalence also refers to whole populations. These characteristics make prevalence especially suitable for the study of individual and group differences.

In the second place, Gordon had performed a meta-analysis of prevalence rates for whites from various studies and had found that when age, sex, race, and a variety of the delinquency criteria were held constant, prevalence rates varied hardly at all from time to time, or by size of community, over most of the urban–rural continuum (Gordon, 1976). (Taking severity into account when comparing studies is necessary because it controls the inclusiveness of the definition of delinquent. For example, among white males, the prevalence of appearance in Juvenile Court at least once by age 18.0 is approximately 18 times the prevalence of commitment to a training school for delinquents.) In these data, there was no evidence for an effect for city size once communities of size 10,000 or so were exceeded; it was the confounding of racial composition with the size of place that created the impression of a widespread association between "urbanism" and crime (Gordon, 1976; Laub, 1983).

The third item of evidence was the fact already referred to, that there is a difference of about one standard deviation between blacks and whites in IQ, and this suggested to Gordon that comparing delinquency rates of blacks and whites was the logical next step in checking for an IQ effect.

The fourth fact, and the crucial one, was that Gordon and Gleser (1974) had already found prevalence rates for blacks and whites in terms of percentiles that were about one standard deviation apart on the cumulative normal probability distribution. This was true both for males and females.

Gordon used this goodness-of-fit statistic to conclude that the black–white difference and prevalence of delinquency is commensurate with black–white differences in IQ parameters or distributions and, ultimately, with black–white differences in the underlying trait that IQ measures. He called this property of well-fitting prevalence traits *IQ-commensurability*. When pairs of prevalence rates are found to have the property of IQ-commersurability, we understand that the usual black–white ratio of three or four to one in prevalence rates has been found to be proportional to black–white differences in IQ. Consequently, the data are in accord with the principle, when deciding causality, that effects should be proportionate to their causes (Einhorn & Hogarth, 1986). Gordon concluded that "although simulations and data indicate that black–white differences in crime and delinquency are not determined solely by the IQs of lone individuals, the difference may be determined entirely by IQ levels of groups nonetheless."

One obvious possible criticism of Gordon's work would be that the IQ effects are secondary to socioeconomic status variables of one kind or another. Gordon has demonstrated that this is not so, exploring alternate hypotheses by substituting SES parameters for IQ parameters in his analysis (Gordon, in press). All known SES status variables relevant for the purpose were employed, including male income, female income, education attainment, and occupational prestige. The mean reduction in variance was 18.6%; IQ averaged a 98.4% reduction! Income for males performed worst of all. Family income did better, but was still below average among SES variables that reduced between-group variance.

These results for income are particularly interesting because group differences in delinquency are often attributed to poverty. No SES variable ever produced a better fit than IQ for the same prevalence rates. The best outcomes were for SES variables best qualified to act as surrogates for IQ in the adult population, such as years of schooling, and the Duncan Index of occupational prestige, which Duncan himself described as measuring something very like the "intelligence demands" of an occupation (Duncan, Featherman, & Duncan, 1972, p. 77). "Thus," Gordon pointed out, "even when SES variables were most successful in the model, such success itself constituted evidence for the importance of IQ to group differences in delinquency."

Gordon concluded his survey by saying that

> the various results reported here, based on six sources of evidence in more than thirty sets of observations representing millions of individuals, are surprisingly consistent in identifying black–white differences in IQ as a source of major black–white differences in the lifetime prevalence of criminals and delinquents of varying degrees of severity.

This clearly negates the prime importance given to social and economic factors by most sociologists, economists, and politicians. It does not, of course, deny the fact that *within* black or white populations factors other than intelligence may be much more important than IQ.

A very recent study by Kendel *et al.* (1988) gives support to the view that it is IQ which may act as a protective factor for subjects at high risk for antisocial behaviour. In their project they compared the characteristics of four groups of men from a Danish birth cohort: (a) those at high-risk for serious criminal involvement (with severely criminal fathers) who nevertheless succeeded in avoiding criminal behavior; (b) those at high-risk who evidenced serious criminal behavior; (c) those at low-risk (with non-criminal fathers) who did not evidence criminal behavior; and (d) those at low-risk who nevertheless evidenced serious criminal behavior. The probands were tested by means of an abbreviated version of the Wechsler Adult Intelligence Scale, and it was found that the first group evidenced a mean IQ score that was significantly higher than that of the other risk groups. This was interpreted by the authors in terms of the possible role of high IQ in protecting high-risk men from criminal involvement, through mediating reinforcing effects of success in the school system. It does seem that low IQ is a potent mediator of criminal conduct, although that mediation may be indirect and comes through affecting success at school.

TEMPERAMENT AND CRIMINALITY

We have already noted the major dimensions of personality in its noncognitive aspects that according to theory are related to criminality. The general theory concerning this relationship has been developed by J. H. Eysenck (1977), and it is this that we will mainly be concerned with here. According to this theory, criminality and antisocial conduct are positively and causally related to high psychoticism, high extraversion, and high neuroticism. The more fundamental, biological aspects of the theory will be discussed in a later chapter. Here let us merely note that the theory posits biologically determined low degrees of arousal and arousability in extraverts and possibly also in persons high on the psychoticism scale. These lead to behaviors (risk taking, sensation seeking, impulsivity, etc.) that increase the cortical level of arousal to a more acceptable amount. Behaviors of this type do not necessarily lead to actual antisocial behavior; they may also lead to participation in sports, adventure, and other arousal-producing activities. Neuroticism-anxiety, as in the Hullian system, acts as a drive that multiplies with the learned behavior patterns based on this biological foundation and in such a way as to increase the antisocial behavior produced by the P and E personality traits.

In this chapter, we will simply look at the evidence suggesting that antisocial behavior is indeed linked with personality in the way suggested; in a later chapter we will deal with the biological aspects of the theory and look at the evidence concerning them. However, one further important aspect of the theory must be mentioned, namely that linking introversion with ease and speed of Pavlovian conditioning (H. J. Eysenck, 1967, 1981). According to this theory, prosocial conduct has to be *learned* by the growing child, and this learning is accomplished through a process of Pavlovian conditioning. Prosocial conduct is praised, antisocial conduct is punished by peers, parents, teachers, and others, and through a thousandfold repetition of such reinforcements, "conscience" becomes established as a conditioned response, leading to prosocial and altruistic behavior. As introverts form conditioned responses of this type more readily than extraverts, they are more easily socialized through Pavlovian conditioning and hence are less likely to indulge in antisocial activities. The theory here presented very briefly is developed extensively elsewhere (H. J. Eysenck, 1967, 1977).

Early studies of the theory, in its original form as presented in the first edition of *Crime and Personality* in 1964, were summarized by Passingham (1972). The general outcome of this analysis was somewhat contradictory. More studies agreed than disagreed with the hypotheses, but on the whole the support was not strong. This is not surprising. Many of the studies were carried out before the hypothesis was put forward and used questionnaires and inventories less than ideally suited for the purpose and sometimes only tangentially relevant. Control groups were not always carefully selected; some investigators, for instance, have used the ubiquitous student groups as controls, which is inadmissible. There was often failure to control for dissimulation through the use of lie scales. Where lie scales were introduced, sometimes very high levels of dissimulation were recorded, but this information was not used in the interpretation of the data. The fact that criminals are not a homogeneous group was disregarded; different investigators have studied different populations, specializing in different types of crime. Other problems are considered by H. J. Eysenck (1977). It would seem better to confine attention to later studies, geared to the theory in question and using inventories directly relevant, such as the EPI and the EPQ. Such a review of later studies is presented by J. H. Eysenck (1977) with much more positive results.

It might seem that a meta-analysis of all available studies would help to decide the issue, but for reasons given elsewhere (H. J. Eysenck, 1984), this would not be appropriate. Meta-analysis throws together with great impartiality good and bad studies, properly and poorly controlled investigations, using relevant or irrelevant measuring instruments, and quite generally cannot replace the scientific judgment so necessary in evaluating evidence. It gives a false sense of objectivity and fairness, particularly in a field where there is a great variety of methodologies, measuring instruments, experimental and control groups, and methods of analysis. What has been done here is to concentrate on studies appearing more recently, using suitable measuring instruments, and employing relatively large samples. Older and less relevant studies will be found in the reviews by Passingham and by Eysenck already mentioned.

Two important points should be noted at this stage. The first relates to *age*. It has usually been found that although P is always relevant to antisocial behavior, E is relevant more in young children and possibly juveniles, as compared with older criminals, whereas the reverse is true of N. This is only a trend, but it may be due to two causes. The first is that older samples are usually incarcerated and younger samples are often tested with self-report inventories. Incarceration itself, particularly when long continued, may produce a reduction in extraverted behavior (H. J. Eysenck, 1977); incarcerated criminals can hardly go to parties, make friends easily, and indulge in other activities characteristic of extraverts! An alternative hypothesis is that extraversion is more relevant at the stage when new habits are acquired; neuroticism as a drive variable more relevant when it multiplies, according to Hullian theory, with already established habits.

A direct study of the possibility that prisoners may understate their extraversion in personality inventories was undertaken by McCue, Booth, and Root (1976). They argued that a negative correlation between L and E might be expected if extraversion was being understated. For their sample of 148 young male prisoners, they reported that "There was no correlation between E and L, and no indication of extraversion being under- or over-stated" (p. 283). In actual fact, as McCue pointed out in a personal communication dated May 14, 1977, there was an error in the calculation, and the r was significant at the .02 level, amounting to $-.29$. Thus the data supports the possibility that prisoners may understate their degree of extraversion.

The other point worth mentioning here is related to the relative *heterogeneity* of criminal groups. It would be unrealistic to assume that murderers must have the same personality as con men, violent offenders the same personality traits as property offenders. S. B. G. Eysenck, Rust, and H. J. Eysenck (1977) have studied five groups of criminals characterized by their respective crimes as con men, property offenders, violent offenders, inadequates, and a residual group guilty of different types of offenses. Figure 12 shows the resulting differentiation in terms of scores on the P, E, and N scales of the EPQ. Thus con men are low on P, low on N, and high on E, whereas inadequates are high on P, high on N, and low on E.

The same study, using EPQ and Galvanic Skin Response (GSR) data for these five groups, showed in a discriminant function analysis a clear separation of the five groups of offenders (Figure 13). These results suggest that in addition to a general factor of antisocial behavior, there are specific factors leading to different *types* of reaction. These also have correlates in personality and will be discussed briefly later.

A study specially directed to the analysis of heterogeneity was published by Bohman, Cloninger, Sigvardsson, and von Knorring (1982), using as subjects 862 Swedish men adopted by nonrelatives at an early age. Criminality was found in 12% of the adopted men, 26% of their biological fathers, and none of their adoptive fathers. There was a marked difference between those whose crime was or was not related to alcohol abuse. Risk for criminality was increased in those men whose biological fathers had no diagnosis of alcoholism but convictions for a small num-

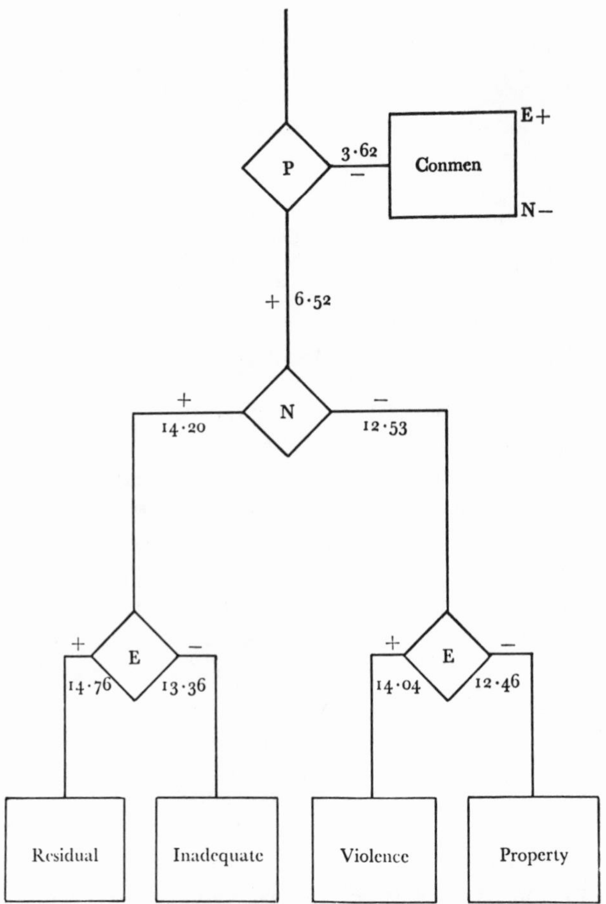

FIGURE 12. Five groups of criminals distinguished in terms of personality (Eysenck, Rust, & Eysenck, 1977).

ber of non violent crimes. In contrast, the sons of biological fathers with a diagnosis of alcoholism and/or convictions for alcohol abuse and violent crimes had a high risk for alcohol abuse but not criminality. A detailed analysis of the data led these authors to conclude that "Criminality without alcohol abuse is characterized by petty property offenses whereas alcohol related criminality is often more violent and highly repetitive" (p. 1246). Thus already from the genetic point of view, crimes involving or not involving violence are clearly differentiated.

In spite of the heterogeneity undoubtedly present in prison populations, it can be shown that there is some generality also. Thus Table

TABLE 2. P, E, and N Scores of Groups of Adult Male Prisoners and Controls: Data from Two Independent Investigations

	n	Psychoticism	Extraversion	Neuroticism
S.B.G. Eysenck				
(a) Prisoners	1301	6.55±3.16	12.51±3.63	11.39±4.97
(b) Controls	1392	4.10±2.53	11.65±4.37	9.73±4.71
		$p<0.001$	$p<0.001$	$p<0.001$
A. MacLean				
(a) Prisoners	569	6.65±3.12	12.47±3.67	11.77±4.98
(b) Controls	595	4.38±2.32	11.54±3.62	8.82±4.50
		$p<0.001$	$p<0.001$	$p<0.001$

Note. From *Crime and Personality*, 3rd ed., by H. J. Eysenck. London: Routledge & Kegan Paul, 1977, p. 60.

2 (H. J. Eysenck, 1977) shows the result of what is probably the largest investigation comparing prisoners and suitable controls (male). There are altogether 1,870 prisoners, and 1,987 controls, in two independent studies carried out by S. B. G. Eysenck and A. MacLean respectively. It will be seen that in both investigations prisoners are very significantly higher on P, E, and N, as expected by the theory. Such a result cannot be invalidated by the usual small-scale studies of groups of a hundred or less prisoners and controls, tested under unspecified motivational conditions, often with unsuitable instruments, and not con-

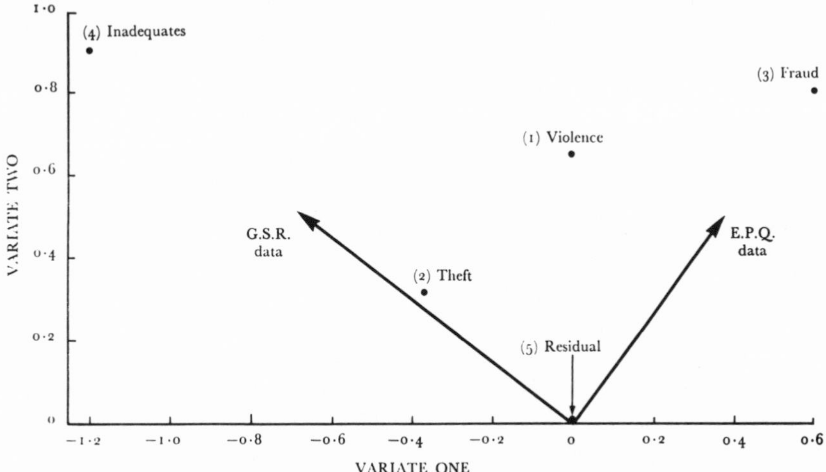

FIGURE 13. Discriminant function analysis of five groups of criminals in terms of personality and psychophysiological reaction (Eysenck, Rust, & Eysenck, 1977).

trolled for such variables as age. Yet this is precisely what meta-analysis would do.

The design of the study just mentioned is a classical one in which a group of convicted offenders, usually incarcerated, is compared with a control group, equated on a number of variables such as age, social status, and sex with respect to personality variables of one kind or another. Such a design, although informative, has one obvious disadvantage in that the control group will almost undoubtedly contain a number of people who should be counted as "criminals" except for the fact that they have not yet been caught! In other words, assuming as we do a continuum of antisocial activity, the two groups overlap possibly to quite a large extent, and hence the differences between them will in truth be much larger than those that emerge from the statistical analysis. In spite of this weakness, this is obviously a valuable paradigm, and we will mention a number of other studies following this paradigm presently.

One additional disadvantage of this paradigm is, of course, that the personality variables measured may be affected by the incarceration; thus being in prison, particularly for a long period of time, may increase the neurotic fears and anxieties of the prisoner and may reduce his extraversion, as already mentioned. If this were so, then longer incarceration should lead to different scoring patterns as compared with short incarcerations, but this has not been found. However, the best proof that it is personality that determines criminality, rather than incarceration determining personality, comes from studies either using nonincarcerated offenders or predicting later criminal behavior in groups followed up over many years from earlier measures of personality. Both these types of investigation will be discussed in this chapter.

Work on self-reported acts of delinquency and antisocial conduct, as related to personality, began with a study by Gibson (1971) of the factorial structure of juvenile delinquency in self-reported acts, in which he found a very prominent general factor as well as other factors indicating a certain amount of heterogeneity. A very detailed discussion of the evidence supporting the validity and reliability of self-report as a measure of criminality is given by Hindelang, Hirschi, and Weis (1979, 1981; see also Singh, 1979).

This work was followed by a study by Allsopp and Feldman (1976) relating to an antisocial behavior inventory constructed on the basis of Gibson's work (ABS scale) to personality. They used two different indices of antisocial behavior. The first was the self-report measure of antisocial behavior (ASB). This subjective index was supplemented by objective records of classroom detention and other punishments inflicted by teachers for misbehavior (Na = naughtiness score). For all the groups

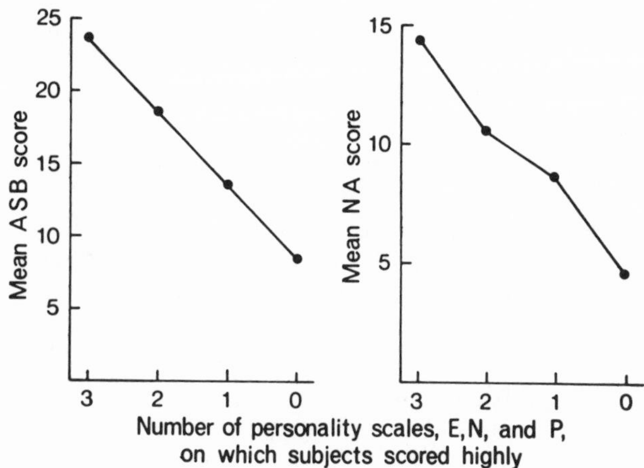

FIGURE 14. Children's scores on ASB (antisocial behavior self-rating scale) and NA (naughtiness score) as determined by their having 0, 1, 2, or all 3 scores on P, E, and N above the mean (Allsopp & Feldman, 1976).

studied by Allsopp and Feldman, these two indices were found to correlate together quite well and to give similar personality differences between normal and antisocial children, a fact that gives us confidence that the apparent subjectivity of the ASB questionnaire does not preclude considerable empirical validity.

In a first study, Allsopp and Feldman (1974) studied four groups of subjects. A total of 197 subjects took part and the major outcome of the study is shown in Figure 14. This groups together children who show high scores on none, one, two, or all three of the personality scales (P, E, and N); on the abscissa are given the mean ASB and Na scores for these four groups. It will be seen that there is a linear or at least monotonic increase in antisocial behavior with increase in P, E, or N; all three scales contribute about equally to the total result.

In a second study Allsopp and Feldman (1976) used 385 boys ranging in age from 11 to 16; these were tested in a grammar school. The analysis in this case was carried out for individual items of the various personality scales, which makes summary of the results somewhat difficult. However, as far as P is concerned, it was found that all 17 P items differentiated between high and low ASB scorers in the predicted manner. On E, all but three of the items differentiated the groups in the predicted manner, the only one showing more than minimal discrimination in the wrong direction being concerned with participation in hobbies and interests, a finding easily explained. On N, the hypothesis is upheld for most items, but there are several that do not conform, for reasons explained by the authors. However, it would be safe to assume from this and other studies that the importance of N is greater for older subjects and less for school children. The general outcome of this study cross-validates the results reported in the earlier work.

Allsopp and Feldman (1976) have reported one further study where they used 461 children between the ages of 13 and 16; of these, results will here be reported only on the 368 white boys. Teachers were asked to rate the behavior of the boys; on this basis, they were divided into well and badly behaved. When these ratings were compared with the personality scale scores, the results indicated that "badly-behaved boys predominate at the high level of P and at the low level of P where there is a combination of high E/high N scores; well-behaved boys predominate at the low level of P except where E and N are simultaneously high." When we turn to the ASB, we may use a factor-analytic subdivision of the scale into 10 factors. All the correlations with P, E, and N were positive, being highest with P and lowest with N. The results certainly bear out the general hypothesis in considerable detail.

A follow-up study to the Allsopp and Feldman one has been reported by Rushton and Chrisjohn (1981), using eight separate samples of high school and university students, totaling 410. Self-report paper-and-pencil questionnaire measures of both personality and delinquency were administered under conditions that ensured anonymity. The evidence showed clear support for the relationship between high delinquency scores and high scores on both extraversion and psychoticism. These relationships held up across diverse samples and different ways of analyzing the data. No support was found for a relationship between delinquency scores and the dimension of neuroticism.

Another replication has been reported by Silva, Martorell, and Clemente (1986) in Spain. An adaptation of the Allsopp and Feldman ASB, the junior version of the EPQ, and the S. B. G. Eysenck and H. J. Eysenck (1980) scales of impulsivity, venturesomeness, and empathy were administered to a Spanish population of children and adolescents. Results of analysis for three groups of low, medium, and high ASB scorers are given in Table 3. It will be seen that both on test and retest the high (antisocial) scorers are significantly higher on P, E, and N, lower on the lie scale (which in this case can probably be regarded as a measure of conformity), and higher on the criminality scale (Saklofske, McKerracher, & Eysenck, 1978), which combines the items in the EPQ most diagnostic of antisocial behavior. High ASB scorers are also very significantly higher on impulsivity and venturesomeness and lower in empathy.

Table 4 shows the results of the study in terms of correlations, for boys and girls separately and for test and retest separately. Also given

TABLE 3. ANOVA for Three Groups

	ASB Test				ASB Retest			
	Low	Medium	High	$P<$	Low	Medium	High	$P<$
P	−1.38	−0.26	1.90	.01	−1.36	−.46	2.38	.001
E	−.48	−.19	0.89	.05	−1.15	.09	.80	.01
N	−1.14	−.06	1.17	.01	−1.90	.25	1.10	.001
L	2.95	44	4.58	.001	2.60	.61	−4.66	.001
C	−1.99	−.47	2.96	.001	3.09	−.31	3.54	.001
Imp.	−2.52	−.47	3.42	.001	−3.31	−.07	3.11	.001
Vent.	−2.05	.17	1.40	.001	−1.71	.20	1.02	.001
Em.	.71	.33	1.45	.001	.55	.50	1.70	.001

ANOVA for 3 groups: Low ASB ($N=72$), Medium ASB ($N=250$), and High ASB ($N=81$). Deviations from mean.

Note. From "Socialization and Personality: Study through Questionnaires in a Preadult Spanish Population" by F. Silva, C. Martorell, and A. Clemente, *Personality and Individual Differences*, 1986, *7*, p. 367.

TABLE 4. Reliability of Scales Test–Retest Used in Silva *et al.* (1986), and Correlations with ASB

		ASB			
		Boys ($N=174$)		Girls ($N=183$)	
	Test–retest reliability	Test	Retest	Test	Retest
P	.56	.44	.51	.43	.32
E	.69	.05	.07	.21	.21
N	.63	.17	.15	.24	.29
L	.75	−.47	−.49	−.62	−.61
C	.55	.42	.53	.47	.40
Imp.	.68	.43	.42	.47	.54
Vent.	.70	.26	.16	.29	.35
Emp.	.69	−.32	−.35	−.12	−.02

are the test–retest reliabilities of the various scales. The results show pretty clearly that P has the highest correlations with the ASB scale, particularly for the boys, with E and N having higher correlations for the girls. The L scale, measuring conformity in this group rather than dissimulation, has very high correlations (negative) particularly for girls, and the criminality scale also has high correlations for both. Impulsivity is clearly correlated with the ASB scale, venturesomeness less so, and empathy has a negative correlation, but negligibly small for girls, reasonably high for boys. In view of the rather low reliability of the trait measures, all these correlations would be much higher if corrected for attenuation. All in all, the figures leave little doubt that there is a strong relationship between antisocial behavior, as reported by the children themselves, and personality. The test–retest reliability of the ASB scale is .67, so that correction for attenuation in the criterion might also be advisable.

How much difference would correction for attenuation make in these data? Let us consider a test correlating .50 with the ASB scale, with a test–retest reliability of .70. Corrected for attenuation, the correlation of test with ASB scores would rise from .50 to .72, doubling the validity ($.50^2 \times 2 < .72^2$). This suggests that several of the personality scales share half the total variance with the ASB scale. It can hardly be said that this is not a valuable and important item of information.

The self-reported antisocial behavior scores cannot be assumed to lack validity. In a later study Silva, Martorell, and Salvador (1987) have shown that on relevant items, the ASB scale correlated .52 with teachers' ratings, based on the actual behavior at school of these boys and girls. Actually, the validity of the ASB scores in this study is probably underestimated because teachers are often ignorant of relevant behaviors of the children in their charge. In a sample of 285 high school boys, Erickson (1972) found a correlation of .72 (Gamma coefficient) between self-reports and court records and a correlation of .66 between self-reported delinquency and future court appearances. This paper discusses the validity of the self-reported delinquency in detail and clearly establishes its value.

Perez and Torrubia (1985) in Spain studied sensation seeking and antisocial behavior in a sample of 349 male and female students, using the Zuckerman (Zuckerman, S. B. G. Eysenck, & H. J. Eysenck, 1978) sensation-seeking scale, a component of E and P, and a Spanish version of self-reported delinquency. The results "bear out the existence of a very high relationship between the sensation seeking trait and antisocial behavior in student populations" (p. 402).

Jamison (1980) obtained results very similar to those of Silva *et al.* (1987) in a study of 1,282 white secondary school children in England. Correlations between the ASB scale for boys and girls separately with the junior EPQ are reported in Table 5; it will be seen that again the highest correlations are with P and L (negative); those with E are reasonably high, those with N quite small but still positive.

A particularly large and well-designed study has been reported by Powell (1977; Powell & Stewart, 1983). The subjects were 808 white nondelinquent children in normal schools, a total of 381 boys and 427

TABLE 5. Correlations of ASB with Personality Variables

	N	P	E	N	L
Boys	781	.58	.31	.10	−.56
Girls	501	.59	.40	.09	−.60

Note. From "Psychoticism, Deviancy and Perception of Risk in Normal Children" by R. N. Jamison, *Personality and Individual Differences*, 1980, *1*, p. 88.

TABLE 6. Correlations of P, E, N, and L with ASB

		Correlation			
	Age	PB	EB	NB	LB
Boys	15 yr	0.51**	0.41**	0.32*	−0.48**
	13 yr	0.52**	0.52**	0.34	−0.61**
	11 yr	0.48**	0.07	0.18	−0.59**
	10 yr	0.42**	0.19	−0.04	−0.52**
	9 yr	0.51**	−0.17	0.09	−0.43**
	8 yr	0.32*	0.17	0.34*	−0.42**
	Senior	0.47**	0.26**	0.18*	−0.64**
	Junior	0.42**	0.04	0.09	−0.48**
Girls	15 yr	0.57**	0.12	0.39**	−0.59**
	13 yr	0.55**	0.38**	0.13	−0.59**
	11 yr	0.13	0.04	0.33**	−0.31**
	10 yr	0.47**	−0.02	0.07	−0.50**
	9 yr	0.58**	0.26**	0.17	−0.47**
	8 yr	0.31	−0.04	0.38*	−0.62**
	Senior	0.44**	0.17*	0.30**	−0.56**
	Junior	0.48**	0.10	0.17*	−0.50**

*$p < 0.05$.
**$p < 0.01$.

Note. From "Psychoticism and Social Deviancy in Children" by G. E. Powell, *Advances in Behavior Research and Therapy*, 1977, *1*, p. 37.

girls, subdivided into six age groups from 8 at the bottom to 15 at the top. For some analyses, a division was made between all senior and all junior children, with average ages of 13 and 9 respectively. Children were given the Junior EPQ and a social attitude test measuring religiosity, ethnocentrism, punitiveness, sex/hedonism, and conservatism. They were also administered a version of the ASB and a teachers' rating scale meant to measure general level of disturbance, antisocial behavior, and neurotic behavior. The main results of this study, in so far as they are relevant to this chapter, are seen in Table 6. Correlations of the

ASB scale, as in other studies, are highest with P and (negatively) with L. Correlations with E and N are in the expected direction, but lower. Powell subdivided extraversion into two factors, impulsivity and sociability, following the suggestion often made the impulsivity is more important for antisocial behavior than sociability.

> There was. . . . absolutely no evidence that the Impulsivity aspect of E is more related to criminality than is the Sociability factor. Neither Impulsivity nor Sociability correlate better with misbehaviour than does the E scale as a whole. It could be argued that treating E as two factors is only relevant when dealing with a prison population when unsociability measures are directly affected by their restricted environment. (p. 38)

Powell also followed up the suggestion by Burgess (1972) that a combination if high E and high N predicts antisocial behavior better than the scales taken separately and that the formula h (hedonism) $= E \times N$ might be used, where h would predict criminality. For senior and junior boys, the values for h were .30 and .12; for girls they were .37 and .20. Clearly, the values are higher for senior boys and girls and assume a reasonable size, although still lower than they are for P.

Using stepwise multiple regression techniques, Powell found multiple correlations for senior and junior boys and senior and junior girls of .72, .54, .64, and .61 respectively.

> The size of these correlations indicates the high degree with which personality predicts self-reported misbehaviour, it being difficult, in fact, to see how the correlations could be much higher unless the reliability of the scales could be substantially improved, with a concomitant reduction in errors of measurement. (p. 38)

Powell reports correlations between the ASB scale and social attitudes, which are of some interest. Table 7 shows these correlations; it will be seen that they are negative with conservatism and religiosity but positive with ethnocentrism, punitiveness, and sex/hedonism. The direction of the correlation is perhaps not surprising, but their size is probably greater than would have been expected.

Almost all these studies using the ASB or similar device of self-reported delinquency have been carried out on children or juveniles. Before turning to work with adults, we may mention briefly some relevant studies using behavior rather than (or as well as) self-reports in relation to personality. In a study by Saklofske, McKerracher, and Eysenck (1978), the EPQ was administered to five groups of adolescent boys, classified into four groups of 20 each by staff ratings and the self-report questionnaire of antisocial behavior. The fifth group of 20 comprised delinquent boys in detention. Well-behaved boys were defined as those who showed few if any behavior problems in the school situation and were considered by teachers as "good to have in their class." Badly

TABLE 7. Correlations of Social Attitudes with ASB

Boys at age	Correlation				
	B Con	B REL	E ETH	B PUN	B SEX
5 yr	−0.47**	−0.40**	0.24	0.25*	0.41**
13 yr	−0.38**	−0.28*	0.20	0.27*	0.47**
11 yr	−0.16	−0.29*	0.29*	0.34**	0.27*
10 yr	−0.43**	−0.23*	0.04	0.16	0.36**
9 yr	−0.25*	−0.31**	0.17	0.26*	0.11
8 yr	−0.29	−0.06	−0.13	0.31*	0.32*
Senior	−0.40**	−0.36**	0.18*	0.22**	0.43**
Junior	−0.36**	−0.26**	0.05	0.22**	0.27**
Girls					
15 yr	−0.53**	−0.47**	0.36**	−0.30*	0.05
13 yr	−0.63**	−0.54**	0.11	0.14	0.36**
11 yr	−0.20	−0.15	0.23*	0.16	0.18
10 yr	−0.33**	−0.09	0.04	−0.13	0.19
9 yr	−0.36**	−0.25*	−0.03	−0.09	0.22*
8 yr	−0.26	−0.26	−0.04	−0.00	0.06
Senior	−0.55**	−0.47**	−0.17*	−0.00	0.30**
Junior	−0.32**	−0.20**	−0.01	−0.08	0.16*

*$p < 0.05$.
**$p < 0.01$.

Note. From "Psychoticism and Social Deviancy in Children" by G. E. Powell, *Advances in Behavior Research and Therapy*, 1977, *1*, p. 42.

behaved boys were so classified when their behavior included a history of general disrespect and defiance of school rules, for example, stealing, fighting, and truancy, resulting in frequent minor punishments, detentions, and temporary suspensions. These boys were characterized as "hard to handle" by teachers. Each of these two groups was subdivided on the basis of the ASB scale into low scoring and high scoring on antisocial behavior. The fifth group was formed from a randomly selected sample of 20 delinquent boys in Borstal, equated for age with the "normal" school boys.

As the hypothesis demands, group E has higher scores on the four scales than groups A and B but not always on N. In addition to groups B and C, it seems that teachers' rating of behavior may not provide an adequate measure of an individual's actual or overall misbehavior. Scores on antisocial behavior in criminal propensity for group C (rated as badly behaved) were lower than for group B (rated as well behaved). Certainly, the mean of the well-behaved boys is lower on all four scales than is the mean of the badly behaved boys or the delinquents, thus using an

TABLE 8. EPQ Scores for Groups of Secondary Pupils with and without Behavior Problems

	P		E		N		L	
	Mean	*SD*	Mean	*SD*	Mean	*SD*	Mean	*SD*
No problem	2.7	2.3	14.4	5.7	14.6	3.7	7.8	2.4
Some problem	2.9	1.8	17.8	3.8	11.7	3.5	5.9	4.4
Severe	3.0	1.6	18.0	3.2	11.4	4.7	7.5	4.1
Impossible	8.9	2.6	20.7	2.0	10.0	6.4	3.8	2.3
N = 40								

Note. From Lane, 1987a, p. 800.

external criterion. Using the ASB as a criterion, only N fails with the badly behaved group; for all the other groups, results are well in line with prediction.

Another study of interest is one by Lane (1987a; Lane and Hymans, 1982). Lane was concerned with the relationship between personality variables and levels of conduct disorder, delinquency, and therapy responsiveness in children, with special regard to the theoretical position of Pierson (1969), who had argued that delinquent youths are resistant to normal pressures to change in the direction of prosocial behavior because they lack anxiety. This hypothesis is clearly contradictory to that advocated in this chapter, as it would predict a *negative* correlation between N and antisocial behavior.

Lane looked at a group of high school pupils who were classified by their teachers as presenting no problems in school, some behavior problems in school, behavior problems severe enough to require expert help, and those who had failed to respond to such expert help and who were regarded as "impossible." There were 10 boys in each group, and the results are shown in Table 8. Clearly P, E, and L behave in the expected manner, but N shows a negative rather than a positive correlation with behavior problems. Response to therapy, however, was more in line with the position taken in this chapter; in a small group of 17, it was found that response to therapy was positively correlated with N and L and negatively with P.

In another study (Lane, 1987a), 120 school children were separated into three groups presenting no problems, some problems, and severe problems. Those with no problems clearly had low P scores, low E scores, and L scores, as expected on the basis of the theory here presented, but high N scores. The differences on N were barely significant at the 5% level; the other differences, particularly those for P and L, were significant at higher levels of P (see Table 9).

TABLE 9. Personality Scores on EPQ for Criminal and Noncriminal Groups of Youths

	Personality	Mean	*SD*	T	2-Tail prob.
P	criminal	6.03	2.80	7.10	0.001
	noncriminal	2.92	2.08		
E	criminal	17.73	3.95		
	noncriminal	17.15	3.89	0.75	0.458
N	criminal	10.07	4.32		
	noncriminal	12.83	4.18	−3.60	0.001
L	criminal	5.58	3.56		
	noncriminal	7.63	3.78	−2.90	0.005

N = 60 pairs

Note. From Lane, 1987a, p. 804.

A long-term follow-up of behavior therapy used on this group was correlated with the EPQ scores of the children. Long-term follow-up correlated −.42 with P and .33 with N; neither E nor L made a significant contribution. These results are well in line with other work on behavior therapy in relation to psychiatric patients showing that P prevents therapy from being accepted (Rahman & S. B. G. Eysenck, 1978). This may be important in considering whether criminals should or should not receive psychiatric therapy of one kind or another.

In a final study (Lane, 1987a), 60 pupils with convictions, matched by age, sex, and social class, were compared with 60 pupils without convictions. All these children had been tested before; some of them were convicted of delinquency during a 5-year follow-up period. In other words, the study tests the extent to which the EPQ factors can be regarded as predictive. P is positively predictive for criminality, N is negatively predictive for criminality, as is L. E shows little (positive) differentiation between the groups. Correlations within the delinquent group showed that P correlated with number of convictions (.34) and violence used (.23). L also showed a correlation with violence used (−.35). These studies by Lane agree with the studies previously discussed with respect to the importance of P, E, and L in their association with antisocial behavior but they show negative correlations with N. It is not clear why this should be so, but as N is in any case only slightly related to delinquency in young children, this may just be a statistical peculiarity in rather small and highly selected samples.

In yet another group of 100 children, the Bristol Social Adjustment Guide (Stott, 1971), a teacher-assessed measure of behavior, was correlated with the EPQ (Lane, 1987). Total score correlated highly with

E (.43) and negatively with N (−.19); the correlation with P was insignificant (.09). Of the correlations with the sub-scales of the BSAG, "inconsequence" correlated .60 with E, hardly at all with the other scales. Hostility correlated .39 with E, .35 with P, and −.27 with N. Here again we find that with the children E is much more important than N, with P in this case, possibly due to the biased coverage of the BSAG, assuming a rather less important role than E.

Support for the view that neuroticism may not correlate positively with criminality in children, and may even correlate negatively, comes from two further studies. Luengo & Nunez (1986) studied 298 normal adolescent males, correlating P, E, and N with two different types of antisocial behavior, "Against property" and "Against rules." P and E were significant in the predicted direction at the $p<.01$ level, but N failed to show significant differences.

J. F. Mitchell (1987) administered the Cattell HSPQ (Cattell & Cattell, 1969) to 5, 763 adjudicated male juveniles whose ages ranged mainly from 9 through 16 years. The HSPQ was administered in a statewide reception and diagnostic center in Joliot, Illinois, from 1966 to 1971, and was given orally on tape to ensure comprehension by those youths whose reading ability was very low. To make comparison possible with the results of Pierson & Kelly (1963a, b), who had found delinquents below average in anxiety, and above average in ego strength, as compared with the standardization population, these two variables were again scored and compared with the standardization population. For anxiety, mean delinquent scores were significantly below the normal groups ($p<.001$), while for ego strength they were significantly above ($p<.001$). Similar results are obtained for a sub-sample of 560 delinquents who were committed for homicide, attempted homicide, rape, attempted rape, and battery. This group was significantly less anxious and had higher ego strength than the other delinquents.

These data, together with similar results by Pierson, Moseley, and Olsen (1967), who studied a more restricted sample of 338 "more aggressively acting out" and "more seriously character disordered" male juveniles, certainly support Pierson's hypothesis. Why young delinquents should differ in this manner from older ones is not known. It is certainly necessary to take age into account in assessing the relation between neuroticism and personality as well as that between extraversion and personality; failure to do so may easily lead to unjustified generalizations.

Neuroticism may assume a more important role, in a positive direction, in connection with conduct disorders, even in young children. Gabrys *et al.* (in press) studied a control group of 354 children, with a mean age of 10.20 and compared them with a group of 330 children diagnosed as "conduct disorders" with a mean age of 11.1 years. The diagnosis of conduct disorder was based on incidents of repeated physical or verbal abuse of individuals or groups of people; incidence of repeated violation of property rights; police attention, or court appearances, or repeated suspensions from school, related to either of the above, and the referral to a social or legal agency for follow-up care. Children meeting all four criteria form the conduct disorder group, which accordingly must definitely be looked upon as antisocial and delinquent. The conduct-disorder group differed from the control groups by showing a higher degree of psychoticism (.001), a higher degree of extraversion (.05), a higher degree of neuroticism (.001), and a lower lie scale score (.001). In these groups, therefore, neuroticism was very significantly higher in the conduct-disorder than in the control group, by about three fifths of a standard deviation.

Before turning to adult criminality, it may be worthwhile to review juvenile crime, which is obviously related to antisocial behavior in children. Juveniles, to some degree, share with children the advantage that antisocial behavior does not necessarily lead to incarceration, so that personality scores are not subject to the possible influence that incarceration may have on personality.

Among nonincarcerated adolescents, the pattern is much the same as among children. R. Foggitt (1974) has published data on a non-institutionalized sample of delinquent and nondelinquent adolescents, 167 in all; these were administered a personality inventory including scales for the measurement of E and N, but not P. From the analysis of the intercorrelations between the crimes and the personality scales, it became clear that they were all positively intercorrelated. A single general factor emerged from the analysis, on which different crimes had loadings as follows: truancy, 0.56; poor work history, 0.62; vagrancy, 0.71; attempted suicide, 0.56; frequency of violence, 0.74; destructiveness of violence, 0.72; heavy drinking, 0.45; excessive drugs, 0.52; theft, 0.71; fraud, 0.50; group delinquency, 0.46; number of convictions, 0.59; and E (0.44) and N (0.42). Age and social class were quite insignificantly related to the other variables (0.17 and 0.06). Clearly, for this group of adolescents also, E and N play an important part in relating to criminal activity.

Much the same result emerges from a long-continued study by Stott, Marston, and Neill, entitled *Taxonomy of Behaviour Disturbance* (1975). This work is based on teachers' ratings, and the instrument employed was a development of the Bristol Social Adjustment Guide. What the writers discovered was the existence of two main syndromes of maladjustment among the children rated, which they called Unract (underreactivity, inhibited behavior; unforthcomingness, withdrawal, depression) and Ovract (overactivity, unhibited behavior, inconsequence, and hostility). These two syndromes resemble quite closely the high N–low E and high N–high E constellations of personality traits, and we would expect, from our general hypothesis, that it would be the Ovract child who would be found to indulge in criminal activities. This is indeed what Stott and his colleagues found.

All those within the city sample who had come to the notice of the police as having committed a delinquent or other deviant act were identified from official records. They differentiated themselves from nondelinquents by scores for overreacting maladjustment, the means for which rose consistently with the number of offenses committed. The mean Ovract score for those who had three or more crimes recorded against them was nearly three times that for the nonoffenders among the boys and over five times among the girls. Even for the first offenders, the Ovract mean for boys and girls together was twice that of the nondelinquents.

This extensive, long-continued follow-up work, relying on teachers' ratings rather than on personality inventories and on court records for assessment of criminality, strongly supports the personality–criminality hypothesis; Ovract ratings seem to combine E and P in equal measure, and the general maladjustment adds a certain amount of N. It is unfortunate that Stott and his co-workers failed to break down their overall ratings into more meaningful dimensional concepts.

Further support for the hypothesis of personality factors being important in criminality comes from the extensive work of W. Belson (1975). In his large-scale inquiry into the criminal and antisocial behavior of 1,425 London boys, Belson sought evidence for the importance of certain factors often thought to be causal in the production of such behavior. He found strong evidence in favor of certain hypotheses relating to the personality of the boys involved in crime, such as "a desire for a lot of fun and excitement and a tendency to go out 'just looking for fun and excitement.' " This seems identical with our postulation of low arousal leading to a search for arousal-producing situations. "Permissiveness on the part of the boy in relation to stealing" was another important factor; this would seem to correspond with our notion of a missing "conscience." "Frequent boredom" was another, though less strong, factor, as was a situation in which the boy's mother had always gone out to work; the former would be related to low arousal, the latter to low levels of conditioning (due to the absence of the person most concerned with carrying out the conditioning program). It was found that boys who engage in stealing are lacking in remorse over acts of theft; again supporting the "lack of conscience" hypothesis.

Association with boys who are already engaged in stealing was found to be an important cause; reasons for this association were that the boys concerned were friendly, lively, easy to get along with, fun—in other words, they were extraverted. It is interesting to note that the existence of a broken home (so frequently suggested as a causal factor) did not emerge as important, though a miserable or uninteresting home did. It seems likely that the latter acted through the intermediary of boredom and low arousal; the former, psychiatric views notwithstanding, failed to exert the supposed adverse influence.

Berman and Paisey (1984) investigated the relationship between antisocial behavior and personality in 30 juvenile males convicted of offenses of assault or confrontations with a victim and 30 juvenile males convicted of offenses involving property without confrontation with the victim. Subjects were administered the EPQ and Zuckerman's Sensation-Seeking Scale. Juveniles convicted of assaultive offenses exhibited significantly higher P, E, and N scores and lower lie scores than those convicted of property offenses only. Sensation-seeking scores were significantly lower for the non assaultive group. These results show that even within a "criminal" group of juvenile offenders, severity of crime is still related in the predicted fashion to P, E, and N.

Other writers (e.g., Farley & Sewell, 1976; Rotenberg & Nackshon, 1979) have correlated traits associated with E or P with antisocial behavior, with positive results. In this review we shall, however, concentrate more on direct measures of these higher order factors and will now go on to look at work with adult subjects, usually incarcerated.

Reviews of the early evidence by Passingham (1972) and Feldman (1977) contain most of the older references, and we have already mentioned studies by S. B. G. Eysenck and by MacLean. In order not to duplicate the existing surveys, we will concentrate here on cross-cultural studies to a large extent, but before doing so it may be of interest to look at some data suggesting the possibility of prediction of adult criminality from childhood personality. The possibility of making such predictions successfully suggests the direction of causality and would seem to rule out the possibility that incarceration or other consequences of criminal conduct might have caused changes in personality. Several such studies have already been mentioned.

The work of Burt (1965) is perhaps the most interesting. He reports on the follow-up of children originally studied over 30 years previously. A total of 763 children, of whom 15% and 18% respectively later became habitual criminals or neurotics. were rated by their teachers for N and for E. Of those who later became habitual offenders, 63% had been rated as high on N; 54% had been rated as high on E, but only 3% as high on introversion. Of those who later became neurotics, 59% had been rated as high on N; 44% had been rated as high on introversion, but only 1%

as high on E. Thus we see that even the probably rather unreliable ratings made by teachers of 10-year-old schoolboys can predict with surprising accuracy the later adult behavior of these children. Note also that these ratings took into account only two of the three major factors we have found associated with criminality; had ratings of P been included, it seems likely that the prediction would have been even more accurate.

Similar results have been reported by Michael (1956). Rather more doubtful, at first sight, seem the results reported by West and Farrington (1973). Their book reports on a longitudinal survey of 411 boys who were aged 8–9 in 1961–1962; they were given the Junior Maudsley Inventory in their primary school at age 10–11 and again in their secondary school at age 14–15. They were also given the EPI at age 16–17, when the majority of them had left school. Almost all the boys were tested at each age, and the authors discuss how the extraversion, neuroticism, and lie scores obtained at these three ages were related to juvenile delinquency, that is, conviction in court for offenses committed between the boys' 10th and 17th birthdays. The results were largely negative, but now analyses are available for the children as young adults; we now know the convictions in court for offenses committed between a boy's 17th and 21st birthdays (Farrington, 1986). A total of 84 boys were classified as juvenile delinquents, 94 as young adult delinquents, and 127 as delinquents at any age. Results are much more encouraging when related to these more extensive data.

As regards extraversion, there was a distinct tendency for above-average E scorers at age 16 to become young adult delinquents–30% as opposed to 16%, with a p level of less than .005. The effect is largely due to the most introverted quarter including significantly *fewer* adult delinquents. This indicates that low E scores genuinely predict a low likelihood of adult delinquency.

As regards neuroticism, there was a significant tendency for those in the lowest quarter of N scores at age 10 not to become adult delinquents and not to be delinquents at any age. Furthermore, there was a significant tendency for those in the highest quarter of N scores at age 14 to be delinquents at any age.

As regards lie scores, those with below average L scores at age 10 were most likely to be delinquents at any age. "Dividing the L scores at this age into quarters showed the effect even more clearly. Of those in the highest quarter, only 19.8% were delinquents, in comparison with 44.1% of those in the lowest quarter" (p. 374). As Farrington points out, "These results back-up what we said in 'Who becomes Delinquent?', namely that high L scores at age 10 probably did not reflect social desirability responding, but were obtained by well-behaved boys telling the truth" (p. 376). The L scores at ages 14 and 16 were not related to any of the delinquency classifications. A quadrant analysis was carried out, showing that "the stable introverts at age 10 included significantly fewer adult delinquents, and significantly fewer delinquents at any age, than the remainder. Neurotic extraverts at age 16 included significantly more adult delinquents, and significantly more delinquents at any age, than the remainder. The neurotic introverts at age 16 included significantly fewer adult delinquents than the remainder."

These data provide some support for the theory considered in this chapter:

> in particular, if one takes the EPI scores at age 16, the extraverts were significantly more likely than the introverts to become adult delinquents, the neurotic extraverts were the most likely of all, and the neurotic introverts were the least likely of all. The results obtained with the NJMI at ages 10 and 14 are less clear-cut, but do include some supportive results. (Farrington, 1986, p. 378)

Farrington, Biron and LeBlanc (1982) give further data on some studies conducted in London and Montreal, as well as a review of some of the studies done on the theory under discussion. In the Montreal study, which presents new data, it was found that for both boys and girls, E and P were significantly related to self-reported delinquency, N was not, but the combination of N and E was. Farrington *et al.* (1982) make some interesting criticism of the EPQ mentioning the fact that P is almost always related to delinquency. They say that "this is only to be expected, bearing in mind how P was constructed" (p. 164). Farrington *et al.* seem to be under the erroneous impression that "the items composing the P scale were selected according to their ability to discriminate between criminals and non-criminals (or, more accurately, prisoners and non-prisoners)" and that "it is only to be expected that criminals should have higher P scores. However, this does not mean that criminals are psychotic in any generally accepted sense of the word, or that we have learned anything about the personalities of criminals." (pp. 155–156). It was indeed *predicted* that criminals would have high P scores, but the scale was not constructed using criminals as criteria, nor were items included or rejected because they did or did not identify criminals.

The question of whether we have learned about the personalities of criminals and whether criminals are psychotic "in any generally accepted sense of the word" is taken up at the end of this chapter, where we shall see that as psychiatric hospitals are closed to send psychotics into the community, the number of prisoners increases *pari passu*, suggesting a definite causal relationship that would be in agreement with our own interpretation of the P scale. Farrington *et al.* (1982) failed to note that P is a continuum in which high scorers do not necessarily have to be classified as certifiably psychotic; this is a necessary consequence of the threshold model of psychosis.

Farrington and his colleagues make another criticism, which may be related to the previous misconception. They look at the items that discriminate best between criminals and noncriminals and suggest that the item content might be related directly to the criminals being prisoners. However, such a criticism seems quite misapplied when we consider that they also conclude that self-report correlates better with personality than does incarceration!

Last but not least in this list of predictive studies we have the Jyvaskyla Prospective Research Investigation (Pitkanen-Pulkkinen, 1981; Pulkkinen, 1982, 1988, in press). This study was based on a two-dimensional analysis of psychosocial behavior, the two dimensions being social activity–passivity, and strong–weak control of behavior, defining four patterns of behavior. These are (1) uncontrolled expression of impulses (high activity and weak control), (2) controlled expression of impulses (high activity and strong control), (3) uncontrolled inhibition of impulses (high passivity and weak control), and (4) controlled inhibition of impulses (high passivity and strong control). Factor analysis using a specially prepared inventory and the JEPI (H. J. Eysenck & S. B. G. Eysenck, 1965) revealed two major bipolar factors, one of them defined by aggressive versus submissive behavior, the other by constructive versus anxious behavior. Combinations of these two factors accounted for the four "types" postulated.

These four patterns emerged in 196 male and 173 female 8-year-old children, who were followed up to the age of 14 using peer nominations, teacher ratings, and semistructured interviews of children and their parents. A high degree of continuity of individual behavior was found, and continuity was also present at a later follow-up at the age of 26.

Special interest in the second follow-up concerned criminal behavior of the probands.

> It was observed that convictions were over-represented in the extreme groups for weak control of behaviour. For instance, nine out of ten extremely aggressive boys at the age of eight had committed offences by the age of 26, but none of the ten submissive boys had done so. No one from the extreme groups for strong control of behaviour ($N=30$) became a "chronic offender" with a criminal "career," but six out of eight male (and one out of two female) "chronic offenders" had belonged to the extreme groups for weak control of behaviour at the age of eight ($N=30$). Two male (one female) "chronic offenders" came from the large none-extreme groups ($N=136$ for males, $N=113$ for females). . . . The results showed that a criminal career in early adulthood was related to weak control of behaviour in childhood. Also in late adolescence, at the age of twenty, offenders and none-offenders differed in their personality ratings in childhood such that offenders had been more aggressive. Especially adolescents who have committed several types of off-

> ences (violence, larceny and alcohol-related offences) differed from the rest. (Pulkkinen, 1983)

It is interesting to note that aggression at the age of 8 correlated very significantly with psychoticism and extraversion on the EPQ at the age of 26 whereas constructiveness correlated even more highly (negatively) with neuroticism. Thus, P, E, and N are all implicated in criminal behavior and are predictable from the age of 8 onwards.

Pulkkinen (1988) went on to a second study in which she showed that aggressive children "had a choleric temperament," that is, were high N and high E in personality. All these results, obtained in Finland, extend our model to yet another country with different laws, customs, and culture.

Another interesting predictive study has been reported by Magnusson (1986) and Magnusson, Klinteberg, and Schalling (1987). They obtained scores on impulsivity at age 26–27 for 77 male subjects, for whom teacher ratings of behavior at age 13 were available. Impulsiveness was significantly and positively correlated with ratings of aggressiveness, motor restlessness, and concentration difficulties, as well as hyperactive behavior in children and impulsiveness in adults. When corrected for attenuation, the multiple R rose to .49.

Impulsiveness in adults was significantly and positively correlated with ratings of aggressiveness, motor restlessness, and concentration difficulties. Hyperactive behavior, using the latter two variables as indicators, was highly related to impulsiveness at adult age. There seems to be little doubt that early childhood behavior persists into adulthood. These results assume particular significant, as will be apparent from a later chapter, because of the connection of hyperactive behavior with low cortical arousal (Satterfield, 1978) and low platelet monoamine oxidase activity (Shekin, Davis, Byland, Brunngraber, Fikes, & Lanham, 1982), both biological indicators of vulnerability to psychopathy (Lidberg, Modlin, Oreland, Tuck, & Gillner, 1985; Schalling, 1978; see also Gittelman, Mannuzza, Shenker, & Bonagura, 1985, and Weiss & Hechtman, 1986).

In the latest study of hyperactive children, Satterfield (1987) found that the rate of teenage antisocial behavior was many times higher in former hyperactive children than in normal control subjects. "This is particularly true for serious types of antisocial behaviour, as reflected by multiple-offender and institutionalization rates, which are more than 25 times greater for hyperactive youths than for normal control" (pp. 161–162). There is, of course, a close connection between hyperactivity and extraversion (H. J. Eysenck, 1977).

Sensation seeking is one aspect of E and P that has often been associated with criminality (e.g., Farley & Farley, 1972; Le Blanc & Tolor, 1972; Wassan, 1980), although not all studies concur (e.g., Thorne, 1971; Karoly, 1975). White, Labonvie, and Bates (1985) report on a sample of 584 male and female adolescents, studied at two points of time with a 3-year interval, to determine the relationship between self-reported delinquency and sensation seeking. The Disinhibition Scale, which has the highest correlation of Zuckerman's 4SS scales with E, significantly predicted later delinquency; Experience Seeking, the only other SS scale employed, failed to do so.

The fact that adult criminality is closely related to juvenile delinquency, and juvenile delinquency to childhood behavior, is, of course, well known (Farrington, 1986; Robins & Ratcliff, 1980) and the stability of aggressive behavior in particular has been equally well established (Olweus, 1979, 1987). As an example, consider the work of Robins and Ratcliff on a sample of black men born in St. Louis. They found that both the number and variety of adult arrests increased with the variety of childhood deviance, indexed by items such as truancy, school failure, early sexual intercourse, illicit drug use, alcohol problems, leaving home, and juvenile arrests. Of those with five or more out of nine kinds of childhood deviance, 69% had three or more adult arrests, 63% had been arrested for theft, 29% for a drug offense, and 27% for violence, as compared with those having no childhood deviance, of whom only 12% had three or more adult arrests, only 10% had been arrested for theft, and none had been arrested for drugs or violence. On a British sample, Farrington (1986) obtained similar results.

These studies, taken in conjunction with those mentioned before that provided predictive data, do suggest that personality can be used as a predictor of future conduct with some degree of success, and considering the unreliability of all the elements entering into this equation, it seems clear that correction for attenuation would be appropriate in giving us a more realistic estimate of the *true* relationships obtaining, which would almost certainly be much closer than those published. For practical applications, of course, we must rest content with the uncorrected figures.

Turning now to adult studies, with particular reference to cross-cultural comparisons, we must note first of all a meta-analysis reported by Steller and Hunze (1984) of 15 empirical studies carried out in Germany, using the Freiburg Personality Inventory (FPI), which is a device measuring nine personality traits in addition to extraversion and neuroticism, and a masculinity scale. The E and N scales are comparable to those employed in the EPI, so that comparisons can be usefully made across countries. Altogether 3,450 delinquent subjects were used in these studies; full details about the works summarized by Steller and Hunze will be found in their article.

On the primary trait scales, delinquents have higher scores primarily on the scales of depression, nervousness, excitability, and aggressiveness. In 15 out of 23 comparisons, delinquents had higher scores on emotional instability (neuroticism). Similarly, extraversion was found more frequently in a delinquent than a nondelinquent group. Sociability was found significantly higher in extraverts in 6 out of 23 comparisons.

Steller and Hunze conclude that

> delinquent compared with non-delinquent probands present themselves on the one hand as characterized by bad humor, low self regard, troubles with psychosomatic reactions, irritable and easily frustrated—altogether as emotionally labile—but on the other hand as spontaneously aggressive, emotionally under-developed, but also sociable and lively—altogether as extraverted. (p. 100)

With respect to age, there is some evidence of higher extraversion in juveniles, higher neuroticism in older delinquents—very much as found in the English-speaking samples.

Duration of incarceration did not seem to have any significant effect on the results of the questionnaire responses. This is an important item of information, contradicting the hypothesis often voiced that incarceration produces changes in personality.

The same conclusion is indicated by the fact that persons guilty of criminal conduct but not incarcerated show personality scale deviations similar to those incarcerated. We see thus that a large number of investigations in Germany, mostly carried out with adults, but some also with juvenile delinquents, using a different inventory from that used in the investigations so far discussed, give results very similar in nature. This is an important conclusion indicating evidence of cross-cultural valdity for the theory in question.

Similar results have been found by Schwenkmetzger (1983) in a study of 107 delinquents, with German delinquents again appearing more neurotic, more aggressive, more depressive, more excitable, more impulsive, more sensation seeking, and more ready to take risks. Differences on extraversion, though in the right direction, were not significant. Amelang and Rodel (1970) obtained similar results.

A final survey of German work, this time of delinquent behavior in juveniles and adolescents, is worthy of mention (Daum & Reitz, in press). These authors summarize their conclusions as follows:

> It can be said that delinquents describe themselves as higher on the depression, nervousness, aggressiveness, excitablity, sociability and dominance scales. Juvenile delinquents also score consistently higher on the extraversion and emotional liability scales. . . . the personality differences. . . . confirm Eysenck's hypothesis of a combination of increased extraversion and neuroticism in delinquent adolescents. The results appear to be independent of the time already spent in detention or sentences still to be served. The general

> picture obtained from studies on self-reported 'hidden' crimes is quite clear: incarcerated juveniles resemble self-reported delinquents who had no official record, and both differ from non-delinquent adolescents on a number of personality traits.

Note that here too sociability appears as a specific predisposing factor; this contradicts hypotheses making impulsivity alone responsible, in the extraversion set of traits, for antisocial behavior.

In addition to these studies carried out in Germany, there is a report by Cote and Leblanc (1982) in France, describing a study of 825 adolescents between the ages of 14 and 19 who had filled in a personality inventory as well as a French version of the antisocial behavior scale. This scale was found to correlate very significantly with psychoticism (.36) and extraversion (.32); the correlation with neuroticism was significant but low (.07). Here again, in a youthful sample, extraversion is clearly more important than neuroticism. Equally clearly, results in France are similar to those in Great Britain, Germany, Spain, and elsewhere.

Studies carried out in Israel by two French criminologists compared two groups of delinquents with two groups of control subjects. The groups were differentiated in terms of age; the young ones were from 17 to 21, the older ones from 22 to 50. All the criminals were incarcerated in Israel. The numbers of young and old criminals were 67 and 46, of young and old controls 51 and 31. For the criminal groups, extraversion scores were 36 and 35, respectively; for the controls they were 33 and 29. As regards neuroticism, the figures for the criminals were 38 and 39, for the controls 32 and 29. These differences are fully significant, but differences within criminal or normal groups due to age are not significant. These data thus confirm that the relationship between criminality, on the one hand, and extraversion and neuroticism, on the other, are characteristic of countries other than the English-speaking ones where the personality system in question was originally evolved.

Studies carried out in Communist countries are of particular interest because of the different social structure in these countries. Two such studies have been summarized in H. J. Eysenck and S. B. G. Eysenck (1976). The first, carried out by Munnich in Hungary, compared 138 Hungarian criminals with 96 Hungarian controls of the EPQ. P scores for controls averaged 4.3, for criminals 7.1; the difference was fully significant statistically. For E and N also, criminals showed higher scores than controls. For the C (criminality) scale, comparative scores were 9.8 as opposed to 15.0; all these differences are very similar to those found in the United Kingdom. The subjects were all male, aged 18 to 25 years. For two small female groups of criminals, Munnich also found very high P and C scores.

TABLE 10. P, E, and N Scores of Delinquent and Nondelinquent Boys and Girls

	P		E		N	
Delinquent boys	8.60		8.70		13.20	
		(.01)		(.01)		(.01)
Nondelinquent boys	6.70		6.61		9.97	
Delinquent girls	8.40		10.50		13.20	
		(.01)		(.05)		(.01)
Nondelinquent girls	6.03		9.30		11.20	

Estimates of p in brackets.

Note. From "A Study of Personality Patterns Among Delinquents" by T. E. Shanmugan, *Indian Journal of Criminology*, 1975, *3*, p. 8.

Cepelak in Czechoslovakia tested 25 prisoners dependent on drugs and 25 nondependent prisoners, finding the forming significantly higher on P and E, but significantly lower on N. H. J. Eysenck and S. B. G. Eysenck (1976) conclude that

> The suggestion, frequently made by sociologists, that criminality is the function of the social system under which a person grows up, would predict that in two so very different systems as the Capitalist and the Communist, no such similarity should be found; the facts tend to disprove the hypothesis. (p. 132)

Continuing our survey of cross-cultural studies, we turn next to India. The work carried out there is of particular interest because, although it might be argued that Germany and France are sufficiently similar to Great Britain and other English-speaking countries to almost guarantee replication of results, India is sufficiently different to make it unlikely that results could be replicated if they were due largely to cultural factors. Narayannan and Mani (1977) tested 50 murderers, 50 ordinary criminals, and 50 normals and found that on various combinations of P, E, and N, along the lines suggested by Burgess (1972), murderers had the highest scores, criminals intermediate, and normals the lowest.

Shanmugan (1975) studied 68 delinquent boys, 73 nondelinquent boys, 60 delinquent girls, and 73 nondelinquent girls. Using the EPQ, differences found for P, E, and N are shown in Table 10. It will be clear that all are significant and in the expected direction.

Rahman and Husain (1984) studied 70 female prisoners in Bangladesh. The expected large differences were found for P and N; for E there was no significant difference, but this is probably explained in terms of the large proportion of murderers with very low E scores. As H. J. Eysenck (1977) has pointed out, "Murderers (of the type that used to be predominant until recently, i.e. done in the family, not terror murders and associated with armed robbery, now so common) tend to be introverted and repressed, until they suddenly break out of their shell" (p. 59). This view had, of course, been most prominently put forward by Megargee (1906). It finds support in a study by Mani (1978), who compared 30 murderers in India with 32 nonmurderers. Murderers had very significantly lower extraversion scores, lower neuroticism scores, and lower psychoticism scores. The nonmurderers in this case were criminals committed for rape and robbery; they are not a normal, noncriminal sample. Compared with normal Indian samples, the nonmurderer delinquents have higher scores on P, E, and N. In another study (Singh, 1979) of murderers, the author found in a comparison with criminals having committed petty crimes that murders were high on P and N but not differentiated in terms of E.

Singh (1980a,b) reported on male and female juvenile delinquents who had been administered the EPI and the Cattell NSQ. In both groups, delinquents scored high on E and N. Similarly, Singh (1978, 1980a,b) found that male and female truants scored higher on E and N than nontruants. Similar positive results are reported by Singh and Aktar (1971) and Aktar and Singh (1972). Ramachandran (1970) found positive results for extraversion but not for neuroticism. All in all, these studies tend to support the view that in India as well as in other countries criminality is linked with the same personality features.

We have concentrated in this chapter on the theory, concepts, and measures associated with P, E, and N scales, but, of course, many other personality inventories have been used in order to discriminate between criminals and noncriminals, to predict criminality, or to assess the likelihood of recidivism. An excellent survey of these other studies is given by Arbuthnot, Gordon, and Jurkovic (1987). The major instruments used have been the following:

1. *The MMPI.* In this multivariate personality inventory, it is the psychopathic deviate (Pd) scale that has been most widely used, although other scales (like the F scale) or combinations of scales have also been used. As Arbuthnot *et al.* (1987) summarize, "Attempts to predict delinquent conduct and recidivism among identified adolescent offenders on the basis of the MMPI have produced equivocal results" (p. 142).
2. *The CPI.* The extensive use of the California Psychological Inventory in relation to criminality has been well documented by Laufer, Skoog, and Day (1982). In this inventory, it has been the So scale (socialization) that has been most widely used, although the self control (Sc) and responsibility (Re) scales have also given positive results.

3. *The JI.* The Jesness (1972) Inventory was designed for assessment purposes with juvenile offenders, and although its reliability has been questioned, there is considerable evidence supporting the concurrent, convergent, and predictive validity of the JI in this respect. D. E. Smith (1974) found evidence for the convergent validity of the JI in terms of expected correlations between it and the EPI. As Arbuthnot *et al.* (1987) say, "The JI promises to represent a valuable addition to the delinquency researcher's armamentarium, and deserves further scrutiny" (p. 144).
4. *The POS.* The POS, which was developed as the result of factor-analytic studies of the patterns of delinquent behavior, contains 100 true-false item scores that give rise to three factors, psychopathic delinquency, neurotic delinquency, and socialized delinquency, somewhat resembling the P, N, and E variables of our own system. The POS has generally been found to be a reliable and valid measure (Quay & Parsons, 1971).

Altogether, there are considerable similarities in all the scales considered here with the EPQ (H. J. Eysenck and M. W. Eysenck, 1985), and scores closely resembling P, E, and N can be derived by suitable formulae for most of them. The large literature associated with the instruments just mentioned tends, on the whole, to support the work done with the EPQ. Many of the studies quoted by Arbuthnot *et al.* (1987) also served to demonstrate the heterogeneity of criminal types, which we have mentioned several times.

We must now return to a consideration of the hetergeneity of criminal populations, which we have also already commented upon. There have been many attempts to subdivide criminal populations into meaningful subgroups. Gibbons (1975) gives a good review of these attempts, demonstrating that they, in turn, suffer from considerable heterogeneity; little agreement is in sight. Perhaps the application of factor analytic methods to this field may improve the situation; a study by Sinclair and Chapman (1973) suggests that this may indeed be so. We will return to their study after considering more recent attempts to investigate directly the homogeneity of prisoners' personality by means of cluster analysis.

McGurk and McDougall (1981) gave the EPQ to 100 delinquent inmates of a detention center and a group of normal youths roughly equal in age and background. The raw scores of the EPQ scales for both samples were each subjected to cluster analysis, resulting in the adoption of a four-cluster solution for both the delinquent and the comparison groups.

The clusters obtained from the delinquent groups support the view that there are homogeneous subgroups in terms of personality profiles within a heterogeneous criminal sample, as there are in the comparison group. Consideration of the descriptions of the clusters in the two populations, however, shows that there are personality types appearing in the delinquent group that do not occur in the comparison group.

Both samples are similar in that they contain a high N–low E subgroup (D 1, C 1) and a low N–high E subgroup (D 2, C 2). The comparison group, however, also has a low N–low E subgroup (C 4) and a subgroup with high scores on P (C 3). This differs from the delinquent sample, which has a high N–high E subgroup (D 3) and a high P–high N and high E subgroup (E 4). Clearly, subgroups D 3 and D 4, which occur only in the delinquent sample, are characterized by combinations of personality factors postulated by Eysenck's criminality theory. The other two groups are similar to those found among the controls and would therefore not be covered by Eysenck's theory.

McEwan (1983) used a similar method of analysis on a random group of 186 delinquents. Again a four-cluster solution was preferred.

> The patterns of scores recorded by two of the clusters. . . . are in line with direct predictions by Eysenck's theory of criminality. One cluster scores on P and E, while the other records high scores on E and N. Another sub-group records a high E but this is accompanied by low scores on P and N. The remaining cluster has its one defining characteristic a low E score and thus would appear to confound Eysenck's theory. (p. 202)

It is interesting to note that the only subgroup characterized by a high P score proved to be the most heavily preconvicted.

In a later study, McEwan and Knowles (1984) carried out another cluster analysis and compared the resulting clusters for age and previous convictions and across both the types of offenses committed in the situational variables operating at the time of the more serious current offenses in each category. Again, four clusters were indicated by these statistical analyses. Again, it was found that the high P-scoring cluster had the highest number of previous convictions and the low P-scoring cluster the fewest. No differences were found across offenses or situational–context variables. Another multi-dimensional approach to the problem is presented by Wardell and Yeudall (1980) also using cluster analysis. They too, ended up with four groups; primary/secondary psychopaths, sub-cultural psychopaths, over controlled, and violent aggressive groups, the latter two both high on inhibition.

These cluster-analysis studies suggest that although some clusters agree with predictions from Eysenck's theory, others do not, and occur equally among noncriminal groups. A possible solution to the problem is given by Sinclair and Chapman (1973), who carried out a factor-analytic study of prisoners resulting in two major factors. The components they found are relatively easy to interpret. The first seemed to them to represent the dimension of working-class criminality corresponding to that found by Marcus (1960) in his study of prisoners at Wakefield. A high scorer on this dimension would tend to be young, not particularly intelligent, and given to drink, violence, and committing offenses with his mates. He would tend to have truanted from school and have low occupational status. This is a type of criminal who fits well into the Eysenck scheme.

The second component would seem to describe a social inadequacy dimension. The socially inadequate individual on this dimension would tend to be older, neurotic, introverted, with a psychiatric history and poor contact with his wife and family. He would tend to commit his offenses on the spur of the moment and sometimes violently while drunk. In general, he would conform to West's (1963) description of the inadequate individual, although he could belong to either the active or the passive variety.

H. J. Eysenck (1977) already drew attention to the existence of a large group of inadequates among prison populations and pointed out that the theory, as far as extraversion was concerned, did not apply to them and that they would be more likely to be introverted in character. The Sinclair and Chapman study does indeed show that although their first component has a positive loading on extraversion, the second component has a very significant negative loading of −.35. Thus it is possible that in general the active type of criminal is more numerous in the samples studied, in a few studies the inadequate individual may be more numerous, giving rise to a negative correlation with extraversion in these groups. This is certainly a differentiation that should be borne in mind in all future studies. It seems to be the most important factor for making for heterogeneity, as far as the relationship between personality and criminality is concerned.

It is sometimes said that although findings such as those discussed in this chapter are of academic interest, they have no practical importance. Such a conclusion would be quite erroneous. The data do have important social consequences such as prediction. Another will be briefly discussed now; the theme will be taken up again in a later chapter. It relates to the mental abnormalities of criminals, as indicated by their high P and N scores.

There has been a tendency in the last 30 years for psychiatric hospitals to be closed down and patients suffering from mental illness to be discharged into the community. If our data showing an association between criminality and mental abnormality (P and N) are correct, then one would predict on this basis an increase in the number of crimes and

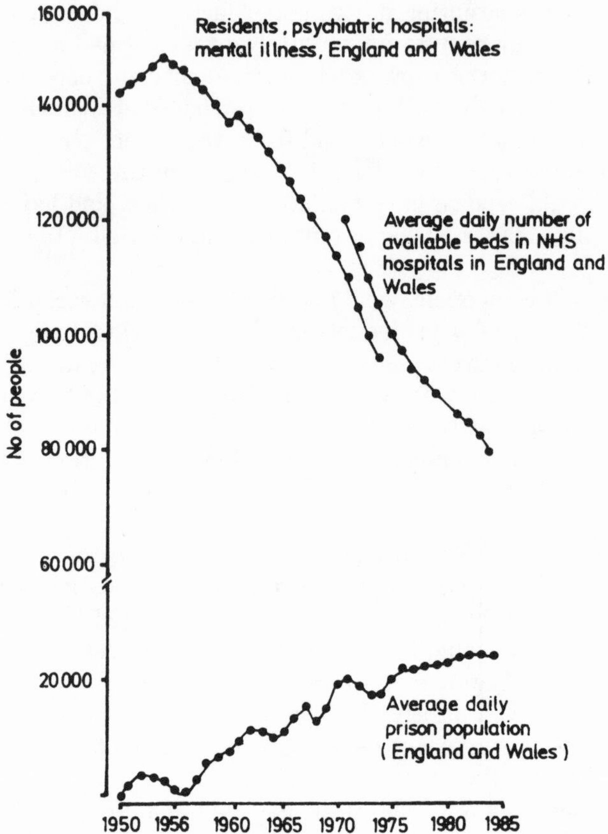

FIGURE 15. Increase in prison population and decrease in psychiatric hospital beds over the years (Weller & Weller, 1986).

an increase in the average daily prison population. Taylor and Gunn (1984) examined people on remand at Brixton Prison on charges of violent offenses and found an overrepresentation of sufferers from schizophrenia exceeding epidemiological expectations by 22.5 times. This is a quite novel situation; earlier surveys had found that the ration of schizophrenic patients charged with or convicted of violent crimes corresponded to the proportion of sufferers in the population (roughly 1%).

Weller and Weller (1986) have plotted psychiatric hospital residence, bed availability, and average daily prison population in England and Wales since 1950, showing that as the former declined, the latter increased, as predicted. Figure 15 shows this trend quite clearly.

Weller and Weller regressed the in-patient psychiatric population

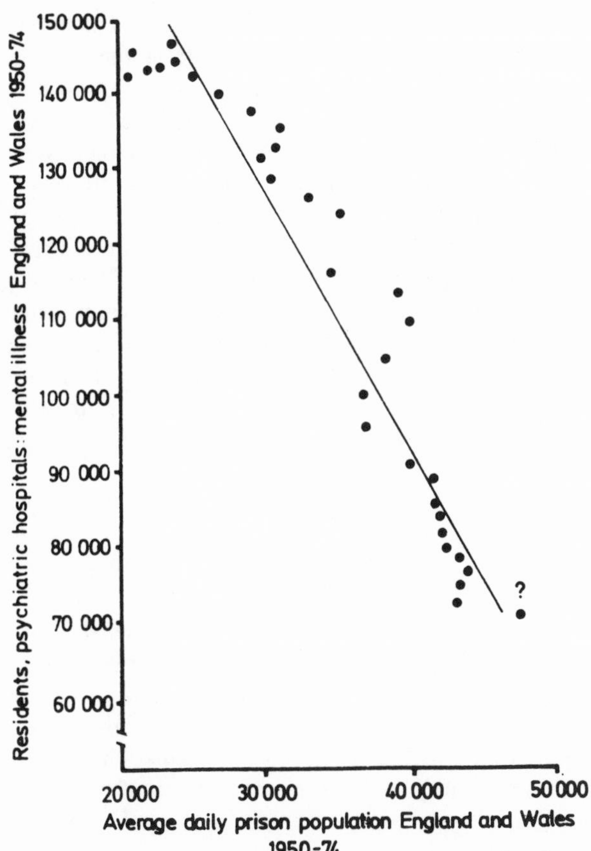

FIGURE 16. Scatter diagram showing relation between number of prisoners and number of psychiatric hospital beds (Weller & Weller, 1986).

against the prison population and found a highly significant correlation of .94! Figure 16 shows the scatter diagram, complete with best-fit regression line. It is quite clear that the results support the prediction; as mental patient are discharged from psychiatric hospitals, so the prison population increases.

Results similar to those reported for Great Britain have been reported for the United States (Teplin, 1984). Deinstitutionalization has had similar effects there. During the period when mental hospital wards were being emptied, prison populations nearly doubled. Furthermore, the data show that the mentally ill contribute disproportionately to arrest rates and criminal justice proceedings. The case made by the Wellers and in Teplin's book is a very strong one. It fits very neatly with the correlation we found between criminality and the mental disorder diathesis measured by the P and N scales. It is such agreements that make us more confident in the meaningfulness of our questionnaire data.*

These results suggest that it might be wise to reverse the trend, particularly in view of the fact that prisoners cost more to maintain than mental patients. Quite apart from such practical considerations, it seems unjust to punish patients suffering from mental disorders by putting them into prison, particularly when there is evidence that psychiatric treatment can very much reduce the probability of mental patients offending (Boker & Hafner, 1973). Other practical recommendations might lead to the introduction of a more active program of psychiatric treatment of suitable criminals in prison. Altogether, it does seem that the results of scientific investigations in this field have more than academic interest and can lead to important practical and political recommendations.

SUMMARY

We are now in a position to summarize, at least tentatively, the large amount of data discussed in this chapter. The following conclusions would seem to be justified. (1) There exists a general behavior pattern of antisocial behavior and criminality, marking the opposite end of a continuum to that constituted by prosocial altruistic behavior (Rushton, 1980). (2) Within the antisocial and criminal type of behavior, there is a certain amount of heterogeneity, marked particularly by the opposition between active and inadequate criminals, but probably also including differences according to type of crime committed. (3) Criminality is related to certain dimensions of personality, in particular that labeled psychoticism, which is apparent in all age groups and under all conditions studied. (4) There is a strong tendency for extraversion to be related to criminality, particularly in younger samples and among more active criminals; inadequate older criminals do not show high extraversion and may indeed be below average on this trait. (5) Most criminals are characterized by a high degree of neuroticism, but this may not be found as markedly in children and youngsters. (6) Scores on the L scale (regarded in these studies as a measure of conformity rather than of dissimulation) tend to correlate negatively with antisocial and criminal conduct, both in children and in adolescents and adults. (7) The criminality scale, made up of the most diagnostic items of the EPQ, tends to dis-

*These results are in line with Penrose's Law which states that if the prison service of a country is extensive, the asylum population is relatively small, and vice versa.

criminate significantly between criminals and noncriminals. (8) Primary personality traits, such as impulsiveness, venturesomeness, risk taking, empathy, and others correlate in predictable directions with antisocial and criminal conduct. (9) These relationships are observed also in conditions where self-report of antisocial behavior is the major criterion. Thus personality–criminality correlations are not confined to legal definitions of crime or incarcerated criminals. (10) The observed personality–criminality correlations have cross-cultural validity, appearing in different countries and cultures with equal prominence. (11) Personality traits characteristic of antisocial and criminal behvior are also found correlated with behavior that is not criminal but is regarded as antisocial, such as smoking (H. J. Eysenck, 1980). Drug users, whether legal (cigarette smoking; H. J. Eysenck, 1980) or illegal tend to show high P, E, and N scores (Shanmugan, 1979). Studies by Gossop (1978) and Gossop and Kirstjansson (1977) show high P and N scores among drug users, but E scores are elevated only among drug users convicted of other crimes.

The results summarized above are incompatible with a purely situational analysis of criminal behavior and suggest an important contribution by dispositional factors.

CHAPTER FOUR

Criminality, Heredity, and Environment

MODERN BEHAVIORAL GENETICS

It is a curious fact that in science we often find a pendulumlike swing from one theory to another and then back again. Huygens's wave theory of light was replaced by Newton's corpuscular theory; this in turn was found to be defective and Young, Fresnel, and others replaced it with a new wave theory. In modern times, physicists found that light had characteristics of both wavelike and corpusclelike nature, and the later theories attempt to combine both properties. Similarly, as far as criminality and personality are concerned, the strong hereditarian theories of the 19th century were followed by equally strong environmentalist theories in the middle years of this century, and it is only in recent years that the realization has set in that both heredity and environment exert a causal influence in this field and that mathematical models have become available to help us break down the total phenotypic variance into components that can be quantatively estimated.

Path models following S. Wright's (1954) formulation (Fuller & Simmel, 1983) and the methods of biometrical genetical analysis of the Birmingham School (Mather & Jinks, 1971) allow us so to partition the variance that a great deal can be learned about the contribution of various genetic and environmental factors to phenotypic behavior. The principles involved are clearly outlined in McClearn and DeFries (1973) and Plomin, DeFries, and McClearn (1980). A knowledge of these principles is indispensable for gaining an understanding of modern ways of looking at the problem of nature and nurture, heredity and environment.

Any discussion of heritability in the context of criminal behavior and personality is handicapped not only by the fact the psychologists are normally not exposed to any systematic teaching of modern genetic theory, but also, and even mainly, because they share a number of erroneous assumptions that make it difficult to discuss such concepts as heritability, interaction, and environmental variance.

The first misconception is that modern behavior genetics is concerned only with genetic causes and hence almost by definition biased in favor of finding such causes. This is quite incorrect. Modern genetic theory, as Fulker (1981) makes clear, is concerned with what he calls "the genetic and environmental architecture" of the causal factors that underlie the phenotypic observations that constitute psychological science. Being concerned with the breakdown of the phenotypic variance, genetic theory cannot arbitrarily restrict itself to the genetic portion of the variance; it must inevitably consider this as a portion of the *total* phenotypic variance and hence assess the contribution of environmental variance also.

The second point to be noted is that both genetic and environmental variance are nowadays broken down into several distinct components, so that the ascertainment of heritability is only one, and probably not the most important, task of modern behavioral genetics. Total genetic variance (V_G) is made up of additive genetic variance, that is, the simple additive action of separate genes making for high or low criminality, neuroticism, altruism, or whatever; this is denoted as V_A. Next we have nonadditive genetic variance due to dominance at the same gene loci (V_D) and nonadditive genetic variance due to interaction between different gene loci, called *epistasis* (V_{EP}). Finally, there is a genetic variance due to *assortative mating*, that is, the increment in total variance attributable to degree of genetic resemblance between mates in the characteristic in question (V_{AM}).

As regards the environmental variance, it is useful to differentiate environmental variance *between* families V_{EB}), and environmental variance *within* families (V_{EW}). The former refers to systematic environmental differences between families, which make for differences between offspring on the trait in question but do not make for differences among offsprings reared together in the same family. Opposed to this, there are differential and environmental influences *within* families, which make for differences among offsprings reared together in the same family.

We can now define heritability, which is given by the formula

$$h^2 = \frac{V_G}{V_P}$$

where V_P is the phenotypic or total variance on the trait of behavior in question. The phenotypic variance is made up as follows:

$$V_P = V_G + V_E + V_{GE} + CovGE + V_e$$

where V_G and V_E refer to the genetic variance and the (additive) environmental variance, which is independent of the genotype, respectively. V_{GE} refers to variance due to interaction, that is nonadditive effects of genotypes and environments, *CovGE* refers to the covariance of genotypes and environments, and V_e refers to the error variance due to unreliability of measurement.

It is important to make a distinction between the two interaction terms. V_{GE} means that different genotypes may respond differently to the same environmental effect. Thus if coaching on an IQ test, say, raises the IQ of every genotype subjected to it by 10 points, the environmental effect is said to be *additive* and the variance contributed by such an environmental effect is included in V_E. If, on the other hand, administration of a drug like glutamic acid causes genotypes with lower IQ to gain more IQ points than genotypes with average IQ and leads to no gain at all among those with superior IQs, then the environmental change *interacts* with genotypes to produce different phenotypic effects in different subgroups. This source of variance is called V_{GE}. The *covariance* between genotypes and environments, *CovGE*, arises when genotypic and environmental effects are correlated in the population. Thus if children with genotypes for high intelligence are also reared in homes with superior environmental advantages for intellectual development, this gives rise to covariance. Some part of it is, of course, itself the product of the genotype, as when an intellectually gifted child spontaneously spends much time in reading or other intellectual activities.

Heritability can, in fact, be defined along different lines. *Narrow* heritability is the proportion of additive genetic variance to total phenotypic variance (*VA/VP*); *broad* heritability has already been defined as *VG/VP*. In the usual formulas, the error variance V_e is included with the environmental variance, and hence the estimate of genetic variance is too low, and a suitable correction should be made. This underestimation can be quite serious, and in what follows attention will be drawn to this point.

Modern methods of analysis, using data from identical twins brought up in separation, comparisons between MZ and DZ twins, studies of adopted children, familial intercorrelations, genetic regression to the mean, inbreeding and heterosis effects, and many other methods enable us to give estimates of the different portions of these formulas (Fuller & Simmel, 1983; Mather & Jinks, 1971). It is also possible to assess the *power* of these methods (Martin, Eaves, Kearsey, & Davies, 1978), and to estimate the numbers of twin pairs, say, that may be required to give a particular set of fiducial limits for one's estimates. This is obviously not the place to go into these technicalities, and the reader is referred to the sources cited.

Another frequent error in this field is to regard estimated heritabilities as applying to *individuals*. As will be clear from the fact that we are using analysis of variance, heritabilities are *population estimates;* in other words, they apply to groups of people, say British people living in Great Britain and born between, say, 1930 and 1960. The error of arguing as if heritability estimates pertained to individuals is clearly brought out by an illustration originally suggested by Donald Hebb, who argued that trying to estimate the relative importance of genetic and environmental factors was as silly as trying to say whether length or width of a field was more important in defining its area. The single field, of course, has no variance, and consequently the comparison does not apply; if we asked whether among a hundred fields length or width contributed more to size, the matter could be easily subjected to a statistical test.

The fact that we are dealing with population estimates also serves to clarify another frequent error that is made by writers in this field. Heritabilities are not given once and for all; they apply to a given population at a given time. Subdividing samples of twins in Norway into age groups widely separated from each other, and looking at heritability of scholastic achievement, Heath *et al.* (1985) found that as expected heritabilities were highest for the youngest age male groups (70%) lowest for the oldest (40%). The obvious explanation is that increasingly greater equality of education in recent years reduced the importance of environmental components over time.

This example also illustrates another common error, namely that any trait or characteristic that is at least in part inherited is thereby *fixed* for all eternity. This is clearly untrue; changing environments will change heritabilities. It is easy to imagine that genetic causes exert a completely deterministic effect on individual behavior, but this obviously is not so. To understand that genetic and environmental factors always work in interaction, in a very complex way, is the beginning of wisdom in approaching the whole topic of behavior genetics.

A slightly fictitious example may make this point clear. At the moment, in conditions of adequate nourishment, the size, the shape, and the consistency of the female bosom is determined largely by genetic factors, and exercise, massage and other measures have little control over it. However, recent advances in hormonal treatment, plastic surgery, and silicone injections have altered the situation to such an extent that it is quite conceivable that in 50 years time, in California, genetic factors will play very little role in determining the size, shape, and consistency of the female bosom! In a similar way, it may be suggested, the introduction of behavior therapy may have altered the strong genetic determination of the neurotic disorders.

GENETICS OF PERSONALITY

Turning now to a substantive account of the genetics of criminality and personality, it may be useful briefly to review the evidence on those aspects of personality (psychoticism, extraversion, neuroticism) that have been found to be related to criminality before actually looking at the genetic analysis of criminal behavior directly. It will be useful to concentrate on the most recent studies in the field, because these have used much larger numbers of twin pairs than previous studies (up to over 12,000 pairs in one study, for instance), and they have used much more sophisticated methods of analysis, as explained above.

These investigations have been carried out in different countries (England, the United States, Scandinavia, and Australia), by investigators using different samples, different questionnaires, different methods of analysis, and starting from different premises; nevertheless, there is a considerable amount of agreement as far as major results are concerned. The British study is discussed in detail in papers by Eaves and Eysenck (1975, 1976a, 1976b, 1977) and recently in book form (Eaves *et al.*, in press). Eaves and Young (1981) have given a detailed account of the development of this work. The American work has been published in book form by Loehlin and Nichols (1976). The Scandinavian work was originally published by Floderus-Myrhed, Pederson, and Rasmuson (1980); this work has been reanalyzed according to the method of the Birmingham School of biometrical genetical analysis by Eaves and Young (1981). Finally, the Australian work has been reported by Jardine, Martin, and Henderson (1984), Kendler, Heath, Martin, and Eaves (1986), and Martin and Jardine (1986). The Scandinavian study, with an unselected sample of 12,889 twin paris of like sex, is undoubtedly the largest, followed by the Australian study, which uses 3,810 pairs of twins. The American and British studies used some 800 and 500 pairs of twins, repsectively.

The following general conclusions may be drawn from this work. (1) All the major dimensions of personality require a model incorporating a strong V_A component in order to fit the data, and this component accounts for some 50% of the variance, which rises to above 60% when corrected for attenuation. (2) There is no evidence of any important contribution by between family environmental variance for any of the personality variables, an important point because traditional theories of personality refer almost exclusively to variables of precisely this type. (3) Within-family factors make up almost exclusively the environmental variance that is found in these studies. (4) Errors of measurement play an important part, and because these are usually confounded with within-family environmental variance, it is important to correct the obtained heritability coefficients for this factor. (5) There is evidence in the larger studies that in extraversion, but not in neuroticism or psychoticism, *dominance* effects are present and must be incorporated in any general theory of the causation of individual differences in this variable. (6) There are in the larger studies important age and sex factors. Heritability seems stronger for females than for males and stronger in the younger than in the older groups. (7) Different parameters in the model give optimal fit for different sex and age groups, suggesting differential genetic effects for these groups.

From the point of view of this chapter, the major conclusion must be that genetic factors exert a predominant influence on the determination of personality factors P, E, and N and that because these are all three implicated in the determination of antisocial and criminal behavior, as can be seen in Chapter 3 it seems likely that genetic factors will also be found in antisocial and criminal conduct. Such a conclusion is not absolutely obligatory, and it is possible to imaging circumstances where it might not be true. However, as we shall see, direct study of antisocial and criminal conduct is in good agreement with this preliminary conclusion.

We have concentrated on P, E, and N in this chapter, primarily because it is these variables that have been particularly closely associated with criminality. However, many traits of temperament and personality have been subjected to a similar genetical analysis, and some of these are quite closely related to our major dimensions of personality, such as impulsive and sensation-seeking behavior (H. J. Eysenck, 1983a; Zuckerman, 1983); a more extended review of studies of a great variety of traits of personality will be found in Buss and Plomin, 1978; Loehlin and Nichols, 1976; and Plomin and DeFries, 1985.

TWIN STUDIES OF CRIMINALITY

A direct study of heredity as a factor in criminality was published in 1929 by Johannes Lange, comparing in a sample of 30 pairs of twins in which at least one had been convicted of a criminal offense, 13 monozygotic and 17 dyzygotic pairs for concordance. In the 13 MZ pairs of twins, the other twin had also been sentenced to imprisonment in 10 cases, whereas this was the case for only 2 out of the 17 DZ pairs. Lange's conclusion was that "Monzygotic twins showed quite considerable concordance with reference to crime, dyzygotes, however, quite considerable discordance. According to the twin method, we must conclude from this that heredity is a very important cause of crime" (p. 14).

In addition to these marked concordance differences between MZ and DZ twins, Lange found special reasons to discount the apparent

TABLE 11. Concordance for Criminality of Monogenetic and Dyzygotic Twins

	MZ		DZ	
	Number of pairs	Concordance %	Number of pairs	Concordance %
Lange (1929)	13	76.9	17	11.8
Legras (1932)	4	100.0	5	0.0
Rosanoff *et al.* (1934)	37	67.6	28	17.9
Kranz (1936)[a]	31	64.5	43	53.5
Stumpfl (1936)[a]	18	64.5	19	36.8
Borgstrom (1939)	4	75.0	5	40.0
Yoshimasu (1961)	28	60.6	18	11.1
Total	135	66.7	135	30.4

[a]One pair of twins common to these two studies is included only in Stumpfl.

discordance in three monozygotic cases. In at least two of these three cases, the criminal partner was though to have suffered serious brain damage, which might have caused his criminality.

Several replications of the Lange's study have been carried out, and the results are reported in Table 11. It will be seen that of 135 MZ twins, 67% are concordant, whereas of 135 DZ twins, only 30% are concordant. This is a very large difference, but it should be noted that these studies are subject to a number of criticisms. Criminality is a quantitative concept, unreliably determined, and it might be considered useful to take degrees of criminality into account in establishing concordance Stumpfl, 1936). Selection of twins is another problem; it is likely that more similar DZ twins are more easily spotted than dissimilar ones (this is a fault in the conservative direction, as greater similarity in DZ twins included in these studies would increase DZ concordance, if anything, thus reducing the difference between MZ and DZ concordance). Another problem is that similarities in type of crime are not covered by the general label of "concordance." Kranz (1936) attempted to analyze his data in line with this concept and found that there were more than twice as many strongly similar MZ as strongly similar DZ twins, whereas where there was moderate or little similarity in crimes committed, DZ twins if anything showed greater concordance.

Another criticism is often made, but appears to have little justification. It is stated that MZ twins are treated more alike by parents and others than are DZ twins, and it is suggested that this greater similarity of treatment may cause greater similarities in intelligence and personality and perhaps criminality. However, Loehlin and Nichols (1976) have shown that when twins who are similarly treated are compared with twins who are not so similarly treated, this makes no difference with respect to congruence in intelligence and personality. Similarities of treatment usually refer to relatively superficial characteristics, such as dressing alike, and it seems unlikely that these would lead to any greater congruence in intelligence, personality, or criminality.

The question of selectivity has been answered by Christiansen (1977a), who has reported on the criminality of a total population of 3,586 twin pairs from a well-defined area in Denmark. This total (non-selected) sample gave 50% concordance for criminal behavior for MZ, and 21% for concordance for DZ twin pairs, using both male and female twins for the comparison and recording serious offenses only. The ratio of MZ concordance over DZ concordance is 2.23 for the seven studies summarized in Table 11 and 2.38 for the Christiansen study; in other words, the selectivity in the seven studies has not resulted in producing a greater concordance among MZ twins then DZ twins when compared with a nonselective study. It seems that we can dismiss this particular criticism as irrelevant (Christiansen, 1977b).

Altogether, these studies powerfully support the view that genetic factors play a large part in the causation of criminal behavior, although the failure of the MZ concordance to be complete suggests a strong environmental influence as well. The data do not allow a strong conclusion in this direction, however, because of the many possible sources of error.

Errors are endemic in studies of this kind. Criminals, in order to be counted, must be caught; yet the rate of detection is only about 20% for the types of criminal conduct here presented, suggesting that many possibly criminal partners of the original proband may be counted as noncriminal in spite of having actually committed (undetected) crimes in the past. This fact alone would significantly decrease the numbers of MZ and DZ concordances. Given the fact that there is a *true* difference between the two groups, any random errors will reduce the observed (absolute) differences. Thus the reported figures, giving a concordance rate of MZ twins of 50% to 70%, must be regarded as a minimum estimate; the true value is probably greater and it may be considerably greater.

It is interesting to see that the importance of this factor does not seem to have occurred even to such a well-known writer on this topic as Christiansen (1977b), who in his review of twin studies comments on the much greater concordance among MZ than DZ twins, and continues: "This does not mean that hereditary factors alone suffice to produce crime, as shown by the relatively high figures of discordance in monozygotic pairs (app. 25%)" (p. 104). Clearly, discordance in MZ pairs can easily be produced by the unreliability of data collection, the failure of actual criminals to be apprehended, and other factors. It is not argued that hereditary factors alone suffice to produce crime; such a position is clearly untenable. However, the reasons given by Christiansen are certainly not those one would choose to argue the case.

Some more recent studies are left out of the table, partly because they were inaccessible (Hayashi, 1963; Sugmati, 1954) or because the results are discussed by the authors in such detail that several breakdowns are given, only one of which might arbitrarily be chose for the table (Dalgard & Kringlen, 1977). Sugmati studied 15 pairs of delinquent twins. Of the 10 MZ twins, 8 were concordant; of the 5 same-sex DZ twins, 1 was concordant; of 4 same sex DZ twins 3 were concordant. Hayashi reported on a sample of 15 male MZ twins of whom 11 pairs were concordant.

Altogether, in these Japanese studies, concordance for MZ twins is 75%, for DZ twins 44%; both are higher than for the data in Table 11, but the *ratio* is approximately the same.

In the Dalgard and Kringlen study, a "complete and representative" sample of 139 male twins formed the basis of the investigation. The authors comment on the ambiguity of the concept of concordance, the final figure depending on the definition of crime. Keeping a strict criterion, the authors found pairwise concordance of 26% for MZ and 15% for DZ twins, a ration of 1.73. There were altogether 31 pairs of MZ and 54 pairs of DZ twins. The MZ/DZ ratio is only 1.24 when a broader concept of crime is used; here the data are based on 49 MZ and 89 DZ pairs of twins. The strict concept of crime is defined according to criminal law, including violence, sexual assault, theft, and robbery; the broad concept includes motor vehicle offenses, military offenses, and cases of treason during World War II.

A study by Tiernari (1963) has not been included because in all his pairs of twins there had been a complaint by one or both of psychic or nervous disturbances, or the twins were excessive users of alcohol or total abstainers. The sample is thus rather odd, and conclusions from it would not necessarily apply to less restricted samples. In any case, all the twins were MZ, making it difficult to make a comparison with DZ twins.

Relying on self-report data rather than on official statistics, Rowe (1983) sent questionnaires by mail to twins in the 8th and 12th grades in almost all the school districts of Ohio along with a promise of a small monetary reward for returning them filled in. Questions asked how often the twin had engaged in several categories of delinquent behavior, the activities of their co-twins and friends, and about physical characteristics useful in deciding on zygocity. Completed questionnaires were obtained from 68 MZ and 97 same-sex DZ twin pairs, and it was found that concordance for self-reported delinquent behavior was greater for MZ than for DZ twins, for both males and females. It was also found that those twins who reported more activities shared with each other were *no more similar* to each other in delinquency than those who reported few shared activities, suggesting that neither the degree of concordance not the difference in concordance between identical and fraternal twins could be explained by how much the twins had to do with each other. Rowe concluded from this data that the prime source of concordance was shared genes rather than shared environment.

An interesting further finding of the study was the substantial correlation between how delinquent the twin was and how many of his or her friends were also delinquent. Rowe and Osgood (1984) suggested that patterns of within-twin differences in delinquency and delinquent associations, compared for MZ and DZ twins, indicated that the correlation between these two variables was largely a result of shared genes, rather than constituting evidence for a "birds of a feather" theory of delinquency. It is not that delinquent friends give rise to delinquency in the proband, but rather that both primarily express the same genetic factor. The inherited traits making some twins susceptible to delinquency also redispose them to friendship with other delinquents.

Analysis of twin data simply in terms of concordance is of course a very primitive method, and modern behavioral genetics suggests more appropriate methods of model building and testing. Such an analysis is provided by Cloninger, Christiansen, Reich, and Gottesman (1978), using the Christiansen data already reviewed.

Cloninger, Christiansen, Reich, and Gottesman (1978) adopt what they call a multifactorial model (Cloninger, Reich & Guze, 1975, 1978), which is in essence similar to the threshold model shown in Figure 4 of our chapter on constitutional factors (Chapter 2), but in their case using *two* thresholds defined by sex. The thresholds for men and women are defined by the population prevalence of the disorder in men and women, respectively. As prevalence is much lower for women than for men, it would follow that their *threshold* would be much higher, and hence female delinquents would be more deviant in liability (diathesis). From this hypothesis, it would follow that the relatives of affected women would be more deviant as a group than the relatives of the affected men. This pattern is what is observed in antisocial personality (Cloninger, Reich, & Guze, 1978).

It is this model that was applied to the Christiansen twin data. The observed data fit the model very well, with correlations between MZ twins (.60) being higher than between DZ twins (.41). Same-sex correlations showed no significant differences either in the MZ or the DZ pairs.

The fact that both criminal and antisocial women are more deviant than criminal and antisocial men in terms of the genotypic and other transmissable influences that contribute to the liability to develop these behaviors agrees well with the findings that psychoticism, a personality trait highly correlated with criminality, shows the same pattern (H. J. Eysenck & S. B. G. Eysenck, 1976). Males have higher P scores than women, but female criminals have higher P scores than male criminals (Eysenck & Eysenck, 1975).

We may use the correlational data in this analysis to make an estimation of the hereditary contribution to criminality, using a formula suggested by D. E. Smith (1974) as the best interpretation of the correlation between twins in genetic terms. Cloninger *et al.* (1978) estimate the heritability to be .59. They add that

> Unfortunately this estimate may be biased in an unpredictable direction by unknown combinations of non-genetic familial effects in which the MZ and DZ pairs differ, non-additive genetic effects, and non-additive gene-environment interactions. However, the data demonstrate little net effect of these complications since r_{MZ} does not differ significantly from $2r_{DZ}$ (.70 versus .82). (p. 949)

The authors discuss several other possible factors that might lead to alternative interpretations but conclude "Our analyses support an additive or linear model without major interactions" (p. 949).

It is interesting to look at the other side of the antisocial continuum, represented by altruistic behavior. The comparative neglect of such prosocial types of behavior has recently been redressed by extensive investigations (Rushton, 1976, 1980), and this work has been extended to the field of genetics (Rushton, Fulker, Neale, Blizard, & H. J. Eysenck, 1984). Three questionnaires measuring altruistic tendency were completed by 573 adult twin pairs in London and a genetic analysis carried out on the data. For the three scales, the intraclass correlations for the 296 MZ pairs were 0.53, 0.54, and 0.49; for the 179 same-sex DZ pairs they were 0.25, 0.20, and 0.14, giving rough estimates of broad heritability of 56%, 68%, and 72%, respectively. (The three questionnaires consisted of a 20-item self-report altruism scale, a 33-item empathy scale, and a 16-item nurturance scale, all of which had previously been shown to have construct validity.)

A maximum-liklihood model-fitting analysis revealed about 50% of the variance on each scale to be associated with genetic effects, virtually none to be due to the twin's common environment, and the remaining 50% to be due to each twin's specific environment and/or error associated with the test. In other words, as one might have expected, genetic effects are equally strong for prosocial as for antisocial behavior.

In another study, in which the authors measured empathy, nurturance, aggressiveness, and assertiveness as well as altruism, they again found, compairing MZ and DZ twins, that approximately 50% of the variance on each scale was associated with genetic effects, a value that rose to approximately 60% when corrections were applied for the unreliability of the tests. Age and sex differences were also found; altruism increased over the age span from 16 to 60, whereas aggressiveness decreased. At each age, women had higher scores than men on altruism and lower scores on aggressiveness (Rushton, Fulker, Neale, Nias, & H. J. Eysenck, 1986).

As a final indication of the importance of genetic factors in criminality, we may refer to the studies of social attitudes. These embrace the analysis of religious values, which tend to favor altruism and go against antisocial conduct (Newman, 1976; Wilson & Herrnstein, 1985), attitudes to crime and punsihment directly, and tender-minded attitudes in general. It is usually assumed that attitudes of this kind are wholly determined by environmental factors. Martin, Eaves, Heath, Jardine, Feingold, and H. J. Eysenck (1986) have shown that data gathered in Australia and England on the social attitudes of spouses and twins are largely consistent with the genetic model for family resemblance and social attitudes. They found substantial assortative mating and little evidence of vertical cultural inheritance. The numbers of subjects involved are quite large, and the agreement between the two separate studies suggests that the results are replicable. Insofar as a person's attitudes are related to his or her behavior, we must come to the conclusion that here too there is evidence for a strong influence of genetic factors.

It is important, before leaving the twin studies, to emphasize that Lange's original interpretation of his results as indicating "crime as destiny" is not a necessary implication of the data and goes very much against modern theories of genetics. Whatever a person's heredity, he or she is not "destined" to become a criminal; everything depends on the interaction of the criminal diathesis with environment. The personality traits and the body build that are associated with the criminal diathesis are similar to those related to becoming a successful sportsman, mercenary, commando, or parachute trooper. The traits we so dislike in criminals we may find admirable in soldiers (when they are fighting on our side!). It would be quite wrong to regard evidence for a partial genetic contribution to phenotypic conduct as fixed and compelling; this is a complete misinterpretation of the data. We will later on, in connection with theories of criminality, go into this more fully.

There are too few MZ twins reared apart to enable one to make much of a comment; the evidence has been reviewed by Christiansen (1977b), and the impression is certainly one of considerable concordance. However, the twins differ so much in the time in which they were separated, the similarity of environment after separation, the definition of criminality, and the amount of information available that it does not seem wise to base any conclusions on these samples.

ADOPTION STUDIES OF CRIMINALITY

We now turn to adoption studies, which differ, of course, in their logic from twin studies. Children adopted at birth derive all their genetic material from their biological parents and their environment from their adoptive parents. We can look at the criminal, sociopathic, or antisocial behavior of the children and see whether it resembles more that of their *biological* parents, indicating a strong genetic component, or that of their *adoptive* parents, indicating a strong environmental component. There are difficulties in this method (as in all methods used in social psychology, which depend on social institutions!), including such factors as matching placement of children. However, these factors are probably not very strong and in any case are completely different from those that might be considered critical in the case of twin studies.

In the first adoptive study to be mentioned, Schulsinger (1972, 1977) in Denmark compared 57 psychopathic adoptees with 57 nonpsychopathic controls, equated for sex, age, social class, and in many cases neighborhood of rearing and age of transfer to the adopting family; carefully defined criteria for psychopathic behavior were used in this study. Next, the investigator examined case records of the biological and adoptive relatives of the psychopathic and of the control subjects. In spite of the fact that adoption took place at an early age, there were no differences whatever between the adoptive families of the psychopathic or the control groups; when it came to the biological family members of these groups, however, relatives of the psychopathic boys showed an incidence of psychopathy two and a half times as great and an incidence of mildly psychopathic behavior also two and a half times as great as was found in relatives of the control boys. In other words, the psychopathic boys had taken after their biological parents, not their adoptive parents.

An interesting finding in the Schulsinger study was that 854 biological and adoptive relatives of 57 psychopathic adoptees and their 57 matched controls showed a frequency of mental disorders higher in the *biological* relatives of the psychopathic probands than among their *adoptive* relatives or than among either group of relative of the controls. The difference is even greater when only psychopathic spectrum disorders are considered. We shall come back to a consideration of the relationship between criminality and psychopathy, on the one hand, and psychiatric disorders (particularly psychoticism and neuroticism) later on (H. J. Eysenck, 1987a).

In a study by Crowe (1972, 1975) in the United States, interest was not in diagnosed psychopathy, but rather in the actual record of arrests. Here the investigators started off by locating 41 female offenders who were inmates of a women's prison reformatory and who had given up their babies for adoption. At the time of the study,they had produced 52 offspring, ranging in age from 15 to 45 years. A properly matched control group of 52 offspring from noncriminal mothers was also studied; these, too, had, of course, been given up for adoption. It was found that the offspring of the criminal mothers had had more criminal arrests and had also received a much greater number of convictions; these differences were fully significant statistically. They also had more "moving traffic violations" recorded against them; this is of importance because of the well-known relationship between criminality and such traffic offenses (H. J. Eysenck, 1977). Here, too, we thus find a much greater resemblance between criminals and biological parents than between criminal and adoptive parents. It is difficult to explain these facts in environmentalistic terms; taken together with the concordance data they seem to prove the implication of genetic mechanisms.

A third important adoption study is one by Hutchings and Mednick (1977). In their sample of 662 adoptive sons, we find that of those where both the biological and adoptive father are criminal, 36% of the sons are criminal, whereas when neither the biological nor the adoptive father was a criminal, only 10% of the adopted sons were criminals. Looking at the sons whose biological but not adoptive father was a criminal, 22% of the sons turned out to be criminal, whereas when the biological father was not a criminal but the adoptive father was, only 12% of the sons were criminal. As the authors say, "this difference falls short of statistical significance, but the direction of the difference favours the strength of the influence of the biological father's criminality" (p. 137).

There were some interesting facts in the more detailed analysis of the data. Thus, for instance, the criminal biological fathers were more criminal when the adoptees themselves were criminal than when the adoptees were not criminal. A similar picture appeared by comparing the criminal and noncriminal adoptees who have criminal adoptive fathers. These findings strengthened the belief in a graded diathesis characteristic of some form of threshold model.

The most sophisticated analysis of adoption study data in relation to criminality has been reported by Baker (1986), using a sample of 2,530 Danish male adoptees and their family members. The statistical procedure used provided estimates of genetic correlations, environmental correlations, and genotype–environment correlations among the measures taken, which were (1) property crimes and (2) a composite psychiatric variable pertaining to hospital admissions for alcohol abuse, drug abuse, and personality disorders. The procedure took into account the facts of selective placement, assortative mating, and cultural transmission from parental phenotypes to offspring environments. Significant heritable influences were found both for property crimes and for the composite psychiatric variables. Both correlated environmental factors and correlated genetic factors important to the different variables accounted for the observed phenotypic relationship between property crime and the antisocial disorders, although significant paternal cultural transmission was found for property crimes. Again, the data leave little doubt about the importance of genetic influences for criminal conduct and also for antisocial conduct and the relationship between these two.

One problem that deserves considerable investigation is the *interaction* of genetic and environmental antecedents of criminality. This was investigated by Cloninger, Sigvardsson, Bohman and von Knorring (1982) using the same population as was used in the study of Bohman *et al.* (1982) mentioned previously. In this work, 862 Swedish men adopted by a nonrelative at an early age were studied and criminality was found to be present in 12% of the adopted men, 26% of their biological fathers, and none of their adoptive fathers. In the present study involving subjects with poor postnatal background alone, the adopted sons had more than twice the rate of petty criminality than a control population of adoptees. When congenital but no postnatal factors predisposed to petty criminality, the risk of such criminality in the sons was increased fourfold. Most important, when both congenital and postnatal factors were present, the risk was 14 times that of the control population! This pattern of results suggests a nonadditive interaction between congenital and postnatal factors, but especially designed analysis based on a linear logistic model showed this interaction to be nonsignificant. A purely additive logistic model proved to give a significant fit for data, suggesting that overall, environmental and genetic factors make separate contributions for risk of petty criminality.

It is useful at this point to reiterate the point that it is not criminality itself that is inherited. Bohman *et al.* (1982) state

> It is important to realize that there are no genes for criminality, but only genes coding for structural proteins and enzymes that influence metabolic, hormonal and other physiological processes, which may indirectly modify the risk of "criminal" behaviour in particular environments. (p. 1234)

INTERPRETATION OF FINDINGS

The data summarized so far from twin studies and from adoptive studies are in good agreement that both genetic and environmental factors are implicated in the genesis of criminal, antisocial, and psychopathic behavior. It has become impossible to deny the importance of either, as indeed might have been expected from simple considerations of what is known about human behavior in general. Whether the estimate of 59% of criminal conduct being associated with genetic causes (Cloninger *et al.*, 1978) is accurate is difficult to say, particularly in view of the standard errors associated with such estimates when the numbers involved are relatively small. What can be said with assurance is that any attempt to disregard genetic factors in criminality would be strictly outside the realm of scientific investigation and would be an ideological statement of no factual relevance. No doubt ongoing studies using larger samples of twins and of adopted children will reduce the fiducial limits of our estimates and will enable us to give a closer estimate of the heritability of criminal and antisocial couduct in our type of society at this point of time; no absolute generality would attach to such estimates, of course, as pointed out at the beginning of this chapter (Cloninger & Gottesman, 1987; Mednick, Gabrielli, & Hutchings, 1987).

We have listed at the beginning of this chapter some of the erroneous views many people have of behavior genetics and the misapprehensions under which they suffer. None of these, perhaps, is more common and more damaging than the notion that because some type of behavior, disorder, or disease is partly determined by heredity, therefore nothing can be done about the hereditary aspect, at least. If this were true, it would seem to follow that one should concentrate on the environmental part of the variance and forget about the genetic part. We have already illustrated the absurdity of this by referring to such environmental steps as hormone treatment, silicone injection, and plastic surgery as means of drastically altering the heritability of female breast size, shape, and consistency. A more realistic example would be phenylketonuria.

This is "a recessive . . . hereditary metabolic anomaly in which the conversion of phenylalanine into tyrosine (i.e., the oxidization of phenylalanines) is disturbed owing to an enzymatic deficiency. The disorder presents as a phenylpyruvic oligophrenia, or various degrees of mental defect, and a tendency to convulsions early in life" (H. J. Eysenck, Arnold, & Meili, 1972, vol. 3, p. 3). It has been known since the disease was first recognized in 1934 that the disorder is inherited, and it is now known to be due to a single recessive gene. Phenylketonuria affects about 1 child in 40,000 in England, and children so affected can be distinguished from other mentally handicapped or from normal children by testing their urine, which yields a green-colored reaction with a solution of ferric chloride, due to the presence of derivatives of phenylalanine. Here we have a perfect example of a disorder produced entirely by hereditary causes, where the cause is simple and well understood, and where the presence of the disorder can be determined with accuracy.

This, however, does not give rise to "therapeutic nihilism." Clearly, knowing that the disease is hereditary is not enough; we must go on to demonstrate in what ways the gene actually produces the mental defect; that is, we must point to the link between DNA on the one hand and the behavioral effects on the other. Now, as mentioned above, children affected by phenylketonuria are unable to convert phenylalaline into tyrosine; they can only break it down to a limited extent. It would seem that some of the incomplete breakdown products of phenylalanine are poisonous to the nervous system. Fortunately, phenylalanine is not an essential part of the diet, provided that tyrosine is present in the diet, and it is possible to maintain these children on a diet that is almost free of phenylalanine, thus eliminating the danger of poisoning to the nervous system. It has been found that when this method of treatment is begun in the first few months of life, there is a very good chance that the child may grow up without the mental handicap that would otherwise have been encountered. In other words, by understanding the *precise* way in which heredity works, and by understanding precisely what it does to the organism, we can arrange a rational method of therapy that will make use of the forces of nature, rather than try to counteract them.

A good analogy here would be the effective methods of treatment for neurotic disorders that have been introduced under the name of behavior therapy (H. J. Eysenck & Martin, 1987). Here, too, personality traits that are strongly inherited have been found to be systematically linked with the disorder, but, nevertheless, a theory was promulgated that appeared to link the genetic predisposition with the observed behavior. This theory made a process of autonomic Pavlovian conditioning responsible for the appearance of neurotic symptoms and suggested the use of Pavlovian extinction as a method of treatment. Results have amply justified this choice of theory and indicate a considerable superiority of behavior therapy methods over the usual psychotherapeutic methods, as far as effectiveness is concerned (Rachman & Wilson, 1980).

It is the hope of ultimately discovering similar methods of treatment for criminal conduct that led to the formulation of theories such as those developed in this book. Only a proper understanding of the links between heredity on the one hand and behavior on the other will enable us to solve this age-old problem of crime and its prevention. Unfortunately, there is one far-reaching difference between neurosis and crime in this respect. Neurotic patients are highly motivated to seek help, because of the suffering that their disorder inflicts upon them. This high degree of motivation is an important factor in leading to a cure. Criminals, on the other hand, are positively reinforced for their behavior in many instances and are hence not likely to seek psychological help of any kind. Indeed, when this is offered, it is often refused. This negative motivation on the part of the criminals and the positive reinforcement they receive from their criminal conduct make theirs a much more difficult problem than that presented by neurotics. To say this is not to suggest that the problem is insoluble. If a solution is to be found, however, it can come about only through a better understanding of the psychological conditions involved in criminal activity and a willingness to adapt social action to any such findings. Genetic factors are equally involved in neurosis as in criminality, but this has not proved an insuperable difficulty in the successful treatment of neurotic disorders. There is equally no reason why the genetic involvement in criminal activities should prove an insuperable obstacle to the successful elimination of criminality.

SUMMARY AND CONCLUSIONS

For many years now, the notion has been widespread that genetic causes have nothing to do with criminality and that environmental influences are all important. The evidence now available conclusively disproves such a view, although, of course, this should not be taken to mean that environmental causes have *no* effect. We are biosocial animals, each influenced both by genetic and environmental factors acting and interacting in complex ways. The analysis of these actions and interactions is necessarily equally complex, but great advances have been made in recent years to enable us to assign numerical values to the various portions of the genetic and the environmental variance and their interaction.

The general finding from studies of twins and adopted children is that genetic causes exert a very strong pull in the direction of prosocial behavior, amounting possibly to something like 60% of the total variance. As we have pointed out, however, it would be quite wrong to regard this as evidence for a view that "crime is destiny." The predisposition to criminal conduct is inborn, but depending on environmental circumstances this predisposition can also lead to quite other types of conduct, which are not regarded as criminal. Equally, the fact that a genetic predisposition exists in some people—stronger in some, weaker in others—does not mean that efforts at rehabilitation or prevention of criminal conduct altogether are doomed to failure. There is no fixed genetic code leading inevitably to crime; other modes of conduct may be suggested by society that will fill the innate needs equally well. The problem is clearly a complex one, but it would be premature to argue that it has no solution. Genetic factors should be understood for what they are and not accepted as an immovable barrier to social progress.

CHAPTER FIVE

A Biological Theory of Criminality

AROUSAL AND CONDITIONING

We have seen in previous chapters that genetic factors play an important part in the causation of criminal behavior, that constitutional factors are strongly implicated, and that personality features are vitally important for the commission of antisocial or altruistic acts. Is it possible to put forward a biological theory of criminality that would bring together all these different aspects and explain more in detail why certain individuals are more predisposed than others to commit antisocial acts? Such a question is not intended to suggest that human behavior is *completely* and *inevitably* conditioned by biological factors; we have already insisted on the biosocial nature of human beings, that is, the combination of biological and social factors in determining behavior. Thus whatever the biological predisposition of a person, it can become activated only in interaction with certain environmental variables. Nevertheless, it is surely important to ask just what the nature of these biological variables might be and to advance theories that might throw light on this biological side of the equation.

One of us has proposed a quite general theory according to which humans (and also animals, although that is irrelevant in this context) differ from each other with respect to the ease or difficulty with which their level of arousal can be increased (arousability), their usual level of arousal, and the ease with which this arousal level can be maintained (H. J. Eysenck, 1963, 1967). Arousal descriptively refers to the different states of consciousness that would be associated with different activities. A tired person sitting in front of the television screen late at night, watching a rather boring program, would be in a low state of arousal. Illustrative of high arousal would be the same person, early in the morning, beginning an important examination and all keyed up to do well. Thus there are differences in arousal within a given person; these can be mirrored psychophysiologically by means of the EEG (high arousal is accompanied by fast, low amplitude alpha waves, low arousal by slow, high amplitude alpha waves, for instance).

The theory asserts that cortical arousal of this kind, although varying for a given person depending on time of day, activity pursued at the time, drug intake, and many other factors, will also characteristically vary from one person to another under *identical* circumstances, so that one person will be highly aroused, another show only average arousal, and a third may be underaroused when offered the same set of stimuli (Strelau & H. J. Eysenck, 1987).

H. J. Eysenck (1967) suggested that cortical arousal, mediated by the so-called ascending reticular formation, was responsible for differences in extraversion and introversion (H. J. Eysenck & M. W. Eysenck, 1985), in the sense that extraverted behavior was characteristic of individuals being difficult to arouse and having low arousal levels, whereas introverts were easy to arouse and had high levels of arousal under identical stimulation conditions. There are many difficulties in identifying and measuring "arousal," and there is a very large literature exploring the relationship between levels of arousal and personality (Stelmack, 1981). On the whole, the evidence is in favor of some such association as has been suggested, although it cannot be said that all deductions from the theory have been verified (H. J. Eysenck & M. W. Eysenck, 1985; Strelau & H. J. Eysenck, 1987). Here we are concerned, not so much with this very large body of literature, but rather with an extension of the theory (H. J. Eysenck, 1964) to criminality. What was suggested was that low arousability/arousal was a biological factor responsible in part for criminal and antisocial behavior and associating criminal behavior with extraverted personality through the operation of the arousal system.

A little earlier, Lykken (1957, 1982) had proposed that psychopathy might be partly due to certain unusual subcortical neurological processes responsible for maintaining an individual's overall arousal level at an unusually low state. We have already commented on the similarities between psychopathy and criminality and also remarked that it is impossible to *identify* the two with each other. Nevertheless, in spite of certain differences, there is some similarity between the two theories, and essentially they implicate the same biological mechanisms, although they have tended to suggest rather different routes for expressing these tendencies. The original suggestion made by H. J. Eysenck (1964) with respect to ways in which different states of arousal might lead to differences in behavior implicated Pavlovian conditioning. To put the matter in its simplest form, Eysenck suggested that socialized and altruistic behavior had to be learned and that this learning was mediated by means of Pavlovian conditioning. The newborn and the young child have no social conscience and behave in a purely egocentric manner. They have to acquire a "conscience" through a process of conditioning; in other words, on thousands of occasions, when they behave in an antisocial manner, parents, teachers, peers, and others punish them in a variety of ways, thus associating through Pavlovian conditioning antisocial thoughts and actions with disagreeable consequences. As a result of this conditioned "conscience," such individuals will refrain from contemplating or carrying out antisocial activities because the contemplation or carrying out is accompanied by conditioned feelings of fear/anxiety, anticipation of punishment, and guilt. Evidence in favor of the theory, both from animal and human experiments, is provided by H. J. Eysenck (1977).

It is well known that Pavlovian conditioning is aided by high arousal, and as a consequence we would expect introverts to condition more readily and hence to socialize better than extraverts. This was the original link proposed by H. J. Eysenck (1964), and the large literature now available linking extraversion with antisocial behavior confirms at least one of the deductions made from the hypothesis. A more direct verification is possible, however, and this is linked with an interesting aspect of the theory that has only recently been given prominence. This aspect of the theory is particularly important because it illustrates the vital role played by social factors, even in dealing with biological theories.

Raine and Venables (1981) argued essentially that if the theory was correct, then the final outcome of the conditioning process should depend not only on the conditionability of the subjects, but also on the prosocial or antisocial conduct to which they were being conditioned. In other words, if the values of the milieu in which a given child grew up were prosocial, then introverted children should emerge as better behaved, but if the values of the milieu were antisocial, as might happen in many socially depressed areas, then it should be the introverted child who would grow up to be less well behaved, having better incorporated the antisocial values of his or her environment.

Using low and high social class as measures of poor and good social milieu as far as prosocial conduct was concerned, they measured both conditionability and pro- or antisocial behavior in their subjects. As Figure 17 shows, prosocial behavior was shown by the offspring of low social class parents who condition poorly and by offspring of high social class parents who conditioned well. Opposite to this was a tendency toward antisocial conduct that was shown by high conditioners from the low social class and low conditioners from the high social class. Thus this experiment confirms both hypotheses, that is, that linking conditioning with social behavior and also that linking type of value system conditioned with social behavior. H. J. Eysenck (1977) has referred to

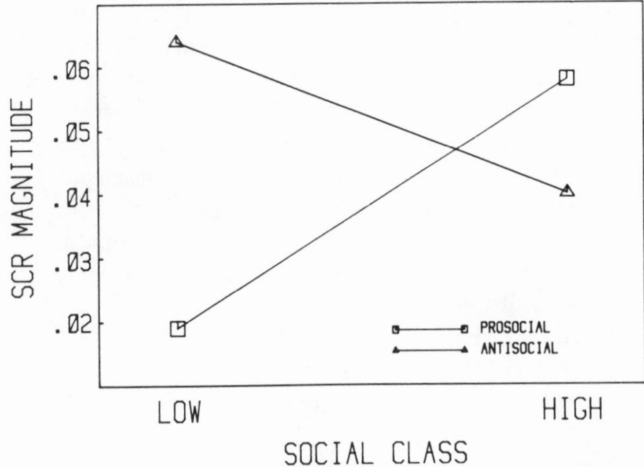

FIGURE 17. Prosocial and antisocial behavior as a function of the interaction of conditionability and social class (Raine &Venables, 1983).

this process of conditioning to antisocial conduct as "anti-socialization," and it must be recognized as inevitably lowering correlations between criminality and extraversion, particularly when it is considered that many criminals come from a milieu that would actively encourage aggressive and other types of antisocial behavior. It is clear that a proper test of the conditioning hypothesis would require some information on the conditioning processes to which a given individual was subjected and the value system giving rise to this conditioning process.

The Raine and Venables study might be faulted in identifying antisocial and prosocial upbringing with low and high social class; it would, of course, be a complete travesty of the truth to say that there is any necessary identity between social class and type of upbringing. Nevertheless, there is undoubtedly a correlation; aggressive behavior, for instance, is much more highly valued in parents of low than of high social class, and similarly a lower value is placed among parents of lower social class on property laws than by parents of higher social class. Future work will have to identify more specifically the degree of antisocial upbringing experienced by given children having high or low conditionability in order to firm up the conclusions of the Raine and Venables study.

Of all the studies that have been done to determine the importance of conditioning on the development of a "conscience," most important has probably been the work of Richard L. Solomon and his colleagues (Solomon, Turner, & Lessac, 1968; see also Mowrer, 1960). In this work, they used 6-month-old puppies, and in other experiments young children were used employing a similar paradigm (Aronfeld & Reber, 1965); here we shall concentrate on the animal experiments. These were conducted in so-called "taboo situations," held in a training room, fairly soundproof, and equipped with a one-way mirror. A chair was placed in a corner of the room and in front of the front legs of the chair were placed two small dishes. The experimenter sat in the chair, holding in his hand a rolled-up newspaper with which he could swat the puppies on the rump. Each of the puppies was deprived of food for two days and was then brought into the experimental room. In one of the dishes had been placed boiled horse meat, which was very much liked by the puppies, whereas in the other dish was placed a much less well-liked commercial dog food. The puppies usually made straight for the horse meat, but as they touched it they were swatted by the experimenter. If one gentle blow was not enough, then the puppies were swatted again and again until they finally gave up their attempts to eat the horse meat. Usually, several further attempts were made, until finally the puppies turned to the commercial dog food, which they could eat without being swatted.

This training was carried on for several days, until the puppies had firmly learned the taboo on horse meat. The experimenter then turned to what was called the "temptation testing" phase. Again the puppies were deprived of food for two days and then brought to the room, but this time with the experimenter absent. Again a choice had to be made between the dish of boiled horse meat and a few pellets of dog food. The puppies soon gobbled up the dog food, then began to react to the large dish of horse meat. In Solomon's words:

> Some puppies would circle the dish over and over again. Some puppies walked around the room with their eyes towards the wall, not looking at the dish. Other puppies got down on their bellies and slowly crawled forward, barking and whining. There was a large range of variability in the emotional behaviour of the puppies in the presence of the tabooed horse meat. We measured resistance to temptation as the number of seconds or minutes which passed by before the subject ate the tabooed food. The puppies were allowed half an hour a day in the experimental room. If they did not eat the horse meat by that time, they were brought back to their home cages, were not fed, and, a day later, were introduced again into the experimental room. This continued until the puppy finally violated the taboo and ate the horse meat, or until he had fasted so long that he had to be fed in his cage, in order to keep him alive.
>
> There was a very great range of resistance to temptation. The shortest period of time it took a puppy to overcome his training and eat the horse meat was six minutes, and the longest period of time was sixteen days without eating, after which time the experiment had to be stopped and the puppy fed in his home cage. This great range of variability made it possible to test the influence of various experimental conditions on the growth of conscience in these puppies. For instance, it was shown that when the puppies were

> hand-fed throughout their early life by the experimenter, then they developed a conscience much more strongly than did other animals which had been machine-fed. (from Mowrer [1960] pp. 399–404)

Solomon separated resistance to temptation from guilt, and he avoided, in his discussion, the use of the term "conscience," which he suggested might be a compound of the two manifestations.

> For example, in the first litter we ran, we found that when a puppy did kick over the traces and eat the horse meat, he did so with his tail wagging the whole time, and after he ate the horse meat, when the experimenter came into the room, the puppy greeted him with tail wags and with no obvious distress. On the other hand, in some preliminary work we did, we noticed that some pups showed much more emotional disturbance after they ate the horse meat than when they were approaching it. We were able to relate this to uncontrolled differences in training techniques.

Apparently when the puppies were walloped just when they *approached* the tabooed food, they built up a high resistance to temptation. However, when such puppies did kick over the traces, they showed no emotional upset following the crime. On the other hand, when the puppies were left to eat half the horse meat before being walloped, then one could still establish an avoidance of the horse meat. In the case of these puppies, however, there was much more emotional disturbance *following* the crime, and these, Solomon suggested, could be called guilt reactions. The presence of the experimenter was not required to elicit these reactions, although his presence seemed to intensify them when he did finally come into the room after the "crime" had been committed.

> Therefore we believe that the conditions for the establishment of strong resistance to temptation as contrasted with the capacity to experience strong guilt reactions, is a function of both the intensity of punishment and the time during the approach and consumatory response-sequence at which the punishment is administered.

Solomon goes on to speculate that delayed punishment is probably not very effective in producing a very high level of resistance to temptation, but might be more effective in producing emotional reactions of guilt after the commission of the crime. On the other hand, he says, it is clear that punishment introduced after the animal eats quite a bit of the horse meat does operate backward in time, and it does produce aversion and the disruption of approach responses. These approach responses, however, do not seem to be as reliably broken up by such delayed punishment.

> We feel that this observation is important, since it represents two major types of socialization techniques used by parents. In one case, the parent traps the child into the commission of the tabooed act, so that the child can be effectively punished, the hope being that this will prevent the child from

> performing it again. The other technique is to watch the child closely, to try to anticipate when the child intends to do something wrong and punish the child during the incipient states. Each of these techniques, according to our observation of these puppies, leads to a very different outcome with regard to the components of "conscience."

Solomon thus assumed that "conscience" has two components, one the ability to resist temptation and the other the susceptibility to guilt reactions. He further assumed that these two components are partially independent and that by appropriate training procedures, organisms can be produced that have high resistance to temptation along with high susceptibility to guilt reactions, low resistance to temptation and low susceptibility to guilt reactions, high resistance to temptation and low susceptibility to guilt reactions, and low resistance to temptation along with high susceptibility to guilt reactions. "It is easy to examine these four classes of outcome and see four clinically important combinations in the neuroses, as well as the creation of a psychopath". Solomon himself does not link up his results particularly with ease of conditioning, but he does refer to the fact that different breeds of dogs differ very much in the ease with which they acquire a "conscience." Thus, for instance, Shetland sheepdogs are especially sensitive to reprimand, and taboos can apparently be established with just one frightening experience and are then extremely resistant to extinction. On the other hand, he reports, Basenjis seem to be constitutional psychopaths and it is very difficult to maintain taboos in such dogs (Scott & Fuller, 1965). All these findings, then, are in very good agreement with our theory.

The theory that the *timing* of the punishment determines whether the outcome will be deterrence or guilt has been much studied in recent years. Aronfeld and Reber (1965), working with children, and Solomon *et al.* (1968), working with dogs, have lent powerful support to this interpretation. We have already discussed at some length Solomon's earlier experiments; we may perhaps continue with a brief account of his most recent work. Using the same paradigm as before, he slapped the dogs who approached the forbidden food either (1) before they could start eating (0 seconds delay), or (2) 5 seconds after beginning to eat (5 seconds delay), or (3) 15 seconds after beginning to eat (15 seconds delay). All three groups learned the avoidance response in roughly similar numbers of conditioning sessions; however, important differences emerged when they were left alone in the room with the two food dishes. The 0 seconds delay group ate the 20 grams of dry chow pellets and then withdrew to the walls of the room far away from the horse meat.

> It was only after several days of starvation that these subjects moved close to the horse meat dish. When they finally broke the taboo, their mood appeared to change abruptly . . . they wagged their tails while eating the

> meat, ate voraciously without pausing, and after finishing the meat did not appear to be apprehensive.

In other words, these dogs feared to approach the forbidden goal, but once the deed was done had no guilt feelings.

The dogs in the groups where punishment had been delayed "behaved *as though the experimenter were still there.*" After eating the few dry chow pellets, they put their forepaws on the experimenter's empty chair, or hid behind the chair, and wagged their tails when they looked at the chair. When they finally broke the taboo and ate the horse meat, they ate in brief intervals and ran away between bites. They appeared to be frightened during and after finishing the meat. These guilt feelings even generalized during training to the dry pellets, which they were permitted to eat; by contrast, the 0 seconds delay dogs during training exhibited fearfulness "only during the approach to the food and not during the eating itself." It may seem fanciful and anthropomorphic to attribute "guilt" to nonhuman experimental subjects such as dogs, but if we judge purely in behavioral terms, then the behavior of the dogs whose punishment was delayed, in their furtiveness, slinking away after brief nibbles at the forbidden food, and general air of doing the wrong thing and being afraid of punishment by some power not present to the senses, reminds one strikingly of human beings acting under some strong guilt feelings.

Furthermore, of course, work with children already mentioned supports the main animal feelings. We may thus conclude that there is some evidence to support the hypothesis regarding the importance of timing in producing either the *avoidance* or the *guilt* reaction. The relevance of this finding to the upbringing of children needs no emphasis; after all, we want them to *avoid* the forbidden act, rather than *feel guilty* after committing it. The former achievement is a useful one, the latter may satisfy our ethical sense of retribution, but is socially pretty useless. It may also be noted that here we have hit upon a mechanism that explains the fact that introverts are not always found to indulge in socially acceptable behavior; it seems possible that in these cases parents and teachers have failed to apply negative reinforcement (punishment) without undue delay, so that these children have grown up, not avoiding temptation, but feeling guilty over succumbing! Guilt feelings are certainly more frequent in introverts, and particularly in neurotics. Empirical support for this view comes from a recent study by Gudjonsson and Singh (1987). Remorse as measured by the Gudjonsson Blame Attribution Inventory correlates positively with introversion and neuroticism and negatively with psychoticism.

Clearly, a theory of the kind here discussed lays equal stress on personality variables, whether in children or dogs, and also the process of conditioning. None of the dogs in Solomon's experiments would have developed avoidance behavior or feelings of guilt if they had not been subjected to a conditioning process, and the strength of the conditioning would determine to a large extent the degree of avoidance or guilt feelings. A biosocial theory must therefore integrate both biologically individual differences and the conditioning and learning program to which the individual is exposed. It follows from the theory that a policy of permissiveness on the part of society would lead to a lack of conditioning of the conscience-building kind, so that it is possible that the recent increments in criminality that have been so noticeable in Western (and other, such as Communist) societies is due to growing permissiveness. It is certainly not suggested that it is due to any kind of genetic changes; clearly, there has been insufficient time for any such changes to occur.

An excellent review of the effects of the general atmosphere of permissiveness in our society, particularly in the field of crime and punishment, has been given by Morgan (1978). As she points out, official attitudes, such as are expressed in the philosophy of the 1969 Children and Young Persons Act, have been characterized by the dogma that delinquency is essentially a symptom of deprivation, emotional, economic, or social. It has been portrayed as a side effect of everything from lack of mother love to substandard housing, from lack of play facilities to low incomes. In her book, Morgan examines these beliefs and, using the results of many research studies, dismisses most of them as irresponsible fantasies. "Their only use lies in comforting those who seek to avoid at all costs the necessity of choosing, transmitting and maintaining rules of social behavior" (p. 8).

As she also states, not only are certain means of reducing delinquency rejected on the basis of this confused ideology, but increasingly there is a rejection of the laws themselves. Those who are charged with preventing delinquency sometimes identify with the delinquent and see him or her as unjustly labeled or even making a valid political protest. The delinquent becomes, to some of them, a creative force helping to break up a society they reject. Comparing the results of our system of conditioning and teaching with the radically different methods of upbringing in traditional and Communist societies, she shows that they appear to be far more successful than our own, not only in reducing delinquency but in increasing the chances of happiness and social adjustment in young people.

In laying emphasis in this book on the more biologically determined aspects of individual differences, we do not of course wish to deny the importance of the environment that teaches and conditions the individual. Morgan's book presents an excellent discussion of both aspects of

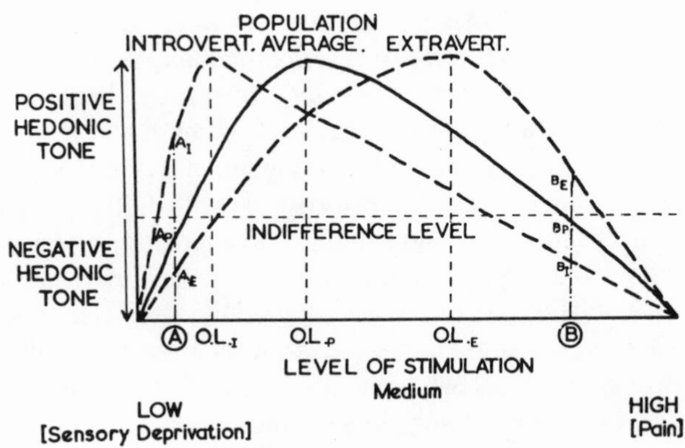

FIGURE 18. Hedonic tone as a function of level of stimulation (H. J. Eysenck, 1967).

criminality and its causation, which we have somewhat neglected in our presentation.

A GENERAL AROUSAL THEORY OF CRIMINALITY

Another direction in which behavioral consequences can be derived from the general theory of low arousal in extraverts and criminals is by way of *pain sensitivity*. This, as we shall see, is not unconnected with our conditioning theory, but it also has features that are quite independent of it. Consider Figure 18. It embodies a relationship between level of sensory stimulation and hedonic tone (i.e., liking and disliking, adience and abience) and dates back to the early days of Wundt (1874). As the central line indicates, when sensory stimulation is too low (sensory deprivation) or when it is too high (pain), it has a negative hedonic tone, arousal levels are too low or too high, and hence such stimuli are avoided if possible. Passing through an indifference level, we have medium levels of stimulation, which have a positive hedonic tone and are sought after. Thus particularly low or high levels of stimulation have motivational features through their effects on arousal. Low levels of arousal are avoided, as are levels of arousal that are too high and are associated with pain.

Berlyne (1974) has greatly elaborated this general theory and discussed its physiological basis in arousal; he has also extended it from sensory stimulation to what he calls "collative" properties of stimulus patterns, that is, such properties as complexity or novelty, which would be similar in their influence on arousal to high levels of sensory stimulation. His own work has mainly dealt with experimental esthetics, but it obviously extends to hedonic everyday life reactions in general.

It will be clear from our discussion of the arousal patterns of extraverts and introverts that the population curve that forms the central part of Figure 18 is displaced toward the left for introverts and the right for extraverts. For introverts, because of their high level of arousal/arousability, even low levels of stimulation will be amplified and considered as satisfactory, whereas extraverts, because of the inhibiting features of their low level of arousal/arousability, will require higher levels of stimulation. In the curve, this is indicated by the different positions of the optimal level (O.L) of introverts, population mean, and extraverts. At levels of stimulation A and B, it will be seen that at A, stimulation is too low for extraverts, indifferent for the mean of the population, and positively acceptable for introverts, whereas at B exactly the opposite is true, the stimulation being too high for introverts and very acceptable for extraverts, with a population mean being again at indifference level. One important consequence of this general theory is that extraverts should suffer pain more readily, that is, experience pain less strongly than introverts, and introverts would tolerate sensory deprivation more readily than extraverts. There is good empirical evidence for both these predictions, summarized in H. J. Eysenck and M. W. Eysenck (1985). Table 12 taken from Barnes (1975) shows results with pain stimulation to date, and H. J. Eysenck (1988) has brought the story up to date. There is no doubt that pain thresholds and pain tolerance are higher for extraverts than for the average person and lower for introverts. This fact has important consequences for criminality.

In the first place, we would expect criminals to be less reactive to pain because of their lower level of arousal. This would be directly relevant to criminal behavior, which often involves physical danger and pain, but its main effect might be on conditioning. Pavlovian conditioning, insofar as it is responsible for the creation of a "conscience," involves repeated application of painful stimuli by parents, teachers, and peers. Principles of Pavlovian conditioning tell us that (within limits) the intensity of the pain is directly correlated with the strength of the conditioned response. Hence, if the intensity of physical punishment is felt less strongly by extraverts, then clearly they should respond less to such types of conditioning than would the average person, and much less so than the introvert.

This deduction, which is implicit in the Eysenck theory, has been explicitly incorporated in Gray's (1981) modification of that theory. Gray's own theory, insofar as it is relevant to our discussion, specifically maintains that extraverts condition better to *positive* (rewarding, pleasant) stimuli whereas introverts condition better to *negative* (painful, harm-

TABLE 12. Relationship between Extraversion and Pain

Study	Subjects	Extraversion measure	Pain or sensation stimulus	Pain or sensation measure	Results
Petrie *et al.* (1960)	42 patients	MPI	Clinical pain	Clinical assessment	Extraverts greater pain tolerance ($P < 0.05$)
Poser (1960)	19 ex'l. pain 18 female students	MPI	Radiant heat Ischemic pain	Pain tolerance Pain tolerance	Significant correlation (0.53) E and pain tolerance
Lynn & Eysenck (1961)	30 female students	MPI	Radiant heat	Pain tolerance	Correlation E and pain tolerance (0.69, $P <$ 0.01)
Schalling & Levander (1964)	20 male delinquents	MPI and clinical assessment	Electric current	Sensation and pain threshold, pain tolerance	Psychopaths less sensitive to pain. Results E and pain n.s. but in right direction.
Martin & Inglis (1965)	24 female ex-addicts 24 female non-addicts	MPI	Cold-pressor test	Pain tolerance	Addicts tolerate more pain. Correlation E and pain tolerance 0.12 (n.s.)
Levine *et al.* (1966)	52 housewives 29 male students	MPI	Electrical stimulation Discrete administration	Sensation threshold, pain tolerance	No significant results E and pain or sensation for either group
Haslam (1967)	19 male students 16 female students	MPI	Radiant heat	Pain threshold	Introverts had a significantly lower pain threshold ($P < 0.002$)
Davidson & McDougal (1969)	60 female students	MPI	Cold pressor and radiant heat	Pain threshold Pain tolerance	No significant results for E and pain
Vando (1969)	80 female students	EPI	Pressure	Pain tolerance	Intoverts low on pain tolerance ($P < 0.01$)
Schalling (1971)	8 male students 18 female students	MNT	Electric current continuous and discrete administration	Pain threshold Pain tolerance	Significant corr. solidity (extraversion) pain tolerance (0.40, $P <$ 0.05)
Brown *et al.* (1973)	52 female students	EPI	Cold stimulus Pressure stimulus	Pain threshold, tolerance, intensity	No significant relationship, pain tolerance and personality variables

[MPI, Maudsley Personality Inventory; EPI, Eysenck Personality Inventory; MNT, Marke–Nyman Temperament Inventory]

Note. From "Extraversion and Pain" by G. Barnes, *British Journal of Social and Clinical Psychology*, 1975, *14*.

ful) stimuli. Although Gray's basic premises are different from Eysenck's, the resulting prediction is the same.

At the other end of the curve, the hypothetical intolerance of extraverts and criminals to low levels of stimulation would be expected to lead them to seek excitement, noise, color, and generally anything that will increase their too-low arousal level. Thus low arousal/arousability should theoretically lead to types of behavior that are typical of extraverts, criminals, and psychopaths. Much work has supported the deductions from our Figure 18, summarized with respect to extraversion by H. J. Eysenck and M. W. Eysenck (1985), to criminals by H. J. Eysenck (1977), and to psychopaths by Hare and Schalling (1978) and H. J. Eysenck (1980) (see also Hare & Cox, 1978).

Particularly striking is the agreement between work on criminality and work on psychopathy. The surprise arises because of the well-known difficulty of defining psychopaths and failure to agree on definition and measurement. Here is the summary of the results of such work by Hare (1970):

> It appears that psychopaths do not develop conditioned responses readily. As a result, they find it difficult to learn responses that are motivated by fear and reinforced by fear reduction. The fact that their behaviour appears to be neither motivated nor guided by the possibility of unpleasant consequences, particularly when the temporal relationship between behaviour and its consequences is relatively great, might be interpreted in this way. There is some evidence that psychopaths are also less influenced than are normal persons by the relationship between past events and the consequences of their present behaviour. (p. 18)

This is in good accord with our theory.

Hare also summarizes evidence on arousal and the attenuation of sensory input, which we have hypothesized in previous chapters to be characteristic of criminals and psychopaths. On arousal, he writes:

> Several lines of research and theory suggest that psychopathy is related to cortical underarousal. As a result, the psychopath actively seeks stimulation unaware of, or inattentive to, many of the subtle cues required for the guidance of behaviour and for adequate social functioning. (p. 37)

He also states that the evidence indicates

> that psychopathy may be related to a general tendency to attenuate sensory input. . . . Besides a general tendency to attenuate sensory input, it is possible that psychopaths may be able to "tune out" or at least greatly attenuate stimulation that is potentially disturbing. The result would be that threats of punishment and cues warning of unpleasant consequences for misbehaviour would not have the same emotional impact that they would have for other individuals. Paradoxically, this would mean that cues that are a source of emotional (and cortical) arousal for normal persons would not have the same function with psychopaths, the very ones who are most in need of this arousal. (p. 56)

On the two crucial deductions from our general principle, then, an independent observer concludes positively, and he also supports the validity of the general principle. The principle is that psychopaths are characterized by low cortical arousal; the deductions are that they condition poorly and that they seek excitement. This accounts for their being subject to temptation (arousal seeking) and having less conscience to save them from temptation (poor conditioning of social mores). Proof is certainly not conclusive (indeed, followers of Popper will realize that conclusive proof in science does not exist), but the results do make it seem possible that this whole line of reasoning is likely to lead to the discovery of worthwhile new facts.

We thus have three (not independent) ways along which the low arousal hypothesized to characterize criminals and those guilty of antisocial behavior in general may give rise to the characteristic behavior of such groups. In the first place, they fail to form the conditioned responses readily that go to make up a socialized "conscience." In the second place, they are more readily tempted to seek arousal in ways that are not socially approved. And in the third place, they are not deterred by pain as much as are other people and overvalue positive reinforcements. Evidence on all these points is by no means conclusive, but tends on the whole to be positive, suggesting that the theory may be worth pursuing further.

We may now look at some of the direct evidence linking low arousal with criminality. Among studies giving direct evidence for such a relationship is the work of Blankenstein (1969), Mathis (1970), Sayed, Lewis and Brittain (1969), and Schalling, Lidberg, Levander, and Dahlin (1973). Blackburn (1975) reports a failure to replicate; but see the most recent studies of Venables (1987) and Volavka (1987). In these studies, it was found that persons with the most serious criminal or psychopathic histories tended to have somewhat lower resting arousal levels than persons without such histories.

Another, much larger, set of studies indicated that seriously criminal or psychopathic persons show signs of a less marked and/or a slower shift toward high arousal when threatened with pain or punishment than do persons with no serious criminal or psychopathic histories. Among authors who can be quoted here are Aniskiewicz (1973), Borkovec (1970), Hare (1970, 1978, 1982), Hare and Craigen (1974), Hare and Quinn (1971), Hare and Schalling, (1978), Hemming (1977), Hinton and O'Neil (1978), Loeb and Mednick (1977), Mathis (1970), Rosen and Schalling (1971), Siddle (1977), Sutker (1970), and Woodman (1979).

Another source of evidence relates to hyperactivity (Satterfield, 1987). This, as will be discussed later, is generally indicative of low arousal, and if criminality partially reflects the same neurological condition, one would expect childhood hyperactivity to be associated with juvenile and adult criminality. Evidence is available to support this view quite strongly (Cantwell, 1981; Halperin & Gittelman, 1982; Mattes, Boswell, & Oliver, 1982; Mendelson, Johnston, & Stewart, 1971; Porges, 1977; Prinz, Connor, and Wilson, 1981; Roff & Wint, 1984; Stewart, 1978; Weiss, Minde, Werry, Douglas, & Nemeth 1971).

Slightly more difficult to explain is the third set of studies in which serious criminals have been found slower than average in recovering to baseline once the threatening situation has been removed (Loeb & Mednick, 1976; Mednick, 1975; Venables, 1975; Siddle, Mednick, Nicol, & Foggitt, 1976). Mednick (1977) explained these results along the following lines. Once a criminal person's arousal has been raised to an unpleasantly high level, it tends to return to a preferred level more slowly than typical, and as a consequence the likelihood of such a person associating his actions with a return to a preferred level of arousal would be considerably less than for persons whose arousal mechanisms are extremely quick to respond to environmental cues. Evidence for this hypothesis, however, is largely lacking.

Ellis (in press d) has argued that criminality and psychopathy are far from the only aspects of behavior influenced by arousal levels. He suggests that a fairly basic test of arousal theory would involve determining to what degree other behavioral symptoms of suboptimal arousal correlated with criminality and psychopathy. To identify what these traits might be he consulted the literature on arousal theory and came up with eight significant behavior patterns besides criminality and psychopathy that should be enhanced by suboptimal arousal. These were as follows:

1. Resistance to punishment or defiance of punishment by parents and other persons in authority (Satinder, 1977)
2. Impulsiveness and nonpersistence at tasks assigned and coordinated by others (Farley, 1986)
3. Childhood hyperactivity (Bell, Alexander, & Schwartzman, 1983; Satterfield & Dawson, 1971; Shouse & Lubar, 1978; Stewart, 1970; Zentall, Gohs, & Culatta, 1983)
4. General risk taking, excitement seeking (including gambling) (Blaszczynski, 1985; Lykken, 1982)
5. Neurologically active recreational drug use, including heavy alcohol use (Tarter, Alterman, & Edwards, 1984)
6. Preference for active, rather than for quiet social interactions (H. J. Eysenck, 1977; McEwan & Devins, 1983; Nichols, 1974)
7. Broad-ranging sexual experiences (or at least a preference for such) and unstable bonding tendency (H. J. Eysenck, 1976; Farley, 1986)

8. Poor academic performance other than that which is attributable to intellectual deficit (H. J. Eysenck & Cookson, 1969; Wankowksi, 1973)

Ellis (in press) reports a meta-analysis that, in effect, covers all published empirical investigations of the relationship between the variables in question published in the English language. He gives a table that summarizes the results of these studies that have correlated criminality and/or psychopathy with the eight other hypothesized behavioral manifestations of suboptimal arousal.

> It shows that large numbers of studies have been conducted, and that, without exception, these studies support the hypothesized relationship between criminality/psychopathy and the other eight reported behavioural manifestations and sub-optimal arousal. Specifically, 10 studies found criminality and/or psychopathy to be significantly associated with defiance of punishment, 44 with poor school performance, 29 with impulsiveness and non-persistence at routine tasks assigned and coordinated by others, 20 with hyperactivity, 10 with risk taking and excitement seeking, 67 with neurologically active drug use (especially the heavy use of alcohol), 6 with preference for active social interactions, and 17 with wide-ranging sex experiences and/or unstable bonding with sexual partners. In all cases, the correlations were in the direction predicted by arousal theory.

Ellis also argues that the hypothesized behavioral manifestations of suboptimal arousal should correlate with each other and gives a table derived from his meta-analysis. This table "strongly supports the view that the 8 variables hypothesized to be reflective of sub-optimal arousal are all inter-correlated with one another just as arousal theory predicts." Minor exceptions are noted in the Ellis article.

Ellis, who strongly endorses the distinction between victimful and victimless crimes, also raises the following question. Why would some types of acts that directly victimize no one also have been made subject to criminal sanctions? What, he asks, would account for the fact that most societies have extended criminal sanctions to cover acts for which there are no victims? He suggests that much of the explanation involves the eight behavioral correlates of criminal behavior and psychopathy identified above. "Specifically, in the efforts to minimize the risk of victimful offences, most governmental bodies have also tried to curb a number of the 8 behavioural correlates of criminality and psychopathy." In a report of this hypothesis, he gives a table, here reprinted as Table 13, in which the first column lists the eight behavioral correlates of criminality and psychopathy and the second column lists various victimless offenses that seem to correspond closely to the eight behavioral correlates.

TABLE 13. Matching of 8 Hypothesized Behavioral Manifestations of Suboptimal Arousal and Various Victimless Acts of Delinquency and Crime

Eight hypothesized behavioral manifestations of suboptimal arousal	Corresponding victimless acts of delinquency and crime
Defiance of punishment	Disobedience to parents and governing authority (incorrigibility, insubordination, resisting arrests)
Poor academic performance at least partially unattributable to intellectual deficiencies	Truancy and leaving school below the minimum age for doing so
Impulsiveness, and nonpersistence at routinized tasks assigned and coordinated by others	Vagrancy; nonsupport of dependents
Hyperactivity	Truancy and leaving school below the minimum age for doing so
Risk taking and excitement seeking	Gambling; reckless driving; speeding; life endangerment; drug trafficking
Neurologically-active recreational drug use	Purchasing and possessing controlled substances
Preference for active, as opposed to solemn, social interactions	Disturbing the peace; child abandonment
Broad-ranging sexual experiences and unstable bonding tendencies	Extramarital copulations; voyeurism; prostitution; indecent exposure; pedophilia and statutory rape; marital desertion

Note. From Ellis (in press d).

AROUSAL, MASCULINITY, AND ANDROGENS

What are the causal factors producing low arousability? There clearly is a relationship with the ascending reticular formation, but again one might ask what causes the reticular formation to behave in different ways for different people in mediating cortical arousal? Ellis (in press a) has advanced a very far-reaching hypothesis that postulates essentially that it is the androgens (male sex hormones) that are responsible not only for differences in arousability, but also for other physiological patterns that mediate criminality. His argument will here be presented in

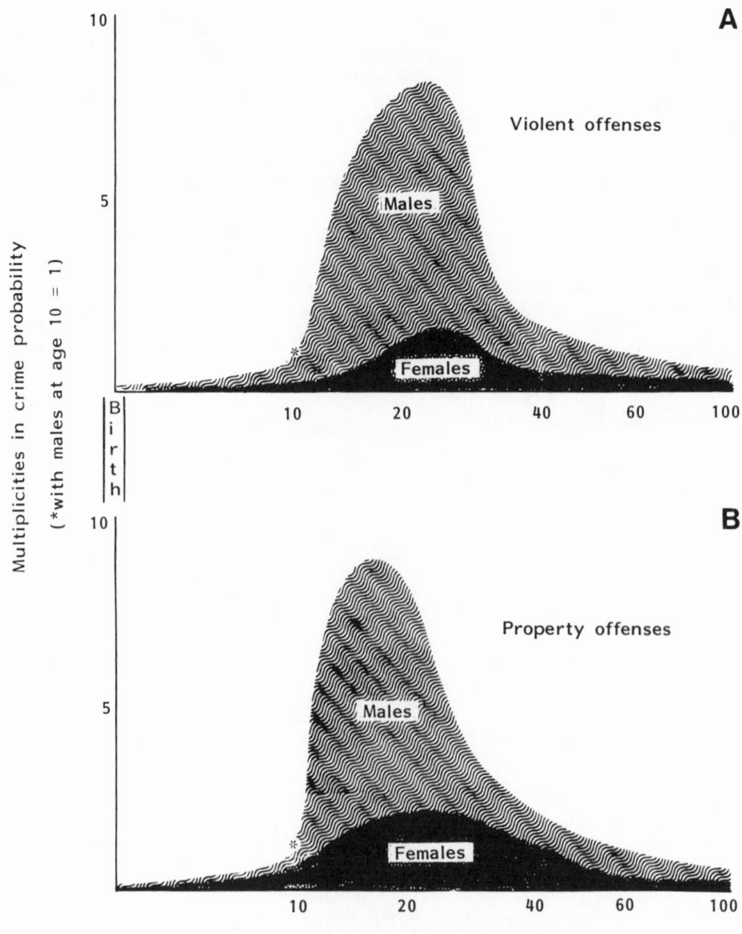

FIGURE 19. The average probability of (A) aggressive-injurious offeses, and (B) "serious" property offenses according to age and sex (Ellis, in press a).

a very abbreviated form; his original presentation should be consulted for consideration of various objections, for clarification of many points, and for extended lists of references.

First, Ellis argues that sex and age have been shown to be the strongest and most consistent correlates of criminal behavior that have yet been found, especially when attention is focused on serious offenses. Figure 19 shows age and sex effects on aggressive–injurious and on property offenses respectively; the figure is a composite arrived at fol-

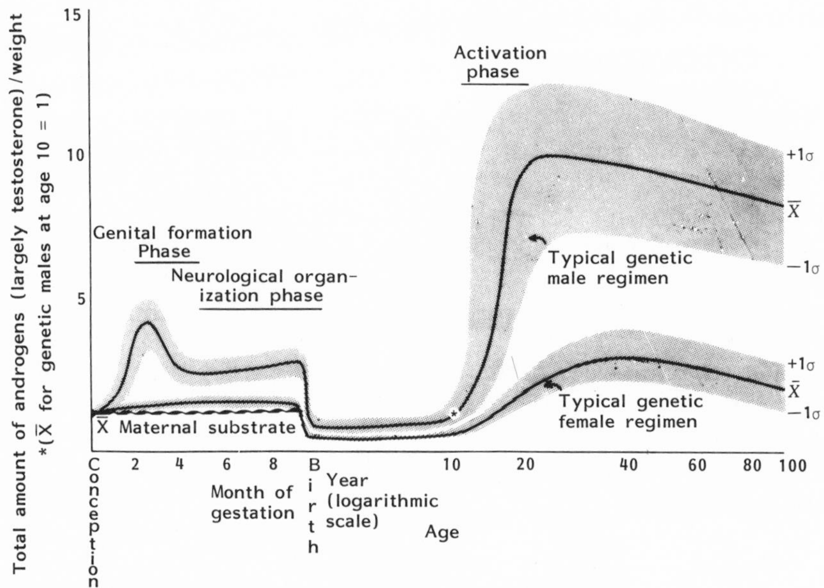

FIGURE 20. Average levels and S.D.s of androgens for human males (XY) and females (XX) according to age (Ellis, in press).

lowing extensive literature reviews of over 50 studies of the relationship between sex, age, and criminality. It is clear that property crime and probabilities are highest somewhere between 15 and 18 years of age and violent crime probabilities are highest somewhere between 21 and 25 years of age. Regarding sex, all studies placed male rates of crime in excess of female rates by a multiple of from 4 to 6 for property offenses and by a multiple of 6 to 10 for violent offenses. Generally, the more serious the offense, the more males tend to dominate in its commission (Giallombardo, 1982; Warr, 1982).

Androgens are produced in the adrenal glands (in both sexes), the ovaries (in females), and, above all, the testes (in males). Average levels and standard deviations of androgens in human males and females, according to age, are shown in Figure 20. It will be apparent that they reach the maximum in males precisely during those periods that show most property and aggressive–injurious offenses. Ellis also discusses in great detail the brain masculinization effects appearing to occur largely between the third and the seventh month of gestation, but to follow him there would take us beyond the main point of this discussion.

Recent evidence of a relation between androgens and aggressivity is not very clear. There are many studies showing positive relationships between testosterone level and aggression, but not all are significant. This occasional failure of results to show significance may be due to the fact that testosterone levels themselves are dependent on environmental factors. Thus in studies of rhesus monkeys, it has been shown that dominant males, exposed to a sudden and decisive defeat by other males, experienced a decrease in plasma testosterone levels (R. M. Rose, 1975). Also, testosterone levels are variable, in that reliability from measurement to measurement is not very high. Nevertheless, the evidence on the whole is positive and supports an association (Olweus, 1987) (see also Schalling, 1987).

Thus Persky, Smith, and Basu (1971) studied 18 healthy young men and found the production rate of testosterone highly correlated with a measure of aggression. Deriving a multivariate regression equation between testosterone production rate and for psychological measures of aggression and hostility, they found that this accounted for 82% of the variance in the production rate of testosterone in their subjects. Similarly, Ehrenkranz, Bliss, and Sheard (1974) determined plasma testosterone levels in 36 male prisoners, 12 of whom showed chronic aggressive behavior, 12 who were socially dominant without physical aggressiveness, and 12 who were neither physically aggressive nor socially dominant. These groups were separated on the basis of psychological tests, and there was a significantly higher level of plasma testosterone in the aggressive group as compared with the other two. The socially dominant group also had a significantly higher level of testosterone than the nonaggressive group. Rada, Laws, and Kellner (1976) classified 52 rapists and 5 child molesters according to degree of violence expressed during the attack. The most violent rapist had a higher mean plasma testosterone than normal subjects, child molester, or other rapists. Monti, Brown, and Corriveau (1977) in a sample of 101 healthy young adult male volunteers, found a test–retest reliability of only .69; correlations with personality inventories were significant, but quite low.

These are some of the positive results, but an equal number of negative results (i.e., very low, insignificant correlations, never negative correlations) could be produced (e.g., Doering, Bordie, Kraemar, Noos, Becker, & Hamburg, 1975; Kreuz & Rose, 1972; Meyer-Bahlburg, Beam, Sharma, & Edwards, 1974). It is perhaps significant that Persky, O'Brien, Fine, Howard, Khan, and Beck (1977), in their study of 40 male alcoholics during one week of abstinence and one week of unlimited alcohol intake, found that plasma testosterone was reduced significantly during the week of alcohol intake; there were only low correlations between testosterone levels and hostility and aggressiveness. If alcohol intake lowers testosterone levels, this would introduce an error into the measurement that would significantly reduce correlations between testosterone and aggressiveness. Altogether, the evidence suggests a positive relationship, but this is not as close as might have been expected. Clearly, antenatal exposure to androgens is the vital factor, rather than androgen level later on.

Ellis (in press a) reviews several lines of information to suggest that low cortical arousal is in part at least produced by androgens. Three of his suggested lines of evidence will be mentioned here. One line of evidence that androgens affect general arousability comes from studies of hyperactive children. They are characterized by an acute inability to concentrate upon tasks for more than a few minutes and by a tendency to be in "perpetual motion." As a result, hyperactive children tend to be unpopular with peers and are frequently punished by parents and teachers for innumerable forms of disruptive behavior (Mendelson, Johnston, & Stewart, 1971; Weiss, Hechtman, & Perlman, 1978). So far, the most effective treatment for childhood hyperactivity involves the daily administration of an amphetamine, called methylphenidate (Ritalin). For about two thirds of children diagnosed as hyperactive, amphetamines have a noticeable calming effect (Connors & Eisenberg, 1963; Connors & Rothschild, 1968; Knights & Hinton, 1969; and Weiss *et al.*, 1971). Even caffeine (equivalent to two or three cups of coffee) a few times each day appears to have calming effects upon many hyperactive children (Anonymous, 1973; Reichard & Elder, 1977; Schnackenberg, 1975). The way stimulant drugs seem to work is by making the reticular activating system (RAS) and its peripheral neuronal support structures more alert and sensitive to incoming stimuli. Thus, drugs that one would intuitively associate with accentuating hyperactive systems, in fact, tend to alleviate many of the behavioral and neurological symptoms of the syndrome (Janes, Hesselbrock, Stern, 1978). Apparently, because of genetic factors (Cantwell, 1975; Lykken, Tellegen, & Thorkelson, 1974; Morrison & Stewart, 1973), hyperactive children are prone to have RAS (and support neuronal) functioning that tends to hover in a "hyporeactive" range (Satterfield & Dawson, 1971; Spring, Greenberg, Scott, & Hopwood, 1974) and more readily habituates to incoming stimuli than in most children (Bell *et al.*, 1983; Shouse & Lubar, 1978; Zentall *et al.*, 1983). For a general discussion of theories linking drugs and personality, see H. J. Eysenck (1983b, 1983c).

Evidence linking androgen exposure with hyperactivity—and by inference, androgen exposure with low arousability of the nervous system—comes from studies showing that hyperactivity is four to six times more common in males than in females throughout the world (Cantwell, 1981; DeFries, Vandenberg, & McClean, 1976; Dubey, 1976; Waldrop, Bell, McLaughlin, & Halverson, 1978).

Another line of evidence that differential exposure to androgens (converted to estradiol) causes low arousability comes from studies of sex differences in pain tolerance. Human males are considerably more likely to tolerate pain at a given intensity than females, both in adulthood (Buchsbaum, Davis, Coppola, & Dieter, 1981a, 1981b; McGrew, 1979; Mechanic, 1975; Woodrow, Freidman, Seigelaub, & Collen, 1977; N. Wright, 1974). and even within a couple of weeks after birth (Barfield, 1976; Bell & Costello, 1964; Freedman, 1980). The same basic sex difference has been found in several other mammalian species (Beatty, 1978; Beatty & Fessler, 1977; Davis, Porter, Burton, & Levine, 1976; Gandelman, 1983; hamsters and gerbils are exceptional in the sense of showing no significant differences, Beatty, 1978). Furthermore, experiments with laboratory animals have shown that the normal sex difference can be largely eliminated by equalizing exposure to androgens during the organization phase of sexual differentiation (Beatty & Fessler, 1977; Marks & Hobbs, 1972; Redmond, Baulu, Murphy, Loriaux, & Zeigler, 1976).

In addition, studies of averaged evoked brain responses indicate that response amplitudes to standard stimuli tend to be greater in females than in males (Eeg-Olofsson, 1971; Matousek & Petersen, 1973; Michalewski *et al.*, 1980; Mochizuki, Go, Ohkubo, Tatara, & Motomura, 1982), indicating a greater sensitivity to most environmental stimuli by females than by males.

Overall, substantial evidence suggests that one of the organizational effects of androgens upon brain functioning is a lowering of the responsiveness of the RAS and probably other arousal control mechanisms in the brain to incoming stimuli (Farley, 1986). Among the results of such a neurological organization effectively is insulation of the higher brain centers from incoming stimuli, accounting for a greater tendency to withstand pain in pursuit of greater environmental input. Some of these effects seem to be apparent at birth, whereas others may not become fully manifested until pubertal activation.

A third line of evidence that is used by Ellis (1987) is based on a recent review of literature in which he concluded that at least 12 behavior patterns exhibited both by humans and other species of mammals showed signs of being androgen influenced. To identify these behavior patterns, he first located behavior patterns for which sex differences had been consistently reported both in humans and in other mammalian species, especially other primates, and found that the following 12 were well documented:

1. Assertive erotic sexual behavior
2. Status-related aggressive behavior
3. Spatial reasoning

4. Spacing behavior (including territoriality)
5. Pain tolerance
6. Retarded acquisition of aversive conditioning
7. Diminished fearful emotional responses to threats
8. Task control-oriented tenacity
9. Transient bonding tendencies
10. Peripheralization
11. Sensation seeking
12. Predatory behavior

Second, evidence was sought from nonhuman experimental studies as to whether or not altering androgen levels—either perinatally, postpubertally, or both—had any influence upon these behavior patterns. Third, this nonhuman experimental evidence was combined with whatever research was available from human clinical experiments and with both human and nonhuman intrasex correlative studies of the same behavior patterns.

The picture that emerged established that the first two behavior patterns in this list—assertive erotic sexual behavior and status-related aggression—were definitely androgen influenced, both in humans and in nonhuman mammals. Evidence that the next four behavior patterns were androgen influenced, at least in some nonhuman species, was also firmly established—spatial reasoning, spacing behavior, pain tolerance, and retarded acquisition of aversive conditioning. Regarding the next three behavior patterns—diminished fearful emotional responses when threatened, task control-oriented tenacity, and transient bonding tendencies—the evidence of androgen influence, at least outside the human species, was strong, although not definitive. For the last three behavior patterns—peripheralization, sensation seeking, and predatory behavior—evidence of androgen influence, at least for some nonhuman species, was suggestive, although not yet proven.

Although none of these behavior patterns are *illegal* in and of themselves, several can be seen as being either frequent components of criminal behavior (assertive erotic sexual behavior, dominance-related aggression) or as making criminal behavior more difficult to deter (greater pain tolerance, retarded acquisition of aversive conditioning, diminished fearful emotional responses to threats) and possibly making criminal behavior more likely to be tried (sensation seeking) or to be continued once tried (task control-oriented tenacity). One of these behavior patterns (peripheralization) could even be seen as a frequent social reaction to the display of disruptive behavior by others, perhaps analogous to ostracism and even imprisonment in humans.

Whereas many of these sex differences may be linked with low cortical arousal (such as increased pain tolerance, sensation seeking, and dominance-related aggression), others might be due to another biological feature associated with androgens, which Ellis calls "rightward shift in neocortical functioning." It is well known that in most people the two hemispheres of the neocortex function differently, the left primarily specializing in serial logical, linguistic reasoning and the right hemisphere inclined to function more intuitively and holistically (Asher, 1983; Sperry, 1982). A further difference is that the right hemisphere is more prone than the left to react to incoming stimuli emotionally (Landis, Graves, & Goodglass, 1982; Morrow, Vrtunski, Kim, & Boller, 1981), particularly in relation to negative emotions (Alford & Alford, 1981; Cacioppo & Petty, 1981; Campbell, 1982; Tucker, Stensile, Roth, & Shearer, 1981).

As Ellis documents, many lines of evidence have converged to indicate that perinatal exposure to high levels of androgens (and estradiol) substantially diminishes the "normal" left hemispheric bias in dominating over fine-motor performance, thus in humans (among other things), shifting hand usage away from the right and toward the left. As a consequence, human males throughout the world have been found to be somewhat more prone to be left and mixed handed than females. There is much evidence to support the conclusion that in many and perhaps all mammals the two hemispheres are organized somewhat differently for males and females and that differential exposure of the brain to androgens and estradiol is the primary reason (Diamond, 1984; Rosen, Berrebi, Yutzey, & Denenberg, 1983). It is these androgenic effects upon hemispheric organization that Ellis calls a "rightward shift in neocortical functioning" (see also Nachshom & Denno, 1987, and Buikhuisen, 1987).

Ellis now turns to the relationship between the rightward shift in neocortical functioning in criminality, pointing out that several interrelated lines of evidence indicate that such a shift *is a cause of criminality*. Thus left- and mixed-handers are more prone to criminality than right-handers; learning disabilities are much more common in persons who are highly prone toward criminality, and these are associated with a rightward shift. Furthermore, left-handedness and learning disabilities are known to be related. The well-documented tendencies for criminally prone persons to do poorly in school is also likely to be due to this rightward shift, as are intellectual deficiencies among delinquents and criminals that arise mainly in regard to the verbal skill portions of aptitude tests, with little or no deficiencies in performance skill portions.

We might also find evidence supporting the hypothesis that androgenic effects upon brain functioning are a cause of criminal behavior from studies of body type, already reviewed in Chapter 2. We found there that mesomorphy is more common among persons with serious criminal records than are other types of physique, and the neuroandrogen hypothesis would predict such an association because musculature is one of the extraneurological indications of high androgen exposure. Specifically, muscle cells, like nerve cells, can be permanently altered by exposure to high organization levels of androgens that subsequently lie relatively dormant until pubertal activities. Theoretically, muscular body build is one of the extraneurological consequences of high androgen exposure, and increased probability of criminal behavior is one of the neurological consequences.

The suggestion thus is that androgens may be responsible for differences in criminal behavior as well as for the intermediary links through low arousal that had previously been suggested. The hypothesis, although attractive, has certain weaknesses that are discussed in some detail by Ellis (in press a), but again one might say that it also has certain intriguing possibilities that would justify further work directed specifically toward testing predictions made from it. It is certainly in agreement with many well-known facts, such as the age and sex distributions of criminal activities, which it would be difficult to explain along any other lines.

Biochemical factors other than androgens have also been found to play a profoundly important part in determining a person's position on the major dimensions of personality (Zuckerman, Ballenger, & Post, 1984). Of all the substances investigated, monoamine oxidase (MAO) has been most consistently linked with personality traits related to criminality, such as psychopathy (Lidberg, Modin, Oreland, Tuck, & Gillner, 1985), childhood hyperactivity (Shekin, Davis, Byland, Brunngraber, Fikes, & Lanham, 1982), alcoholism (Wiberg, Gottfries, & Oreland, 1977), sensation seeking (Klinteberg, Levander, Oreland, Asberg, & Schalling, in press), and impulsivity (Schalling, Edman, Asberg & Oreland, in press). A general review of work with MAO has been given by Oreland, van Knorring, and Schalling (1984).

All these traits tend to be extraversion related, and extraversion itself also appears to be associated with low MAO activity (Gattaz & Beckman, 1981). MAO is a mitochondrial enzyme present in all tissues and responsible for the oxidative deamination of the endogenous neurotransmitters as well as of exogenous monoamines. There is some evidence that low platelet MAO activity reflects low serotonin turnover in the brain, possibly because of a common genetic control. There is also a positive correlation between platelet MAO activity and the concentration on the serotonin metabolite 5-hydroxyindoleacetic acid (5-HIAA) in the cerebrospinal fluid (CSF) in chronic pain patients (van Knorring, Oreland, Haggendal, Magnusson, Almay, & Johansson, 1984). This is important because higher sensation seeking and impulsivity has been found low in 5-HIAA subjects, and G. L. Brown *et al.* (1982) have reported negative correlations between 5-HIAA and the MMPI Scale psychopathic deviate. Similarly, Schalling *et al.* (in press) have reported a positive correlation between socialization and 5-HIAA as well as a strong negative correlation with EPQ extraversion.

These data and others discussed by Schalling *et al.* (in press) point to a close relationship between antisocial, psychopathic, and impulsive behavior on the one hand and low MAO platelet activity and low 5-HIAA concentration on the other. These relationships can be quite close, as some data from the paper by Schalling *et al.* (in press) document. These investigators divided their subjects into groups of 12 low, 34 intermediate, and 12 high platelet MAO activity subjects and reported the number of "yes" answers of the three groups to various items on an impulsivity scale. Thus low, intermediate, and high MAO subgroups answered "yes" 83%, 41%, and 8% respectively to the question "Do you often do things on the spur of the moment?". Percentages were 75, 44, and 8 respectively in answering the question "Do you mostly speak before thinking things out?". "Yes" answers to the question "Do you often get involved in things you later wish you could get out of?" were reported in 42% of the low, 15% of the intermediate, and 0% of the high MAO subgroups.

It is clear that the study of hormones like androgens, enzymes like MAO, and peptides like ACTH and cortisol must receive a high priority in future research on the biological causes of antisocial and criminal activity (Rubin, 1987; Virkkunen, 1987). A good review of related work is given by Venables and Raine (1987).

SOCIOBIOLOGY OF HUMAN REPRODUCTION AND CRIMINALITY

The association of criminality and low arousal with androgens and the male sex generally has been taken one step further by Ellis in a very original manner. In order to understand the theory, we must first take a slight detour to the sociobiology of human reproduction. In particular, we shall be concerned with r- versus K- selection, terms that refer to a theoretical continuum in which all living things (or, more precisely, the genes they carry) function (McNaughton, 1975). The contrast between the two extremes of this continuum refers, at the r-selected end, to organisms that produce tens or even hundreds of thousands of offspring in a lifetime but invest almost no time or energy in gestating, feeding, and rearing any one of their offspring. Most insect species are extreme examples of this tendency. At the other extreme, are animals, for example, most primate species, who rarely produce more than five

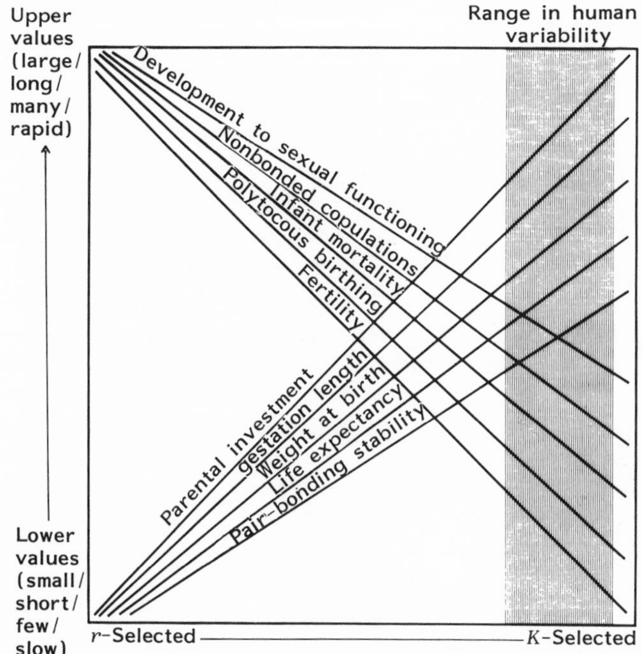

FIGURE 21. Traits associated with r- versus K-selection (Ellis, in press).

or six offspring in a lifetime but who tend to invest great amounts of time and energy gestating, feeding, protecting, and often training each offspring. Most species are intermediate on this continuum, and it is important also to realize that the concept is applicable not only to the differentiation between species, but also can be applied to individuals *within* species (Gadgil & Solbrig, 1972; Jolly, 1985; Rushton, 1985b).

A good example of intraspecies variability arises in the case of the gender. Sex differences in the size and numbers of gametes produced over a lifetime clearly imply that males are less K-selected than females. This reflects the fact that males may reproductively benefit more from mating with numerous sex partners than females can, particularly among mammals with extended gestation periods. In addition, because males can identify their offspring with less certainty than females, natural selection favors males who devote greater time and energy seeking copulatory activity and less time and energy gestating, feeding, protecting, and rearing offspring relative to females (Barash, 1977; H. J. Eysenck & Wilson, 1979; Hagen, 1979; Hrdy, 1981).

Ellis (in press b) gives a model of the r- versus K-selection concept, which is reproduced above as Figure 21. Traits that vary along the r–K continuum are represented by lines tilted roughly in the direction and

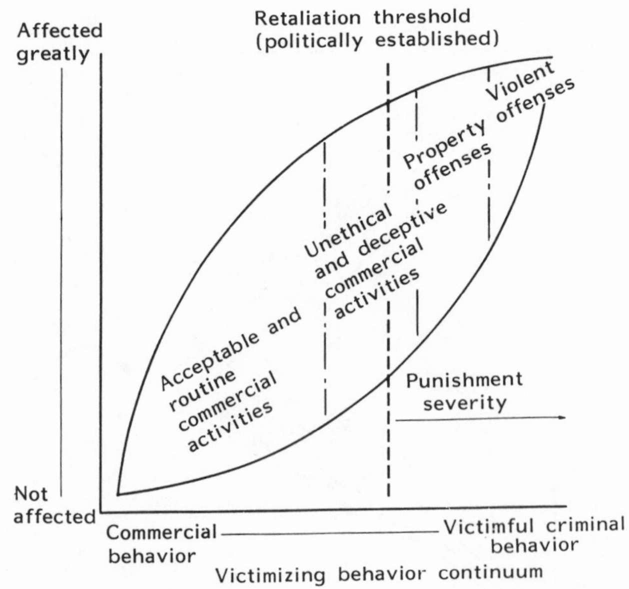

FIGURE 22. Representation of victimizing behavior and the effects of such behavior on reproductive fitness (Ellis, in press).

with the slope that seems to correspond to their bearing upon the r–K continuum. The figure also contains a shaded area that is meant to represent the approximate range in human variation along the continuum.

Ellis relates this concept to another one, illustrated in Figure 22. As he points out, violent and property offenses may be conceived of as part of a continuum of intentional victimizing acts. At the most trivial end of this continuum, he places victimizing acts that have imperceptible adverse effects upon the reproductive fitness of either the "victim" or the "perpetrator." At the most serious extreme are property and especially violent criminal offenses, which often have considerable impact upon the reproductive fitness of the victim (nearly always negative) and/or the offender (fairly often positive). The *retaliation threshold* is also positive; this is politically defined as the point beyond which a victimizing act becomes *criminal*. As Ellis points out,

> Property and violent offenses are extreme manifestations of the victimizing behaviour continuum, but, to varying degree, many profit-making commercial activities and lucrative occupational pursuits have victimizing qualities as well, and, in some societies, may be considered criminal. . . . Property offenses, in particular, are close to a number of deceptive business practices, whether the latter happen to exceed the retaliation threshold within a given society or not.

What Ellis is proposing is "that all classes of victimizing acts are r-selected, and that victimful criminal offenses are especially so." This view is consistent with the proposition that altruistic behavior is K-selected (Rushton, 1980, 1985b) and with a conclusion that victimful criminal behavior is essentially the opposite of altruism (Dickstein, 1979; McKissack, 1975).

Ellis continues his argument by saying that if victimful criminal behavior is r-selected, all, or nearly all, of the more fundamental r-selected traits shown in Figure should correlate with victimful criminality. In a review of the literature, Ellis looked for universal demographic correlates of criminal behavior, that is, demographic variables related to criminality in essentially the same way in at least 10 studies from a minimum of five different countries. He found seven such variables and discovered the following parallels with r- versus K-selection concept:

1. *Number of siblings.* Persons who came from families with large numbers of siblings (or half-siblings) committed more victimful crimes than those from small families. This pattern was reported by all three studies of serious victimful criminality bearing on the relationship, and by all but one of eleven studies pertaining to trivial and/or victimless offenses.
2. *Intactness of parent's marital bond.* Persons who came from families in which parents no longer living together were more likely to engage in victimful crimes than persons from maritally intact families. Six studies of serious victimful criminality reported this pattern, and no exceptions were found. Seventy-six studies of the relationship between "broken homes" and less serious offenses were located; of these, all but nine reported the same pattern.
3. *Sex.* Males were more likely to commit victimful crimes than females. With regard to sex (and age) sufficient information was available to draw separate generalizations for property and violent offenses. Of 12 studies of property offenses and 35 studies of violent offenses, all indicated males were more involved than females. Even for 71 studies of fairly trivial offenses (including a few that were vague as to seriousness), the same pattern emerged without exception, although to a less extreme degree than in the case of serious victimful offenses.
4. *Age.* Victimful criminality was most likely during the second and third decades of life. Of 17 studies of property offenses and 12 studies of violent offenses, all indicated that the most crime-prone ages were between 12 to 30 years of age. An additional 59 studies reported on offenses of mixed degrees of seriousness and/or

victimfulness, and they too indicated that the most crime-prone ages were during the second and third decades of life.

The first two of these universal correlates are the same variables as two of those listed in Figure 19. Both sex and age appear to reflect r-selection for reasons outlined above.

Although the number of relevant studies fell short of the criteria set for being universal correlates, studies were found to indicate that all but one of the other r-selected traits shown in Figure 19 also were associated with criminal behavior (at least regarding serious victimful offenses). Specifically, compared with the general population (even the general male population), persons with histories of serious delinquency/criminality appear to have the following r-selected traits:

1. Shorter gestation periods (more premature births) (Douglas, 1960; Douglas & Ross, 1968)
2. More rapid development to sexual functioning (Ellis, in press a)
3. Greater copulatory frequency outside of bonded relationships (or at least a preference for such) (Farrington, 1982; Robins, 1966; Wilson & McLean, 1974)
4. Less stable bonding (Handler & Schuett, 1979; Hurwitz & Christiansen, 1983)
5. Lower parental investment in offspring (as evidenced by higher rates of child abandonment, neglect, and abuse) (Bush, 1970; Glueck & Glueck, 1950; Kempe, Silverman, Steel, Droegemueller, & Silver, 1962; Sendi & Blomgren, 1975)
6. Shorter life expectancy (Robins, 1966)

The one r-selected trait for which no evidence was found either for or against its association with delinquency/criminality was multiparous birthing (e.g., twinning).

The three remaining universal demographic correlates of criminal behavior were (5) race, (6) socioeconomic status, and (7) urban–rural residency. The possible relevance of the first two of these variables to r-K selection was recently suggested by Rushton (1985a). Regarding race, he reviewed evidence that blacks were more r-selected than whites and that whites were more so than orientals (with a great deal of intraracial variability within each broad grouping) (Rushton & Bogaert, in press). Concerning socioeconomic status, lower strata were hypothesized to be more r-selected than middle and especially upper strata (of course, with a great deal of intraclass variability). References to research consistent with his hypothesis are presented by Ellis (in press c).

If race and social status are r-K selected as suggested by Ellis, then involvement in victimful criminality should be related to race and social status in essentially the same way as they are for the more basic r-selected traits. This was exactly what the literature search revealed. Specifically regarding race, blacks had higher victimful crime rates than whites, and whites in turn had higher rates than persons of oriental background. No societies were found for which this pattern had not been reported, except in the case of the most trivial and/or victimless offenses (for which little or no race and social status differences were frequently reported). Although certainly controversial, this observation is consistent with Wilson and Herrnstein's (1985) recent proposal that biological factors may underlie some ethnoracial differences in crime rates.

Concerning social status, using all of the four most common indicators (education, income, occupational prestige, housing conditions), the data again fit the r-selection hypothesis extremely well. Individuals (and, to a lesser degree, their families and their neighborhoods) of low social status exhibited higher probabilities of victimful crime than those of middle and especially high social status. There is only one universal correlate of victimful criminal behavior (urban–rural residency) that is difficult to relate to the r-K selection concept. Rural residents usually have lower crime rates than urbanites, thus suggesting that they are more K-selected. However, with respect to at least one key r-K trait, namely fertility rates, rural residents consistently have more children on average than adjacent urban dwellers, thus conforming to r-selected patterns relative to urbanites. It is easy to suggest reasons why there should be this apparent anomaly, and it certainly does not detract from the impressiveness of the evidence relating to the other six variables mentioned.

SUMMARY AND CONCLUSIONS

How can we summarize the contents of this chapter? It was more difficult to write than any of the others and will probably be more difficult to understand. The reason for this is not obscure; it relates to a variety of different disciplines, from biochemistry to sociobiology, from physiology to demography, from Darwinian selection to hemispheric differences, and any attempt to link together all these theoretical and conceptual notions into a coherent whole would be bound to run into considerable difficulties.

Another reason for the possible difficulties encountered by the reader may be that the lines of argument here presented have not been favored during the past 50 years, when most efforts have gone into the building of sociological theories and the investigation of nonbiological hypotheses. Hence there is a paucity of evidence on many of the points considered and little or no effort to bring them together and devise tests for the evaluation of such a more generalized theory. What we are dealing with is clearly a paradigm in the making, and as Barnes (1982) points out, there is always considerable inadequacy in a paradigm as it is initially formulated and accepted, in its crudity, its unsatisfactory predictive power, and its limited scope, which may in some case amount to but a single application.

> In agreeing upon a paradigm scientists do not accept a finished product: rather, they agree to accept a basis for future work, and to treat as illusory or eliminable all its apparent inadequacies and defects. Paradigms are refined and elaborated in normal science. And they are used in the development of further problem-solutions, thus extending the scope of scientific competence and procedures. . . . (p. 46)

In other words, the budding paradigm here discussed will need a lengthy period of "normal science" in order to eliminate all the anomalies, bring together all the fruitful ideas into a more general conception, and thus serve as a lawful statement of human criminal behavior. The theory is not here offered as a finished product, but there are too many facts supporting the various notions here discussed to dismiss it out of hand.

What is suggested by these facts is that criminal and antisocial behaviors, forming the opposite end to altruism on a continuous scale ranging from one extreme to the other, are in part the product of genetic features of the organism related to the masculinization of the brain and the degree to which androgens are present in the individual. These androgens influence behavior through their effect on the arousal system, primarily, but also in other ways, for example, through producing a right hemispheric shift, masculine physique, and other characteristics discussed. Low arousal, thus related to androgen secretion, affects conditioning, brain sensitivity, and other variables that are expressed in human conduct, in particular the intensity of temptation, the absence of a "conscience," a failure to be deterred by painful punishments, and so on. All these factors, of course, interact with social pressures, social temptations, and social consequences; they do not guarantee antisocial or altruistic behavior, but merely point the individual in one direction or the other.

What we have explored are the biological factors acting on the biosocial unit that is the human individual. A better understanding of these biological features underlying antisocial behavior does not suffice to explain it completely, but will certainly lead to a better understanding, particularly when more research is directed toward the interaction between biological and social factors, an area at present almost completely neglected.

PART TWO

SENTENCING, PUNISHMENT, AND REHABILITATION

CHAPTER SIX

The Function and Effectiveness of Sentencing

INTRODUCTION

The prevention and control of delinquency can be attempted at different stages of the judicial process. Each stage can be associated with different procedures and techniques, although on occasion the same techniques may be applied at the various stages of the judicial system, as will become evident in the next chapter. Lundman (1984) argues that it is possible to identify three major prevention and control intervention points. The first stage comprises "predelinquent intervention": that is, the primary objective is to prevent delinquency commencing in the first place. The second stage, "preadjudication intervention," involves formal attempts to "divert" juveniles away from the judicial system into some form of counseling or crisis intervention. Finally, there is "post-adjudication intervention," which is the central theme of this chapter, and this comprises the sentencing options available to judges and magistrates once the person has pleaded or been found guilty of an offense.

Predelinquent and preadjudication measures will be reviewed in the next chapter, in addition to the rehabilitation and treatment programs that are commonly applied at the postadjudication stage. This chapter is directly concerned with different sentencing procedures and their effectiveness. We use the English legal system as a frame of reference for reviewing different sentencing options, but there is considerable overlap with the American legal system and many of the studies we review are based on American work. Whenever appropriate we make comparisons between the British and American data.

THE FUNCTION OF SENTENCING

Curzon (1986), in *A Dictionary of Law,* defines a sentence as "punishment or penalty imposed on a person found guilty by the court." Punishment within the context of the criminal law is defined by Fitzgerald (1962) as the "authoritative infliction of suffering for an offence," implying that punishment comprises three major components: that is, (1) it must be imposed by someone in authority, (2) it involves the infliction of something unpleasant on the person concerned, and (3) it must be imposed as a punishment for some specific offense.

In his thought-provoking book *Punishment, Danger and Stigma,* Walker (1980) discusses the three generally proposed justifications for inflicting criminal penalties. These are labeled the "retributive," the "reductive," and the "expressive" justification. The retributive argument holds that the offender deserves to be punished because of the offense he or she has committed. The reductive justification maintains that penalizing offenses reduces their frequency. The expressive argument is that by penalizing an offender an important general statement is being made about the offense: that is, society communicates that it is not going to tolerate this type of offense. A good example of the expressive function is the current public concern in England about the "lenient" sentences imposed in the Ealing vicarage rape case (Gibb, 1987; Sapstead, 1987) and the move toward more severe sentences for rapists (Gledhill, 1987). Although the retributive and expressive functions are clearly important with respect to sentencing, it is the reductive justification that is central to the theme of this chapter.

Assuming that penalties are effective in reducing crime, it is important to look at the different ways in which this may be achieved. According to Walker (1980), the supporters of the reductive justification argument maintain that penalties reduce the frequency of offending in one or more of the following ways:

1. *By individual or "specific" deterrents.* This is achieved by reminding the offender, by inflicting direct punishment, that he or she should in the future refrain from further offending.
2. *By reforming the offender.* This consists of improving the offender's character and thereby making it less likely that he or she will reoffend. This is linked to the idea of "treatment" or "rehabilitation." Some authors (e.g., M. Wright, 1982) prefer to use the term *rehabilitation* rather than *treatment* because the latter implies that the person is suffering "from some malfunction of personality or attitude" and requires treatment. Rehabil-

itation is more commonly associated with attempts to help the person overcome a particular problem or disability.

3. *By general deterrents.* This involves punishment discouraging the criminal behavior of potential offenders other than those convicted. Its impact is measured in terms of the impact it has on the population as a whole. An evaluation of the effectiveness of general deterrents requires an analysis of the offending behavior of large numbers of people in relation to changes in statutes or legal policy (Bartol, 1983).
4. *By educating the public about the seriousness of offending.* If this is achieved, then people take a more serious view of certain offenses and the frequency of offending is subsequently reduced.
5. *By protecting the public.* The argument is that the potential future victims are protected when offenders are taken out of circulation and incarcerated.

In a recent proposed reform of sentencing in Canada, the Report of the Canadian Sentencing Commission (1987) argued that the overall purpose of sentencing has to achieve two separate objectives: (1) it has to be realistic and (2) it has to emphasize the principle of justice. This means that the sentence should be proportionate to the gravity of the offense and the degree of responsibility of the individual offender. The commission identified two serious problems with sentencing in Canada. First, there appeared to be overreliance on custodial sentences. Second, there was a very large and undesirable disparity in sentencing practices.

THE COURT HIERARCHY

When a person has been convicted of an offense in a court of law, certain basic penalties are available to the court to impose. The range of penalties and sentencing options available varies from one country to another. In England and Wales over 90% of all criminal cases are tried in the Magistrates' Courts, and therefore without a jury, which in 1983 heard 2.3 million cases and sentenced about 2 million offenders (Home Office, 1986c). The magistrates' powers to try cases and to pass sentences are limited and the most serious cases are dealt with by the Crown Court. In 1983, a total of 99,000 cases were heard by the Crown Court and sentences were passed on 83,000 offenders (Home Office, 1986c). A trial by magistrates is known as a "summary trial" whereas in the Crown Court cases must be tired on "indictment." An indictment is a written or printed accusation of a crime, prepared by the Crown and read out at the beginning of the trial. In many instances, the distinction between indictable and summary offenses reflects the seriousness of the offense. However, some offenses (e.g., theft, burglary, indecent assault) can be tried either summarily or on indictment depending on the circumstances of the case. These are known as offenses "triable either way." In practice, one of the most important distinctions between an indictment and a summary trial relates to the question of trial with or without jury. All indictable cases must be heard before a jury, whereas all summary trials are conducted by magistrates and without a jury. A more detailed discussion of the above threefold classification of criminal offenses is provided by J. C. Smith and Hogan (1986).

In the United States, there is a distinction made between the "state" and "federal" courts. This means that the courts may be sponsored by either the state or the federal government. Many of the procedures and rules are similar for the two types of courts, although each has some unique features (Blau, 1984). Unlike in England where magistrates and judges are appointed, in America the selection procedures for state judges vary from state to state (Bartol, 1983). The lower courts (municipal or magistrates) deal with minor violations of the law and are similar to the Magistrates' Courts in England in that they are tried without a jury. In England sentencing is always performed by a magistrate or a judge. This is also the general rule in America although in several states sentencing with respect to certain offences may be performed by juries (Bartol, 1983).

TYPES OF SENTENCING AVAILABLE

The types of sentence available to the courts in England and Wales are documented in *The Sentence of the Court* (Home Office, 1986c). Basically, these fall into two groups, custodial and noncustodial sentences.

Custodial Sentences

In the "developed" countries, custodial sentences are generally regarded as the most severe form of penalty imposed by a court. Of all available sentencing options, custodial sentences require most resources (Home Office, 1986c) and are, except for capital punishment in countries where it is available, alleged to have the greatest deleterious side effects (M. Wright, 1982). The types of custodial sentence available in England and Wales are as follows.

Imprisonment

Offenders may be sentenced to prison only if they are 21 years of age or over. Those under 21 may be sent to youth custody or detention centers (see below). Although the penalty of imprisonment is available for a large number of offenses, all imprisonment offenses except for murder, which carries a mandatory sentence of life imprisonment, can be dealt with by noncustodial measures. This is, of course, at the discretion of the trial judge, who has to consider the circumstances and merit of the offense and offender in question.

Suspended Sentences

Fully suspended prison sentences were introduced into the Criminal Justice Act 1967, with some modifications in the 1972 and 1982 Acts, and gave the courts the power, when passing a sentence of not more than 2 years, to fully suspend such sentences. This means that the serving of the sentence does not take effect unless the offender commits a further imprisonable offense during the "operational period" (i.e., the period the sentence is suspended for). The operational period is for a minimum of 1 year and a maximum of 2 years. There is no direct relationship between the length of the suspended prison term and the duration of the operational period. The former depends primarily on the seriousness of the offense, whereas the latter is viewed with respect to the circumstances of the offender (Home Office, 1986c). The Criminal Justice Act of 1982 abolished fully suspended sentences for offenders aged 17 to 20.

An offender who is given a fully suspended sentence cannot at the same time be given a probation order, but in cases where the Crown Court believes the offender needs assistance from a probation officer, a "suspended sentence supervision order" may be added if the sentence is for more than 6 months. Unlike a probation order, this does not require the consent of the offender and lasts for a period, not exceeding the operational period, specified by the court. According to the Home Office (1986c), the court should not pass a suspended sentence unless an immediate prison sentence would have been appropriate in the absence of the power to suspend it.

Partly Suspended Sentences

Partly suspended sentences are used when the court decides that the offense is so serious as to merit a prison term of between 3 months and 2 years and it would not be appropriate to suspend the sentence fully. It may, therefore, instruct that a part of the sentence, a minimum of 28 days and a maximum of three quarters of the full sentence, be served immediately and the rest be suspended.

Youth Custody

Youth custody centers are defined in the Criminal Justice Act of 1982 as "places in which offenders not less than 15 but under 21 years of age may be detained and given training, instruction and work and prepared for their release."

The centers are divided into open, closed, and long-term establishments. Some provide specialized medical, psychiatric, and educational facilities. They replace a previous custodial sentence referred to as "Borstal Training," which was available under Section 20 of the Criminal Justice Act 1948.

The maximum sentence in youth custody is 12 months and sentences of less than 4 months are normally dealt with by a Detention Center Order (see below). There are some exceptions to this. For example, a juvenile who has been found guilty of an offense that in the case of an adult would be punishable with a prison sentence of 14 or more years may be detained under Section 53(2) of the Children and Young Persons Act of 1933. Such an order must be issued by the Crown Court on indictment and the young offender is not eligible for the one third remission as in the case of the ordinary terms of imprisonment. The Home Secretary has the power to release the offender on license at the recommendation of the Parole Board.

A person found guilty of murder under the age of 18 years must be sentenced to detention during Her Majesty's pleasure. Offenders aged 18 to 20 are sentenced to custody for life and normally serve their sentence in prison.

Detention Center Orders

According to the Criminal Justice Act 1982, Detention Center Orders are available only for male offenders who are "not less than 14 and under 21 years of age." The minimum is 21 days and the maximum is 4 months. Offenders who are considered by the court to be unsuitable for detention because of physical and mental problems may be sent to youth custody. Those who have previously been sentenced to detention under Section 53(2) of the Children and Young Persons Act of 1933 may be sentenced to a detention center only in special circumstances (Home Office, 1986a).

Noncustodial Sentences

A number of noncustodial sentences are available to the courts. The most common ones are discussed below.

Absolute and Conditional Discharges

An absolute discharge is used by courts for offenders found guilty of the offense charged, but it is considered unnecessary to take any further action (i.e., impose a specific sentence). This may be related to such factors as the triviality of the offense or the specific circumstances of the offense or the offender. A conditional discharge means that if the offender commits another offense during the period of discharge (a period of not more than 3 years specified by the court), then he or she is liable to be sentenced for the original offense. There is, however, no statutory requirement to do so.

Probation Orders

The development of the probation service in England and the United States is comprehensively discussed by Bochel (1976) and Chute and Bell (1956) respectively. Basically, probation provides offenders with the opportunity of being rehabilitated while living in the community and it is commonly imposed as an alternative to incarceration. An individual who is placed on probation is assigned to a probation officer, who is an official member of the court and has the task of supervising and assisting the offender in the community. In England and Wales, an offender can be placed on probation only if he or she is aged 17 or over. The minimum period of a probation order is 6 months and the maximum is 3 years.

In addition to being intended as rehabilitative, a probation order contains two additional and central features. First, the offender has to officially agree to the probation and its requirements. Second, the court will impose certain conditions of behavior that the offender has to fulfill. In some instances, the offender may be required to submit to psychiatric treatment under Section 3 of the Powers of Criminal Courts Act of 1973. The offender may also be required to reside in an approved probation hostel for a period not exceeding the term of the probation order. If the conditions of the order are breached, then the offender can be brought back to the court at the discretion of his or her probation officer. The strength of the probation order appears to lie in the flexibility of the conditions, which can be adjusted to meet the offender's individual needs.

Supervison Orders

Supervision orders were introduced by Section 7 of the Children and Young Persons Act of 1969, which gives courts the power to place a person under the age of 17 who has committed an offense under official supervision for a period of 3 years. It is in some ways similar to a probation order given to persons who are 17 or older, but it differs in that the offender does not have to consent to the order. Consent may, however, be necessary when certain requirements are included in the order.

Following the Children and Young Persons Act of 1969, intensive community-based programs, commonly known as "Intermediate Treatment" or "IT," were developed in Britain in an attempt to prevent delinquency and recidivism. They consist of a variety of recreational, educational, and socially constructive activities within the community.

Preston (1982) argues that IT developed into two different approaches: (1) new facilities in the community aimed primarily at the day care of juvenile offenders and (2) utilization of existing facilities to provide evening and weekend intervention for those juveniles who were attending either school or work in the daytime.

Care Orders

Like supervision orders, care orders in criminal proceedings are governed by Section 7 of the Children and Young Persons Act of 1969. They are available to courts dealing with offenders under the age of 18 who have been convicted of an offense punishable by imprisonment if committed by adults. The effect of the order is to transfer certain rights from the parents to the local authority. The local authority will decide how the order is to be implemented. Depending on the individual case, the juvenile may be allowed to reside at home, be boarded with foster parents, or be required to reside in a community voluntary home. In criminal cases, certain conditions must be satisfied, such as, the court must be satisfied that a care order is appropriate with respect to the seriousness of the offense and that the juvenile is in need of care and control that he or she is unlikely to receive without the order. The Children and Young Persons Act of 1969 abolished the existing approved school order. Instead, the Juvenile Court places the child in the care of the local authority, who in turn can place the child, if it is considered appropriate, in a Community Home, which is the successor of the Approved School. The abolition of the Approved School Order means that the distinction between deprived and delinquent children is no longer legally recognized (Tutt, 1974).

ATTENDANCE CENTER ORDERS

According to the Criminal Justice Act of 1982, an Attendance Center is a place at which offenders under 21 years of age may be required to attend and be given appropriate occupation or instruction. The minimum number of hours served is 12, but this can be reduced in the case of those under the age of 14. The maximum number of hours is 36, except if the offender is under 17 years of age, in which case the maximum is 24 hours. The order may be given to a young person who has been found guilty of an offense that carries a prison sentence if committed by adults. However, an Attendance Center order may also be made in cases where the offender has failed to comply with another order, such as a breach of probation or failing to pay a fine.

COMMUNITY SERVICE ORDER

Experimental schemes for community service by offenders in certain probation and after-care areas came into operation in 1973, following the introduction of the Powers of Criminal Courts Act of 1973. Since March 1979, community service arrangements have existed throughout England and Wales.

Community service orders are available for offenders over 16 years of age who have been convicted of an offense punishable with imprisonment. The offender, who has to consent to the order, spends a specified number of hours performing unpaid work within the community. Suitable work must, of course, be available in the community for the order to be made. The order involves a minimum number of 40 hours and a maximum of 240 hours. Offenders aged 16 years must not do more than 120 hours. Regardless of the number of hours required, all the work must be completed within 12 months. If the order is revoked, the offender may be resentenced for the original offense.

FINES

A fine is available for all offenses except murder and treason. The amount fined is unlimited in the Crown Court, whereas in the Magistrates' Court the maximum amount for either-way offenses is £2,000. The amount of fine depends on such factors as the gravity of the offense and the offender's age and means. In some instances, a fine may be imposed in addition to a prison sentence. When an individual is in default of payment, a warrant may be issued for him or her to serve a period of imprisonment. There clearly are limitations with respect to the level of fine that can be imposed in the case of some offenders, including juveniles. Fines imposed on children under the age of 14 have to be paid by their parents.

REMISSION AND PAROLE

Remission of a sentence is available to any prisoner serving more than 5 days. The Prison Rules allow remission of one third of the sentence imposed by the court provided the prisoner has not been ordered a loss of remission by a prison disciplinary body, for example, for bad behavior while in prison.

Parole is a discretionary early method of release and is subject to the following criteria: (1) the prisoner must have served at least one third of the sentence imposed by the court, (2) at least 6 months must have been served in prison, and (3) the prisoner must have been recommended for release by the Parole Board and the release must be approved by the Home Secretary.

A life sentence is indeterminate and without remission and normal parole arrangements. It is the mandatory sentence for murder, but can theoretically be imposed at the discretion of the trial judge in no fewer than 50 statutory offenses and 14 common law offenses (Advisory Council on the Penal System, 1978). However, it tends to be reserved for especially grave offenses. Of 257 life sentences imposed in 1981, 190 (74%) were for murder, 28 (11%) for manslaughter, 18 (7%) for rape, and 9 (3.5%) were for arson (Coker & Martin, 1985). In the same year, 107 prisoners were released on license.

Until the early 1980s, those sentenced to life imprisonment commonly served between 9 and 10 years, but in 1983 the Home Secretary announced in Parliment that certain classes of prisoners serving life sentences should serve at least 20 years in prison (Coker & Martin, 1985). It is also quite common for trial judges, when sentencing lifers, to recommend the minimum sentence they think the prisoner should serve. The lifer may be considered for release on license at any stage, but this would be at the recommendation of the Parole Board and with the authority of the Home Secretary. Lifers remain on license for the rest of their lives and may be recalled to prison at any time if considered necessary by the Home Secretary or Parole Board.

MENTALLY DISORDERED OFFENDERS

Mental disorder is defined in the British Mental Health Act of 1983 as "mental illness, arrested or incomplete development of mind, psychopathic disorder and any other disorder or disability of mind." The great majority of people charged with a criminal offense are not suffering from a mental disorder within the meaning of the Mental Health Act (Bluglass, 1984). Some suffer from a minor mental disorder, which may be treated in prison or by a psychiatric probation order. In cases of serious disorder where treatment is required, the court may consider making a hospital order or a guardianship order under Section 37 of the Act, which is a therapeutic disposal and not a punitive sentence. The courts have the power to deal on occasion with disordered offenders without proceeding to conviction (Home Office, 1986c). For example, the Crown Court may remand the accused to the hospital for assessment and/or treatment while the accused is waiting to be tried or sentenced if already convicted. Magistrates' Courts have the power to make a hospital order without convicting the offender provided they are satisfied of his or her commission of a criminal act (Ashworth & Gostin, 1984).

Gostin (1986) argues that the courts often fail to employ therapeutic disposal options for mentally disordered offenders and many of them consequently go to prison. He makes several important, although undoubtedly controversial, proposals for reform that he thinks would improve the mental health care of mentally disordered offenders. The main argument is that mentally ill and handicapped offenders are deleteriously affected by being placed in prisons and other secure institutions (e.g., security hospitals), and staff in local hospitals and residential setting should be provided with the necessary resources to deal with periodic outbursts of difficult and dangerous behavior.

Teplin (1983), with reference to the United States, argues that more mentally disordered people are at liberty in the community than in the past. The reasons given for this are classic deinstitutionalisations of mental hospitals, more stringent criteria for involuntary hospital admissions, and reduced resources in social services departments. There is some evidence that this may have resulted in increased numbers of mentally disordered people coming into contact with the criminal justice systems (Monahan & Monahan, 1986). In a recent study, Teplin (1984) found that between 3% and 6% of citizens encountered by the police were mentally disturbed. In the United States, mentally disordered offenders comprise 7.3% of the institutionalized mentally disordered populations and 3.2% of the institutionalized offender population (Monahan & Monahan, 1986).

JUVENILE DELINQUENCY

The term *juvenile delinquency* is generally used to describe illegal acts committed by "young people." However, social scientists do not agree on the precise definition of *juvenile delinquency*. Two different areas of disagreement can be identified. These are related to the age of the offender and the type or seriousness of the offense.

According to English law, a "juvenile" is a young person under the age of 17 (Mitchell & Richardson, 1986). However, "no child under the age of ten years can be guilty of any offense." This is known as the "age of criminal responsibility." A juvenile between 10 and 13 is in common law not presumed to have reached the age of discretion, but this may be rebutted by the prosecution in some cases. The prosecution has to satisfy the court that the juvenile knew the act was wrong and was aware of the probable consequences of his or her actions. A boy under the age of 14 is in law presumed to be unable to commit a rape and cannot be found guilty of such an offense. In England, most juveniles are tried by Juvenile Courts, which are specially constituted Magistrates' Courts and may try a much wider range of offenses than the adult Magistrates' Courts (Home Office, 1986c). The purpose of specially designed courts for juveniles is to remove the adversarial nature of adult proceedings and place greater emphasis on protecting the juveniles' welfare.

In the United States, there is some variation by jurisdication in the age at which juveniles can be tried in a juvenile court, but in the majority of states the maximum age is 17 (Lundman, 1984). Whereas some scientists use the age under 18 as the cutoff point for the definition of delinquency (e.g., Bartollas & Miller, 1978), others (e.g., Kaplan, 1984; Rutter & Giller, 1983) fail to refer to a specific age limit in their definition of juvenile delinquency.

Various definitions are used in the literature with respect to defining *delinquency* (Olczak, Parcell, & Stott, 1983). A common distinction is made between "status" and "index" offenses (Lundman, 1984). The former comprise offenses such as truancy from school, running away, and consuming alcoholic beverages under age and are only applicable to juveniles. Index offenses are offenses that would be criminal if committed by adults.

It is unclear from the literature as to what extent there is a progression from status to index offenses. Kobrin, Hellum, and Peterson (1980) found that status offenders comprise three distinguishable groups. One group consists of status offenders who have little tendency to commit the more serious index offenses. The second group show a mixture of status and index offenses, with a predominance for the latter. The final and largest group comprise those who have a single conviction for a status offense without any prior or subsequent conviction for either a status or index offense. The main conclusion that can be drawn from the work of Kobrin *et al.* (1980) is that there is a small group of persistent status offenders who are, in due course, likely to engage in index offenses. The majority of status offenders do not seem to progress to committing serious index offenses. It is perhaps for this reason that Erickson and Gibbs (1980) argue that there should be a separate penal policy for status offenses and victimless crimes. Olczak *et al.* (1983) argue that the legal charge, whether status offense, misdemeanor, or felony, gives a useful indication about the seriousness of the offense. They further recommend that researchers should clearly specify the behavioral and legal dimensions of their samples in order to make comparisons across studies more meaningful. It is interesting, however, that Olczak *et al.* (1983) do not offer a definition of juvenile delinquency, quoting Hallock's (1972) pessimistic conclusion that "it is impossible to derive a comprehensive or logical definition of delinquency."

The Juvenile Court was introduced in the United States in 1899 (Empey, 1980b) and in Britain with the Children's Act of 1908 (Lane, 1987b). The ideology behind the introduction of the Juvenile Court was paternalistic and rehabilitative; that is, children were seen as vulnerable individuals, requiring special care and protection. During the 1960s and 1970s, there was growing concern in the United States about the apparent failure of the Juvenile Courts in preventing delinquency and some revolutionary changes took place (Empey, 1978, 1980b; Erickson & Gibbs, 1980). There has been a significant movement in many states toward more severe punishment when dealing with juvenile offenders, lowering the age at which adult penal sanctions are applicable and abolishing the special status of the Juvenile Court; these and other recent changes are discussed by Empey (1978, 1980b) under the headings of due process, decriminalization, diversion, and deinstitutionalization.

THE MEASUREMENT OF CRIMINAL BEHAVIOR

Information about the frequency and type of delinquent and criminal behavior can be obtained from four different sources: (1) official criminal statistics, (2) self-report studies, (3) surveys carried out on victims, and (4) direct observational studies. We shall discuss each of these in turn.

CRIMINAL STATISTICS

In England, detailed statistics of notifiable offenses recorded by the police are presented annually in the series *Criminal Statistics, England and Wales*. In 1985, over 3.6 million notifiable offenses were recorded by 43 police forces in England and Wales and about 35% of these offenses were "cleared up" (Home Office, 1986a). Table 14 gives the num-

TABLE 14. Notifiable Offenses Recorded by the Police in 1985

Type of offense	No. of offenses (in thousands)
Violence against the person	121.7 (3.4%)
Sexual offenses	21.5 (0.6%)
Robbery	27.5 (0.8%)
Burglary	871.3 (24.1%)
Theft and handling stolen goods	1884.1 (52.3%)
Fraud and forgery	134.8 (3.7%)
Criminal damage	539.0 (14.8%)
Other notifiable offenses	12.2 (0.3%)
Total	3611.9 (100%)

Note. From *Criminal Statistics: England and Wales 1985*, Home Office. London: H.M.S.O., 1986b, pp. 22–24.

ber of notifiable offenses recorded by the police in 1985, categorized according to the type of offense. It is evident that theft and handling stolen goods comprised the largest category of offenses (52.3%), followed by burglary (24.1%) and criminal damage (14.8%).

The clearup rate for the different type of offenses showed large variation. The rate for violence against the person and sexual offenses was over 70%, whereas for burglary and robbery the clearup rate was just over 20%. The rate among the theft offenses showed large variation, ranging from 13% for theft from the person to 87% from shops and nearly 100% for handling stolen goods. These statistics are, of course, dependent on offenses being recorded by the police, and a large number of offenses go unreported. There are at least three reasons for this. First, some offenses (e.g., shoplifting) go largely undetected and are reported to the police only when a suspect has been apprehended (Buckle & Farrington, 1984). Second, the police may use their discretion not to record certain crimes they observe. Third, victims of crime may not report crimes to the police. Razinowicz (1964) suggested that only about 15% of crimes committed in England are officially recorded. More recent data, based on victim surveys, will be discussed below, but they clearly show that the great majority of many offenses are not reported to the police.

In the United States, *Uniform Crime Reports* are issued annually by the Federal Bureau of Investigation and they show that only about 21% of all "index" offenses are cleared by arrest (Federal Bureau of Investigation, 1985). The overall clearance rate in 1985 was 48% for violent crime and 18% for property offenses. The total number of index offenses in the United States in 1985 was over 11.6 million. Over 10.4 million of these were property offenses and about 1.3 million comprised violent crime. Similar to the British data in Table 14, about 56% of the Crime Index total was made up of larceny–theft and an additional 25% comprised burglary. Index offenses constitute the most serious offenses (e.g., murder, rape, burglary, robbery, aggravated assault, and arson), whereas "nonindex" offenses, which are most common among juveniles, relate to such offenses as vandalism, drug abuse, licensing laws violation, curfew violation, running away, and disorderly conduct. According to Lundman (1984), fewer than 10% of delinquent acts lead to apprehension by the police, and out of those apprehended only about 20% are convicted. There clearly are many problems involved in relying on the official statistics as a measure of crime and delinquency, but in spite of their limitations they undoubtedly give a reasonably good indication of the involvement in delinquency and criminal behavior and provide the most independent outcome measure, whether based on arrest or conviction rates.

Self-Report Studies

Self-report studies consist of asking offenders about their involvement in delinquency or criminal activity. The original systematic work begun in the late 1950s as researchers realized the inherent limitations of the official methods and developed a reliable and valid method of measuring self-reported delinquency (Short & Nye, 1958). The argument was that self-report measures administered to the general juvenile population were more representative of delinquency than samples of the official statistics. Subsequent researchers have relied heavily on the original pool of items developed by Short and Nye, but there has been a lack of attempts to utilize a standard instrument (Hirschi, Hindeland, & Weis, 1980). The usual approach is to administer a questionnaire covering various delinquent activities (Riley & Shaw, 1985). This often gives a useful and valid indication of the frequency, type, and seriousness of delinquent activity.

The scores on self-report questionnaires have been shown to predict subsequent court appearances (e.g., Farrington, 1973; Shapland, 1978) and juveniles officially classified as delinquent on the basis of the seriousness of their delinquency (West & Farrington, 1973).

Hood and Sparks (1970) indicate that self-report studies of delinquency serve three important functions: (1) they make possible an assessment of the overall number of people in the population that have committed delinquent acts and the frequency with which they have done so, (2) they make unnecessary the artificial distinction between delinquents and nondelinquents, and (3) they enable a comparison between those officially labeled delinquent and those labeled nondelinquent.

In addition to the functions identified by Hood and Sparks, experience with self-report measures has shown that they can be applied very flexibly to fit the specific requirement of the particular theory or study (Hirschi *et al.*, 1980). However, self-report measures are not without problems. One drawback is that they rely entirely upon the cooperation and honesty of the sample studied and, as Cernkovich, Giordano, and Pugn (1985) have argued, they tend to underestimate the criminal activity of "chronic offenders" who are involved in the most serious and persistent delinquent activity.

The results from self-report studies indicate that annually most juveniles commit some delinquent acts but these tend to be nonindex and minor offenses. Furthermore, a very small proportion of these offenses result in arrest, court appearance, or conviction. However, the proportion varies markedly according to the type of offense (West & Farrington, 1977). When juveniles commit index offenses, they are most commonly property offenses (Lundman, 1984), vandalism (Gladstone, 1978), traveling on public transport without paying, and damage to property (West & Farrington, 1973).

Victims Surveys

Victims surveys consist of asking "potential" victims about crimes they have been victims of within a given period. Many such surveys have been carried out since the mid-1960s. In an early national survey, carried out by the National Research Center at the University of Chicago, 10,000 households were asked about victimization of a member of their household during the preceding year (Ennis, 1967). It was found that the majority of common crime was not reported to the police, but this varied for the type of crime committed, with about 90% of consumer fraud not being reported and 11% of car theft.

More recent studies (e.g., Hindelang, 1976; Hough & Mayhew, 1985; Law Enforcement Assistance Administration, 1979) support the findings from the early work indicating that the official statistics give a gross underestimate of the number of offenses committed every year. For example, the results from the 1984 British Crime Survey (Hough & Mayhew, 1985) indicate that the overall reporting of crime is 38%. Particularly low reporting was noted for vandalism, certain types of household theft, and sexual offenses. In contrast, almost all theft of motor vehicles was reported to the police. Very similar findings are evident from the American 1977 National Crime Survey (Law Enforcement Assistance

Administration, 1979). It seems that, overall, about two thirds of criminal offenses go unreported. The most common reasons given for not reporting the crime were (1) it was considered too trivial and (2) the crime was not considered amenable to police action.

It is reasonable to assume that, in general, the less serious the offense the less likely it is to be reported. There may, however, be some exceptions to this general rule with respect to sex offenses, such as rape. In a recent English Survey (Hall, 1985), 2,000 questionnaires were distributed to women in 32 London boroughs and they were asked 76 questions relevant to sexual victimization. Out of the 1,236 women who completed the questionnaire, 17% reported having been raped and 31% said they had been sexually assaulted. When the person who committed the rape was a stranger, one in six (17%) incidents was reported to the police, but this dropped to one in 19 (5%) when the assailant was known to the victim. In a recent American survey (Russell, 1982), 44% of a sample of 930 women reported having been subjected to at least one rape or attempted rape. Few of these incidents were reported to the police. Rape committed by strangers was most likely to be reported.

One of the most important discoveries from recent victim surveys is the often long-lasting and deleterious effect upon the victim. In a recent study funded by the Home Office (Maguire & Corbett, 1987), it was evident that severe fear reaction, sleep disturbance, and weight loss were experienced by nearly all rape victims. Furthermore, most of these interviewed more than a year after the attack were still seriously disturbed by the experience. Marked psychological reactions were also noted with respect to other offenses, such as robbery, assault, and burglary.

Observational Studies

Direct and systematic observation of offending is difficult to arrange without inadvertently influencing the behavior being observed (McCall, 1975). Buckle and Farrington (1984) report that direct observation is probably easiest with respect to offenses that occur relatively frequently and are committed in public. They describe two different approaches to systematic observation of offending. One approach involves providing members of the public with the opportunity for offending. In a study by Farrington and Kidd (1977), members of the public were given the opportunity to dishonestly claim coins that had apparently been dropped on the pavement. Farrington and Knight (1980) provided people with the opportunity of stealing money found in apparently lost letters. As these studies "incite" people to offend, they raise serious ethical issues (Farrington, 1979). The alternative approach is to dis-

TABLE 15. Types of Sentences Passed in 1985 for All Groups of Offenses

Type of sentence or order	Sentences passed in 1985 (in thousands)	
	All offenses	Indictable offenses
1. *Custodial*		
(i) Imprisonment	42.7 (2.2%)	39.4 (8.8%)
(ii) Detention center order	11.7 (0.6%)	10.9 (2.4%)
(iii) Youth custody	20.3 (1.0%)	19.7 (4.4%)
(iv) Suspended sentence	29.2 (1.5%)	26.3 (5.8%)
(v) Partly suspended sentence	4.0 (0.2%)	3.9 (0.9%)
2. *Noncustodial*		
(i) Absolute discharge	20.2 (1.0%)	2.6 (0.6%)
(ii) Conditional discharge	80.6 (4.1%)	57.4 (12.8%)
(iii) Probation order	40.9 (2.1%)	36.0 (8.0%)
(iv) Supervision order	13.4 (0.7%)	12.4 (2.8%)
(v) Fine	1633.4 (83.2%)	186.8 (41.5%)
(vi) Community service order	37.9 (2.1%)	33.6 (7.5%)
(vii) Attendance service order	15.3 (0.8%)	13.8 (3.1%)
(viii) Care orders	1.8 (0.1%)	1.7 (0.4%)
3. *Otherwise dealt with*	12.0 (0.6%)	5.4 (1.2%)
Total	1963.4 (100%)	449.9 (100%)

Note. Primary source, *The Sentence of the Courts:* Handbook for Courts on the Treatment of Offenders, 1986c, p. 98.

creetly observe naturally occurring offending, as in the case of shoplifting (Buckle & Farrington, 1984). The information obtained from such studies has greatly advanced our understanding of the frequency and nature of offending.

POLICE CAUTIONING

Police cautioning is a formal warning given to a person as an alternative to prosecution. It was legally introduced in 1969 and is most commonly used for first offenders (Pratt, 1986). The Children and Young Persons Act of 1969 and the Home Office's guide to Part 1 of the Act encouraged police forces to consider procedures that were primarily for the welfare of children and to try and keep them out of the judicial system as far as possible. This has meant increased use of cautioning and more routine consultation with other social agencies (Laycock & Tarling, 1985).

Cautioning is usually given orally by a senior police officer at a police station. There are four criteria for a caution (Rutter & Giller, 1983): (1) the available evidence must be sufficient to secure a successful prosecution; (2) the juvenile must admit the offense and know that it was wrong; (3) the parent(s) must consent to the use of cautioning; and (4) the victim of the crime must agree to leave the matter to the police.

The Home Office (1986a) gives the most recent statistics for the number of cautions given by police forces in England and Wales. In 1985, about 589,000 and 487,000 offenders were cautioned or found guilty of indictable and summary (excluding motoring) offenses respectively. Over 80% of these offenders were male. For all indictable offenses, 26% of the offenders were cautioned compared with 15% for summary offenses. For the indictable offenses, about one quarter of those cautioned were females and about three quarters of all cautioned were under the age of 17 years. Cautioning is, therefore, mainly used for offenders between the ages of 10 to 16, with younger children and girls being more likely to receive caution (see Table 16 below). For offenders 17 years and over, 18% were cautioned for indictable offenses and 10% for summary offenses.

In 1985, of all offenders cautioned or found guilty of indictable offenses 54% were under 21 years. About 30% were juveniles under 17 (29% for males and 36% for females).

TYPE OF SENTENCES GIVEN

It is evident from the above discussion that the courts have a number of sentencing options available to them when dealing with convicted offenders. When sentencing offenders, magistrates and judges may take into account such factors as the age and sex of the offender, the type and seriousness of the offense, the offender's previous convictions, and his or her financial and domestic circumstances (Home Office, 1986a).

Table 15 shows sentences passed in 1985 for all offenses and indictable offenses. A fine was the most common sentence (83.2% for all offenses and 41.5% for indictable offenses) followed by conditional discharge, imprisonment, probation, and community service order. Custodial sentences were most commonly used for indictable offenses.

It is evident from the official statistics (Home Office, 1986a) that age and sex are important with respect to the sentence given. This is clearly evident from Table 16, which shows the proportionate use of sentences given for different sex and age groups with respect to indictable offenses.

TABLE 16. Percentage Use of Sentences for Indictable Offenses in 1985 Grouped by Age and Sex

	Age Group							
	10 and under 14		14 and under 17		17 and under 21		21 and over	
	M	F	M	F	M	F	M	F
Immediate custody	*	*	12	2	22	5	21	7
Fully suspended sentence	*	*	*	*	*	*	12	8
Attendance center order	22	3	16	7	*	*	*	*
Supervision order	18	18	17	20	*	*	*	*
Care order	4	3	2	3	*	*	*	*
Probation order	*	*	*	*	11	21	7	18
Community service order	*	*	4	1	13	5	7	3
Fine	16	18	25	28	42	43	43	41
Conditional/absolute discharge	39	55	22	30	9	24	9	23
Otherwise dealt with	1		2	1	2	1	1	1
Caution	79	93	50	78	6		6	19
Caution or discharge	87	97	61	86	15	33	15	38

*Not applicable
M = Male
F = Female

Note. From *Criminal Statistics: England and Wales 1985*, Home Office. London: H.M.S.O., 1986a, pp. 146–149.

Table 16 shows that the offenders under 14 years of age, 87% of boys and 97% of girls, are dealt with by caution or a discharge. The figures for the age group 14 and under 17 are 61% and 86% respectively. For offenders 17 and over, only a small minority (15%) of male offenders are dealt with by caution or discharge compared with about a third of females. Furthermore, males much more commonly receive custodial sentences than females and are less likely to be placed on a probation order.

The British data given above are consistent with American research. That is, judicial statistics indicate that women comprise a small proportion of all known offenders. According to the Uniform Crime Reports for 1985, about two thirds of all people arrested for property offenses in America were male; with respect to violent crime the male–female ratio was 8:1. These results indicate that females commit less serious offenses than their male counterparts. The sex ratio for self-reported delinquency seems to be considerably smaller than for the official statistics (Feyerherm, 1981; Widom, 1986). Feyerherm (1981) gives two alternative explanations for the discrepancy between official and self-reporting studies. The first is that victims or observers of female offenders are less likely to report the offense to the police than in the case of male offenders. In addition, police officers are more reluctant to arrest female offenders and the courts give them more lenient sentences. The second argument is that part of the sex ratio differences between self-report and official statistics is caused by methodological weakness, especially in the case of self-report research. There is evidence from the work of Tjaden and Tjaden (1981) that female offenders receive differential treatment with respect to two areas. First, males are more likely to be arrested and detained in custody than females, even when the type of offense has been taken into account. Second, females are more likely than males to receive probation or a deferred sentence, despite the control for variables known to influence sentencing decisions. It is worth noting that the disparity between male and female cases coming before the courts has been narrowing steadily over the years and this is explained in terms of increased equal opportunities for females (Giallombardo, 1980).

RECONVICTION

The most common way of measuring recidivism is by analysis of reconviction rates. This means looking at whether or not the offender under investigation has been reconvicted by a court within a specified follow-up period. Although reconviction rates are a crude way of evaluating sentence effectiveness (Brody, 1976) and often fail to reveal important relative improvements (Rutter & Giller, 1983), they are the most objective and informative outcome measure presently available for criminological research. Problems are particularly likely to arise when comparisons are made across different studies, because studies commonly use different length of follow-up and select subjects in different ways. Furthermore, as will become evident later, the type of sentence given is only one of several variables that may influence reconviction rates.

The Length of Follow-up

In his review of the reconviction literature, Brody (1976) provides evidence from three studies that most offenders are reconvicted within 2 years of freedom and very few indeed are caught after 5 years. For example, Mannheim and Wilkins (1955) found that between 75% and 80% of Borstal boys who were subsequently found guilty were reconvicted within 3½ years. Broadly similar findings were reported more recently by Gibbens (1984), who followed up Borstal boys for 25 years and found that 85% had been reconvicted during this period. Of those, 68% were reconvicted within 3 years and 85% within 5 years. In view of these and other similar findings, many scientists accept that a 2- or 3-year period will give a reasonable estimate of comparative rates.

There is evidence that for common property offenders a 3- to 5-year follow-up period is quite adequate, but for certain sex offenders, short follow-up periods can be very misleading. For example, Soothill and Gibbens (1978) showed that among a group of sex offenders only about half of those reconvicted within 22 years had been reconvicted within the first 5 years of freedom.

Age, Sex, Previous Convictions, and Type of Offense

With respect to reconviction rates, age, sex, and the number of previous convictions are highly significant variables. This can be clearly seen from the work of Phillpotts and Lancucki (1979), who carried out a 6-year follow-up of 5,000 English offenders convicted of "standard list" offenses in January 1971. The main results from the study are shown in Table 17. Overall, 50% of the males and 22% of females were reconvicted within the 6-year follow-up period. The general trend for both males and females was for the offenders to be more likely to be reconvicted the younger they were. Similarly, the larger the number of previous convictions the offenders had had, the more likely they were to be reconvicted. The offenders convicted of burglary and robbery had the highest reconviction rate and the lowest was found for those who had been convicted of driving offenses. Identical findings have been reported for the Netherlands by van der Werff (1981), who looked at the reconviction rate for 2,035 offenders convicted of serious offenses in 1966. At 6-year follow-up, 41% of the offenders had been reconvicted. The reconviction rate for burglary was 68% compared with less than 40% for traffic offenses. In addition, the study confirms previous findings that age, sex, and the number of previous convictions are significantly related to reconviction. The results from these studies indicate that over 50% of all offenders are never reconvicted; therefore, the general effectiveness of sentencing is at least 50%, although we do not know how many would have continued to reoffend if they had not been apprehended.

The marked effects of age and the number of previous convictions on the reconviction rates is also clearly seen in an early study conducted by the Home Office (Hammond, 1964). The study, which had a follow-

TABLE 17. Percentage of Offenders Reconvicted within Six Years by Sex

	Reconvictions Rate	
	Males	Females
(a) *Age when convicted in January 1971*		
10 and under 17	63	31
17 and under 21	56	29
21 and under 30	49	19
30 and over	38	19
(b) *Number of previous convictions*		
0	29	15
1	54	29
2 to 4	70	58
5 or more	87	86
(c) *Offense in January 1971*		
Violence against person	49	35
Sexual offenses	44	*
Burglary and robbery	68	42
Thefts and handling stolen goods	49	20
Fraud and forgery	50	20
Malicious damage	26	*
Motoring offenses	26	*
Other offenses	47	31
Total for all offenders	50	22

*Not reported due to insufficient number of cases.

Note. From *Previous Convictions, Sentence and Reconviction* by G. J. O. Philpotts and L. B. Lancucki, Home Office Research Study No. 53. London: H.M.S.O., 1979, p. 15.

up period of 5 years and a smaller geographical area than the Phillpotts and Lancucki study, unfortunately did not give separate figures for males and females, which limits some of the comparisons one can make with the Phillpotts and Lancucki (1979) study.

In an interesting study, Soothill, Way, and Gibbens (1980) compared subsequent offending of those convicted and those acquitted of rape in 1961. The study shows that both groups had a very similar rate of subsequent convictions for sex offenses and pattern of criminal career. There are, of course, many different interpretations possible for this interesting finding. In view of the fact that rape tends to have an exceptionally high acquittal rate (Soothill, 1986), one interpretation is that many of those acquitted of rape are probably guilty. The majority of those found guilty received prison sentences. Thus one may also wonder what such findings tell us about the effectiveness of prison sentences as an individual deterrent.

TABLE 18. Reconviction Rates According to Type of Sentence Given

Types of sentence	Phillpotts & Lancucki (1979) (Reconv. 6 yrs within conviction)		Home Office (1986b) (2-yr follow-up)	
	Males %	Females %	Males %	Females %
Discharge	44	22		
Fine	39	16		
Probation or supervision	63	33		
Care order	88	*		
Borstal training	84	*	71	42
Detention Center	73	*	68	
Attendance Center	65	*		
Suspended sentence	62	31		
Imprisonment	67	*	69	39
(Custodial sentence)	71	(50)[a]		

*No data available or does not apply This comprises all types of custodial sentences both juvenile and adults.

[a]Based on 9 cases only.

Note. From *Previous Convictions, Sentence and Reconviction* by G. J. O. Phillpotts and L. B. Lancucki, Home Office Research Study No. 53. London: H.M.S.O., 1979, p. 15, and *Prison Statistics: England and Wales 1985*, Home Office. London: H.M.S.O., 1986b, pp. 98–107.

The Effectiveness of Different Sentences

Hammond (1964) attempted to compare the effectiveness of different types of sentences among offenders of varied ages. A total of 4,239 offenders convicted in the Metropolitan Police District between March and April 1957 were followed up, and it was found that for first offenders a fine and discharge were associated with lower reconviction rates than custodial sentences. For offenders with previous convictions, the pattern was somewhat different in that discharge became relatively less effective and was, overall, similar to that of probation.

The results of the more methodologically sound study of Phillpotts and Lancucki (1979) are, in general, similar to those of Hammond and can be seen in summarized Table 18. The table also gives reconviction statistics for over 6,000 offenders discharged in 1982 from custodial sentences of over 3 months (Home Office, 1986b). It is evident that the reconviction rates for custodial sentences are consistently lower in the 1986 study, which is undoubtedly due to the difference in the length of the follow-up period, that is, 2 years in contrast to 6 years. On the whole, custodial sentences are associated with high reconviction rates, which become markedly more pronounced the younger the offenders are and the more previous convictions they have had.

Walker, Farrington, and Tucker (1981) reanalyzed the data used in the Phillpotts and Lancucki study and concluded that both sentence and reconviction varied markedly according to the offender's previous criminal record. For example, they found that probation was less effective than imprisonment for first offenders but more effective for those with between one and four previous convictions. The findings show that imprisonment is not necessarily associated with higher than average reconviction rates. We discuss this point in more detail later in this chapter.

COMMUNITY SERVICE ORDERS

The basic idea behind community service orders is that the offender should make up for the harm he or she caused by providing constructive service to the community. In addition, one could argue that it possibly provides a useful life experience for some offenders. Pease (1981) believes that community service still attracts a great deal of public support and there is no doubt that in theory such an approach to sentencing is a sound one.

However, the evidence that is available does not indicate that community service is an effective rehabilitative exercise. For example, Pease, Billingham, and Earnshaw (1977) looked at the reconviction rates of early community service orders and found that 44% of those sentenced to community service in six experimental areas during the first year of the scheme were reconvictioned within a year. A comparison group of offenders who had been recommended for community service but were not so sentenced, had a reconviction rate of 33%. Over half (62%) of the comparison subjects were given custodial sentences. This suggests that community service orders are less effective in reducing reoffending than alternative sentences. Unfortunately, the subjects in the comparison group were significantly older than the community service group, which may have accounted for their relatively lower reconviction rate.

TRUANCY AND THE COURTS

Children up to the age of 16 are required by law in Britain to attend school and may be taken to the Juvenile Court under care proceedings if they persistently fail to attend school. The reason why we wish to focus on truancy and its prevention is twofold. First, there is a close relationship between truancy and delinquency, with the former perhaps preceding the latter (Robins, 1978; Farrington, 1980). Second, changes in sentencing in Leeds (England) have been shown to have marked effects on improved school attendance and delinquency (Hullin, 1985).

Most truants who are taken to court in Britain are placed under the supervision of the social services of the Probation Department (Berg, Hullin, McGuire, & Tyrer, 1977). The procedure used is a supervision order described earlier in this chapter. In the more serious cases, the child or juvenile may be placed on a care order, which gives the social services the power to remove the child from home. This involves the magistrate adjourning the court proceedings and bringing the child back to court repeatedly at a few weeks' intervals. When improvement in school attendance has been satisfactory, the time interval between adjournments is lengthened. If no improvement has been achieved, an interim care order may be made by the court for the child to be placed in a residential establishment for an assessment. Accompanying the adjournment procedure in the study quoted below was the threat that if the children did not attend school on a regular basis they would be automatically sent into residential care when they next appeared in the court (Hullin, 1983).

Berg *et al.* (1977) carried out a retrospective study of 179 children (103 boys and 76 girls) who had been taken before the Juvenile Court in Leeds for truancy in 1972/3. It was found that both supervision and adjournment were commonly used by the magistrates. In spite of the lack of obvious presentencing differences between the two samples before sentencing, adjournment was found to be markedly more effective in improving school attendance than supervision orders. This finding was subsequently confirmed by a prospective study utilizing a randomly controlled trial into the effectiveness of the two procedures (Berg, Consterdine, Hullin, McGuire, & Tyrer, 1978). In this study, 45 children received adjournment and 51 supervision orders. The average absence from school of those on supervision orders was 51% compared with 35% of those on adjournment 6 months after the original court appearance (see Figure 23). Furthermore, whereas the children given supervision orders continued to commit delinquent acts at about the same rate as before, those on adjournment evidenced an 80% fall in delinquency. These very impressive results could not be accounted for by presentencing differences. These studies indicate that court officials in Leeds were prepared to cooperate with a systematic and randomly allocated experimental design. Furthermore, the results from these studies provide strong evidence for differential effects of varied sentences in the case of juveniles with persistent truancy problems. There is no reason why similar ex-

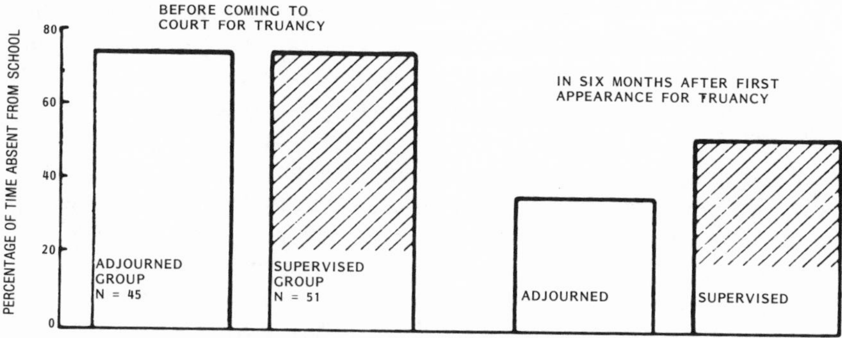

FIGURE 23. The effectiveness of adjournment and supervision orders in improving school attendance.

perimental procedures could not be applied in other areas and countries and for a wider range of acts.

Following the results from the above studies, magistrates in Leeds virtually abandoned the use of supervision orders for truancy and instead relied on adjournment (Hullin, 1985). Hullin argues that this has reduced the number of new cases brought before the courts in Leeds and the average school attendance is now twice as high as it was at the end of the 1970s. Perhaps related to this is the finding that juvenile delinquency has progressively dropped in Leeds in recent years and currently stands at only 18% compared with 25% for the rest of West Yorkshire (Hullin, 1985).

The reason why adjournment worked better than supervision in reducing truancy is unclear. West (1982) speculates that being repeatedly brought back to court, with the prospect each time of being sent away under a court order, was a greater deterrent than regularly reporting to a supervisor. Another possible explanation is that the adjournment actually influenced the parents' behavior, encouraging them to ensure that the child actually attended school regularly.

PRISON SENTENCES

When discussing prison sentences, it is important to remember that the prison population is largely composed of four different types of prisoners: (1) untried criminal prisoners, (2) convicted but unsentenced prisoners, (3) prisoners under sentence, and (4) noncriminal prisoners, which includes those on reception under the Immigration Act and committals by magistrates' courts for nonpayments of maintenance or fines. The average prison population in England and Wales in 1985 was 46,233 (Home Office, 1986b). Of these, 44,701 (97%) were male and 1,532 (3%) female. Prisoners under sentence are the largest group (79%), followed by those who are on remand awaiting trial (18%). Over 20,000 people (19,108 males and 1,395 females) were committed to prison in 1985 for defaulting payments of fines, the average population of defaulters being 663. About 34% of women and 54% of men who are remanded in custody are sentenced to prison for their offenses (Evans, 1987).

When attempting to evaluate the deterrent effect of incarceration, it is important to consider the following questions: (1) to what extent can crime be prevented by sending more offenders to prison, (2) what are the preventive effects of longer sentences, and (3) if certain "career criminals" are responsible for a disproportionate amount of crime, should they be specially selected for incarceration?

The Incapacitation Effect

Only about 4% of offenders sentenced for all types of offense are given custodial sentences (Home Office, 1986a). Although this figure is considerably higher for indictable offenses, the fact remains that the great majority of offenders are not given custodial sentences. The average length of sentence is about 12 months and nearly 60% of all male offenders over 21 years of age receive a sentence of 6 months or less. Therefore, short-term sentences, as an individual deterrent, are clearly limited in the extent to which they can be directly expected to influence the crime rate. Indeed, Brody and Tarling (1980) argue that "modest reductions in the lengths of prison sentences awarded, or in the length of time served by each offender, would not lead to a large number of additional convictions but would significantly decrease the size of the prison population." They estimated that where remission increased from one third to one half for adult prisoners serving determinate sentences, convictions would be likely to increase by only 1.2% per year. S. H. Clarke (1975) estimated that only about 1% to 4% of all index crimes were prevented by the custodial sentences served by juveniles. Similarly, Greenberg (1975) estimated that if prison sentences were entirely eliminated, this would lead to an increase in index crimes by only between 1.2% and 8%. At the other extreme, Shinnar and Shinnar (1975) considered that in 1970 custodial sentences potentially reduced the crime rate in New York by about 20%. In a study of 624 prisoners in California, Greenwood (1979) estimated on the basis of self-report data of criminal activities prior to the current sentence, that a 3-year mandatory custodial sentence for burglary would reduce the rate of burglary by 50%.

Brody and Tarling (1980) identify a number of methodological problems involved in comparing the findings from different studies. One major problem is that often very little is known about the actual rate of offending of the sample studied and those studies that base their estimates on conviction rates undoubtedly give a gross underestimate of the potential incapacitation effect of custodial sentences. Furthermore, preventing prisoners from reoffending while they are in custody is only one form of deterrent. Other types of deterrents are related to (1) the effects of criminal sanctions on the preceived threat of future punishment with respect to the individual offender (e.g., Bridges & Stone, 1986) and (2) the general deterrence effect on potential offenders other than the prisoner.

Time in Custody and Reconvictions

We discussed earlier the finding that custodial sentences were commonly associated with higher than average reconviction rates, although there are exceptions in the case of first offenders, as indicated by Walker *et al.* (1981). In the study by Phillpotts and Lancucki (1979), 71% of males and 50% of females were reconvicted within 6 years. (We should point out that the 50% figure for females is based on nine cases only and may therefore be unreliable and probably gives a slight overestimate of the true reconviction rate for females.) With respect to the length of sentence given, the potential benefits of longer sentences are threefold (Lewis, 1986): (1) while serving sentences in prison, offenders do not have the opportunity to commit offenses (except against other prisoners and prison staff), (2) those who have served longer sentences may be less likely to reoffend than other prisoners, and (3) longer sentences may deter potential offenders from committing offenses.

One major problem with comparing the effectiveness of different sentences is that the salient presentencing variables, such as the seriousness of the offense, the age of the offender, and the number of previous convictions, are not randomly controlled. Indeed, randomization in the field of sentencing is very rare (Farrington, 1983b). It is undoubtedly the case that the most serious offenders and those who are perceived as most likely to reoffend are particularly likely to be given custodial sentences. The length of custodial sentence given is probably also related to similar presentence variables in addition to the broader aspects of public policy. A further complicating variable is the fact that many long-term prisoners are given parole or are out on license, which means that they are generally receiving some supervision during the follow-up period. Certainly, in the case of life-sentence prisoners, the Parliamentary All-Party Penal Affairs Group (1985) has recommended that the conditions of the license should not be canceled for at least 4 to 6 years after release. It is also worth bearing in mind that it is probably the length of sentence served rather than the sentence passed that is of critical importance.

It is for the above reasons that the effectiveness of prison sentences and their length is particularly difficult to evaluate with respect to individual deterrence. In his thorough review of the literature, Brody (1976) discussed nine studies addressing the relative effectiveness of institutional sentences of varying length. Five of the nine studies found that the length of time served in custody did not appear to affect reconviction. The results from two studies (Florida Division of Corrections, 1966; Jaman, 1968) indicated that prisoners released early from prison had somewhat better outcomes than those released later. A further two studies (Weeks, 1958; Garrity, 1961) provided some evidence for an interaction effect; that is, for some individuals, early release from prison is beneficial, whereas for others it is the reverse. Although such findings make sense intuitively, there are major problems with identifying the salient intervening variables and mechanisms.

The Prison Statistics (Home Office, 1986b) provide reconviction data for different lengths of custodial sentences. It is evident from the figures provided that the reconviction rate is highest for those given the shortest sentences and lowest for the lifers. This is true both for young offenders (those under the age of 21 on date of reception on sentence) and for adult offenders as well as for males and females. However, there are problems with accepting these findings at face value because those serving long sentences are undoubtedly older when they are discharged, which is likely to affect the reconviction rate. Furthermore, life-sentence prisoners, who generally have a very low reconviction rate (about 4% after 2 years, Home Office, 1986b; and 27% after more than 5 years, Coker & Martin, 1985) are a highly selected group, having often committed a single major offense, such as homicide, and are considered a "safe bet" on release. Coker and Martin found that out of 239 lifers, only 2 (0.8 %) committed a further homicide after release.

Although the deterrent effect of varying length of sentences on the individual offender is uncertain, Lewis (1986) in his detailed review of the literature, provides some evidence for the general deterrent effect of longer sentences on potential offenders. He looked at 15 individual studies in which an attempt had been made to "quantify empirically the magnitude of the deterrent effect of longer sentences while holding constant other variables which affect the crime rate" (p. 48). Data were derived from different countries and time periods. Twelve of the studies provided substantial support for the deterrent effect of longer sentences, two studies provided mixed results, and only one study was unsupportive. The findings of the majority of the studies clearly show that longer sentences deter most types of crimes. The deterrent effect is strongest for such crimes as rape and assault and weakest for fraud and hijacking. Homicide, robbery, burglary, and theft fall in the middle range. The above findings reinforce the conclusions of Nagin (1978) that for the majority of crimes there is a negative association between crime rates and the severity of sentences imposed.

The Career Criminals

There is growing evidence that a relatively small number of offenders are responsible for a disproportionate amount of crime (Dinitz & Conrad, 1980; Wolfgang, Figlio, & Sellin, 1972). For example, Wolfgang *et al.* (1972) found that the chronic offenders in their study (those with five or more arrests, which comprise 6% of the sample) were responsible for over half of all the crimes officially committed by the cohort and about two thirds of all the most serious offenses. In a later study, the 70% who were classified as chronic offenders accounted for 61% of all the arrests (Wolfgang & Tracy, 1982; quoted by Farrington, Ohlin, & Wilson, 1986). Very similar findings have been reported in other studies (e.g., Shannon, 1981; Farrington, 1983b). The implication of the findings is that prisons can be made more effective by careful selection of serious career criminals and giving them long-term prison sentences. Although one must accept the views of Brody and Tarling (1980) that the prediction of dangerousness is problematic, it is true to say that the serious habitual offenders are becoming easier to identify as our knowledge of the salient prediction variables develops (Blumstein, Farrington, & Moitra, 1985; Dinitz & Conrad, 1980; Farrington, 1986; Methvin, 1986). Therefore, one effective way of reducing certain crimes is to identify persistent criminals as quickly as possible and take them out of circulation. This requires close cooperation between scientists, law enforcement agencies, and judicial officials.

Type of Prison and Reconviction

Rule 1 of the Prison Rules (Home Office, 1964) states that the objective of prisons is "to hold (securely) those people admitted to custody and to encourage and assist them to lead a good and useful life." Since prisons vary immensely in terms of the care and facilities they provide, it would not be surprising to find that some are better able to fulfill their aims than others. As we will discuss later, one important variable influencing prison effectiveness is overcrowding. Another important compo-

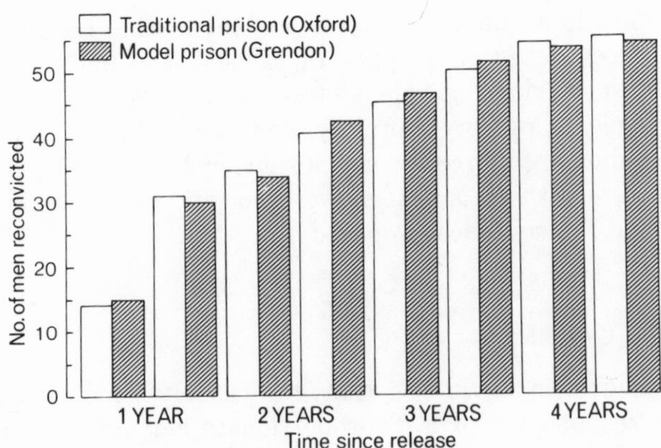

FIGURE 24. A comparison in reconviction rates between a traditional prison (Oxford) and a psychotherapeutic prison (Grendon).

nent could be the therapeutic orientation of the penal institution concerned. For example, do prisons who offer substantial psychiatric and therapeutic input to the inmates succeed better in terms of subsequent reconvictions than the more traditional prisons? In order to test this, Newton (1971) compared the reconviction rate of 87 inmates at Grendon "Psychiatric Prison" with 87 matched controls from a local neighboring prison (Oxford), run along traditional lines. The findings of a 4-year follow-up are illustrated in Figure 24.

It is evident from the results that the reconviction rates for the two groups correspond very closely at all points. As Williams (1976) points out, these results make it difficult to argue that the treatment offered at Grendon has in itself any marked effect on subsequent reconviction.

In a more recent study, Robertson and Gunn (1987) carried out a 10-year follow-up on the criminal records of men discharged from Grendon. The results were compared with a matched control group of inmates from a traditional prison. No significant difference was found between the two groups with regard to the frequency or severity of postdischarge convictions. The majority of men (92%) of the Grendon sample and 85% of the control group had been reconvicted during the 10-year period. Those that seemed to benefit more from the Grendon therapeutic regime were the more intelligent and motivated subjects. Robertson and Gunn (1987) argue that a prison like Grendon provides inmates with the opportunity to work on their current problems, and for some motivated subjects it can substantially improve their behavior following discharge.

Delayed Deterrence

When evaluating the deterrence effect of different penal sanctions, it is important to remember that the effects may be delayed and cumulative. Cusson and Pinsonneault (1986) define delayed deterrence as "the gradual wearing down of the criminal drive caused by the accumulation of punishments." They argue, on the basis of their research, that the succession of arrests and incarceration over a long period of time leads to increased fear of punishment and makes criminal behavior more difficult. Cusson and Pinsonneault present an interesting theoretical model of delayed deterrence and discuss four salient components: (1) a higher estimate of the cumulative probability of punishment, as criminals become known to the police and more readily arrested, (2) the increased difficulty of coping with and accepting imprisonment as people become older, (3) an awareness of the weight of previous convictions on the severity of future sentences, and (4) increased spreading of fear into the criminal's everyday life. The above theoretical components imply that career criminals gradually become increasingly dissatisfied with the consequences of their criminal way of life. The rewards of nonoffending (e.g., making more constructive and purposeful uses of their time) and the painful consequences of punishment influence their decision to give up their criminal activities. These can be meaningfully interpreted within the theory of conditioning discussed in earlier chapters.

The Harmful Effects of Imprisonment

There is no doubt that for most offenders, a period of imprisonment is an unpleasant experience. As Sykes (1962) points out, the individual's self-concept and respect are seriously threatened, in addition to the deprivation of autonomy, heterosexual relationships, and normal interactions with friends and relatives. Family life and work may be seriously interrupted, and in the case of women, over 50% of them have dependent children living with them immediately prior to incarceration (Glick & Neto, 1977). The effects on the children as a result of a parent going to prison may be serious, but little attention is paid to this in court proceedings (Stanton, 1980).

M. Wright (1982) argues that many aspects of imprisonment are inhumane and degrading. The physical conditions of many prisons are deplorable and there are often poor safeguards against ill-treatment and physical abuse. According to Wright, overcrowding is a major problem in most prisons and with the increase of the crime rate and the length of prison sentences of about one third every decade, the physical conditions are unlikely to improve in the foreseeable future. Cox, Paulus, and

McCain (1984) have shown that overcrowding in prison is related to markedly increased pathology among the inmates. Furthermore, the larger the size of the prison, the higher the suicide rate (and other premature deaths), and the greater the number of psychiatric problems. Farrington and Nuttall (1980) provide some evidence from data collected in England that there is a negative relationship between prison effectiveness in terms of reconviction and overcrowding in prison. That is, the greater the degree of overcrowding, the poorer the correctional effectiveness after discharge. The size of the prison did not prove to be a significant variable.

The literature referred to above briefly highlights some of the common experiences associated with imprisonment and the potential deleterious side effects. Undoubtedly, for some offenders the experiences encountered in prison are painful and potentially damaging to the individual. Furthermore, there is evidence from the work of Cohen and Taylor (1972) that long-term prisoners fear mental deterioration but this does not mean that it necessarily occurs. Indeed, research on the effects of long periods of imprisonment has failed to demonstrate clear evidence of intellectual and personality deterioration (Home Office, 1985). Furthermore, many "petty persistent offenders" are mentally disordered before being sentenced to prison and incarceration provides them with periods of shelter (Fairhead, 1981). There is some evidence from a study by Bolton, Smith, Heskin, and Banister (1976) that the experience of imprisonment may actually be psychologically beneficial for some prisoners. Much may depend on what educational and other facilities are available in prison. Sapsford (1983) argues from the results of a longitudinal study of 60 lifers that prisoners do not deteriorate mentally because they find ways of coping with the prison environment and use it to their advantage.

The above studies are in sharp contrast to West's (1982) conclusions that "most previous research suggests that severity of punishment, and especially commitment to a penal institution, is more likely than leniency to produce an escalation of delinquency." The studies quoted by West to support his argument (Dinitz & Conrad, 1980; Home Office, 1970; Wolfgang *et al.*, 1972), when looked at in detail, do not warrant the conclusion he makes. West makes the common error of overlooking the fact that the most troublesome offenders are generally given the most severe sentences. Even the finding by Dinitz and Conrad (1980) that "with all else controlled, there is a moderate to high inverse relationship between the severity of the sanctions for the first in every pair of crimes and the arrest for the second in the pair" does not, as indeed Dinitz and Conrad acknowledge, necessarily mean that severe sentences in themselves increase the likelihood of future offending.

First, there is no way of knowing how many of the offenders would have reoffended without the threat of returning to penal institution. Second, although important variables, such as number of previous convictions, type of offense, age, sex, race, and socioeconomic status were controlled, other variables not controlled for in the study (e.g., judges being able to identify by other criteria the most troublesome offenders) may have influenced the type of sentence given. Furthermore, Dinitz and Conrad do not provide sufficient information about the statistical procedures used in their analysis of the data for an independent evaluation of their findings to be made. At best, their findings suggest that with certain types of offenders, incarceration does not appear to have more positive effect with respect to reconviction than more lenient sentences.

THE DEATH PENALTY

The death penalty is an ancient form of punishment and a few centuries ago it was imposed in a large number of countries for a variety of offenses, some of which would seem quite trivial nowadays. Many countries have abolished the death penalty during this century, but it is commonly retained for certain crimes, such as treason and special murders. The Amnesty International Report (1979) considers the death penalty to be a "cruel, inhuman and degrading punishment and a violation of the right to life." In addition to moral arguments presented by the abolitionists, the death penalty comprises an irreversible procedure and there are cases reported in the literature of innocent people having been wrongfully executed because of the fallibility of the criminal justice system (e.g., Borchard, 1970). Another problem with the death penalty is that it may actually in some instances provoke murder and therefore offset the deterrent effect. According to Frost (1983), there are at least two reasons for this. First, the fear of detection and execution may encourage some offenders to murder witnesses and people likely to be instrumental in bringing about their arrest. Second, judges and juries may be more reluctant to convict offenders who risk the death penalty.

From a social learning theory point of view, one could argue that executions may have "negative modeling" effect. That is, executions may on occasions increase homicide rates rather than reduce them as potential murderers become inclined to display or copy the behavior of the legitimate authority. Evidence for this comes from the study of Bowers and Pierce (1975). They looked at the monthly homicide rates in New York State between 1907 and 1963 and discovered an average increase of two homicides in the month after an execution.

There has been much controversy in the literature about the possible deterrent effect of the death penalty. The critical question is whether or not capital punishment is more effective as a general deterrent than the alternative sentence of life imprisonment. Until the influential work of Ehrlich (1975), there was no significant empirical support for the general deterrent effect of the death penalty. Using a sophisticated econometric analysis, Ehrlich claimed that the death penalty is a more effective general deterrent in the case of murder than imprisonment. Furthermore, he estimated that each execution in the United States for the period 1935 to 1969 deterred seven or eight murders. In 1977, Ehrlich produced further empirical evidence that he claimed supported his previous findings (Ehrlich, 1977).

Ehrlich's findings and basic assumptions have been criticized in the literature on various methodological grounds (Beyleveld, 1982; Bowers & Pierce, 1975; Brier & Fienberg, 1980; Symposium on Current Death Penalty Issues, 1983), but they are not without some independent support (Frost, 1983). Nor do studies failing to find support for the deterrent effect necessarily invalidate Ehrlich's conclusions.

Bandura (1986) questions the efficacy of capital punishment on the basis that the death penalty has failed to produce a marked drop in the rate of capital crimes in the United States where it has been reinstated, and homicide rates do not appear to differ in neighboring states with and without capital punishment. Baron (1987) makes the point that this is not a surprising finding in view of the fact that the incidence of executions in those states is very low and there is usually a very long delay between the commission of the capital crime and the ultimate punishment. Baron quotes recent data from China, where over 5,000 executions for capital offenses were during one summer carried out immediately after the courts' verdict. There was a very noticeable fall in the incidence of capital crimes. How lasting such a fall in the crime rate would be it is not possible to say. However, the findings suggest that in order for capital punishment to be maximally effective it has to be carried out immediately after the courts' verdict and there must be certainties that it will take place if the person is convicted of a capital offense.

CONCLUSIONS

It is evident from this chapter that there are a number of sentencing options available to magistrates and judges and we have discussed these within the framework of the English legal system. Sentencing practices undoubtedly differ markedly cross-culturally and even within countries, but sufficient similarities exist for certain generalizations to be made. Indeed, many of the studies referred to in this chapter from different countries give similar results, particularly with respect to the relative outcome of different types of sentence. We have primarily focused on the reductive justification for punishment, only briefly mentioning the restitutive and expressive functions.

Our review of the criminal statistics reveals that the sentences given vary widely according to the age and sex of the offender. The great majority of juvenile offenders (i.e., those under the age of 17) are given a caution or a discharge, although there are clear sex differences in favor of females that become more marked with age. In the case of adult offenders and those between 17 and 20, only 15% of the males and about a third of the females receive a caution or a discharge. Female offenders are much less likely to receive custodial sentences than males and in the case of adults, are more likely to receive caution, discharge, or probation. The number of previous convictions and type of offense also markedly affect the type of sentence given. In general, the more serious the offense and the larger the number of previous convictions, the greater the likelihood that the offender will receive a custodial sentence. About 4% of all adult offenders receive a custodial sentence, with the average length of sentence for males being about 12 months. Females are generally given shorter sentences than males. Just over 20% of all males and 5% of females convicted of indictable offenses are given prison sentences.

Prior to the 1960s, fines and probation were the main alternatives to custodial sentences in England (Stanley & Baginsky, 1984). Subsequently, several new alternative sentences have been introduced, such as care and supervision orders, suspended prison sentences, and community service orders. The last two were specifically designed as alternatives to prison. There is no evidence that these alternative sentences and increased use of formal police cautioning have reduced recidivism. Indeed, as will become evident in the next chapter, there is evidence from both British and American studies that the new sentencing initiatives and diversion programs introduced in the past two decades have resulted in "net widening" and place more people at risk of a prison sentence.

A comparison of the effectiveness of different sentences is very difficult because offenders are generally not randomly allocated to different sentences. As the least serious offenders are likely to be given the most lenient sentences, such as discharge or a fine, and the most serious and persistent offenders custodial sentences, it is not surprising that some differences in reconviction rates are noted with respect to these sentences. There is some evidence from the literature for interaction effects in that certain offenders may "benefit" most from certain types of sentences, but our present knowledge about what sentence best suits each individual is far too limited to have much predictive validity.

There is considerable controversy in the literature about the deterrent effects of custodial sentences and capital punishment. The specific deterrence of custodial sentences is limited by the fact that relatively few offenders are given such sentences, and when they are, the sentences tend to be quite short so that they soon have further opportunity for offending. Furthermore, it is the sentence served rather than the sentence given that needs to be considered. The threat of a prison sentence may deter some offenders, and there is growing evidence that the effect of prison sentences is cumulative, which means that one has to consider the number and duration of previous sentences rather than studying each sentence in isolation. With respect to general deterrence, there is evidence that longer sentences do deter certain types of crimes, such as rape, assault, murder, burglary, and robbery. The death penalty poses many moral and ethical problems, and its effectiveness as a general deterrence when compared with the alternative sentence of life imprisonment has not been firmly established. However, the work of Ehrlich, suggesting that each execution saves several potential victims from murder, is impressive and should not be underestimated. It is also worth mentioning that nearly 1% of murderers carefully selected for release on a license commit a further murder. This means that, although very few murderers released from a life sentence commit another murder, their rate of dangerousness remains much higher than that for the general population.

Considering the fact that the prisons in most industrial countries are overcrowded and very expensive to run, it is unlikely that the prison population can be markedly increased in the short term. Probably a better alternative than sending more people to prison is to carefully select those given prison sentences and thereby improve the effectiveness of such sentences. There is growing knowledge about how to identify "hardcore" or career criminals early in their criminal careers and the law enforcement agencies should concentrate on arresting such offenders and taking them out of circulation. The courts must cooperate by giving these offenders long sentences and their parole applications should be very cautiously considered.

The low clearup rate of some offenses (e.g., below 20% for burglary) undoubtedly reduces the deterrent value of the sentences imposed. In addition, the majority of young offenders arrested are given either a caution or a discharge, even in the case of some recidivists. Stumphauzer (1986) makes the important point that increased legal rights of youths and more restrictions on police and prosecutions in recent years are likely to reduce the number of offenders prosecuted and convicted in the future. Whereas unnecessarily harsh sentences are impractical and unlikely to cure the delinquency problems, sentences that are perceived by the victims, the police, and the public as too lenient may have serious repercussions in terms of lowered morale and members of the public taking the law into their own hands.

One of the most exciting findings in recent years with respect to the sentencing of juveniles is the success of adjournment in cases of truancy. There is no reason why such procedures could not be applied equally effectively to other delinquent behaviors. But above all, the studies in question underline emphatically the need for better empirical investigation of the effects of different types of sentencing. Cooperation between psychologists and the judiciary has been almost completely missing, and without it, a greater understanding on the part of judges and magistrates of the requirements of scientific investigation and the promise of better understanding and more appropriate sentencing, there is little likelihood of a solution being found for the problems being discussed in this chapter.

CHAPTER SEVEN

The Prevention and Treatment of Illegal Behavior

INTRODUCTION

This chapter is concerned with predelinquent and preadjudication methods for preventing and controlling delinquency and adult offending. We shall also discuss in some detail the rehabilitation and treatment that have been applied at the postadjudication stage. Throughout the chapter we emphasize the importance of a proper scientific enquiry.

While reviewing the literature, we became aware of the negativism that generally exists with respect to the potential impact of prevention and rehabilitation programs. This is not surprising in view of the fact that successful programs are the exception rather than the rule. However, there is growing evidence that some treatment programs do work. That notion that "nothing works" is erroneous and misleading. What is important is identifying factors that can differentiate between successful and unsuccessful intervention outcome.

WAYS OF STUDYING INTERVENTION EFFECTS

A number of different research strategies have been used in studying criminal behavior and its control. These include case studies, cross-sectional surveys, experimental studies, and participant observations. The three most common methods consist of cross-sectional, longitudinal, and experimental research designs.

Farrington, Ohlin, and Wilson (1986) have recently produced a comprehensive and informative account of these three research methods. Their book is important because it provides researchers with a clear conceptual and methodological framework for carrying out future research on the prevention and control of criminal behavior. They argue that what is needed are ways of combining rigorous experiments with longitudinal studies. Before discussing how this could be achieved, we wish to briefly illustrate the salient components of the cross-sectional, longitudinal, and experimental methods.

Cross-sectional research involves examining the similarities and differences among a cross-section of offenders and their families at any one point of time. It can provide some important information about delinquency and criminal behavior, but cross-section research is limited and cannot answer questions about causality.

Longitudinal studies involve following the development of subjects over time. That is, subjects are interviewed and tested at regular intervals and this provides useful information about the course of development of a particular behavioral pattern, such as repeated offending. Detailed information about the pattern of offending can be collected at different stages of development and this has greatly advanced our knowledge about criminal careers. On the basis of their detailed review of longitudinal research projects that meet acceptable scientific criteria, Farrington *et al.* (1986) make the following conclusions:

1. The participation in offending peaks between the ages of 15 and 18.
2. The earlier the offenders commence delinquent activity the more offenses they tend to commit and the longer their criminal career.
3. Criminal parents tend to have delinquent children.
4. The best predictors of the onset of offending are parental child-rearing techniques, the child's poor educational achievement, and generally troublesome early behavior.
5. Offending is concentrated in a small deviant minority of high-rate offenders. They can be predicted at an early age by such variables as criminal parents, poor school performance, economic deprivation, low intelligence, and poor parental child-rearing behavior.

Farrington *et al.* rightly point out that although criminal behavior tends to occur disproportionately among people who have low income, are unemployed, and of low intelligence, this does not prove that these variables *cause* the criminal behavior. A number of alternative explanations are possible, including the possibility that people with criminal propensities are poorly motivated to seek employment.

Experimental research involves a planned and systematic intervention that is assigned to a subject at random. Those who receive the intervention become the "experimental" subjects and those who do not become the "controls." When random matching is not possible, a quasiexperimental procedure may be used. This commonly involves some form of matching the experimental and control subjects with respect to certain variables (e.g., age, sex). Unfortunately, in spite of careful matching, the two groups may differ in important ways and seriously confound the results.

Most of what is known about the effects of treatment interventions is derived from experimental and quasiexperimental studies. These will be reviewed in detail later in this chapter.

Farrington *et al.* (1986) list 10 key issues that are relevant to the prevention and control of delinquency and criminal behavior:

1. Can delinquency be prevented by parent training or by a preschool intellectual program?
2. Can delinquency be prevented by exposure to a prosocial peer group?
3. How far can "chronic offenders" be predicted?
4. What are the effects of diverting offenders from the court?
5. What are the effects on offending of juvenile as opposed to adult processing?
6. What are the effects on adult court decision making of providing juvenile records?
7. What are the effects of different sentences on offenders?
8. What interactions are there between the effectiveness of correctional treatments and types of offenders?
9. What are the effects of imprisonment on prisoners?
10. Can the recidivism rate of released prisoners be reduced by providing welfare benefits or special assistance with employment?

Issues number 3, 7, and 9 were discussed in the previous chapter. We shall attempt to answer some of the remaining questions later in this chapter.

Farrington *et al.* (1986) argue that the best method of investigating the 10 issues is by means of longitudinal-experimental surveys. That is, people are followed up over a period of time while the effects of different experimental interventions are periodically investigated. According to Farrington *et al.* (1986), such longitudinal-experimental surveys would have two distinct aims. First, they would inform us about the course of development of criminal careers, especially with regard to the onset, duration, and termination of offending. Second, they would enable us to establish the importance of specific events in the causes of criminal behavior and help us study the impact of different interventions with regard to the development of criminal careers.

The ideal scientific approach involves assigning subjects in a cohort at random to a particular intervention and objectively monitoring the outcome for the experimental and control subjects respectively. The aim would be to observe the results of a specific intervention, implemented at a particular point in time, on the normal course of development of criminal careers. Data could be gathered from different surveys carried out within a longitudinal study in order to construct a complete picture of the development of criminal careers. Ideally, research should be based on sound theoretical principles and in turn research findings should stimulate theoretical ideas. In practice, most evaluative research has not been concerned with theory testing.

Sechrest and Rosenblatt (1987) point out that many studies fail to distinguish between *process* evaluations and *outcome* evaluations. Most studies have focused on outcome evaluations without any consideration of the developmental phases or individual components of a program. Process evaluation helps to identify the salient elements that make a program work. Undoubtedly, in future research there will be much greater emphasis on clearly defining and identifying the treatment process and providing programs that suit the specific needs of the individual offender.

REQUIREMENTS FOR EVALUATION RESEARCH

The literature on the evaluation of different intervention approaches to delinquent and criminal behavior is immense. However, in order for the findings of a study to be accepted on scientific grounds, it must fulfill certain methodological requirements.

In an early attempt to evaluate the effectiveness of preventive and intervention studies, Bailey (1966) reviewed 100 empirical studies published between 1940 and 1960. The studies were subjected to content analysis in order to evaluate the status of correctional treatment. Most of the studies were carried out in "formal treatment" settings (prison, parole, probation) and involved group therapy or psychotherapy. Although about half of the studies reported "some improvement," Bailey's (1966) conclusion was that most of the studies were based on inadequately conceptualized treatment and research designs, rendering any interpretation of positive outcome highly questionable.

A major problem with Bailey's (1966) review is that the criteria used to evaluate the different studies were not sufficiently well defined or specific to make a meaningful evaluation of treatment and research design deficiencies. For this we have to turn to the review study of Logan (1972).

Logan (1972) presents seven minimum methodological requirements that studies with offenders must meet in order to be considered scientifically adequate. These minimum requirements are

1. The program or set of techniques whose effectiveness is being tested must be adequately defined so that the individual components can be readily identified. This helps to establish *what it was* that resulted in success or failure. What should be avoided is a treatment package that is too broad; that is, a whole range of different activities are covered and it becomes difficult to evaluate the contribution of each activity.
2. The study must be capable of replication; that is, it can be repeated with different subjects and therapists and is not dependent on the unique attributes of the participants.
3. The offenders should be selected randomly into treatment and control groups or they must be matched as far as possible with respect to variables that may influence outcome (e.g., age, IQ, social class).
4. Care must be taken so that only the treatment group is receiving the treatment. On no account should the control group be allowed to receive important elements of the treatment.
5. There should be "before-and-after" measurements with respect to the behavior that is subject to modification. The measurements must be made for both the treatment and control groups and the two groups should be measured at the same times or comparable points in their case histories.
6. Reliable and valid criteria for measuring "success" or "failure" in terms of criminal behavior must be employed. "Success" should refer to the prevention or reduction in criminal behavior, not to such variables as personal adjustment, mental health, or educational achievements. These latter variables may be important for various reasons but they are often too indirect to allow us to make relevant interpretations about criminal conduct.
7. There should be adequate follow-up in the community for both the treatment and control groups. This is particularly important with respect to criminal behavior because (a) the opportunity for exhibiting the criminal conduct while the offender is in an institutional setting and under close supervision is very limited, (b) some criminal behavior occurs infrequently and a long follow-up period is therefore essential, and (c) not all criminal conduct is

TABLE 19. Methodological Criteria Fulfilled in 100 Evaluation Studies

Methodological criteria	Criterion		
	Fulfilled	Partly fulfilled	Total
1. Adequate definition of program or technique	9	3	12
2. Capable of replication	9	2	11
3. Provision of a control group	41	1	42
4. Only treatment group receiving treatment	5	0	5
5. Before and After comparisons	31	0	31
6. Measurable definition of "success"	50	9	59
7. Follow-up in the community	30	0	30

Note. Raw data from "Evaluation Research in Crime and Delinquency: A Reappraisal" by C. H. Logan, *Journal of Criminal Law, Criminology and Police Science, 1972, 63,* pp. 378–387.

detected and the offender may be caught for only some of his or her offenses.

Logan (1972) reviewed 100 intervention studies, published between 1930 and 1967, with reference to the seven minimum requirement criteria. In Table 19 we present Logan's (1972) raw data with respect to the seven criteria.

None of the studies of correctional or preventive effectiveness fulfilled all seven minimum requirements. Only 42 of the studies used some kind of control group. The figure is reduced to 31 if one limits it to control groups that were either selected at random or through proper matching. This is clearly a very serious methodological limitation, but a more common problem was that very few studies (12%) defined their techniques or program sufficiently clearly to make replications possible. When the two criteria (a proper control group and adequately defined program/technique) are combined, only three studies survive. This is reduced to one study if a measurable definition of "success" is included, which becomes eliminated if a follow-up in the community is added as a minimum criterion.

Thirty-seven of the studies involved the use of psychiatric treatment, psychiatric social work, and psychotherapy. This was followed by 20 studies utilizing probation, parole, and institutionalization. Seven studies involved educational programs and a further eight used counseling. The majority of studies made subjective and unsupported claims of success; only 16 admitted to failure. Educational programs made the highest claims of success while fulfilling fewest of the methodological criteria.

THE CONCEPT OF PREVENTION

In its broadest sense, any method that reduces the likelihood of future offending can be labeled as "preventive." This may consist of preventing offending from occurring in the first place or, alternatively, preventing recidivism. Intervening once offenders have been apprehended, prosecuted, or sentenced in order to prevent recidivism is more appropriately referred to as "treatment," "rehabilitation," or "disposal." It should be clearly differentiated from those interventions that focus on predelinquent strategies.

According to Nietzel and Himelein (1986), there are two types of prevention with respect to delinquent and adult offending: *primary* and *secondary* prevention. Primary prevention comprises methods intended to prevent delinquent and criminal behavior from commencing in the first place. This can be achieved by (1) modifying factors known to contribute or facilitate criminal behavior or (2) designing methods that promote prosocial behavior. Secondary prevention refers to focusing on "at-risk" (predelinquent) individuals (i.e., those considered to be most likely to offend at some future date but have not yet engaged in delinquent or criminal activity). Nietzel and Himelein (1986) equate primary and secondary prevention with the terms *general immunology* and *special immunology* described by Glueck and Glueck (1972).

Nietzel and Himelein (1986) believe that there is sufficient knowledge available about the causes of crime to justify intervention at the following targets:

1. Diversion of predelinquent youngsters.
2. Reductions of family violence.
3. Development of better parental discipline techniques.
4. Development of cognitive, behavior, academic, and occupational competencies, which are considered important for helping the youngster to cope with social, academic, and occupational stressors.
5. Modification of the environmental opportunities and victim vulnerabilities.

Diversion is given as an example of secondary prevention, whereas the remaining four areas are considered to fall under primary prevention when delivered proactively. When targeted for "at-risk" groups, they fulfill the criterion for secondary prevention.

We are in slight disagreement with Neitzel and Himelein about the classification of diversion as predelinquent intervention. The term is generally used in describing the attempt to "divert" from judicial processing those juveniles who have already committed offenses and been arrested. Such juveniles can hardly be described as "predelinquent." The major purpose of the diversion is to discourage them from further offending. Furthermore, diversion is not exclusively used for first offenders, which makes it meaningless to call them "predelinquent."

A potential confusion exists with respect to target 4. Cognitive, behavioral, academic, and occupational competencies can be subjected to intervention in order to prevent recidivism rather than initial offending. In practice both types of intervention take place.

The primary objective of predelinquent intervention is to prevent delinquency commencing in the first place. Broadly speaking, prevention techniques fall into three distinct groups:

(1) Individual treatment techniques, which are based on the assumption that delinquency and criminal behavior are rooted within the personality of the individual. An early advocate of this approach was Healy (1915), who asserted that delinquency was caused by individual personality problems, such as those related to "mental dissatisfaction"; the development of criminalistic imagery and ideas; and mental instability, conflicts, and defect.

Two factors are central to the success of the individual treatment approach. First, those juveniles that are likely to become delinquent need to be properly identified so that steps can be taken to prevent them from offending. Second, individually tailored treatment techniques need to be implemented that counteract their flawed personalities. The more common practice is for juveniles to be offered regular contact with social workers and other mental health professionals.

It is worth pointing out that although our knowledge about the factors that seem to precipitate delinquency is increasing, any reliable prediction equation needs to consider a combination of variables rather than relying on any single one (Lorion, Tolan, & Wahler, 1987).

(2) Social or community-based interventions that attempt to identify and alter some of the social and environmental forces thought to facilitate or cause delinquency. Among the most important projects under this heading are the "area projects," which have their theoretical origins in the pioneering work of Shaw, Zorbaugh, McKay, and Cottrell (1929), who argued that delinquency is geographically located. In other words, neighborhoods shape the attitudes and behavior of their residents and, on occasions, these are supportive of delinquent and criminal behavior. Shaw *et al.* (1929) plotted rates of delinquency in different areas of the city of Chicago in order to study the origin of urban delinquency for the period from 1900 to 1926. Their main conclusion was that delinquency was caused by "social disorganization." In their more extended work of 22 cities, Shaw and McKay (1942) discuss the process whereby delinquent traditions emerge in socially disorganized neighbor-

hoods. Basically, residents in such neighborhoods are thought to lack access to conventional means of reaching important cultural and economic goals and consequently resort to illegitimate means.

Lundman (1984) argues that one of the most important contributions of Shaw and McKay was establishing the foundation for the area-project approach to the prevention of juvenile delinquency. Such efforts attempt to prevent delinquency by implementing some form of social reorganization, such as stimulating the development of self-help community committees in high-delinquency neighborhoods.

(3) Physical and situational measures intended to reduce opportunity for offending. The most recent development in the prevention of delinquency, this approach does not deny the importance of inheritance, personality, and social factors in explaining criminal behavior, but because these are often difficult to modify satisfactorily it is thought more effective to manipulate factors immediately contingent on the criminal event (Clarke, 1977). The main proposition of this "environmental/learning theory" (Clarke, 1985; Cornish & Clarke, 1975) is that the critical determinants of delinquent behavior are situated in the person's current environment, which provides the cues, stimuli, and reinforcement for delinquency. Once the delinquent act has been committed, reinforcement and opportunity become essential to its performance and maintenance.

Other theories that emphasize situational determinants of delinquency are the "opportunity theory" (Cohen & Felson, 1979) and the "situational control theory" (Downes & Rock, 1982). Both of these theories are based on assumptions about the causes of delinquency similar to those of the environmental/learning theory.

THE EFFECTIVENESS OF PREDELINQUENT MEASURES

One of the best-known studies of the prevention of delinquent behavior is the Cambridge-Somerville Youth Study (Powers & Witmer, 1951). The study attempted to prevent delinquency by providing individual counseling to 325 experimental subjects and 325 untreated controls. The treatment hypothesis was that attempts of adult counselors to improve juveniles' school performance, personality development, and family functioning would prevent juvenile delinquency. The project lasted from 1937 to 1945, and at the end of the treatment period, only a minority was still receiving treatment. Follow-up data are available for three periods: 1948 (Powers & Witmer, 1951), 1955 (McCord, McCord, & Zola, 1959), and 1976 (McCord, 1978). It is evident from these follow-up studies that the counseling, or the semistructured treatment offered, was completely ineffective in preventing future delinquency. Efforts to replicate the Cambridge-Somerville Youth Study have proved similarly ineffective in preventing delinquency (Lundman, 1984).

Several attempts have been made to use mental health, group counseling, or special education programs in schools in order to prevent problem behavior and delinquency, but in most instances no significant benefits have emerged from these programs (Rutter & Giller, 1983). Rutter and Giller quote the work of Rose and Marshall (1974) and Schweinhart and Weikart (1980) as evidence that educational benefits may on occasions have some, although probably small, spinoff effects on delinquent behavior.

Farrington (1985) argues that Rutter and Giller place insufficient emphasis on the work of Schweinhart and Weikart (1980). He considers this to be the most important study published in recent years. The study gives clear support for the idea that preschool enrichment programs can lead to a significant increase in school achievement and reduce risk of future delinquency. In this study an experimental group received a daily preschool program, followed by weekly home visits. The primary aim of the program was to increase intellectual abilities and school performance among the experimental group. A further follow-up of the Perry preschool project (Berrueta-Clement, Schweinhart, Barnett, Epstein, & Weikart, 1984) shows that 51% of the control group by age 19 had been apprehended by the police compared with only 31% of the experimental subjects. In addition to less likelihood of offending, the control group had experienced significantly higher rates of unemployment than the experimental group after leaving school.

The findings of the Perry project demonstrate the long-term beneficial effects of preschool intellectual enrichment programs. However, attempts at preventing delinquency in older children by such methods as social work intervention and special classes designed to improve self-concept have not been successful. For example, the two major school experiments on delinquency prevention carried out by Meyer, Borgatta, and Jones (1965) and Reckless and Dinitz (1972) failed to find any differences in delinquency at follow-up between the experimental and control groups. These results point to the importance of separating the variables of age and type of intervention. It is possible that intervention at an early age (i.e., preschool) has more effects on preventing later delinquency than intervention with older children. In addition, programs focusing on specific skills (e.g., intellectual or cognitive) may have more powerful effects than less specific programs.

Efforts in the United States to prevent delinquency by changing or improving the social environment have proved little or no more effective. For example, attempts to prevent delinquency by improving the quality of people's lives by setting up neighborhood self-help community programs, as in the Chicago Area Project (Sorrentino, 1977; Witmer & Tufts, 1954) and the Midcity Project (Miller, 1962), have not proved successful by objective criteria (Lundman, 1984; Wright & Dixon, 1977).

Somewhat more encouraging results about the effectiveness of community intervention programs are perhaps evident from a British study, called The Wincroft Youth Project (Smith, Farrant, & Merchant, 1972). Fifty-four boys, selected on the basis of their scores on the British Social Adjustment Guides, were compared with matched controls who came from a similarly socially deprived area. Two follow-ups (one year apart) showed the experimental group to be less delinquent on the basis of official convictions and self-report data than the matched controls, but the difference was not very marked (e.g., at second follow-up, conviction rates were 50% versus 62%).

In the British Community Development projects, attempts were made to deal with poverty and social deprivation by mobilizing unused local resources and encouraging the community to develop its own systems of support (Rutter & Madge, 1976) but no data are available to indicate how effective, if at all, these projects were in reducing delinquency (Rutter & Giller, 1983).

The most recent innovation in preventing delinquency is the attempt to reduce the opportunity for offending. This can take one of two forms. First, juveniles can be kept occupied in order to reduce the time they have for offending, but there is no evidence that this is effective because they are still left with ample time to offend (Clarke, 1985). However, Hills and Walter (1979) provide some evidence that a combined "behavioral-employment program" can successfully reduce recidivism among delinquents. Such a program comprises a multiple-treatment package (e.g., job opportunities, recruiting and training employers, and shaping proemployment behaviors), which makes it impossible to determine precisely what facilitates the improvement. Second, situational and opportunity-reducing measures of crime prevention may be implemented (Clarke & Mayhew, 1980). Clarke (1983) indicates that there are many effective ways of making crimes more difficult to commit (i.e., "target hardening"), including the use of cheque guarantee cards, the control of alcohol sales at football matches, closed-circuit television surveillance, routine security screening at airports, and the presence of caretakers in blocks of flats.

In spite of the undoubtedly important effects of situational opportunities, the effectiveness of environmental manipulations in markedly reducing the crime rate is unclear. Furthermore, Rutter and Giller (1983) point out, "we remain ignorant of the extent to which situational factors truly reduce crime rather than just displace it from one area to another or from one activity to another." We accept Clarke's (1985) argument that displacement is by no means the inevitable consequence of blocked opportunities because fresh and harder effort may be required of the offender.

PREADJUDICATION INTERVENTION

Preadjudication intervention consists of formal attempts to divert juveniles from the juvenile court. The main reasoning behind diversion is that judicial processing has potentially stigmatizing and deleterious effects on juveniles. Not only may their self-concept be affected by labeling, but the association with other, perhaps more serious offenders, may be positively harmful (Lundman, 1984). Farrington *et al.* (1986) quote research findings supporting the view that an official conviction can have a "deviance amplification" effect, but there appear to be large individual variations in how people are affected by the labeling process.

A number of diversion projects have been carried out in the United States, including the Sacramento County Diversion Project (Baron, Feeney, & Thornton, 1973) and the National Evaluation of Diversion Projects (Dunford, Osgood, & Weichselbaum, 1981). Although some marginal beneficial effects were reported for the Sacramento project, it suffered from methodological problems that made it difficult to interpret the findings (Lundman, 1984). The National Evaluation of Diversion Projects appears to have suffered from fewer methodological problems. It compared at 6 and 12 month follow-up rearrest figures for those *released*, those *diverted*, and those *processed* through the juvenile court. The rearrest rates for the three groups were almost identical (i.e., about 22% at 6-month follow-up and 30% to 32% at 12-month follow-up).

One major problem with diversion projects is that they appear to increase the overall number of juveniles who would otherwise have been processed through the judicial system (Klein, 1979; Sarri & Bradley, 1980).

Rutter and Giller (1983) argue that formal cautioning in Britain seems to have succeeded in diverting young people from the Juvenile Court but it has been accompanied by an increase in the number of juveniles arrested and brought into the legal processing net. Some evidence for the "net widening" effect is provided by Ditchfield (1976), Farrington and Bennett (1981), and Pearson (1984). One possible reason for this, discussed by Tutt and Giller (1983), is that since 1978 Home Office Guidelines make it a requirement that previous cautions are cited in the juvenile court, making it less likely that juveniles who have been cautioned are given conditional discharges or a fine. Unfortunately for many juveniles, the formal cautioning procedure makes them drawn into the judicial system where they would otherwise have been dealt with informally by the use of police discretion.

Tutt and Giller (1983) suggest that the increase in recent years in the use of diversion is generally envisaged as part of the development of a "welfare"-based system for dealing with offenders. They present evidence from 15 different police forces in England and Wales that wide variations across forces still exist in the organizations, practice, and rates of cautioning. However, in spite of great variation among police forces, cautioning is a very commonly used preadjudication intervention, particularly for first offenders and those committing minor delinquent acts.

POSTADJUDICATION INTERVENTION

Postadjudication interventions include the sentencing options of judges and magistrates once the person has pleaded or been found guilty of an offense in a court of law. However, on many occasions, postadjudication intervention is not directly related to judicial sentencing decisions. For example, many offenders are treated on a voluntary basis in outpatient clinics, in the community, or in prison. In this chapter we shall focus on the outcome of treatment and rehabilitation studies with offenders that have been reported in the literature. Some of the studies were carried out as part of the sentencing procedure and others were not.

In the preceding chapter we discussed the various sentencing options available to English courts. We would like to discuss the use of probation orders in some detail in this chapter because it is one of the most important alternatives to a prison sentence. Furthermore, its effectiveness is commonly evaluated in reviews on psychological and rehabilitative methods, although, in our view, probation is not based on systematic scientific principles.

Lundman (1984) argues that the main problem with probation orders is the large caseload that many probation officers have to carry, which makes it difficult for them to maintain frequent and effective rehabilitative contact. However, there is no evidence that frequency of contact with the probation officer significantly reduces recidivism. Indeed no difference in overall level of effectiveness was found in the IMPACT study (Folkard, 1981) between intensive and ordinary probation supervision, although some interaction effects were found. That is, criminal offenders with personal problems did better under intensive supervision, whereas the criminal offenders with fewer personal problems did better with ordinary supervision.

In their recent evaluation of the effectiveness of probation, Goldberg and Stanley (1985) provide data to support the importance of task-centered probation casework with offenders. This involves helping clients carry out problem-alleviating tasks within a specified time period. They give 3-year follow-up data for 96 offenders who had engaged in a task-centered casework project. The reconviction rate after 3 years was 42% in contrast with 53% reported for ordinary probation in the Phillpotts and Lancucki (1979) study. Goldberg and Stanley (1985) conclude that short-term task-centered probation may be more effective with offenders than long-term probation not conducted along task-centered lines. Another interesting finding was that the offenders' acknowledgment of problems and their readiness to work on them, in conjunction with low criminal tendencies, seemed to be associated with the most favorable outcome.

Stumphauzer (1986) points out four major problems with probation that make it relatively ineffective in relieving recidivism. These are (1) the probation "contract" is commonly vague and poorly structured; (2) the threat of punishment is the only learning principle utilized; (3) probation officers generally get little training in how to modify behavior; and (4) probation officers carry incapacitatingly large caseloads.

Lundman (1984) describes community-based treatment (e.g., Fox, 1977) as a sentencing option that bridges the gap between the loose supervision of routine probation and the secure custody of correctional facilities. He reviews community-based treatment programs, such as the Provo Experiment (Empey & Erickson, 1972) and the Silverlake Experiment (Empey & Lubeck, 1971).

The Provo Experiment compared the effectiveness of three different interventions with serious delinquents: a community-based program (approximately 5 to 6 months of treatment), probation, and a State Industrial School. The follow-up period lasted 4 years. No noticeable difference in outcome was found between probation and the community-based program, and the State Training School had the highest recidivism rate. Unfortunately, unlike the probation group, the State Training group was a nonrandom control group so the differences in outcome may have at least partly resulted from intake differences.

Kobrin and Klein (1982) evaluated the effectiveness of deinstitutionalization (i.e., attempts to keep status offenders out of correctional facilities) and found that it marginally increased recidivism. Nevertheless, in view of the small difference, Kobrin and Klein recommended deinstitutionalization because of greater cost effectiveness.

One major problem with many treatment programs implemented within institutional settings is lack of *generalization* of the desirable behavior once the person leaves the institution (Ayllon & Milan, 1979).

Indeed, on occasions, there may be a poor relationship between the behavior exhibited within the institution and subsequent behavior in the community. For example, Ross and Mckay (1976), in their study of delinquent girls treated by a token economy program in an institution, found a high recidivism rate after discharge in spite of improved behavior while in the institution.

An important attempt to link the desirable behavior to external environment contingencies is the establishment of residential group homes that are integrated within the community (Burchard & Harig, 1976). A good example of behaviorally oriented group homes for delinquents is the Achievement Place in Kansas, a community based family-style home for six to eight delinquents in the 12–15-year-old age group (Kirigin, Wolf, Braukmann, Fixsen, & Phillips, 1979; Phillips, 1968). The program was developed in order to provide an "effective, humane, replicable, and less costly alternative to institutional treatment." The treatment, which is based on a (token economy) behavioral model, is administered by a well-trained couple, who provide the juveniles, through reinforcement, modeling, and intervention, with behavioral skills in social, interpersonal, academic, and occupational areas. The assumption is that after learning these skills the juveniles will become more successful in their endeavors and relationships, which will be maintained by reinforcement. As they gradually earn more "points," they will spend more and more time in their natural, family environment, a process that is greatly facilitated by the nature of the behavioral program.

A preliminary outcome evaluation of the Achievement Place (Kirigin, Wolf, Braukmann, Fixsen, & Phillips, 1979) seems favorable with respect to target behavior and subsequent institutionalization but unfortunately follow-up data concerning recidivism is very limited and difficult to interpret and provides no clear evidence about effectiveness. In another study (Eitzen, 1979), highly favorable changes in attitudes, self-esteem, and locus of control were noted in juveniles who had been at Achievement Place. These improvements were maintained during treatment but unfortunately no follow-up data are reported.

Liberman, Ferris, Salgado, and Salgado (1975) attempted to replicate the procedures from Achievement Place with 16 delinquent boys referred by a juvenile court. Token economy procedures were used to modify the juveniles' saving behavior, promptness, conversational interruptions, and table setting while they resided in a home-style, community-based, treatment setting. Point rewards and fines were found to be effective in modifying the target behaviors. In their paper, the authors refer to an unpublished study by Liberman and Ferris (1974), where outcome data showed improvement in the juvenile's academic records and recidivism. Unfortunately, insufficient data are provided to objectively evaluate the significance of this outcome study. Indeed, a more recent outcome evaluation study by Kirigin, Braukmann, Atwater, and Wolf (1982) suggests that an Achievement Place approach to the control of delinquency is of limited value.

These authors evaluated the outcome of the original Achievement Place program in conjunction with 12 subsequent replications and compared it with that of more conventional community-based residential programs in Kansas. Although some significant differences in offending emerged between the two groups during treatment, these differences were not significant at 1-year follow-up. The reported offenses for boys at 1-year follow-up were 57% and 73% for the Achievement Place and conventional residential programs respectively. The corresponding figures for girls were 27% and 47% respectively perhaps indicating that residential treatment intervention is more effective for delinquent girls than for boys. This possibility was not discussed by Kirigin *et al.* (1982) and one needs to be careful in making generalizations from this study in view of the relatively small samples and nonrandom allocation of subjects.

Applications of partial replication of the Achievement approach have been attempted in the United Kingdom. In an earlier effort to partly replicate features of the Achievement Place approach, staff at the Glenthorne Youth Treatment Centre (GYTC) visited the Achievement Place in the United and adopted some of its main social learning theory features (Reid, 1982). The unit has now operated for several years but no published outcome data are yet available.

Brown (1985) describes a community-based residential program for young offenders in London. The program applies some of the social reinforcement and self-government aspects of the original Achievement Place approach and reports success in terms of no further offending 1 year following for five out of eight juvenile offenders. In view of the small sample studied and absence of a control group, this study gives no clear evidence for the success of a social learning theory approach to the treatment of delinquency.

Ostapiuk (1982) provides a thought-provoking review of community-based behavior programs in the United Kingdom and the United States and considers that the most important advantages of community-based rehabilitation is the potential of such programs to facilitate generalization of newly required skills. This is consistent with the views of Ayllon and Milan (1979), who argue that a major problem with behavioral change achieved within institutional settings is that it is commonly not maintained once the person returns to his or her natural environment. These authors discuss two general procedures—"fading" and "attenuation of reinforcing consequences"—that can sometimes ensure that behavioral change will generalize across settings. In spite of these procedures, generalization is often ineffective because the natural environment may not contain contingencies that support the behavioral change and the inappropriate behavior may remain more reinforcing within the natural environment than the newly established alternatives.

Following the introduction of the Children's and Young Persons Act (1969), intensive community-based programs, commonly referred to as "intermediate treatment" (IT), were developed in the United Kingdom in an attempt to prevent delinquency, recidivism, and institutionalization. This new approach to community care and various Youth Centre projects have been discussed and evaluated by Preston (1982). Most projects appear to have been inadequately evaluated and one has to agree with the conclusions of Bottoms and Sheffield (1980) that the limited available evidence suggests that IT programs have no marked and lasting effects on recidivism.

However, more recently Feldman, Caplinger, and Wodarski (1983) provide some promising results from a large-scale community-based project in St. Louis, which included delinquent and nondelinquent youths between the ages of 8 and 17 years. The results indicated that both the delinquent (referred) and nondelinquent (nonreferred) youths benefited. Most promising results were associated with (1) an experienced leader conducting the program, (2) treatment being based on a social learning theory approach, and (3) treatment being implemented in a mixed group of referred and nonreferred youths. Unfortunately, the 1-year follow-up data included only a portion of the sample subjected to the program, limiting the generalizations that can be drawn from this finding.

One recent attempt to control delinquency in the United States has been the use of "Scare Straight" projects (Lundman, 1984). These projects are based on the idea that an intensive confrontation session of juvenile offenders with prisoners serving long sentences will alter the former's perceptions of the severity of punishment and make them more aware of the many unhappy consequences of imprisonment. Lundman (1984) reviews four such projects carried out in the United States: (1) the Juvenile Awareness Project (Finckenauer, 1982), (2) the Michigan Reformatory Visitation Program (Michigan Department of Corrections, 1967), (3) Juvenile Offenders Learn Truth (JOLT) (Yarborough, 1979), and (4) the Insiders Juvenile Crime Prevention Program (Orchowsky & Taylor, 1981).

The influence of these programs on recidivism has been mixed. In the first two projects, the experimental subjects became worse than the controls. There was no significant difference between the experimental and control group in the JOLT program. The Insiders Juvenile Prevention Program had the advantage over other projects of having longer follow-up (at 6, 9, and 12 months) and demonstrated favorable differences between the experimental and control groups at 9-month and 12-month follow-up but not at 6-month follow-up. One apparent limitation of all these studies is that, although a large number of juveniles had participated in the projects, owing to various methodological difficulties the follow-up measures were available only for very small groups (i.e., 17 to 46). The results, therefore, tell us very little about overall effectiveness of these projects. The evidence, as it stands, does not appear to justify such projects, especially since they may actually result in increased recidivism.

OVERALL EFFECTIVENESS OF TREATMENT/REHABILITATION

The status of treatment programs with offenders in institutional and community settings was seriously challenged in the early 1970s by Martinson (1974). His conclusion that virtually no treatment approach had been found to significantly reduce recidivism was based on data later published in more detail by Lipton, Martinson, and Wilks (1975). The study assessed the outcome of 231 experimental studies carried out between 1945 and 1967, and involved a wide range of treatment methods (e.g., medical therapy, individual psychotherapy, group therapy, milieu therapy, educational/vocational training, probation, imprisonment). For each category of treatment Martinson (1974) found across studies a mixture of positive and negative findings, which indicated to him that no single category of treatment was likely to be effective for the majority of offenders. In a later publication (Martinson, 1976), he asserted that only one category of treatment—probation—had given encouraging results. The remaining 10 treatment approaches were rejected by Martinson because they contained many contradictory results.

Palmer (1975, 1978, 1983) has critically evaluated Martinson's findings and conclusions and argues that Martinson was unnecessarily rejecting of many important positive research findings. Moreover, he disagrees with Martinson that only probation gave positive results; several of the categories of treatment, when looked at carefully, contained many encouraging results. Martinson stated that for most of the positive studies there was only a trivial drop in recidivism. Palmer (1978) argues that this is not true when one looks at the 48 studies evaluated by Lipton, Martinson, and Wilks (1975) that showed positive results and included a behavioral measure of recidivism. Here, the average reduction of recidivism is 32%, which is well above that suggested by Martinson.

Martinson is alleged to have failed to distinguish between a "percentage point drop" and a "percentage difference." The latter is synonymous with "percent reduction," not the former, as Martinson implied. To illustrate the difference, Palmer gives the following example: For all treatment categories combined, 36% of the experimental subjects and 53% of the control subjects had been rearrested with 19 months. This reflects a 17% point drop and a 32% reduction in illegal behavior. In view of his failure to integrate the results that were obtained across all individual studies, Martinson was unable to separate out and focus on specific conditions that facilitated positive results (e.g., offender, worker, and treatment setting characteristics).

In 1977, a "Special Panel on Research on Rehabilitative Techniques" was set up in the United States in order to assess the state of knowledge about the effectiveness of rehabilitation. There have been two separate volumes of work published following the panel's investigation. In the first volume (Sechrest, White, & Brown, 1979), the emphasis was on evaluating rehabilitation programs within correctional institutions; the second volume (Martin, Sechrest, & Redner, 1981) focused primarily on noninstitutional rehabilitation and suggestions for future programs and research. The overall aim of the panel was to evaluate the current state of knowledge about rehabilitation, in view of the work and pessimistic conclusions of Lipton, Martinson, and Wilks (1975), which covered studies up to 1968. The panel focused on more recent studies and reported on a number of studies published in the 1970s.

Sechrest, White, and Brown (1979) concluded that studies in the area had generally been so inadequate that "only a relatively few studies warrant any unequivocal interpretation." Furthermore, it was evident that no intervention program of any type could be guaranteed to reduce the criminal activity of released offenders. The two main problems with rehabilitation research were identified by the panel as "problems of implementation" and "problems of evaluation." The former related to difficulties in implementing treatment programs and research in institutions because of other priorities and concerns. "Problems of evaluation" included poor planning and lack of theoretical rationale for the research with techniques being evaluated as isolated entities when what was required was analysis of the combination of techniques, the implementation of weak and inadequate interventions, and lack of attention to individual needs. Sechrest, White, and Brown (1979) came to similar pessimistic conclusions, as Lipton, Martinson, and Wilks (1975) had, except that they had come across some successful rehabilitative efforts and believed that some treatments might, in the future, prove effective with certain subgroups of offenders.

The review of the panel's work on rehabilitative efforts in extrainstitutional settings (Martin, Sechrest, & Redner, 1981) was no more favorable than that for conventional institutions. The main conclusion drawn was that instead of concluding that nothing works, it is more accurate to state that we do not know what works.

The emphasis in the panel's second volume is on theoretical issues related to rehabilitative efforts. It is concluded that there is no theory of offender rehabilitation but many theories of criminal behavior developed in several disciplines. It is recommended that "greater efforts should be made to draw propositions from one or several theories of crime into a causal model, employ that model as a guide in designing intervention strategies, and test the asssumptions on which the programs are based." Another recommendation is that there should be more systematic, long-term, and focused research undertaken with the aim of improving techniques and programs so that definite conclusions can be reached about their effectiveness.

Romig (1978) reviewed about 170 studies that met the following two criteria: (1) They utilized either a randomly assigned control group or a matched control group and (2) they included some measurement of program effectiveness in terms of specific behavior (e.g., reconviction, improved institutional behavior). These studies, fulfilling the necessary criteria, were then divided according to the rehabilitation methods they had used (e.g., behavior therapy, individual psychotherapy, juvenile probation).

It appeared that, with a few isolated exceptions, the studies reviewed were ineffective in reducing recidivisim. When comparing the "successful" with the "unsuccessful" studies, certain trends emerge about the treatment intervention. Basically, the most successful programs included teaching specific behavioral and communication skills, sometimes involving other members of the family.

Blackburn (1980) evaluated the outcome of 40 psychological rehabilitation studies reported in the literature from 1973 to 1978. They were examined in terms of therapeutic method, target population, therapeutic goals, evaluative treatment designs, treatment setting, and reduction of recidivism. The majority of programs (70%) utilized behavioral methods, and the therapeutic goals more commonly involved "convenience behaviors" (i.e., activities convenient for the management of the institution). Only three studies attempted to directly reduce antisocial or illegal behavior, which suggests that most studies focus on targets that are, at best, indirectly related to illegal behavior. Most of the studies did not individualize their treatment procedures, applying a single method to the same target for all the subjects studied. At the completion of the program, two thirds of the studies showed significant changes with respect to target behaviors (e.g., academic achievement, observer ratings of behavior, self-reported adjustment), but unfortunately only half of the studies gave follow-up data beyond the termination of treatment. Five studies followed up their subjects for more than 2 years. Eleven (28% of the total) can claim success in that the experimental subjects recidivated significantly less than the untreated controls or comparison groups. Blackburn (1980) considered these results to be encouraging, but points to some problems with respect to interpreting the results.

First, only a minority of studies appeared to meet Logan's (1972) minimum methodological criteria, but of those five that did, all reported successful results. The second problem relates to the use of statistical criteria of success. That is, although some significant results were evident, the overall reduction in recidivism was often quite small.

Blackburn (1980) concludes, on the basis of his review, that psychological approaches can achieve some success with offenders but the extent of reduction in recidivism is quite limited. He examines three reasons why treatment effects have been so limited with offenders: (1) those treatment interventions with offenders are carried out in the wrong setting, (2) they are based on the wrong models of crime and psychological change, and (3) they focus on inappropriate targets.

Blackburn (1980) argues that penal institutions are commonly unsympathetic to therapeutic programs. This view is also expressed by Logan (1972), who maintains that the factor that commonly interferes with adequate design and implementation of research in the area is the politics of the institutional staff. Ross and Price (1976) similarly argue that the social climate and organizational structure of prisons inevitably hinder the successful implementation of behavioral programs. However, there is no evidence that rehabilitation programs are less successful in institutional settings than in open residential and community settings. This is clearly documented by the work of the Panel on Research on Rehabilitative Techniques (Martin, Sechrest, & Redner, 1981), which was discussed earlier.

The studies reviewed by Blackburn (1980) lead to similar conclusions, and he argues that the failures cannot be attributed solely to the setting. Furthermore, programs in extrainstitutional settings appear to fail for reasons similar to those for programs carried out in institutions. These, according to Blackburn (1980), include lack of control by therapists over administrative resources, poor motivation or sabotage on the part of the primary change agent, and failure to gain control over other sources of influence (e.g., the peer group). Blackburn's review also highlights the conclusion of Feldman (1977) that therapists *should* direct their attention to criminal behavior *per se*, rather than institutional behavior.

Thornton (1987) has recently reviewed the 38 out of 231 studies from the Lipton *et al.* (1975) paper that met the following criteria: (1)

recidivism was used as an outcome variable; (2) the experimental designs involved either random allocation or matching of subjects; (3) the experimental designs were classified as methodologically acceptable. Thirty-four of the 38 studies involved psychological therapy of some kind (e.g., counseling, intensive case work, psychotherapy). Thornton found that (1) significant differences emerged in about half the studies, (2) all but one of the studies with significant results involved psychological therapy, and (3) in contrast to the "nothing works" conclusions of Martinson (1974), those studies he and his colleagues reviewed that met "acceptable" scientific criteria indicate that psychological therapy can significantly reduce recidivism.

Garrett (1984, 1985) provides some of the most convincing evidence for the effectiveness of treatment with adjudicated delinquents in residential settings. She carried out meta-analyses on 111 studies that had used some form of control procedure and had been conducted between 1960 and 1983. Outcome measures included recidivism, psychological adjustment, institutional adjustment, and academic achievement. The overall average "effect size" (i.e, the amount that the treatment groups differed from the control group following treatment) was +.37 across treatments, settings, offense types, and outcome measures used. This means that the subjects who received treatment performed at the 64th percentile rank on the outcome measures in contrast with the 50th percentile for those not receiving any treatment. The importance of Garrett's meta-analysis is that it provides us with information about how much change has taken place in relation to "differential treatment." For example, improvement in psychological, institutional, and community adjustment was more noticeable than reduction in recidivism. Of all the treatments studied, cognitive-behavioral and contingency management programs were most effective.

Gottschalk, Davidson, Gensheimer, and Mayer (1987) provide a meta-analysis study to assess the size of treatment effects with delinquents in community settings. It was found that treatments in community settings generally had small effects on outcome. Gottschalk *et al.* conclude that community interventions with delinquents may be effective under certain circumstances (e.g., when the treatment is of sufficient duration and intensity and is properly implemented). A major problem with conducting meta-analysis studies on the treatment literature appears to be the inadequate reporting about the relevant research variables. Hopefully, in the future, studies will provide a more complete data base, which will help to establish through meta-analysis the specific effects of different treatment techniques or components.

Clarke (1985) recently reviewed (British) Home Office research into delinquency and prevention. The two main research questions were "How can crime and delinquency be prevented?" and "How can those delinquents who come to the attention of the authorities best be dealt with?" The evaluative research was in three separate stages, each distinguished by the methodology used: (1) prediction studies related to reconviction rates, (2) experimental studies of different types of personal treatment, and (3) "cross-institutional" studies.

Prediction Studies

The Home Office prediction studies had a number of objectives, including identifying high-risk groups, gaining further understanding about the causes of delinquency by studying variables associated with reconviction, and determining potentially effective treatments by comparing the risk of reconviction scores with eventual outcome.

According to Clarke (1985) the best example of this phase of research was the Mannheim-Wilkins Borstal (reform school) prediction study (Mannheim & Wilkins, 1955), which successfully identified variables (e.g., previous work record and previous criminal behavior) as being predictive of reconviction. In addition, the study produced some evidence that Borstals run on "open" lines were significantly more successful than "closed" ones. In another study, Hammond (1964) found that for first offenders, fines and then probation were more effective than being sent to Approved Schools. Unfortunately, these studies are limited in that there was no random allocation of subjects between treatments (Clarke, 1983).

Experimental Studies

During the 1960s, there was increased emphasis in American and British research on random allocation of subjects to different treatment groups. In one important British study (Clarke & Cornish, 1978), 280 boys sent to an "Approved School" (now called "Community Homes") over a 4-year period were randomly allocated into three different houses of the schools: (1) a "therapeutic community" based on the four principles of democratization, communalism, permissiveness, and reality confrontation suggested by Rapoport (1960); (2) a "control house" with a traditional paternalistic regime; and (3) boys considered "unsuitable" for the therapeutic community and control house. At 2-year follow-up, the reconviction rate for the three different houses was almost identical (i.e., about 70%). The reconviction rates for this particular Approved School are very similar to those found for similar juvenile institutions in Britain (Dunlop, 1974; Millham, Bullock & Cherrett, 1975; Brody, 1976), the United States (Lundman, 1984), and Iceland (Gudjonsson, 1982a).

Cross-Institutional Studies

In the third phase of treatment research, the Home Office research began to compare a number of institutions within the context of a single study. The first study into probation hostels was carried out by Sinclair (1971, 1975). It was found that there were marked differences between hostels with respect to residents' misbehavior (e.g., absconding, further offenses), which could not be accounted for by differences in intake characteristics and which provided evidence for the importance of hostel staff. When comparisons were made, using the Jesness Staff Attitudes Questionnaire (Jesness, 1965), it was found that the wardens with the facilities having the lowest rates of absconding were those who ran a strictly disciplined hostel, accompanied by expressed warmth toward the boys.

Further evidence for the importance of cross-institutional differences comes from the studies of Sinclair and Clarke (1973) and Dunlop (1974). In the former study, a small but significant relationship was found between absconding from Approved Schools and subsequent rate of reconviction. Dunlop interviewed several hundred boys in eight Approved Schools and followed them up for 5 years after their release. The results indicate that the schools that emphasized trade training and responsible behavior had lower rates of absconding and other kinds of misbehavior during residence and marginally lower reconviction rates at follow-up.

Clarke (1985) concludes that the three phases of Home Office treatment research suggest the following. First, *prediction studies* indicate that only a small proportion of the variance in reconviction can be explained on the basis of pretreatment factors for any group of offenders. The most important factors are age and history of offending. Second, the *treatment experiments* indicate that there is little difference in the long-term effectiveness of different types of intervention. Third, cross-institutional studies were able to identify some longer term treatment effects, but these were quite small and appeared to relate to misbehavior in the particular institution.

Kazdin (1987) reviewed the current status of treatment for antisocial behavior among children. He discusses the therapeutic focus and presence of major types of treatment and concludes that several promising techniques are currently available, including "parent management training" (PMT) and "functional family therapy" (FFT). The former technique is based on the assumption that conduct disorder is developed and maintained in the home by maladaptive parent–child interactions. The goal of treatment is to improve these maladaptive interactions and help parents develop prosocial behavior in the child. The technique appears to be particularly effective with children who have problems with aggression (Patterson, 1982).

Functional family therapy in some ways resembles PMT, but its emphasis is more on viewing the child's problems as serving some function within the family system. As in the case of PMT, the main problems are thought to relate to maladaptive interactional and communicative processes. The main goals of FFT are to make the family more aware of the function the conduct problems serves within the family and help identify solutions to interpersonal problems, to increase reciprocity and positive reinforcements among the family members, and to improve effective communication. Alexander and Parsons (1973) found FFT to be more effective in reducing recidivism among delinquents than some alternative treatments. In addition, the siblings of those treated by FFT showed significantly lower rates of referral to the juvenile courts (Klein, Alexander, & Parsons, 1977).

It is important to note that both PMT and FFT are principally based on social learning principles. It is to those that we now turn in more detail.

Nietzel (1979) reviews the status of rehabilitative programs derived from a social learning perspective in relation to reducing criminal behavior. Behavioral approaches with adult criminals in three settings (penal institutions, nonresidential therapies, and community programs) are described by Nietzel in some detail, and the conclusion he comes to is that behavioral techniques are reasonably effective with many types of criminal conduct and superior to most alternative techniques.

McGuire and Priestley (1985) provide a working manual for dealing with offenders. The importance of this work is the emphasis the authors place on treating offending behavior directly rather than focusing on peripheral convenience behaviors. They illustrate techniques aimed to help offenders bring about changes in their offense-related attitudes and behaviors. The main focus of treatment is to help offenders develop skills that facilitate their ability to resist peer group pressure, defuse tense situations, and acquire better self-control and decision-making skills. The psychological techniques recommended are largely based on a social learning theory approach.

SOCIAL LEARNING APPROACH

Stumphauzer (1986), in his book *Helping Delinquents Change*, provides an excellent account of how social learning theory can be used to modify delinquent behavior. According to this approach, "delinquent behavior is acquired through psychological learning principles in a social context, and changing delinquent behavior requires application and variation of the same principles also in a social context" (p. 6). Following his earlier work (1977), Stumphauzer developed a training manual based on some basic psychological principles such as "reinforcement" and "modelling" (aimed at increasing desirable behavior), "extinction," and "punishment" (aimed at decreasing undesirable behavior). Stumphauzer (1986) argues that "punishment alone is never the most effective method of changing delinquent behavior" and it should be used only in conjunction with other more effective social learning principles, such as positive reinforcement and modeling. He maintains that the types of punishment with the fewest ethical and legal problems are "time-out" from positive reinforcement and "response cost" (Stumphauzer, 1977). The latter commonly involves the loss of a reinforcer following the targetted delinquent behavior.

Positive reinforcement can be used in two different ways to modify delinquent behavior. First, instances and times when the delinquent behavior *does not occur* can be reinforced. Second, behavior *that is incompatible* with delinquent behavior can be reinforced. An example of the way positive reinforcement has been applied, with some success, is the case of Achievement Place-style homes for delinquents. Although such homes have achieved some success in the short term, as discussed earlier in this chapter, the long-term effects have been more pessimistic. Stumphauzer (1986) defends the use of such homes as alternatives to institutions on a cost-effectiveness basis and considers that they should be evaluated in the following ways: (1) the residents should be "hard-core" delinquents rather than predelinquents and petty offenders and (2) subjects should be *randomly* assigned to behavioral group homes and institutions so that proper scientific comparisons can be made.

Stumphauzer (1986) lists a number of disadvantages, in addition to cost, of institutional treatment of delinquents. First, the delinquent youths are removed from the "natural environment" to which they should learn to adapt. Second, offenders placed in institutional settings are exposed to delinquent peers who may encourage future offending through the processes of modeling and reinforcement. He cites the study of Buehler, Patterson, and Furniss (1966), which documents the importance of the peer group in shaping and controlling behavior.

In a series of three studies, Buehler *et al.* (1966) identified and measured social reinforcers given by staff and inmates during prosocial and antisocial behavior. Staff members were found to be inconsistent in their handling of the delinquent girls, alternatively rewarding and punishing them for the same type of behavior. The peer delinquents, on the other hand, consistently reinforced antisocial acts and "punished' or showed disappointment or a lack of interest of prosocial behavior. The reinforcement of the peer groups was for antisocial acts mainly communicated at nonverbal level.

We accept that peer behavior may be important on occasion in shaping and controlling antisocial acts, but believe that Stumphauzer (1986) places too much weight on the findings from the Beuhler *et al.* (1966) study. First, the studies do not demonstrate that peer group reinforcement increased the delinquent behavior of the group. All the findings indicate is that staff members in an institution tend to reinforce and punish behavior more indiscriminately than peer group members. Second, there is no data provided to indicate that the postrelease behavior of the subjects was at all affected by the reinforcement and punishment given by the peer group. Third, there are many methodological problems with the three studies, including small sample size, inadequate definition of methods used, and uncertain reliability of the observational techniques applied, which makes independent replication of the studies impossible and limits the generalizations of the findings. This does not mean that peer group pressure should be considered as unimportant in encouraging delinquent behavior. Indeed, there is empirical evidence that an association with delinquent peers is positively related with delinquency (e.g., Burkett & Jenson, 1975; Gudjonsson, 1982a; Skinner, 1986; Voss, 1964). Such findings support the "differential association" theory of Sutherland and Cressey (1978).

PUNISHMENT: DOES IT WORK?

The primary purpose of any punishment technique is to remove an unwanted response from the person's behavioral repertoire. Punishment techniques comprise two different types of negative sanctions. First, rewards and privileges may be withdrawn. Second, an aversive stimulus is presented (a verbal reprimand, physical punishment, being arrested, convicted, sent to prison). The former type of sanction is commonly seen in clinical and institutional settings where inappropriate or misbehavior results in removal from positive reinforcement (e.g., "time-out") and loss of certain privileges (e.g., not being allowed to go out or participate in social activities that would otherwise be permitted).

Punishment as a technique for behavioral change has met with considerable criticism in the literature. For example, as we mentioned earlier, Stumphauzer (1986) argues that punishment is the "least effective" way of changing delinquent behavior. In fact, he argues that on occasion an arrest and short-term detention may serve as a reward by increasing the status of the youth within the peer group (Stumphauzer, Aiken, & Veloz, 1977). When this occurs, the legal sanction functions as a reward rather than a punisher. Stumphauzer (1986) further asserts that one reason why punishment has traditionally been popular as a method of controlling criminal behavior is the "temporary suppression" effect that sometimes follows punishment.

We disagree with Stumphauzer's conclusion that positive reinforcement of desirable alternative behavior is invariable more effective than punishment in controlling delinquent behavior. Indeed, Walters and Grusec (1977) have shown that positive reinforcement has its own limitations as a technique for behavioral change and under certain conditions, it is less effective than punishment. The critical questions with regard to behavioral control are

1. What are the conditions that maximize the effectiveness of punishment?
2. What are the "side effects" of punishment techniques?
3. Is punishment more effective with some offenders than others? If so, can the critical components be identified?

When considering the general effectiveness of punishment in modifying behavior, it is important to remember that punishment has complex and varied effects on behavior (Church, 1963). It is therefore important to look at some of the conditions that determine the effectiveness of punishment. The circumstances that have been found to maximize the effectiveness of punishment are summarized by Azrin and Holz (1966) and Walters and Grusec (1977). The most important of these for the control of antisocial behavior are as follows:

1. The offender should not be able to escape the punishment.
2. The punishment should be as intense as possible. We would use the words "appropriately intense" because the intensity needs to be determined with reference to the seriousness and the nature of the offense rather than in isolation.
3. The punishment should be administered as soon as possible after the commission of the criminal act. The greater the delay between the criminal act and the punishment (e.g., arrest, conviction, sentence) the less effective the punishment is likely to be.
4. The punishment should be consistently applied. Continuous punishment is more effective in suppressing or eliminating undesirable behavior than intermittent punishment.
5. Attempts should be made to ensure that the delivery of the punishing stimulus is not differentially associated with the delivery of the reinforcement. Gudjonsson and Drinkwater (1986) describe a case in point where, during a time-out program, the punishment stimulus (time-out of reinforcement) acquired condi-

tioned reinforcing properties (i.e., sexual arousal and gratification).

The above points have important implications for crime control. Whereas the rewards gained from committing offenses are generally fairly immediately received, the potential punishment from arrest, conviction, and sentence are unpredictable and usually much delayed. The majority of offenders are never apprehended for their offenses and when they are, they are inconsistently dealt with by the police and the courts. One way of controlling crime would be to improve the detection rate and the certainty of a legal sanction. A recent approach that seems to have worked very well in Canada involves giving payments to anonymous informants. At present (Moon, 1987) there are 29 "Crime Stopper Programs" operating across Canada and they have drastically increased the number of offenders apprehended and the amount of stolen property recovered. Although in certain circumstances an arrest may act as a reward by enhancing the offender's peer group status (Stumphauzer, 1977), increased certainty of arrest is likely to act as a deterrent for most offenders. On occasion, the mere act of an arrest, without the likelihood of a conviction and sentence, may be sufficient to deter some people from further offending. For example, in Iceland, shoplifters are very rarely prosecuted but the mere fact that they have been arrested seems to deter them from further offending (Gudjonsson, 1982b). In a larger community, where the detection rate is lower and the arrest is more easily concealed from family and friends, legal sanctions may be much more important as a form of deterrent.

The extent to which punishment techniques have unwanted side effects has been reviewed by Walters and Grusec (1977) and more recently by Bandura (1986). The general effects of punishment, regardless of type, is to temporarily increase arousal and the vigor of responding. Physical punishment appears to have the strongest long-term side effects and may, through "negative modeling," reinforce aggressive behavior. A common example is that of children brought up by aggressive parents who tend to become assaultive with their own children when they grow up (Silver, Dublin, & Lourie, 1969). Bandura (1973) argues that punishment used for the purposes of social control may lead to collective aggression when grievances are justifiable. Two further unintended effects of punishment are worth mentioning. First, aversive punishment tends to result in avoidance of the punishing agent. On occasion, this interpersonal avoidance may reduce opportunities for constructive social influence. Second, legal sanctions may, in exceptional circumstances, create or exacerbate emotional disturbance and depression, resulting in the offender committing suicide.

It is evident that punishment is quite complex in its effects on behavior and it is therefore not surprising that punishment works with some offenders and not with others. Gray (1981) provides an interesting model about individual differences in the "susceptibility to punishment" and the "susceptibility to reward." The basic implications of Gray's model are that within Eysenck's neurotic-stable and introverted-extraverted dimensions, the neurotic-introvert is most sensitive to potential punishment whereas the neurotic-extravert is most sensitive to the potential of reward. The stable-introvert and the stable-extravert would be relatively unresponsive to either punishment or reward. Of course, most individuals would fall within the average scores for neuroticism and extraversion, being moderately susceptible to both punishment and reward. Gray's dimensions of anxiety (ANX-D) and impulsivity (Imp-D) are rotated 45 degrees from Eysenck's two dimensions. The individual high on Imp-D (the neurotic-extravert) would be expected to be highly sensitive to the rewards gained from criminal activity and relatively insensitive to the threat of punishment if apprehended.

Gray's model could be extended to look at the susceptibility to punishment and reward within a treatment context. That is, many current comprehensive treatment programs with offenders have two separate objectives. The undesirable antisocial behavior can be suppressed by aversive-conditioning procedures while alternative desirable prosocial behaviors are reinforced. When this is possible, the effects of the punishment paradigm can be very durable (Walters & Grusec, 1977). The balance between the aversive and reward components of the treatment may need to be considered with regard to individual differences, such as differences in introversion-extraversion and neuroticism. A case where such a consideration was helpful is reported by Gudjonsson (1987). It involved a middle-aged woman who had over a 20-year history of shoplifting. She had been treated unsuccessfully in the past by an aversive-conditioning procedure. Her high extraversion score and a moderately high neuroticism score on the Eysenck Personality Questionnaire indicated that she might be more responsive to a treatment package that focused on reinforcing alternative purposeful and constructive behavior rather than suppressing her shoplifting urges by aversive procedures. This proved to be the case and the woman was successfully treated.

The failure of extraverts to respond to and learn from punishment has been interpreted within the framework of deficient "passive avoidance learning" (Patterson, Kosson, & Newman, 1987). The implications of the work in this area are that extraverts are particularly unresponsive to punishment when they are required to inhibit behavior that has previously been associated with reward.

COGNITIVE–BEHAVIORAL TECHNIQUES

There is growing evidence that, among the psychological methods, cognitive-behavioral techniques are most effective in reducing delinquency and adult offending.

In their detailed analysis of the difference between successful and unsuccessful intervention programs with offenders, Ross and Fabiano (1985) present a conceptual model for delinquency and rehabilitation programs. The major premise of the model is that cognitive variables (i.e., what and how offenders think, their views of the world, their reasoning, values, understanding of others, and their coping skills) play an important part in criminal behavior. Ross and Fabiano argue that criminal behavior is associated with delayed or impaired cognitive development and the enhancement of cognitive skills decreases criminal behavior. The most likely explanation is that adequate cognitive skills protect the person from engaging in criminal activity. Ross and Fabiano suggest that this may be achieved by the cognitive skills insulating the individual from personal, social, and environmental pressures toward criminal behavior.

The major implication of the Ross and Fabiano model is that offenders require individual programs depending on their idiosyncratic characteristics and problems, the nature of the treatment setting, and the goal of the intervention. The specific skills that are required for social competence and the deficits they are designed to overcome are given in Table 20.

It can be seen from Table 20 that there are a number of varied cognitive skills that can be modified in order to improve the offender's social competence. What we do not know is what specific type of cognitive inadequacy is most commonly associated with a particular type of offender or type of offense. It is likely that some of the seven skill areas listed in Table 20 are interrelated, such as "Social Perspective Taking" and "Values." A further problem is that we do not know what proportion of offenders are likely to suffer from cognitive inadequacy. It would surely be erroneous to assume that all offenders have some type of cognitive deficit, nor is it likely that all those who are cognitively inadequate will become offenders. Ross and Fabiano speculate that young and persistent offenders are more likely to suffer from cognitive inadequacy. They point out that many of the studies that have found a positive relationship between cognitive functioning and crime involve recidivists.

It is also worth noting that cognitive–behavior techniques form an important part of the management of anger aggression. Howells (1987) has just completed a detailed review of the effectiveness of anger-man-

TABLE 20. Cognitive Skills for Social Competence

Interpersonal problem solving	Cognitive skill	Social perspective-taking	Critical reasoning	Values	Meta-cognition	Self-control
Deficits in: –problem recognition	Deficits in: –concrete	Deficits in: –egocentric	Deficits in: –thinking errors	Deficits in: –egocentric	Deficits in: –limited awareness of their thinking	Deficits in: –impulsive
–consequential thinking –alternative thinking –means-end reasoning	–external –present oriented	–non-empathetic –role taking		–non-empathetic		–non-reflective

Note. From *Time to Think: A Cognitive Model of Delinquency Prevention and Offender Rehabilitation* by R. R. Ross and E. A. Fabiano. Johnson City, N.J.: Institute of Social Sciences and Arts, 1985, p. 179.

TABLE 21. The Outcome of Programs in Terms of the Presence and Absence of Cognitive Program Components

	Treatment	
Outcome	Cognitive	Noncognitive
Effective	15 (94%)	10 (29%)
Ineffective	1 (6%)	24 (71%)
Total	16 (100%)	34 (100%)

Note. From *Time to Think: A Cognitive Model of Delinquency Prevention and Offender Rehabilitation* by R. R. Ross and E. A. Fabiano. Johnson City, N.J.: Institute of Social Sciences and Arts, 1985, p. 114.

agement methods, based on Novaco's (1975, 1978) model of anger and anger management. He concludes that the studies carried out so far are encouraging and indicate the cognitive–behavioral intervention with angry aggressiveness is likely to become very important in the future.

Ross and Fabiano give the results of a differential component analysis of 25 effective and 25 ineffective treatment programs with offenders. The results can be seen in Table 21.

It is clear from Table 21 that the presence of cognitive program components was significantly associated with effective outcome ($\chi^2 = 18.02$, df=1, $p < .001$). Indeed, out of the 16 programs, only one was ineffective compared with 71% of the programs that did not contain cognitive components as treatment targets. The findings give strong support for the effectiveness of cognitive training with offenders. Ross and Fabiano cite the meta-analysis study of Garret (1984) as further evidence for the importance of cognitive training in the rehabilitation of offenders. Garret's study attempted to determine which program characteristics were associated with the most successful outcome. Out of 111 programs reported between 1960 and 1983, Garret found that the cognitive-behavioral programs had been most successful.

According to Ross and Fabiano, successful cognitive-behavior programs emphasize such techniques as (1) rational self-analysis (teaching people to critically assess their thinking), (2) self-control (teaching people to learn to think before acting), (3) means–end reasoning (teaching offenders more appropriate ways of satisfying their needs), and (4) critical thinking (teaching offenders to think rationally, logically, and objectively). One of the most important training components is considered to be interpersonal cognitive problem solving (see Table 20), which teaches people how to utilize prosocial rather than antisocial ways of coping with interpersonal conflict.

INDIVIDUAL DIFFERENCES IN TREATMENT EFFECTIVENESS

There is considerable controversy in the literature about whether or not there are predictable individual differences in response to different intervention methods. There clearly are individual differences in the sense that some offenders reoffend and others do not. The extent to which this may be due to subsequent differences in situational variables, such as opportunity and environmental pressure, or motivational and personality factors, is not clear. Palmer (1978) indicates that there may be certain conditions associated with the offender, therapist, or treatment setting that can potentially facilitate positive results. What exactly these variables are remains to be determined in future research.

Martinson (1976) argues that there is no point in looking for differential effects of treatment before it is established that one has an effective treatment. Other authors, for example, Rutter and Giller (1983), view the examination of differential effects as part of the tests of efficacy, and one should not assume that an intervention must, to some extent, work for everybody. Our view is that individual differences in response to different treatments is an important area to be researched as certain treatments may be effective only with certain selected individuals. Evidence for this comes from a recent study by Copas, O'Brien, Roberts, and Whiteley (1984). They followed up, after 3 and 5 years, "personality disordered" patients admitted to a therapeutic community in England and found a number of variables that facilitated positive outcome (i.e., no subsequent criminal conviction or psychiatric hospital admission) such as high anxiety and intropunitiveness, having had only one previous conviction, and at least 6 months' treatment in the therapeutic community. In personality terms, the extrapunitive neurotic had the poorest outcome. The finding is consistent with the conclusions of Rutter and Giller (1983) that intensive counseling is likely to be of value only with rather anxious, introspective youths who are aware of their personal problems and want help with them.

Shaw (1974) and Sinclair, Shaw, and Troop (1974) found that highly introverted prisoners serving long-term sentences responded better to casework counseling than extraverts, which was reflected in significantly lower reconviction rates at follow-up. In a subsequent study by Fowler (1978), this finding was not confirmed for short-term prisoners.

There is some evidence from a study by Rahman and S. B. G. Eysenck (1978) that psychoticism, as measured by the EPQ, is important in the treatment of neurotic patients. Patients with high P scores took significantly longer to improve and doctors rated them as harder to treat at final assessment. The main treatment given was psychotherapy. There was some tendency for the P score to be lowered by antidepressants, making the subjects more responsive to psychotherapy. Lane (1977) found a token economy behavior therapy to be the most appropriate treatment for troublesome children. In a more recent study, Lane (1987) looked at the relationship between failure of behavior therapy and P scores among conduct-disordered children. The P scale for a group of 100 children was found to correlate negatively with both short-term and long-term follow-up. This indicates that psychoticism, as measured by EPQ, plays an important part in the outcome of behavior therapy.

MENTAL ILLNESS AND CRIME

There is no doubt that the mentally ill do sometimes act in a criminal manner, and on many occasions convicted criminals are found to be suffering from psychiatric problems. However, this does not mean that there is a causal relationship between the mental disorder and the criminal behavior because both the mental disorder and the criminal behavior may occur coincidentally within the same individual.

Studies looking at the relationship between mental disorder and crime have tended to be of two kinds. First, a large number of studies have monitored mental disorder among various criminal groups. The second group of studies have monitored the criminal behavior among various mentally disordered groups. The two major methodological problems with all these studies is that mental disorder and crime are differently defined, and it is very difficult in most instances to establish a satisfactory link between mental disorder and crime.

Prins (1980) summarized a number of studies that have examined the prevalence of psychiatric disorder in penal institutions. He grouped the studies according to type of mental disorder (i.e., psychosis, mental subnormality, psychopathy, neurosis, and alcoholism) and showed that substantial disparities in the reported percentages exist between studies. The disparity was evident for the diagnosis of psychopathy (5.6% to 70%) and alcoholism (11% to 80%) and lowest for neurosis (2% to 7.9%), psychosis (0.5% to 26%), and mental subnormality (2.4% to 28%). Gunn, Robertson, Dell, and Way (1978), in their study of psychiatric disturbance in two English prisons (Grendon and Wandsworth), found that about one third of the criminals suffered from marked psychiatric disorder. More recently, Monahan and Monahan (1986) argue that mentally disordered offenders in the United States comprise 3.2% of the institutionalized offender population.

The disparities between the different studies could be related to at least four different factors: (1) different definitions of mental disorder and crime, (2) different penal setting, (3) different offender groups, and (4) different assessment points in time (e.g., pretrial, at time of admission to prison, after having been in prison for a while).

We indicated in Chapter 6 that a very small proportion of all offenders go to prison and they are therefore likely to comprise a rather specialized group of offenders. Certainly, they are extremely unlikely to give a representative indication about mental disorder in the general offender population. For example, there is some evidence that psychiatrically disturbed offenders are likely to gravitate toward institutions (prison, mental hospitals), whereas stable offenders will not (Howells, 1982).

The type of institution studied, the offenders, and the nature of their offense may be relevant to the diagnosis of mental disorder. First, different institutions may admit different types of offenders. For example, the regime at Grendon Prison in Britain is based on a modified therapeutic community model and has its own selection criteria (Gunn *et al.*, 1978). Second, the more serious the offense committed the more likely the offender is to be diagnosed as mentally disordered (Petursson & Gudjonsson, 1981). Third, institutions may cause some offenders a great deal of stress and increase the likelihood that they will develop mental disorder while in prison (e.g., Gunn *et al.*, 1978).

Studies investigating the frequency of criminal behavior among mentally disordered patients have not consistently shown a higher rate for mental patients (Howells, 1982). There is some indication of an elevated risk for mental patients, but this seems to be due to a high rate of prior criminality in a small proportion of mental patients rather than the mental illness itself (Rabkin, 1979). Monahan and Steadman (1983) argue that the factors associated with crime among the mentally disordered are similar to those associated with crime among other groups (e.g., age, gender, jail, prior criminal behavior, and social class). Likewise, factors associated with mental disorder among criminal offenders are similar to those associated with mental disorder in other groups (e.g., age, social class, previous history of mental disorder).

Once these demographic variables have been controlled for, there appears to be no significant relationship between mental illness and crime. However, it must be remembered that group comparisons ignore individual differences. This means that in some instances mental disorder may reduce offenders' propensity to crime, whereas in other cases mental disorder may be strongly associated with criminal behavior. Particular diagnostic categories (e.g., schizophrenia, depressive illness) may be associated with an elevated risk of offending, but the overall rate of criminal behavior (e.g., violent behaviors) remains quite low (e.g., Hafner & Boker, 1982; Prins, 1980). Even within specific diagnostic categories, there may be large individual variations. For example, research by Fottrell (1980) showed that depressives had a low propensity for violence in hospital settings. Howells (1982) interprets this finding to suggest that depressives are most likely to become violent in intimate relationships where they are unable to assert themselves appropriately during a prolonged period of time.

What can be concluded is that the relationship between criminal behavior and mental disorder is very complex, and it is the exception rather than the rule for criminal behavior to be largely attributable in a simple way to a specific psychiatric diagnosis. Gudjonsson and MacKeith (1983), in their discussion of the relationship between mental illness and crime, make the point that different patients suffering from similar illnesses, even with similar symptomatology and delusions, often resort to entirely different modes of behavior, which highlights the importance of social, interpersonal, and personality factors even when florid illness is present.

CONCLUSIONS

In this chapter, we have reviewed studies regarding the prevention and control of delinquency and adult offending. We have done this by focusing on the three major prevention and control intervention points identified by Lundman (1984). These are *predelinquent*, *preadjudication*, and *postadjudication* interventions. In some instances the distinction between these three points of intervention has proved quite arbitrary as similar techniques and programs have been applied at more than one level. Nevertheless, the identification of different intervention points provides a useful conceptual framework for presenting and interpreting general findings.

The primary objective of predelinquent interventions is the prevention of offending in the first place. This requires being able to readily identify potential offenders at a very early stage or the social and environmental forces that precipitate delinquent behavior. The best predictors of the onset of offending are parental child-rearing techniques, a family history of criminal behavior, the child's educational, intellectual, and cognitive skills, and early troublesome behavior exhibited by the child.

Studies attempting to provide counseling and social work for children and juveniles "at risk" and efforts to prevent delinquency by setting up community programs, have met with poor results. Some encouraging results were obtained in the Wincroft Youth Project, but the difference in offending between the experimental and control group was quite small.

The most encouraging results with respect to predelinquent prevention have come from preschool enrichment programs. The long-term effects of such programs appear to be multifaceted. That is, not only does school performance improve but employment records after leaving school are also markedly improved. The effects on future offending are impressive, particularly with respect to the persistency of offending (Berrueta-Clement *et al.*, 1984). It could be that preschool enrichment programs are important because they provide the child with cognitive skills that help him or her to cope more appropriately with personal and social pressures and conflicts that commonly precipitate delinquency.

There have been some attempts made to prevent offending by applying situational and opportunity-reducing measures, generally through "target hardening" (i.e., making offending more difficult to achieve). The effectiveness of such environmental manipulation is uncertain at the moment.

Preadjudication intervention comprises such methods as "diversion," that is, offenders are directed away from detention and juvenile proceedings by providing them, as an alternative, with either some kind of crisis intervention or formal caution (warning). The limited evidence available indicates that diversion and police cautioning have not been markedly effective in reducing recidivism and may indeed have resulted in "net widening" (i.e., increasing the number of juveniles formally dealt with).

Postadjudication intervention comprises ways of reducing recidivism once the person has been convicted of an offense. Many innovative techniques and programs have been developed and implemented during the past two or three decades, either as an alternative to incarceration and other judicial sentences or in addition to it. It seems clear from the literature that the majority of programs have been unsuccessful in significantly reducing recidivism. However, we do not believe that this indicates that nothing works. Indeed, when one compares the programs that succeed with those that fail, there is a clear trend for the former techniques to comprise a range of different treatment components, often involving a combination of more than one technique. Cognitive–behavioral techniques seem to offer the greatest promise for the future. Here the offenders' cognitive deficits (i.e., their reasoning, expectations, understanding, and attributions) and lack of social competence need to become the focus of the treatment intervention.

Finally, we have emphasized the importance of individual differences in treatment responsiveness. This is an important but neglected area. The available evidence suggests that treatment programs are most effective when they are made to suit the offender's individual needs and personality. The balance between the aversive and reward components of the treatment should be considered with regard to individual differences, such as introversion–extraversion and neuroticism.

CHAPTER EIGHT

Sexual Deviations

INTRODUCTION: RECENT TRENDS

What constitutes sexually deviant behavior varies considerably across different societies and is subject to changes over time. When such behavior violates cultural norms and seriously offends its members, legal sanctions may be developed and implemented. The behavior thereby becomes labeled as a "crime."

There have been very marked changes with respect to sexuality in Western societies during the past 25 years as the result of "sexual liberalization" (Schmidt, 1983). Sexuality has become more freely expressed, attitudes toward sexual minorities have improved, and there have been legal changes to accommodate this increased "liberalisation." The trend in law has been to focus on crimes of sexual violence and pay less attention to sexual conduct involving consenting adults and where there has been no violence. This is most clearly seen with respect to the legal changes that have taken place in cases of homosexual conduct among consenting adults and the increased emphasis on severe prison sentences for males convicted of violent sexual assaults (Walmsley, 1986).

Sexual deviance is clearly a social rather than a medical phenomenon and comprises both victimful (e.g., rape, pedophilia) and victimless (e.g., fetishism, consenting sadomasochistic acts) behaviors. For this reason, and in view of the sensitive nature of sexual matters generally, the investigation of and intervention in sexual deviations raise many moral and ethical issues that are not easily resolved.

Sexual deviations are of interest to mental health professionals for a variety of reasons, including the common finding that the behavior arouses great concern among the people who have to deal with sexual deviates (Bluglass, 1982). West (1987) states that, unlike ordinary criminals, many sex offenders believe there is something wrong with them and therefore welcome professional help. However, only a very small proportion of people who commit sexually deviant acts do so because of mental illness. Even among the more serious sexual offenders few carry out such acts because of diagnostically clear mental illness problems. For example, Able, Rouleau, and Cunningham-Rathner (1986) estimate that fewer than 5% of males charged with sexually aggressive acts do so because of underlying psychotic illness. This does not, of course, rule out the possibility of high P scores. We are dealing with a dimension of personality not a categorical either–or diagnosis.

Sexual deviations are particularly poorly documented among females. The literature on female deviations is very limited but it is evident that females are rarely charged with sexual offenses (O'Connor, 1987). In the case of adolescent sex offenders, girls account for less than 5% of all cases (Davis and Leitenberg, 1987). When females are charged with sexually aggressive acts, they are usually alleged to be accomplices of males, acting to lure the victim into the proximity of the male who subsequently forces himself on the victim (Abel *et al.*, 1986). In view of the relatively infrequent reporting of sexual deviations among females, accompanied by apparent lack of academic and clinical interest, very little is known about the actual frequency, determinants, maintenance, and consequences of their deviations, other than prostitution and related offenses (Bargon, 1982). We shall therefore mainly focus on sexual deviations among males but when necessary refer to the relevant and available female literature. In view of the academic and clinical interest that male sexual deviations commonly attract, a considerable amount of empirical research has been carried out in the area during the past 20 years. This has been a very desirable development because the empirical findings are beginning to replace the unsubstantiated theories and speculations of the past.

DEFINITIONS AND CONCEPTUALIZATIONS

The terms *sexual deviation*, *sexual variation*, *sexual anomaly*, and *parophilia* have similar meanings and refer to some kind of unusual imagery or acts necessary for sexual excitement. The particular fantasy or act has to be repeatedly preferred as the exclusive method of achieving the sexual excitement (American Psychiatric Association, 1980). There is controversy among experts whether a diagnosis should be given on the basis of some unusual sexual thought and physiological arousal without it being accompanied by some tangible behavioral action (Dietz, 1986). A person who has repeated sexual fantasies of a deviant nature (e.g., rape, pedophilia) commits no offense unless he or she acts on those fantasies, no matter how deviant they may be. However, if he or she is very distressed by the fantasy, sexual preference, or physiological arousal, then clinicians may classify the deviation as "abnormal" on the basis of what it signifies to the sexually deviant individual (Gudjonsson, 1986).

There are many reasons why a sexually deviant person may seek help or be referred to treatment for his or her deviations. The most common reason is that the person, a member of his or her family, or a judicial agency are concerned about the person's sexual fantasies or practices. This usually happens after the person has been arrested for a sexual offense. There may even have been several previous convictions for similar offenses.

Walmsley and White (1979) specify five circumstances whereby sexual behavior constitutes an offense. These relate to nonconsensual sexual behavior (e.g., rape), sexual behavior with a person below the age of consent (e.g., pedophilia), homosexual behavior carried out in public, homosexual behavior with a male below the age of 21, and sexual behavior specifically prohibited by law (e.g., incest, bestiality, sodomy with a female). Not all traditionally classified sexually deviant behaviors are illegal, but many are. Examples of legal sexually deviant behaviors are fetishism and transvestism. The former occurs in private whereas the latter may occur in public but it is usually considered to be a fairly nonthreatening conduct. There are over 30 separate indictable sexual offenses, most of which are addressed in the Sexual Offenses Act of 1956, representing about 1% of all offenses recorded by the police in England and Wales (Craft, Craft, & Spencer, 1984). In the United States, laws sometimes take on a bizarre character, as in Georgia where oral sex is prohibited.

The sexually deviant individual typically exhibits sexual arousal or responses to inappropriate people (e.g., minors), objects (e.g., leather, rubber, garments), or activities (e.g., exposure in public, coercion, violence). Deficient sexual and social responses to appropriate people or situations may also be present in such individuals. Indeed it is evident from clinical data that deviant sexual behavior is not simply a problem of sexual arousal to deviant stimuli (Crawford, 1979). The sexually deviant individual, although not mentally ill, often has a wide range of problems related to sexual, social, and interpersonal skills, in addition to broader personality and attitudinal difficulties. For this reason, it is important to carry out a comprehensive assessment on such individuals so that their particular behavioral patterns, difficulties, and deficits are fully understood. Descriptions of specific assessment methods are beyond the scope of this book; Gudjonsson (1986) provides a detailed account of the different techniques available for the comprehensive assessment of sexually deviant individuals.

TABLE 22. Stimulus–Response Matrix of Sexual Behavior

The stimuli	The responses
1. Body characteristics	1. Intercourse
A. Mature	A. Vaginal
B. Immature	B. Anal
C. Male shape	2. Oral–genital
D. Female shape	3. Masturbation
2. Gender behavior	
A. Masculine	4. Exhibiting
B. Feminine	5. Peeping
3. Other behaviors	
A. Pleasure–pain	6. Rape
B. Dominance–submission	7. Touching
C. Courtship	8. Frottage
4. Miscellany	9. Obscene calls
A. Fetish—garments, hair, fire, etc.	10. Cross gender dressing
	A. Transvestism
	B. Transsexualism

Note. From *Sexual Strands: Understanding and Treating Sexual Anomalies in Men* by R. Langevin. London: Faber & Faber, 1983, p. 2.

One problem with the scientific study of sexual deviations has been the lack of an adequate conceptual framework for the assessment and treatment of the phenomena. For this reason, Langevin (1983) has recently organized what is known about sexual deviations into an important conceptual model, referred to as a "stimulus response matrix." The model seeks to answer two separate questions:

1. *What* is the sexually deviant male erotically reacting to?
2. *How* is he reacting?

The first question refers to the stimulus properties of the model, whereas the latter focuses on the specific responses and actions of the individual who has been aroused erotically.

Table 22 shows the range of stimuli and responses that Langevin (1983) considers important with respect to sexual behavior. The content of the stimulus response matrix may need to be elaborated as the result of further research into the nature of sexual deviations but the model provides the researcher and clinician with a conceptual framework that seems to cover most deviations and helps to focus assessment and treatment evaluations and organize data. A detailed description of the content of the stimulus response matrix is given by Langevin (1983) and it is not necessary to discuss these specifically here in order to appreciate the implications of the model. What is important is that each sexual deviation is viewed as a preference for certain stimuli and a preference to respond "orgasmically" in certain ways. Each sexual deviation may produce a range of stimulus–response connections that are of both theoretical and clinical significance. The most salient stimuli and responses for a few common sexual deviations and the accompanying psychological characteristics will become evident below.

Before discussing the individual types of sexual deviation it is important to remember that some sexual deviations are interrelated. That is, the presence of one increases the likelihood that the individual will develop others. Flor-Henry (1987) argues that this is due to the fact that many sexual deviations (e.g., voyeurism, exhibitionism, fetishism, mild sadomasochism) represent fragments of normal sexuality. In normal males, they are peripheral to sexual arousal but in sexual deviations they become central and exclusive.

TYPES OF SEXUAL DEVIATIONS

Genital Exhibitionism

Genital exhibitionism refers to a male who exposes his genitals to an unsuspecting female outside an intimate relationship for the purpose of achieving sexual excitement or to insult the female. It is one of the most common sexual offenses and is legally classified as "indecent exposure." It accounts for about one third of all recorded sexual offenses in Canada, the United States, and England and Wales (Dietz, Cox, & Wegener, 1986). Exhibitionism is the second most common sexual deviation seen in psychiatric hospitals in England (Bancroft, 1976), although little is known about the prevalence in the population.

West (1987) quotes recent findings from a National Population Survey in Canada, in which nearly 20% of the females questioned had been unwilling witnesses to indecent exposure. In a British study of 100 psychiatric female staff (Gittleson, Eacott, & Mehta, 1978), 44% reported having been victims of indecent exposure. From these surveys, it seems that adolescent and prepubertal girls are more commonly exposed to.

Exhibitionists are typically seen in psychiatric hospitals only after they have been apprehended for their conduct. Only between 15% and 25% of all indecent exposures are reported to the police and detected recidivism rates vary from 17% to 41% depending on the study (Dietz *et al.*, 1986). Genital exposure in females is very rare and is generally associated with mental retardation or mental illness (Hollender, Brown & Roback, 1977). This is interesting when one considers that male exhibitionists tend to be reasonably intelligent (Mohr, Turner, & Jerry, 1964).

West (1987) argues on the basis of data from the National Survey in Canada mentioned above that indecent exposure is more common among females than previously thought, but such incidents are very rarely reported to the police.

Genital exhibitionism, which appears rare outside Europe and America (Rooth, 1973a), is viewed by some authors (e.g., Gayford, 1981) as a protest against Victorian gentility and sexual repression and causes more nuisance than danger to society. Rooth (1971) described exhibitionists as "immature" young men who are reluctant to accept responsibility.

With respect to the stimulus response matrix, there is experimental evidence that the stimulus choice for the exhibitionist involves a physically mature female similar to the choice of normal males (Langevin, 1983). Many exhibitionists are married and appear to have adequate heterosexual social skills and experiences, but for some reason have a preference for being watched while masturbating, indicating some tendency toward narcissism. However, narcissism has not been systematically studied in exhibitionists and no consistent differences between them and normal controls have been found with respect to personality traits.

In a study of 30 exhibitionists, Rooth (1973b) found some overlap between exhibitionism and pedophilia but a history of sexual violence was exceptional. Such an overlap is not supported by the recent work of Myers and Berah (1983), on which exhibitionists were found to be significantly younger, came from more stable family backgrounds, had superior school and work records, and had done less heavy drinking than pedophiles. In addition, only 4% of the exhibitionists had been intoxicated at the time of their offense, compared with 49% of the pedophiles. The findings suggest that pedophiles' aberrant sexual behavior may be more associated with alcohol than that of exhibitionists. It may be that, as McCreary (1975) has shown, abnormal personality features among exhibitionists are evident only among chronic recidivists. Apprehension and court appearance seem to have a strong deterrent effect on the majority of indecent exposures (Gebhard, Gagnon, Pomeroy, & Christenson, 1965).

Flor-Henry (1987) has recently reported EEG and neuropsychological abnormalities in a group of exhibitionists. There were reduced "overall EEG coherence, slower oscillations and reduced intra- and interhemispheric phase relations bilaterally" (p. 75). Most of the effects were seen in the alpha band and none emerged in the beta frequencies. The neuropsychological tests carried out on 109 sex offenders showed an overall pattern of cerebral dysfunction in the bilateral frontotemporal (left→right) area. In the case of 23 exhibitionists, the dysfunction was most discrete, giving strong support for "focal left frontotemporal dysfunction."

Fetishism

Fetishism refers to the repeated use of inanimate objects for achieving sexual excitement. The fetishes often include female clothing and may include rubber and leather (Gosselin & Wilson, 1980). Fetishes are common in normal males as a means of achieving arousal. Fetishism is a private activity that may interfere with "normal" sexual activity and therefore cause the person to seek help. However, fetishists are rarely seen in clinical settings, which means that there are few studies and empirical findings available. There is evidence that fetishism is a conditioned response (Rachman, 1966), but it is unlikely to be the whole explanation as males are much more likely to develop fetishism than females. Temporal lobe abnormality has been associated with fetishism (Kolarsky, Freund, Machek, & Polak, 1967; Epstein, 1969). Gosselin and Wilson (1980) studied sexual fantasies among sadomasochists, fetishists, transvestites, and controls. The fetishistic group (comprising rubberites and leatherites) showed a high degree of sadomasochistic fantasy, establishing important similarities in fantasy between fetishists and sadomasochists.

Fetishism is not a criminal offense but some fetishists are arrested and brought to the attention of mental health professionals because of the theft of female clothing.

Homosexuality

Homosexuality is an erotic preference for a person of the same sex. Homosexual behavior is quite common particularly among males and may occur in the absence of settled homosexual orientation (Kinsey, Pomeroy, & Martin, 1948). Kinsey and his colleagues found that 37% of American white males had had some homosexual experience to the point of orgasm since adolescence. About 10% had been almost exclusively homosexual for at least 3 years between ages 16 and 55; 4% appeared to remain exclusively homosexual all their lives. They presumably represented men with an established erotic preference for a member of their own sex. The figures for females were much lower than for males but are unlikely to be entirely comparable (West, 1983).

Bancroft (1983) cogently argues that the true incidence of homosexuality may be impossible to obtain and gives a clear account of the many problems involved in interpreting Kinsey's data. The law with respect to homosexuality has changed in some countries, including Britain, during the past 20 years, making homosexual acts in private between consenting adults no longer a criminal offense. Within mental health classification, homosexuality is nowadays seen more as a "sexual orientation disturbance" than a psychological entity. Langevin (1983) has looked at the erotic profile of the "typical" homosexual and states that he responds sexually more to a mature male body and to a lesser extent the developing and immature male body. He generally shows some feminine interests and behaviors and a moderate degree of feminine gender identity. His preferred outlets are through oral-genital contact, mutual masturbation, and anal intercourse. Homosexuality has not been found to be associated with any particular psychiatric abnormality (Langevin, 1983).

The causes of homosexuality are unknown. West (1987) argues that both biological and environmental factors are relevant in varying proportions, according to the type of homosexual behavior being considered.

Incest

In England and Wales, it is an offense for a man to have sexual intercourse with a woman whom he knows to be his granddaughter, daughter, sister, or mother. A woman commits incest if she is of, or above, the age of 16 and with consent allows her grandfather, father, brother, or son to have sexual intercourse with her. About 300 cases of incest are brought to the attention of the British police annually and the conviction rate is about 50% (Prins, 1986). The custodial rate for adults in England and Wales convicted of incest between 1976 and 1980 was 72% (Walmsley, 1984). Katz and Mazur (1979) have estimated that about 90% of all incest cases are undetected. In reported cases, the majority involve intercourse between father and pubescent or postpubescent daughter (Weiner, 1964). The second largest number of reported cases involves sexual intercourse between brother and sister. Mother–son, father–son, and multiple relationships account for only 2 to 3% of cases.

Incestuous behavior commonly indicates interpersonal problems within the family and Prins (1986) has identified five incest-promoting situations (overcrowding, impaired intelligence, absence of wife, aggressive and dominating father, and "object fixation"). Maisch (1972), in a detailed study of 78 German incest cases, found that the major difference between incest and other forms of child molestation was its extended duration. That is, it was common for the fathers to have sexually assaulted their daughters on many previous occasions, commonly beginning at a young age by fondling and progressing to full sexual intercourse as the daughter becomes older.

The empirical evidence on incest is very scarce because of a number of methodoligical problems (Meiselman, 1978). Incestuous men in general seem to have a normal erotic profile (Langevin, 1983). That is, their sexual preference involves the appropriate sexual stimuli and responses and it is the nature of the socially defined relationship that generates the legal problem. However, although not predominant, some incestuous fathers are pedophilic, exhibit serious violent behavior, and abuse alcohol and drugs (Langevin, Handy, Russon, & Day, 1985).

Pedophilia

Strictly speaking, the term *pedophilia* means "love of children" and in its broadest sense refers to a sexual act (sodomy, intercourse, indecent assault, gross indecency) performed against a person below the age of consent, this being 16 for heterosexual behavior and 21 for homosexual behavior. Genital touching seems to be the most common sexual outlet among pedophiles but other sexual behaviors are also evident (Langevin, Hucker, Ben-Aron, Purins, & Hook, 1985). Academics, clinicians, and researchers generally do not rely on the legal criteria for consent but there is uncertainty about the age used to distinguish a "child" from an "adult." Various authors have suggested from 12 to 18 years as a cutoff point, which has made it difficult to compare the results from different studies. With respect to the Clarke Sexual History questionnaire (Langevin, 1985), the term *pedophilia* is used to refer to sexual encounters with children 12 years or younger (i.e., prepubertal). The terms *hebephilia* and *ephebilia* apply to children, male and female respectively, between the ages of 13 to 15 (i.e., those who are pubertal or in the process of physical maturity). Bancroft (1983) also considers the age of 12 as being important in distinguishing pedophilia offenders from others in the case of female victims, but suggests that the comparable age for boys is 14 years. According to DSM–III, the essential feature of pedophilia is "the act or fantasy of engaging in sexual activity with prepubertal children as a repeatedly preferred or exclusive method of achieving sexual excitement" (American Psychiatric Association, 1980).

Three further potentially confusing factors need to be considered when studying and treating pedophiles. First, one may need to separate "incest offenders" from pedophiles as the former exhibit two types of "violation," that is, sexually interacting with a minor of one's own kin. Second, pedophiles can be heterosexual, homosexual, or bisexual. Each group may have different etiologies and erotic profiles and require different treatment approaches. The proportion of pedophiles who choose a male victim may in some instances, be as high as 30% or more compared with the 5% of adult males who choose an adult male partner (see Quinsey, 1986, for a review). Third, some men who sexually assault children erotically prefer adults and only act out with children under special circumstances (Langevin, 1983). This means that sexual offenses against children include a heterogeneous group of adult men, some of whom are not "true" pedophiles in terms of sexual preferences.

With respect to the stimulus–response matrix, the most important feature among some pedophiles is the young age and immature body shape of the preferred sex objects (Langevin, 1983). Further support of a preference for immature body shape comes from Howells' (1979) "Repertory Grid" study of heterosexual pedophiles and non-sex-offender controls. The pedophiles often rated adults as overbearing whereas children were seen as nonthreatening and submissive. In personality terms, pedophiles are commonly found to be shy and introverted (Quinsey, 1986; Wilson & Cox, 1983), which may prevent them from interacting sexually with mature women (Langevin, Hucker, Handy, Purins, Russon, & Hook, 1985). Pedophiles, whether heterosexual, homosexual, or bisexual, commonly show evidence of personality disturbance (e.g., MMPI psychopathic scale) and other abnormalities on personality tests (Quinsey, 1986).

Rape

In law, rape is sexual intercourse with a woman without her consent. The intercourse must be vaginal and carried out by a person who is fully aware that the woman does not consent. The maximum sentence is life imprisonment but this is rarely imposed. Rape is regarded by the courts as the most serious of sexual offenses and 93% of the convicted adults in England and Wales receive a custodial sentence (Walmsley, 1984). During the past few years, this figure has risen to 97% and the sentences are becoming increasingly severe (Walmsley, 1986). Rape is the sexual offense that has shown the largest increase in frequency over the past 20 years. A varied amount of force and violence is used by rapists, ranging from mild force or threat to extreme violence. The rapist commonly has a history of theft, common assault, and indecent assault as well as rape (Langevin, 1983). Sexual assault, including rape, is predominantly heterosexual. Langevin, Paitich, and Russon (1985), in their study of 40 rapists, found inordinate interest in 13- to 15-year-old females, and several of the rapists had engaged in transvestism. Most of the rapists had had a wide range of heterosexual outlets and 55% were married. The main conclusion from this study was that violent history, alcohol abuse, poor socialization in childhood, and strong sex drive seem major factors that predispose rapists collectively to rape. Another interesting finding was that frottage (rubbing against females in crowds) and transvestism were common among the rapists. Quinsey (1984a) argues that although rapists' attitudes toward women may not be particularly unusual, their specific attitude toward rape itself may be important.

Several authors have shown that rapists have sexual arousal patterns that are different from those of non-sex offenders (e.g., Barbaree, Marshall, & Lanthier, 1979; Quinsey, Chaplin, & Upfold, 1984). Basically, rapists are much more sexually responsive to descriptions of rape than non-sex offenders. This appears to be particularly true among sadistic rapists, who are commonly found to be obsessed with aggressive sexual imagery (Quinsey, 1984a). There are three interpretations of such findings. First, it could be that for rapists the coercion by violence is itself sexually arousing. Second, nonsexual violence is not sexually arousing in itself but elicits a sexual response because it shares elements with violent sexual fantasies. Third, coercion or violence may not necessarily evoke rapists' sexual arousal but rather fails to inhibit it as it does in "normal" males.

Evidence for the last interpretation comes from a study by Barbaree *et al.* (1979). On this study, the inhibition of the erectile response in the controls was directly related to the degree of violence used in the verbal descriptions of the rape, whereas the rapists gave equal erectile arousal to none, mild, and severe degrees of violence. In a more recent study, Quinsey *et al.* (1984) found that rapists showed more sexual arousal to rape descriptions than consenting sex stories, and the degree of violence was important in differentiating the rapists from non-sex offenders. It was also evident that the rapists showed marked sexual arousal to nonsexual violence, giving support for the first interpretation mentioned above.

Groth, Burgess, and Holmstrom (1977) studied 133 convicted rapists and 92 victims of rape and concluded that three motives operate in every rape—power, anger, and sexuality—one being dominant in each instance. Power rape was the most common, followed by anger rape. There was no rape in which sex was a dominant issue; sexuality always seemed to be instrumental to the service of nonsexual needs. These findings support the view that in many instances rape is an aggressive rather than a sexual act. Psychoticism (P), as expected, has been shown to be related to arousal by rape-related stimuli (Barnes, Malamuth, & Check, 1984).

Sadism and Masochism

Sadism and masochism are two related behaviors that involve sexual gratification obtained in association with humiliation, enslavement, domination, and, on occasion, physical pain (Langevin, 1983). The sadist is the donor and the masochist is the recipient of the degrading act. As the two paradoxical behaviors are commonly thought to co-occur within the same individual, the term *sadomasochism* is often used. For example, Wilson (1978) found a close connection between sadistic and masochistic fantasies in normal males and females. Similar association was found among fetishists, transvestites, and sadomasochists (Gosselin & Wilson, 1980). However, when the fantasy scores for sadism and masochism were separated, it was evident that all groups had a preference for masochism. Another finding was that subjects who had predominant sadistic fantasies had a more extraverted and masculine personality profile than the masochists. Crepault and Couture (1980) found that many "normal" males have sexual fantasies that are controlling and sadistic but they do not act out their specific fantasies. Why some people act out their sadistic fantasies is poorly understood. Although females commonly report sadomasochistic fantasies, they rarely engage in serious sadomasochistic activities (Spengler, 1977).

MacCulloch, Snowden, Wood, and Mills (1983) studied the relationship between sadistic fantasy and behavior in 16 Special Hospital patients who had committed sadistic sexual offenses. These authors cogently argue that it is the "wish to control" that is the primary motivating force in sadism. Temporal lobe abnormality has been found in a significant number of sadists (Langevin, 1985).

Transsexualism

Transsexualism is primarily a disturbance in "gender identity" in which the person, most commonly a male, wishes to become a member of the opposite sex, and consequently requests hormone treatment and surgical operations for a sex change. The disturbance in gender development is typically manifested before puberty (Christie-Brown, 1983). Many transsexuals are disturbed emotionally and require psychiatric intervention (Langevin, 1983).

Transvestism

Transvestism or cross-dressing bridges the gap between fetishism and transsexualism and may be defined as sexual pleasure obtained from dressing in the clothes of the opposite sex (Christie-Brown, 1983). The number of transvestites with transsexual tendencies is probably quite low (Bancroft, 1983). The majority of transvestites are married, although cross-dressing may cause problems in their marriage (Brierley, 1979). Bancroft (1983) describes four typical examples of cross-dressing individuals, each illustrating a particular aspect of the phenomenon: (1) "the fetishistic transvestite," who wears female clothes as fetish objects for the purposes of sexual arousal, commonly resulting in masturbation; (2) "the transsexual," who cross-dresses as part of expressing one's professed gender; (3) "the double-role transvestite," who has no desire to change his or her gender role permanently but likes on occasions to dress and "pass" as a member of the appropriate sex; and (4) "the homosexual transvestite," a person who is sexually attracted to members of the same sex and cross-dresses not necessarily for sexual reasons. According to Bancroft (1983), the above four examples demonstrate the three salient dimensions of the cross-dressing experience: (1) the fetish component, (2) the cross-gender identity and role, and (3) sexual orientation and preference.

Most cross-dressing behavior can be accounted for by the interaction of these three dimensions. Bancroft states that major differences emerge from the literature with respect to males and females. For the male, the two most important factors with respect to cross-dressing are a search for a female identity and a fetishistic response to women's clothes. In the female transsexual, the cross-dressing has no fetishistic component, highlighting the fact that it is invariably men who develop an inanimate sexual extension of the body.

Some differences have been noted in the personality of transvestites and transsexuals. For example, Steiner, Langevin, and Sanders (1985) found the former to be more introverted, supporting the work of Gosselin and Wilson (1980). They also found that a history of exhibitionism, voyeurism, toucherism, frottage, and rape was quite common among the transvestites but not among the transsexuals. About half the transvestites had previously engaged in one or more of these sexual activities.

Voyeurism

Voyeurism (or "peeping") refers to the surreptitious observing of sexual activity or naked people as the preferred means of sexual arousal and outlet. It is commonly accompanied by masturbation (Langevin, 1983). Legally, voyeurism comes under the heading of "breach of the peace" or "being a public nuisance" (if several victims are involved). The desire to look at sexually exciting things is very common and it can be difficult to distinguish between the normal and abnormal individual doing it when the term is used in its broadest sense. Generally, the voyeur is the person who repeatedly prefers to look at sexual activity rather than actually participating, presumably because the real contact is perceived as too threatening or frightening. There is some support for this view from the work of Gebhard, Gagnon, Pomeroy, and Christenson (1965) on sex offenders, who found the voyeurs to have marked heterosexual social skills deficits and lack of sexual experience. However, voyeurism may not represent a discrete clinical entity as it is frequently reported in combination with other sexually variant behaviors, particularly exhibitionism (Langevin, 1983).

Elderly Sex Offenders

Most sex offenses are committed by young males (Gebhard *et al.*, 1965; Radzinowicz, 1957). However, a small percentage of offenses is committed by males aged 60 years or older. Although the actual numbers are very small, elderly offenders are of special interest to clinicians. Hucker and Ben-Aron (1985) have recently reviewed the literature and presented data of their own in which they compare 43 elderly sex offenders with 43 young offenders with respect to various characteristics. The most common psychiatric diagnoses among elderly offenders were alcoholism, personality disorder other than the antisocial type, neurosis, and organic brain syndrome. There was absence of rape and violence in this group and their offenses most commonly involved touching an acquaintance or exposing the genitals, usually to a minor (i.e., a child below the age of 12). Twenty-three percent had had previous convictions for sex offenses, which may have indicated underlying sexual disturbance of long duration. The main conclusion one can draw from the literature is that elderly sex offenders tend to have a number of problems including mental disturbance, social isolation and loneliness, and organic brain pathology.

It is evident with respect to the range of deviations discussed above that there is considerable overlap between different deviations (i.e., they are interrelated). For example, Flor-Henry (1987) argues that voyeurism, exhibitionism, fetishism, and mild sadomasochism are all to some extent part of a normal sexual experience, but they are peripheral, whereas in sexual deviations they become central. It is for this reason that the presence of one may increase the probability that others become evident in the affected individual. In their recent chapter on "courtship disorders," which comprise voyeurism, exhibitionism, obscene phone calls, toucheurism, and rape, Langevin and Lang (1987) discuss some important overlapping features and common underlying etiology but nevertheless emphasize the unique characteristics of each deviation.

INTERVENTION TECHNIQUES AND THEIR EVALUATION

It is evident that sexually variant individuals, including sex offenders, comprise a heterogeneous group of people with a wide range of different problems. For this reason, Crawford (1979) argues for a comprehensive treatment package, covering such problems as sexual dysfunction, anxiety, deficient social skills, inadequate sexual knowledge, poor self-control, lack of nondeviant sexual arousal, as well as the presence of deviant sexual arousal. This implies that the therapist should

TABLE 23. Classification of Some Techniques Used in Treating Sexually Deviant Behavior

	Increasing desirable behavior	Decreasing undesirable behavior
Overt behavior	Social skills training Sexual education	Aversion therapy Shame aversion Self-control techniques
Subjective cognitions/emotions	Systematic desensitization Aversion relief Positive conditioning Fading Shaping Attitude change Psychotherapy Group therapy Family–systems approaches	Covert sensitization
Physiological responses	Orgasmic reconditioning	Satiation therapy Chemotherapy Castration

focus on two different objectives: (1) reduce the undesirable or inappropriate thoughts, feelings, and behaviors and (2) increase alternative thoughts, feelings, and behaviors. Each type of response can be treated at one or more of three levels, as shown in Table 23. Some of the treatment approaches are behavioral (i.e., they are based on learning theory and principles), whereas others involve psychotherapy, group therapy, or chemotherapy. The distinction between the three levels is sometimes arbitrary because a particular technique may be administered at more than one level.

Modifying Overt Behavior

Increasing Desirable Behavior

At an overt behavioral level, the main objective is to increase *heterosocial–heterosexual skills* in patients whose skills are deficient, preventing them from interacting satisfactorily with, for example, adult women. A primary prerequisite for motivation to change is that the patient actually has some interests and preferably also positive experiences that he wants to cultivate. Social skills training may be carried out individually or in a group and commonly involves rehearsal and feedback in role plays relevant to the offender's circumstances, often incorporating therapist modeling and videotape playback (Perkins, 1986). Crawford and Allen (1979) have described a social skills program carried out with patients in a maximum-security hospital. The training program was effective in improving the social skills of the patients, assessed by questionnaires and standardized role-playing tests. The effects of such treatment on reoffending are not known.

Unfortunately, there are many problems with implementing and evaluating social skills programs in institutional settings that reduces the validity of such techniques (Abel, Blanchard, & Becker, 1976). According to case studies (e.g., Stevenson & Wolpe, 1960), assertiveness training may have some beneficial effects with patients whose sexual offending results from their inability to assert themselves appropriately in heterosexual situations, as in the case of rapists (Abel, Blanchard, & Becker, 1976).

Helzel and Rice (1985) assessed the social skills of 64 male patients in a maximum-security hospital and found that assertion and conversational role plays correlated highly with independent ratings by nursing staff, supporting the external validity of role-played interventions among psychiatric patients.

Some positive effects from structured *sex education programs* have been reported. For example, Crawford and Howells (1982) found that sex education significantly improved sexual knowledge and reduced anxiety associated with sexual intercourse, although no significant effect was noted with respect to sexual interests and preferences. Wanlass, Kilmann, Bella, and Tarnowski (1983) point out that in addition to increased sexual knowledge, sex education has been commonly found to increase positive sexual attitudes.

Quinsey (1984b) argues that deviant sexual behaviors are the result of skill deficits and/or inappropriate behaviors acquired through previous learning. The offender should therefore be provided with requisite skills and techniques for the self-management of his future sexual behavior. Quinsey provides data to show that a behavioral program focusing on skill acquisition and self-management techniques is useful in the treatment of sex offenders. Improvement with patients in a maximum-security hospital was noted on theoretically relevant measures, such as sexual knowledge, heterosocial skills, and sexual arousal patterns, and the program appeared to reduce recidivism in the short term.

Decreasing Undesirable Behavior

Aversion therapy has been commonly used since the 1960s to reduce sexual arousal to undesirable stimuli. Its use with sexual deviates was first reported by Max (1935), who found that the application of electric shocks was successful in reducing "homosexual fixations." Aversion techniques involve the pairing of an aversive stimulus (e.g., electric shock, nausea-inducing drug) with sexually deviant fantasy or behavior that is subject to modification. Aversion therapy is generally conceptualized as falling within both classical and operant conditioning paradigms (Crawford, 1981). It has long been shown to be moderately effective with a range of sexual deviations. For example, Marks, Gelder, and Bancroft (1970) followed up 24 sexual deviants who had been treated 2 years previously by electric aversion therapy for 2 to 3 weeks as inpatients. After treatment and follow-up, deviant acts and fantasies had diminished markedly in transvestites, fetishists, and sadomasochists (over 60% were "much improved"). Other studies reviewed by Bancroft (1974), Crawford (1981), Hallam and Rachman (1976), and Langevin (1983) suggest that the "success rate" at follow-up of sexual deviates treated by aversion therapy is commonly reported to be between 30% and 50%.

Shame aversion is a technique that has been used to treat exhibitionism and transvestism (Serber, 1970). The patient is instructed to perform the undesirable sexual act in front of an audience and aversion is considered to arise from embarrassment and anxiety (Jones & Frei, 1977). Langevin (1983) states that two or three sessions are usually sufficient but care must be taken not to use this technique with patients who are already depressed as it may increase the likelihood of suicide. In a variant of this approach, Wickramasekera (1972) had exhibitionists rehearse their deviant activity while verbalizing their feelings to prevent dissociation. The advantage of shame aversion is the brevity of treatment accompanied by favorable outcome. More studies with adequate follow-up are required before definite conclusions can be drawn about the effectiveness of this technique.

Modifying Cognitions/Emotions

Many attempts aimed at modifying cognitions and emotions are indirect ways of influencing behavior. Often these pose fewer practical and ethical problems than the more direct techniques.

Increasing Desirable Behavior

Systematic desensitization is a relaxation technique that has been used with sex offenders in order to reduce some of their heterosocial and heterosexual anxieties (James, 1978). Nowadays, it often forms part of a more comprehensive treatment package rather than being used on its own.

Aversion relief consists of pairing heterosexual stimuli with the relief from noxious stimuli (Thorpe, Schmidt, Brown, & Castell, 1964). The relief from "tension" might, for example, be associated with fantasies or pictures of adult women, thereby increasing heterosexual interest. Because of the nature of the technique it is invariably used in conjunction with aversion therapy. Barlow (1973) argues that the technique lacks empirical support. It may also have certain undesirable side effects, such as avoidance reaction to both the shock and females (Langevin, 1983). Alternative methods for enhancing heterosexual behavior are therefore preferable.

Positive classical conditioning has been used as an alternative approach to aversion relief. The idea is to pair desirable neutral stimuli with those that are sexually arousing. For example, in the case of pedophiles, pictures of children are arousing and by pairing them with pictures of females as conditioning stimuli, the latter become arousing. Crawford (1984) argues that the results from classical conditioning studies have been mixed, which may be due to the fact that the precise timing necessary for classical conditioning to take effect is difficult to arrange when the response to be conditioned is sexual arousal. In addition, the conditioned reaction is inevitably always going to be smaller than the reaction to the unconditioned stimulus (Langevin, 1983).

Fading is a procedure developed by Barlow and Agras (1973) and overcomes some of the problems associated with weak conditioned reactions in classical conditioning paradigms. They used it to increase heterosexual responsiveness in three homosexual males. The technique consists of gradually changing an undesirable stimulus (e.g., males, children) to a heterosexual stimulus (e.g., adult women) by superimposing one slide over another. As the patient responds sexually the brightness of the female slide is increased and that of the male slide decreased. The procedure can also be based on imagery by instructing the patient to gradually change the content of his erotic fantasies (Bancroft, 1971). There are some practical problems with the procedure. For example, when using slides many subjects are unresponsive sexually (Laws, 1984), which limits the utility of the procedure. Laws and Pawlowski (1974) failed to use the technique successfully with two pedophiles.

Shaping has been reported in one study (Quinn, Harbison, & McAllister, 1970) as a method of modifying sexual arousal. In this study, iced lime juice was used to reward increased penile response of a homosexual to heterosexual stimuli, resulting in increased heterosexual fantasy and responsiveness. The method is based on systematically reinforcing desirable increases in penile response.

Marks and Sartorius (1968) have looked at the importance of attitude change among sexually variant patients, showing it to be a valid indicator of clinical change. From the point of view of treatment, attitude change may be attempted at three different levels: (1) attitude toward the sexual object, (2) attitude toward interpersonal relationships, and (3) attitude toward one's sexually deviant behavior. Attitude change may result indirectly from several different treatment approaches. For example, negative attitude and arrogance may become evident during social skills training sessions and may be modified by appropriate modeling, coaching, and feedback. Problems in attitudes may be dealt with directly by psychotherapy or group therapy, especially by confronting the patient with the consequences of and responsibility for his actions (Abel, Blanchard, & Becker, 1976). Attitudes and beliefs can also be modified along cognitive–behavioral lines (Watts, Powell, & Austin, 1973), which provides an important scope for new therapeutic developments relevant to sexual deviations.

Individual psychoanalytic therapy was the main psychological method for treating sexual offenders before behavioral methods began to be explored more extensively in the 1960s. In general, psychoanalysis and individual psychotherapy have been poorly assessed for outcome in the case of sexually deviant behavior and the empirical evidence for their effectiveness is very limited (Crawford, 1981; Langevin, 1983). Craft and Craft (1984) discuss several of the difficulties involved in treating sex offenders with psychotherapy and point out the advantages of utilizing group therapy instead. Unfortunately, however, group therapy has not yet demonstrated its effectiveness in the case of sex offenders, although promising results have been reported in one study. MacDonald and Di Furia (1971) obtained an 87% success rate in their group treatment program with highly motivated sex offenders. Group therapy is often very time consuming and about one third of the patients who commence treatment fail to continue treatment (Mathias & Collins, 1971).

Lanyon (1986) has reviewed the evidence for the use of *family-systems approaches* in cases of incestuous child molestation. Treatment comprises a combination of individual therapy for each family member, followed by therapy for each dyad, and then family therapy. This is supplemented by group therapy and self-help support groups. Evaluating a family systems program, Giarretto (1982) reports less than 1% recidivism rate for children returned home after the offense.

Decreasing Undesirable Behavior

Covert sensitization is a variant of aversion therapy, introduced for the treatment of sexual variations by Cautela and Wisocki (1971). It relies on the patient being able to imagine himself engaging in sexually deviant behavior. Once vivid imagery is achieved, the patient is instructed to imagine an unpleasant scene or event (e.g., nausea, vomiting, being caught, arrested), which will inhibit his erotic arousal to the undesirable stimulus. The technique is easy to implement provided the patient is capable of vivid imagery and one can establish an effective aversive stimulus. The disadvantage of the technique is that the imagined stimuli are unobservable and the procedure requires genuine cooperation from the patient.

Covert sensitization has been used effectively with many different deviations (Brownell, Hayes, & Barlow, 1977; Cautela & Wisocki, 1971) and some further ingredients have been added. For example, Maletzky (1974) paired smell aversion (valeric acid) with the undesirable images and reported excellent success with exhibitionists. At 1-year follow-up, none of the exhibitionists has been reapprehended and their overt exposing behavior, fantasies, and urges were markedly reduced. None of the patients dropped out during treatment, which is quite exceptional. In a more recent publication, Maletzky (1980) reports the success rate for "assisted" covert sensitization among 38 homosexual pedophiles and 62 exhibitionists, who were either self referred or court referred. The outcome criteria comprised self-report data, penile plethysmograph recordings, and legal records. At 36-month follow-up, only eight patients had been recharged, giving a success rate of 92% in terms of the legal criterion. No significant difference was noted with respect to type of referral or type of offending. One reasons for the exceptional success in the study may relate to the fact that the 24-week treatment was followed by "booster" sessions every 3 months for 3 years. It is also worth noting that in addition to the covert sensitization technique employed, adjunctive techniques (e.g., environmental manipulation, masturbatory fantasy change) were carried out via homework assignments during the active phase of treatment.

Able, Rouleau, and Cunningham-Rathner (1986) report a high success rate with sexual offenders seen on a voluntary out-patient basis, employing a broad-based behavioral treatment package. At 1-year follow-up 82% of the patients reported no longer being involved in deviant sexual behavior. Poor outcomes were evident in the case of homosexual pedophiles. Incest offenders and heterosexual pedophiles had very low recidivism rates. Unfortunately, the authors give insufficient information for a proper evaluation of their findings.

Perkins (1984) reports on a number of sexual offenders treated in prison and the community by a behavioral package. Out of 145 sexual offenders 65 (45%) refused to participate in treatment. Out of those who commenced treatment only 12 (18%) completed the entire treatment package. A further 35 offenders (54%) completed parts of the treatment. No data are given for reconviction rates but the author concluded that those who completed treatment appeared to do better in the community at follow-up than those who did not complete or participate in treatment. Unfortunately, the number of subjects in their study is too small for meaningful analysis but the study clearly demonstrated the lack of motivation often found among sexual offenders in clinical practice resulting in the majority of sexual offenders never satisfactorily completing treatment. In a more recent study, Perkins (1987) provides reconviction data for his samples and convincing evidence that those sex offenders who complete treatment have superior outcome compared with those who did not want treatment or did not complete it.

One factor that may influence the effectiveness of some psychological techniques (e.g., covert sensitization) with sex offenders is that, as a group, they tend to be of lower intelligence than other types of offenders (Power, 1987). This may relate to the common finding that sex offenders often lack social skills and sexual knowledge. The level of intelligence of the offender is likely to affect the content and sophistication of the treatment package constructed, but at present there is no evidence that intelligence *per se* makes sex offenders unresponsive to treatment.

Modifying Physiological Responses

These techniques specifically refer to modifying the penile response in males.

Increasing Desirable Behavior

Orgasmic reconditioning refers to methods of modifying sexual fantasies during masturbation. McGuire, Carlisle, and Young (1965) emphasized the important role of undesirable sexual fantasies in maintaining undesirable arousal, whereas Marquis (1970) introduced the theory and practice of orgasmic reconditioning, during which patients are instructed to shift their masturbation fantasy from an undesirable one to a desirable one at the point of orgasmic inevitability. Subsequently, the patient is instructed to make the shift at earlier stages of masturbation. However, in spite of its frequent clinical use and empirical support from case studies, there are theoretical problems involved with the procedure (i.e., it involves "backward" rather than "forward" conditioning), which makes the outcome of the procedure questionable in terms of learning theory (Keller & Goldstein, 1977). Laws and O'Neil (1981) found orgasmic reconditioning to be successful with a variety of sexual deviations but recommended some modifications to Marquis' (1970) procedure in which the fantasy content within a single session was not altered.

Instead, switching back and forth of fantasy themes between sessions was considered to be a more effective way of confronting patients with the inappropriateness of their deviant fantasy. A further problem is that sexual deviates often find it difficult to switch from deviant to nondeviant fantasy prior to orgasm (Crawford, 1981), which limits the usefulness of the technique.

Decreasing Undesirable Arousal

Satiation therapy was developed by Marshall and Barbaree (1978). The objective is to reduce deviant sexual arousal by satiation, which means that the patient is instructed to continue to masturbate for a long time (i.e., one hour) after orgasm while verbalizing his deviant fantasies. Marshall (1979) presented two successful single-case experiments where satiation therapy had been used with two adult males who had longstanding deviant sexual interests.

A number of *antilibidinal* drugs have been used to help offenders control their sex drive. These include the female hormone *estrogen*, the neuroleptic drug *benperidol*, and *cyproterone acetate*. The last two appear to produce the least harmful side effects (Bancroft, Tennent, Loucas, & Cass, 1974). None of these drugs or hormones are effective in changing the person's basic sexual preferences, but they commonly reduce sex drive and erectile and ejaculatory responses while the person is on the medication (Bancroft *et al.*, 1974).

Several outcome studies have been carried out regarding the effectiveness of these drugs in reducing recidivism. The general finding is that these drugs are highly effective in suppressing libido and in reducing the reconviction rate (e.g., Field, 1973; Field & Williams, 1971; Ortmann, 1980). For example, Ortmann (1980) reviewed seven studies from six samples and concluded that cyproterone acetate decreased recidivism rates remarkably among mixed groups. However, most of the studies investigating the effectiveness of antilibidinal drugs are difficult to evaluate properly because of poorly selected control groups and not all studies have produced encouraging results (Tennent, Bancroft, & Cass, 1974; Torpy & Tomison, 1986). Furthermore, the drugs are likely to be effective in reducing libido and recidivism only while the person is on the medication and other treatments are therefore essential to achieve long-term changes in deviant behavior.

Castration involves removing the testicles in males surgically in order to reduce the level of testosterone in the body, which in turn may reduce the person's sex drive and ability to respond sexually. In many countries, castration is prohibited by law and it is normally used only for persistent and dangerous offenders whose prognosis is very poor. In spite of the serious ethical, physical, and psychological problems castration may pose, it has been shown to be the single most effective method of reducing recidivism among persistent sex offenders (Sturup, 1972). Heim and Hursch (1979) reviewed the recent European literature on surgical castration in the treatment of sex offenders. The results from the most important empirical studies conducted in Germany, Switzerland, Norway, and Denmark are presented. It is evident that the recidivism rate among castrated males at follow-up is very low (commonly about 2%), but Heim and Hursch (1979) argue that in other respects the sexual responsiveness of castrated males is often very variable and unpredictable, reducing the scientific basis for the use of castration with sexual offenders. During the past two or three decades the number of legally castrated sexual offenders has been steadily falling and since 1972 no sexual offenders have been castrated in Denmark (Ortmann, 1980). It seems extremely unlikely that castration will ever become legally, medically, and ethically acceptable in Great Britain and the United States.

CONCLUSIONS

With respect to individual treatment techniques, the available empirical evidence indicates that the most effective methods employ some kind of an aversive element, aimed at reducing deviant sexual arousal. The most dramatic form of treatment, castration, appears to be the only consistently effective method of significantly reducing the recidivism rate among some of the most serious and repetitive offenders. However, castration, despite its effectiveness, cannot be used for legal, ethical, and complicated side-effect reasons. As an alternative form of treatment, antiandrogens, such as cyproterone acetate, have been used with considerable, although varied, success. The main problems with using antiandrogens is that they reduce the deviant behavior only while the person is on medication. It is not possible for medical and ethical reasons to keep the person on the drug indefinitely. We therefore recommend that antiandrogens be principally used in the short term to facilitate improvements in the sexual deviate's deficient heterosexual and heterosocial skills and relevant clinical problems. That is, while the deviant urges and fantasies are reduced or eliminated by the medication, efforts should be made to improve those areas in the individual's life that may facilitate more acceptable behaviors and reduce his needs for engaging in unacceptable behaviors.

Of the psychological techniques, behavioral approaches appear to be most effective. An important component of a behavioral treatment package is an aversive conditioning element. This may be presented in the form of an electric shock, a chemical substance, or an imagined event as in the case of covert sensitization. The objective is to reduce sexual arousal to deviant stimuli. However, many sexual deviates are reluctant to give up their existing sexual outlets without some alternative outlets being facilitated (Gudjonsson, 1986). For this reason, aversion therapy or covert sensitization are most effective when they form part of a broader-based treatment package simultaneously aiming to improve heterosexual interests, deficient social skills, negative interpersonal attitudes, and anxiety and marital problems. The importance of maintaining therapeutic contact after the termination of treatment is evident from the literature and "booster sessions" may have to be provided if the deviant urges and fantasies return. Furthermore, the nature of the treatment setting is of vital importance for a variety of reasons and special problems exist for sex offenders treated in institutional settings (Perkins, 1984; Quinsey, 1984b).

It is evident from the above discussion that sexual deviates differ markedly in terms of their therapeutic responsiveness. No one treatment has been found to be effective across all deviations or individuals. It is becoming increasingly common in clinical practice and evaluation research to implement a comprehensive treatment package, comprising a combination of techniques aimed to modify several different target behaviors. The multidimensional approach generally includes interventions designed to reduce deviant sexual arousal, techniques for increasing appropriate sexual arousal, heterosexual skills training, training in self-control, and sex education (Earls & Quinsey, 1985). Unfortunately, the evaluation of a broad-based treatment program is very complicated because techniques are specifically selected to suit the individual patient rather than on the basis of rigid research criteria. What is needed is further understanding of the factors that enhance therapeutic change in different individuals and with different deviations. In other words, in what type of patient and under what circumstances are different techniques, or a combination of techniques, most effective in facilitating and maintaining therapeutic change?

There are further obstacles to the adequate evaluation of treatment effectiveness with sexual deviates. First, most of the studies reported in the literature have inadequate follow-up for proper evaluation. This is particularly serious in the case of sex offenders, where recidivism and reconviction rates are used as the effectiveness criterion requiring long follow-up periods. Second, many studies employ relatively few subjects or are single-case studies. More large-scale studies are needed. Third, very few of the studies reported in the literature employ control groups and the patients treated are often specially rather than randomly selected for treatment.

Most treatment studies focus only on those patients who complete treatment programs and this gives misleading information about the average success rate because a large proportion of patients fail to complete the treatment satisfactorily and are not included in the figures. Furthermore, many sex offenders who are referred to outpatient clinics never turn up for their appointments and therefore never engage in treatment. This means that many treatment studies are biased in that they evaluate the effectiveness of treatment programs only among patients who are motivated, for whatever reason, to complete treatment. It is also important to note that most sex offenders are never referred for treatment and are dealt with by the criminal justice system. Those who are referred, or refer themselves, are unlikely to be representative of sex offenders in general.

In conclusion, during the last two decades, the understanding of the nature of sexual deviations and their appropriate assessment and treatment has advanced immensely. Many treatment techniques have been shown to be effective but more evaluation studies are clearly required. There are many difficulties with evaluating studies reported in the literature and because of methodological weaknesses many studies have reported success rates that may overstate the effectiveness of psychological methods with sex offenders.

CHAPTER NINE

Summary and Conclusions

In this chapter we draw together the main themes and findings from the previous chapters. In the first four chapters we concentrated predominantly on theoretical issues about the causes of crime, whereas the last three chapters dealt mainly with interventions. Inevitably, there are certain overlaps between the two parts of the book. That is, the chapters on the causes of crime, personality, and individual differences also broach findings from studies about sentencing and treatment effectiveness when this is appropriate within the context and scope of the individual chapter. Conversely, the chapters on sentencing, punishment, and rehabilitation broach issues about the causes of crime and the importance of personality and individual differences. The main theme that runs through the book is that *psychological factors and individual differences related to the personality are of central importance in relation to both the causes of crime and its control.* This does not mean to say that other factors, such as sociological and economic ones, are not important. Indeed, in many instances they are. We believe that sociological theories are particularly relevant in relation to victimless crimes and less so in the case of victimful crimes.

Psychological factors in criminality, we argue, relate to genetic and constitutional causes and to personality and other sources of individual differences. This does not mean that some people are *destined* to commit crimes. Criminal behavior as such is not innate. What is inherited are certain peculiarities of the brain and nervous system that interact with certain environmental factors and thereby increase the likelihood that a given person will act in a particular antisocial manner in a given situation.

When discussing the causes and control of criminal behavior, it is important to take into account the *type* of crime committed. For example, in terms of personality, extraversion may be an important predisposing factor in the case of certain property offenses (e.g., burglary, robbery, con operations), whereas in the case of some sex offenders, family murderers, and "social inadequates," introversion and social isolation seem more important. This indicates that offenders comprise a heterogeneous group of people and that no single theory of crime can explain all criminal activity.

We agree with Farrington (1986) that much criminal behavior may be construed as the end product of a chain of processes. The first stage consists of the desire for certain goods or outlets. Most commonly, this involves a desire for material goods, status among peers, excitement, sexual gratification, and the relief of anger and hostility. Second, illegal and socially disapproved methods are chosen as acceptable means for satisfying these needs and desires. The reasons for this may be manyfold. They may involve faulty learning and inadequate moral development, the tendency to respond to stress in a particular way, and dissorted attitudes and attributions. The third and final stage involves a number of situational and opportunity factors, where the criminal act is the outcome of a decision-making process involving perceptions of benefits and costs at any one point in time.

The prevention and control of illegal behavior can be attempted at three stages of the judicial process. These are identified as "predelinquent," "preadjudication," and "postadjudication" interventions, respectively. Preschool enrichment programs have given the most promising results as far as predelinquent measures are concerned. Such programs seem to provide children with certain cognitive skills and competencies that help them cope more appropriately with the conflicts and pressures that commonly precipitate delinquency. Situational and opportunity-reducing measures—for example, through "target hardening" and other environmental manipulations—may hold some promise for the future, but more research is needed to prove their effectiveness. Preadjudication measures (such as cautioning and diversion) appear to have resulted in "net widening" (i.e., increased the number of juveniles being formally dealt with by the judicial system), and there is no evidence that they have reduced reoffending.

Postadjudication intervention focuses on ways of reducing recidivism once the person has been convicted of an offense. Many techniques and programs have been tried over the past 20–30 years, either as an alternative to sentencing (e.g., incarceration) or in addition to it. It is evident that many of these therapeutic interventions have been unsuccessful in markedly reducing recidivism.

One major problem with treating or rehabilitating many offenders is their poor motivation and resistance to change. This resistance is perhaps not surprising when one considers that most offenses are probably predominantly committed on the basis of rational choice. That is, the commission of the offense provides immediate pleasure and reinforcement, and the likelihood of detection and punishment are perceived as very low. Therefore, the payoff is perceived as exceeding the likely punishment, which in any case is uncertain and much delayed even if offenders are eventually caught. The resistance to change may take the form of refusal or reluctance to attend therapeutic meetings or appointments, failure to comply with homework, and unwillingness to apply the skills that offenders have been taught to help them resist the temptation to offend. All that mental health workers can do is provide offenders with the opportunity to work on their problems, and if they are sufficiently motivated to change, much can sometimes be achieved. The therapeutic package needs to be constructed in close cooperation with the individual offender. Most success seems to be achieved when the offenders themselves are actively involved in selecting the goals and behaviors to work on. Cognitive therapy may on occasion be helpful in modifying the offenders' perceptions, beliefs, reasoning, and attitudes that form part of their motivational problem.

Although the majority of treatment and rehabilitation programs have been unsuccessful in markedly reducing recidivism, this does not mean that nothing works. When one compares the successful and unsuccessful programs, it is evident that the programs commonly contain identifiable components that explain their effectiveness. These are

1. They are individually tailored to suit the offender's specific personality needs and problems.
2. The treatment package consists of a range of different treatment components, often involving a combination of more than one technique.
3. Cognitive–behavioral techniques appear to be most successful with a range of offenses, including anger and aggression. Here the offenders' cognitive deficits (e.g., reasoning, attitudes, and attributions) and lack of social competence become the direct focus of the treatment intervention.
4. The individual offenders take an active part in choosing the goals and behaviors to be modified.
5. Therapeutic contact is maintained *after* the termination of treatment, with "booster sessions" and long-term counseling being provided if necessary.

Throughout the book we have emphasized the importance of *individual differences* in treatment responsiveness. We believe that this is an important area that is much neglected and underresearched. The balance between *aversive* and *reward* components of the treatment package needs to be considered with regard to the individual differences. The personality dimensions of introversion–extraversion and neuroticism–stability are particularly useful in this respect. Neurotic introverts are most responsive to potential punishment whereas neurotic extraverts are most responsive to potential reward. Many offenders have average scores for neuroticism and extraversion and are therefore moderately responsive to both punishment and reward.

In many instances, a combination of punishment and reinforcement procedures are most effective in reducing recidivism. The punishment component may be of two different types. First, it sometimes forms part of the sentencing of the offender, as in the case of a probation order or a suspended sentence, which may be attached to a psychological or psychiatric treatment package. The mental health professional may then primarily focus on building up a reinforcing desirable alternative behavior in the criminal. The use of a probation order or a suspended sentence in conjunction with voluntary treatment is a good example of how psychologists and the courts can work together in an attempt to reduce recidivism for individual offenders who are considered suitable and motivated for such a disposal. The second and more common way punishment is utilized within a treatment program is to apply some aversive stimulus paradigm (e.g., covert sensitization) in order to suppress the undesirable behavior. We argue that with some offenders (e.g., pedophiles) an aversive component to the treatment program is essential in conjunction with reinforcement-based components. It is erroneous to think that punishment is always less effective than reinforcement in reducing offending.

There are several major problems with the implementation of punishment, with respect to both sentencing and treatment, which limits its effectiveness. That is, in order for punishment to be maximally effective in reducing offending, it must be applied as soon after the criminal act as possible. Its implementation must be certain and consistent. In practice, these criteria are very rarely met. Offenders often escape arrest (the overall detection rate for offenses is no more than 20%). Even when they are apprehended, they are commonly not prosecuted and convicted. Those convicted are typically inconsistently dealt with by the courts.

Although the detection rate for most offenses is very low, the law of averages would predict that the most persistent offenders will eventually be caught. Our knowledge about how to identify the potential persistent offenders at an early age is steadily increasing. Taking them out of circulation early in their criminal career can have marked effects on the crime rate. The courts must cooperate by giving the persistent offenders long prison sentences and their parole applications should be cautiously considered.

One potentially useful way of improving the detection rate for many crimes is by making more use of informants. In some countries the use of paid informants is on the increase with promising results.

A comparison of the effectiveness of different sentences is very difficult because offenders are not randomly allocated to different sentences. The most serious offenders tend to be given the most severe sentence. There appear to be some interaction effects with respect to sentencing. That is, certain offenders may benefit most from certain types of sentences, but our knowledge about what type of sentence best suits each offender is at present very limited. There is some evidence that the effects of prison sentences are cumulative, which means that one has to consider the number and duration of the previous sentences served rather than studying each sentence in isolation. With respect to general deterrence, longer sentences do appear to deter certain types of crime, such as rape, certain murders, burglary, and robbery.

Our investigation has convinced us of the importance of certain general conclusions that at the present moment are more honored in their breach than their observance. The first is the widespread belief that punishment, particularly prison, does not deter. Allied with this is the belief that stricter punishment does not deter any more than soft punishment. Both beliefs are clearly wrong. Half of the criminals sent to prison will go back again; this amount of recidivism may be regarded as proof of the inadequacy of prison as a deterrent. However, as in the case of the glass that may be considered half full or half empty, we should also regard the fact that half of the criminals sentenced to prison do *not* become recidivists! Prison is certainly less than 100% successful in preventing recidivism and deterring criminals, but even a 50% success rate is not negligible. We have some idea of what would happen if legal punishments did not exist when we look at the events following strikes of the police force or their ineffectiveness during the early stages of a riot. Large numbers of people who would probably not normally be criminals take to looting, arson, destruction of property, aggression against persons, and other serious criminal acts, and the fact that there is no retribution is certainly an important factor in all this. Prison is an ineluctable part of the legal system; it can certainly be improved by being more selective in deciding who is to go to prison and for how long, but it is not as ineffective as is sometimes made out.

Similarly, the notion that harsh treatment does not deter is clearly and absolutely wrong. As a typical example, consider the Arab states where theft is punished by cutting off the thief's right hand or adultery by stoning the guilty woman. We are *not* suggesting that these penalties should be introduced into our legal system, but there is no question that they have worked extremely well in reducing theft and adultery to an absolute minimum.

Another example is Singapore. There was a good deal of crime of all sorts when the Japanese marched in and decreed the death penalty for any form of crime, however small and unimportant. As soon as it became apparent that they were actually going to execute anyone committing a crime, crime practically ceased in Singapore. Again, we are not suggesting that the death penalty should be introduced in this manner; we are only concerned to show that severity of sentencing may have a very salutary effect on prospective criminals.

A third point: We have no doubt that much could be done to improve the present state of our prisons, where overcrowding and other similar evils are rife at the moment. It seems to us incredible that anyone responsible for prisons should urge judges and magistrates to avoid prison sentences, or make them shorter, or release prisoners earlier, because there is not sufficient accommodation for prisoners. That the inefficiency of politicians in foreseeing the obvious need for building prisons should alter the legal duties of judges and magistrates to apply the law seems a completely unacceptable novelty in constitutional practice. Here is obviously an area where improvements could be made.

A fourth point is the self-defeating policy of forcing mentally ill people into the community by closing down hospital beds and reducing outpatient facilities, thus making these individuals reemerge in prisons, having done considerable damage to law-abiding members of the community and requiring a great deal of money for their capture, sentencing, and maintenance in prison! This penny-wise, pound-foolish behavior is typical of politicians who fail to think through the consequences of their actions: If psychotic and severely neurotic patients are to be sent out into the community, the state has a duty to provide proper accommodation and care, in order to avoid their drifting into crime and possibly costing the state far more money than they would have done had they remained in the hospital!

A fifth point would be for the state to give up prosecution of those who are engaged in what we called "victimless crimes" and devote the time and energy of the police to the more important business of bringing to justice real criminals who have done harm to real victims. Prostitution—to take but one example—can be easily and effectively regulated, as for instance in Germany; the American practice of outlawing prostitution in theory but allowing it in practice, subject to ineffective routine prosecutions, is as absurd as the British one of legalizing prostitution but making it illegal for the prostitute and her client to get together!

Hypocrisy may be the homage vice pays to virtue, as La Rochefoucauld said over 300 years ago, but it is not a good counselor or effective legislation, and the prevalence of bribery and corruption among members of the vice squads in many countries is another powerful argument for restricting the influence of the law to victimful crimes. Setting the police free to increase the likelihood of detection of such victimful crimes by ceasing to employ them in the service of hypocritical righteousness might be a useful contribution to the general improvement of law and order.

Another issue on which we would like to lay particular stress is the need for the experimental study of the consequences of legal actions. What we have at the moment is simply the propagation of individual ideas and views, often held with great sincerity and proclaimed with considerable fervor but lacking completely in any kind of factual support. Arguments about the death penalty present a good example of the failure of both sides to consider the evidence. We encounter opinionated declarations that the death penalty does not deter, met by equally opinionated declarations that it does; none of the participants seem to be familiar with such evidence as the statistical studies of Professor Ehrlich mentioned in an earlier chapter. We do not here argue that Ehrlich is necessarily right, or that even if he were it would be desirable to introduce the death penalty. There are many ethical, religious, and other arguments involved in such a debate, but surely the factual issue of the effectiveness of the death penalty as a deterrent for certain types of murder is fundamental to any such discussion. Quite generally we advocate a much greater appeal to empirical evidence, a much greater appreciation of the importance of facts and figures, and a much greater readiness to carry out experimental studies, than can be found at present.

It is only by supporting rigorously controlled experimental investigations that we can find out the kind of answer that will enable us to improve our present practices, which are universally acknowledged to be faulty and rather ineffective. We have given one example of this type of investigation, looking at the respective effects of adjournment and supervision on later truancy and criminality. Could we have predicted the much greater effectiveness of adjournment over supervision in reducing truancy and criminality?

It is only by suitable experiments, based on realistic and meaningful psychological theories, that we will gain a better knowledge of the kind of punishment most likely to avoid recidivism. Such a process would have to look critically and seriously at many "sacred cows," including, for instance, the effectiveness of probation, which is often taken for granted but which has very little direct proof in its favor. It seems quite likely that there are important *interactions* between the personality of the criminal, the personality of the probation officer, and the methods used that will determine the outcome. If the nature of this interaction is not known—and at present it is merely surmised—then no effective intervention is likely to be forthcoming. We must be hard-nosed in our search for facts if we want to improve our efforts at redemption of the criminal and protection of society.

Much the same is true of probation, bail, and other elements of the legal system of dealing with criminals. All these processes are far too subjective to be even minimally effective in sorting the wheat from the chaff, and the constant findings that criminals on bail or parole continue undeterred in their habits of stealing, raping, and murdering suggest that all may not be well in these respects. Proper psychometric research could unearth factual evidence to improve the present unsatisfactory and entirely subjective methods immeasurably, but the will to carry out such research—and abide by the results—is lacking. Of course, research costs money, and in particular the longitudinal studies so urgently needed are not inexpensive to carry out. However, given the enormous amount of money that crime is costing the nation, the amounts involved in financing decent research are infinitesimally small. What is lacking is not the money, but the will: There is little realization of the need for research, the power of research, or the improvement that it could bring to this seemingly hopeless area of social intervention.

We do, of course, realize the ethical and social problems that make research difficult in this area, and we are fully cognizant of the very negative attitude of many prison governors, prison officers, and others with respect to the carrying out of such research. Clearly, it will be a long time yet before we see a change in these attitudes and can welcome the first fruits of such large-scale research. Difficulties are here to be overcome, and the end result may well be worth all the effort that has to be put into it.

We are convinced that without undue expenditure, and possibly even with the saving of money, considerable improvements could be made in our dealings with criminals. We do not, of course, suggest any foolish optimism that anything we are suggesting could be other than a palliative, although, of course, palliatives are better than nothing! Crime, if our general theory be correct, is essentially a function of the ethos of the society in which we live; it reflects the practices of positive and negative reinforcement, of reward and punishment, of teaching and conditioning, which are prevalent, and these in turn are mirrored and reflected by the types of films we see, television programs we watch, books and newspapers we read, and teaching and example we receive at school.

If parents do not insist on decent and moral behavior in their children; if schools do not maintain discipline, and even preach rebellion and resistance to authority; if criminals and vice generally are constantly portrayed in a positive fashion in films and on television; and if even the representatives of organized religion fail to speak up for obedience to the law and refuse to condemn terrorism—then clearly the task of enforcing law and order will be all the more difficult, and will possibly become impossible. Add to this the leniency of punishment so often preached by those who erroneously assume that it is society rather than the individual who is guilty of criminal conduct, and we have a situation where anything that can be done directly to improve the rule of law can only be a palliative. The permissive society is earning the rewards it deserves: "The fathers have eaten sour grapes, and the children's teeth are set on edge." All this does not suggest that our recommendations are useless—merely that they can only go a little way to improve the situation.

Some of our main recommendations, such as the need to improve the likelihood of detection and increase the severity of punishment, are very much in line with common sense. They would undoubtedly enjoy great popular favor. They are also not new, and we may close our book by quoting some words Francis Bacon spoke in the Star Chamber almost 400 years ago:

> There is a rising of robberies more now than in former times was wont: and there are two causes hereof; the one is that men are too loose in taking of the committers of them, and the other is they are negligent in suffering them to go away; for now hue and cries are of no consequence, only a little paper is sent up and down with a soft pace, whereas they should be prosecuted with horse and foot, and hunted as a thief.

"Books must follow sciences, and not sciences books."

Sir Francis Bacon
(Proposition touching Amendment of Laws)

References

Abel, G. G., & Blanchard, E. B. The role of fantasy in the treatment of sexual deviation. *Archives of General Psychiatry*, 1974, *30*, 467–475.

Abel, G. G., Blanchard, E. B., & Becker, J. V. Psychological treatment of rapists. In M. J. Walker & S. L. Brodsky (Eds.), *Sexual assaults*. London: Lexington Books, 1976.

Able, G. G., Rouleau, J., & Cunningham-Rathner, J. Sexually aggressive behavior. In W. Curran, A. L. McGarry & S. Shah (Eds.), *Modern legal psychiatry and psychology*. Philadelphia: F. A. Davis Co., 1984.

Abel, G. G., Rouleau, J. L. & Cunningham-Rathner, J. Sexually aggressive behavior. In W. J. Curran, A. L. McGarry & S. A. Shah (Eds.), *Forensic psychiatry and psychology*. Philadelphia: F. A. Davis Co., 1986, pp. 289–313.

Adcock, C. J. A factorial examination of Sheldon's type. *Journal of Personality*, 1948, *16*, 312–319.

Addad, M., & Benezech, M. Jugement moral, extraversion, neurosisme et delinquance. *L'Evolution Psychiatrique*, 1987, *52*, 703–727.

Advisory Council on the Penal System. *Sentences of imprisonment: A review of maximum penalties*. London: H. M. S. O., 1978.

Aktar, S. N., & Singh, U. P. The temporary stability of MPI scores in normal and criminal populations. *Behaviour Metrica*, 1972, *2*, 2–26.

Alexander, J. F. & Parsons, B. V. Short-term behavioral intervention with delinquent families: Impact on family process and recidivism. *Journal of Abnormal Psychology*, 1973, *81*, 219–225.

Alford, R., & Alford, F. Sex differences in asymmetry in the facial expression of emotion. *Neuropsychologia*, 1981, *19*, 605–608.

Allsopp, J. F. *Investigations into the applicability of Eysenck's theory of criminality to the antisocial behaviour of school children*. Unpublished Ph.D. thesis, University of London, 1975.

Allsopp, J. F. & Feldman, M. P. Extraversion, neuroticism, psychoticism and antisocial behaviour in school girls. *Social Behaviour and Personality*, 1974, *2*, 184–189.

Allsopp, J. F., & Feldman, M. P. Item analyses of questionnaire measures of personality and anti-social behaviour in school. *British Journal of Criminology*, 1976, *16*, 337–351.

Amelang, M., & Rodel, G. Personlichkeits-und Einstellungskorrelate krimineller Verhaltensweisen. *Psychologische Rundschau*, 1970, *21*, 157–179.

American Psychiatric Association. *Diagnostic and statistical manual of mental disorders*, (3rd ed.). Washington, D. C.: American Psychiatric Association, 1980.

Amnesty International Report. *The death penalty*. London: Amnesty International Publications, 1979.

Aniskiewicz, A. *Autonomic components of vicarious conditioning and psychopathy*. Unpublished Ph.D. dissertation, Purdue University, 1973.

Anonymous. How coffee calms kids. *Newsweek*, 1973, *8*, (Oct.), 76.

Arbuthnot, J., Gordon, D., & Jurkovic, G. Personality. In H. C. Quay (Ed.), *Handbook of juvenile delinquency*. New York: Wiley, 1987 pp. 87–106.

Aronfeld, J., & Reber, A. Internalized behavioral suppression and the timing of social punishment. *Journal of Personality and Social Psychology*, 1965, *5*, 13–16.

Asher, J. Mapping mental illness. *Alcohol, Drug Abuse and Mental Health News*, 1983, (9, (Feb.), 51–58.

Ashworth, A., & Gostin, L. Mentally disordered offenders and the sentencing process. *Criminal Law Review*, *23* 1984, 195–212.

Ayllon, T., & Milan, M. A. *Correctional rehabilitation and management: A psychological approach*. Chichester: Wiley, 1979.

Azrin, N. H. & Holz, W. C. Punishment. In W. K. Honig (Ed.), *Operant behavior: Areas of research and application*. New York: Appleton-Century-Crofts, 1966, pp. 215–234.

Bailey, W. C. Correctional outcome: An evaluation of 100 reports. *Journal of Criminal Law, Criminology and Police Science*, 1966, *57*, 153–160.

Baker, L. Estimating genetic correlations among discontinuous phenotypes: An analysis of criminal convictions and psychiatric diagnoses in Danish adoptees. *Behaviour Genetics*, 1986, *16*, 127–172.

Bancroft, H. Behavioral treatment of sexual deviations. In H. Leitenberg (Ed.), *Handbook of behavior modification and behavior therapy* (pp. 115–138). New York: Prentice-Hall, 1976.

Bancroft J. The application of psychophysiological methods to the assessment and modification of sexual behaviour. *Behaviour Research and Therapy*, 1971, *9*, 119–130.

Bancroft, J. *Deviant sexual behavior: Modification and assessment*. Oxford: Clarendon Press, 1974.

Bancroft, J. The nature of the patient–therapist relationship: Its relevance to behaviour modification of offenders. *British Journal of Criminology*, 1979, *19*, 416–419.

Bancroft, J. *Human sexuality and its problems*. London: Churchill Livingstone, 1983.

Bancroft, J., & Marks, I. Electric aversion therapy of sexual deviations. *Procedures of the Royal Society of Medicine*, 1968, *61*, 796–799.

Bancroft, J., Tennent, G., Loucas, K., & Cass, J. The control of deviant sexual behaviour by drugs: 1. Behavioural changes following oestrogens and antiandrogens. *British Journal of Psychiatry*, 1974, *125*, 310–315.

Bandura, A. *Aggression: A social-learning analysis*. Englewood Cliffs, N. J.: Prentice-Hall, 1973.

Bandura, A. *Social foundations of thought and action: A social cognitive theory*. Englewood Cliffs, N. J: Prentice-Hall, 1986.

Banister, P. A., Smith, E. V., Heskin, K. J. & Bolton, N. Psychological correlates of long-term imprisonment. *British Journal of Criminology*, 1973, *13*, 312–322.

Barack, L. I., & Widom, C. S. Eysenck's theory of criminality applied to women awaiting trial. *British Journal of Psychiatry*, 1978, *133*, 452–456.

Barash, D. P. *Sociobiology and behaviour*. Amsterdam: Elsevier, 1977.

Barbaree, H. E., Marshall, W. L., & Lanthier, R. D. Deviant sexual arousal in rapists. *Behaviour Research and Therapy*, 1979, *17*, 215–222.

Barfield, A. Biological influences on sex differences in behaviour. In M. S. Teitelbaum (Ed.), *Sex differences*. Garden City, N. Y.: Anchor, 1976, pp. 62–121.

Bargon, M. *Prostitution and Zuhalterei*. Lubeck: Schmidt-Romhild, 1982.

Barlow, D. H. Increasing heterosexual responsiveness in the treatment of sexual deviation: A review of the clinical and experimental evidence. *Behaviour Therapy*, 1973, *4*, 655–671.

Barlow, D. H. Assessment of sexual behaviour. In R. A. Ciminero, K. S. Calhoun, & H. E. Adams (Eds.), *Handbook of behavioral assessment*. New York: Wiley, 1977, pp. 134–151.

Barlow, D. H. & Agras, W. S. Fading to increase heterosexual responsiveness in homosexuals. *Journal of Applied Behavior Analysis*, 1973, *6*, 355–366.

Barnes, B. *T. S. Kuhn and social science*. London: Macmillan, 1982.

Barnes, G. Extraversion and pain. *British Journal of Social and Clinical Psychology*, 1975, *14*, 303–308.

Barnes. G. E. Malamuth, N. M., & Check, J. V. P. Personality and sexuality. *Personality and Individual Differences*, 1984, *5*, 159–172.

Baron, R. A. Outlines of a “Grand Theory.” *Contemporary Psychology*, 1987, *32*, 413–415.

Baron, R., Feeney, F., & Thornton, W. Preventing delinquency through diversion. *Federal Probation*, 1973, *37*, 13–18.

Barrett, P., & Eysenck., S. B. G. The assessment of personality factors across 25 countries. *Personality and Individual Differences*, 1984, *5*, 615–632.

Bartol, C. R. *Psychology and the American law*. Belmont, Calif.: Wadsworth Publishing Co., 1983.

Bartollas, C., & Miller, S. J. *The juvenile offender: Control, correction and treatment*. Boston & London: Holbrook Press, 1978.

Bauer J. *Vorlesungen uber allgemeine Konstitutions-Vererbungslehre*. Berlin: Springer, 1923.

Beatty, W. W. DRL behaviour in gerbils and hamsters of both sexes. *Bulletin of the Psychonomic society*, 1978, *11*, 41–42.

Beatty, W. W., & Fessler, R. G. Sex differences in sensitivity to electric shock in rats and hamsters. *Bulletin of the Psychonomic Society*, 1977, *10*, 189–190.

Beck, E. A., & McIntrye, S. C. MMPI patterns of shoplifters within a college population. *Psychological Reports*, 1977, *41*, 1035–1040.

Bell, R. D., Alexander, B. M., & Schwartzman, P. J. Methylphenidate decreases local gluclose metabolism in the motor cortex. *Pharmacological Biochemistry and Behaviour*, 1983, *18*, 1–15.

Bell, R. Q. A reinterpretation of the direction of effects in studies of socialization. *Psychological Review*, 1968, *75*, 81–95.

Bell, R. Q., & Costello, N. S. Three tests for sex differences in the tactile sensitivity of the newborn. *Biology of the Neonate*, 1964, *7*, 335–337.

Bell, R. Q., & Waldrop, M. F. Temperament and minor physical anomalies. In R. Porter & G. M. Collins (Eds.), Temperamental differences in infants and young children (Ciba Symposium No. 89, pp. 206–220). London: Pitman, 1982.

Belson, W. A. *Juvenile theft: The causal factors*. London: Harper & Row, 1975.

Berah, E. F., & Myers, R. G. The offense records of a sample of convicted exhibitionists. *Bulletin of the American Academy of Psychiatry and Law*, 1983, *11*, 365–374.

Berg, I., Consterdine, M., Hullin, R., McGuire, R., & Tyrer, S. The effects of two randomly allocated court procedures on truancy. *British Journal of Criminology*, 1978, *18*, 232–244.

Berg, I., Hullin, R., McGuire, R., & Tyrer, S. Truancy and the courts: Research note. *Journal of Child Psychology and Psychiatry*, 1977, *18*, 359–365.

Berlyne, D. E. *Studies in the new experimental aesthetics*. London: Wiley, 1974.

Berman, T., & Paisey, T. Personality in assaultive and non-assaultive juvenile male offenders. *Psychological Reports*, 1984, *54*, 527–530.

Beshai, J. A. Behavioural correlates of the EEG in delinquents. *Journal of Psychology*, 1971, *79*, 141–146.

Bessonet-Favre, A. *La typologie: Méthode d'observation des types humains*. Paris, 1910.

Berrueta-Clement, J. R., Schweinhart, L. J., Barnett, W. S., Epstein, A. S., & Weikart, D. P. *Changed lives*. Ypsilanti, Mich.: High/Scope, 1984.

Beyleveld, D. Ehrlich's analysis of deterrence. *British Journal of Criminology*, 1982, *22*, 101–123.

Blackburn, R. in relation to extreme aggression in psychiatric offenders. *British Journal of Psychiatry*, 1968, *114*, 821–828.

Blackburn, R. Personality types among abnormal homicides. *Special Hospitals Research Report*, No. 1. London: DHSS 1970.

Blackburn, R. Aggression and the EEG: A quantitative analysis. *Journal of Abnormal Psychology*, 1975, *84*, 358–365.

Blackburn, R. *Still not working? A look at recent outcomes in offender rehabilitation*. Paper presented at the Scottish Branch of the British Psychological Society Conference on Deviance, University of Stirling, February, 1980.

Blair, C. D. & Lanyon, R. I. Exhibitionism: Etiology and treatment. *Psychological Bulletin*, 1981, *89*, 439–463.

Blankenstein, K. R. Patterns of autonomic functioning in primary and secondary psychopaths. Unpublished M. A. thesis, University of Waterloo, 1969.

Blaszczynski, A. P. A winning bet: Treatment for compulsive gambling. *Psychology Today*, 1985, *19* (Dec.), 38–46.

Blau, T. H. *The psychologist as expert witness*. New York: Wiley, 1984.

Blomberg, T. G. Widening the net: An anomaly in the evaluation of diversion programs. In M. W. Klein & K. S. Teilmann (Eds.), *Handbook of Criminal Justice Evaluation*. London: Sage, 1980, pp. 572–592.

Bluglass, R. Incest. *British Journal of Hospital Medicine*, 1979, *22*, 152–157.

Bluglass, R. Assessing dangerousness in sex offenders. In J. R. Hamilton & H. Freeman (Eds.), *Dangerousness: Psychiatric assessment and management*. London: Royal College of Psychiatrists Special Publication 2. Gaskeel, 1982, pp. 68–72.

Bluglass, R. *A guide to the Mental Health Act 1983*. London: Churchill Livingstone, 1984.

Blumstein, A., Farrington, D. P., & Moitra, S. Delinquency careers: Innocents, desisters, and persisters. In M. Tonry & N. Morris (Eds.), *Crime and justice: An annual review of research* (Vol. 6). Chicago: University of Chicago Press, 1985, pp. 187–219.

Bochel, D. *Probation and after-care: Its development in England and Wales*. Edinburgh: Scottish Academic Press, 1976.

Bockner, S. Psychiatric aspects of shoplifting. *British Medical Journal*, 1976, *1*, 710.

Bohman, M., Cloninger, C. R., Sigvardsson, S., & von Knorring, A. L. Predisposition to petty criminalities in Swedish adoptees: Genetic and environmental heterogeneity. *Archives of General Psychiatry*, 1982, *39*, 1233–1241.

Bohmer, K. Untersuchungen über den Körperbau des Verbrechers. Quoted by Exner, 1939.

Roker, W., & Hafner, H. *Gewalttaten Geistesgestorter*. Berlin: Springer, 1973.

Bolton, N., Smith, F. V., Heskin, K. J., & Banister, P. A. Psychological correlates of long-term imprisonment. *British Journal of Criminology*, 1976, *16*, 38–47.

Borchard, E. M. *Convicting the innocent*. New York: Da Capo Press, 1970.

Borgstrom, C. A. Ein Serie von Kriminellen Zwillingen. *Archiv fur Rassenbiologie*, 1939.

Borkovec, T. Autonomic reactivity to sensory stimulation in psychopaths, neurotic and normal juvenile delinquents. *Journal of Consulting and Clinical Psychology*, 1970, *35*, 216–222.

Bottoms, A. E., & Sheffield, C. *Report on feasibility of research into intermediate treatment*. London: Report to the Department of Health and Social Security, 1980.

Bowers, W. J. & Pierce, G. L. The illusion of deterrence in Isaac Ehrlich's research on capital punishment. *Yale Law Journal*, 1975, *85*, 187–208.

Bridges, G. S. & Stone, J. A. Effects of criminal punishment on perceived threat of punishment: Toward an understanding of specific deterrence. *Journal of Research in Crime and Delinquency*, 1986, *23*, 207–239.

Brier, S. S., & Feinberg, S. E. Recent econometric modeling of crime and punishment: Support for the deterrence hypothesis? In S. E. Fienberg & A. J. Reiss (Eds.), *Indicators of Crime and Criminal Justice: Quantitative Studies*. Washington, D. C.: U. S. Government Printing Office, 1980, pp. 82–97.

Brierley, H. *Transvestism: A handbook with case studies for psychologists, psychiatrists and counsellors*. Oxford: Pergamon Press, 1979.

Brittain, R. P. The sadistic murderer. *Medicine, Science and the Law*, 1970, *10*, 198–207.

Brody, S. R. *The effectiveness of sentencing*. Home Office Research Study No. 35. London: H. M. S. O., 1976.

Brody, S., & Tarling, R. *Taking offenders out of circulation*. Home Office Research Study No. 64. London: H. M. S. O., 1980.

Brown, B. An application of social learning methods in a residential programme for young offenders. *Journal of Adolescence*, 1985, *8*, 321–331.

Brown, B. S., & Courtless, T. F. *The mentally retarded offender*. Reference document reproduced by the President's Commission on Law Enforcement and Administration of Justice, Washington, D. C., 1967.

Brown, E. J., Flanagan, T. J. & McLeod, M. (Eds.) *Sourcebook of criminal justice statistics—1983*. Washington, D. C.: Bureau of Justice Statistics, 1984.

Brown, G. L., Ebert, M. H., Goyer, P. F., Jimerson, D., Klein, W. J., Bunney, W. E., & Goodwin, F. K. Aggression, suicide and serotonin: Relationships to cerebrospinal fluid amine metabolites. *American Journal of Psychiatry*, 1982, *139*, 741–746.

Brown, R. A., Fader, K., & Barber, T. X. Responsiveness to pain: Stimulus-specificity versus generality. *Psychological Record*, 1973, *23*, 1–7.

Brownell, K. D., Hayes, S., & Barlow, D. H., Patterns of appropriate and deviant sexual arousal: The behavioral treatment of multiple sexual deviants. *Journal of Consulting and Clinical Psychology*, 1977, *45*, 1144–1155.

Buchsbaum, M. S., Davis, G. C., Coppola, R., & Dieter, N. Opiate pharmacology and individual differences: 1. Psychophysical pain measurement. *Pain*, 1981, *10*, 357–366.(a)

Buchsbaum, M. S., Davis, G. C., Coppola, R., & Dieter, N. Opiate pharmacology and individual differences: 2. Somatosensory evoked potentials. *Pain*, 1981, *10*, 367–377.(b)

Buckle, A., & Farrington, D. P. An observational study of shoplifting. *British Journal of Criminology*, 1984, *24*, 63–73.

Buehler, R. E., Patterson, G. R., & Furniss, J. M. The reinforcement of behaviour in institutional settings. *Behaviour Research and Therapy*, 1966, *4*, 157–167.

Buikhuisen, W. Cerebral dysfunctions and persistent juvenile delinquency. In S. A. Mednic, T. E. Moffitt., & S. A. Stack (Eds.), *The causes of crime*. Cambridge: Cambridge University Press, 1987, pp. 168–184.

Burchard, J. D., & Harig, P. T. Behaviour modification and juvenile delinquency. In H. Leiternberg (Ed.), *Handbook of behavior modification and behavior therapy*. Englewood Cliffs, N.J.: Prentice-Hall, 1976, pp. 405–452.

Burchard, J., & Vernon, T. The modification of delinquent behaviour through operant conditioning. *Behaviour Research and Therapy*, 1965, *2*, 245–250.

Burg, C., Hart, D., Quinn, P., & Rapaport, J. L. Newborn minor physical anomalies and prediction of infant behaviour. *Journal of Autism and Childhood Schizophrenia*, 1978, *8*, 427–439.

Burgess, P. K. Eysenck's theory of criminality: A new approach. *British Journal of Criminality*, 1972, *12*, 74–82.

Burkett, S., & Jenson, E. Conventional ties, peer influence, and fear of apprehension: A study of adolescent marijuana use. *Sociological Quarterly*, 1975, *16*, 522–533.

Burt, C. Factorial studies of personality and their bearing on the work of the teacher. *British Journal of Educational Psychology*, 1965, *35*, 308-328.

Bush, S. Predicting and parenting child abuse. *Psychology Today*, 1970, *11*,(Jan.), 99.

Buss. A. H., & Plomin, R. *Temperament: Early developing personality traits*. Hillsdale, N. J.: Lawrence Erlbaum, 1978.

Cacioppo, J. T., & Petty, R. E. Lateral asymmetry in the expression of cognition and emotion. *Journal of Experimental Psychology*, 1981, *7*, 333–341.

Cadoret, R. J., Cain, C. A., & Crowe, R. R. Evidence for gene-environment interaction in the development of adolescent and antisocial behaviour. *Behaviour Genetics*, 1983, *13*, 301–310.

Campbell, M., Geller, B., Small, A., Petti, T., & Ferris, S. Minor physical anomalies in young psychotic children. *American Journal of Psychiatry*, 1978, *135*, 573–575.

Campbell, R. The laterilisation of emotion: A critical review. *International Journal of Psychology*, 1982, *17*, 211–229.

Cantwell, D. Genetic studies of hyperactive children: Psychiatric illness in biological and adopting parents. In R. Fieve, D. Rosentahl, & H. Brill (Eds.), *Genetic research in psychiatry*. Baltimore: Johns Hopkins University Press, 1975.

Cantwell, D. P. Hyperactivity and antisocial behaviour revisited: A critical review of the literature. In D. O. Lewis (Ed.), *Vulnerabilities to delinquency*. New York: SP Medical & Scientific Books, 1981, pp. 21–38.

Castellino, D. *La costituzione individuale: La personalita*. Naples, 1927.

Cattell, R. B., & Cattell, M. D. L. *Handbook for the High School Personality Questionnaire*. Champaign, Ill.: IPAT, 1969.

Cautela, J. R., & Wisocki, P. A. Covert sensitisation for the treatment of sexual deviations. *Psychological Record*, 1971, *21*, 37–48.

Cavior, H. E., & Schmidt, A. A test of the effectiveness of a differential treatment strategy at the Robert F. Kennedy Center. *Criminal Justice and Behavior*, 1978, *5*, 131–139.

Cernkovich, S. A., Giordano, P. C., & Pugh, M. D. Chronic offenders: The missing cases in self-report delinquency research. *Journal of Criminal Law and Criminology*, 1985, *76*, 705–732.

Child, I. L. The relation of somatotype to self-ratings on Sheldon's temperamental traits. *Journal of Personality*, 1950, *18*, 440–453.

Chiswick, D. Sex crimes. *British Journal of Psychiatry*, 1983, *143*, 236–242.

Christiansen, K. O. A preliminary study of criminality among twins. In S. A. Mednick & K. O. Christiansen (Eds.), *Biosocial bases of criminal behaviour*. New York: Gardner Press, 1977(a), pp. 89–108.

Christiansen, K. O. a review of studies of criminality among twins. In S. A. Mednick & K. O. Christiansen (Eds.), *Biosocial bases of criminal behaviour*. New York: Gardner Press, 1977(b), pp. 45–88.

Christie-Brown, J. R. W. Parophilias: Sadomasochism, fetishism, transvestism and transexuality. *British Journal of Psychiatry*, 1983, *143*, 227–231.

Church, R. M. The varied effects of punishment on behaviour. *Psychological Review*, 1963, *70*, 369–402.

Chute, C. L., & Bell, M. *Crime, courts and probation*. New York: Macmillan, 1956.

Clarke, R. V. G. Psychology and crime. *Bulletin of the British Psychological Society*, 1977, *30*, 280–283.

Clarke, R. V. G. Situational crime prevention: Its theoretical basis and pratical scope. In N. Morris & M. Tonry (Eds.), *Crime and Justice* (Vol. 4). Chicago: University of Chicago, Press, 1983.

Clarke, R. V. G. Jack Tizard Memorial Lecture: Delinquency, environment and intervention. *Journal of Child Psychology and Psychiatry*, 1985, *26*, 505–523.

Clarke, R. V. G., & Cornish, D. B. The effectiveness of residential treatments for delinquents. In Hersov, L. A., Berger, M., & Shaffer, D. (Eds.), *Aggression and anti-social behaviour in childhood and adolescence*. Oxford: Pergamon Press, 1978.

Clarke, R. V. G., & Mayhew, P. (Eds.) *Designing out crime*. London: H. M. S. O., 1980.

Clarke, S. H. Getting 'em out of circulation: Does incarceration of juvenile offenders reduce crime? *Journal of Criminal Law and Criminilogy*, 1975, *65*, 528–535.

Cleckley, H. J. *The mark of sanity*. St. Louis, Mosby, 1976.

Cloninger, C. R., Christiansen, K. O., Reich, T., & Gottesman, I. I. Implications of sex differences in the prevalence of antisocial personality, alcoholism and criminality for familial transmission. *Archives of General Psychiatry*, 1978, *35*, 941–951.

Cloninger, C. R., & Gottesman, I. I. Genetic and environmental factors in antisocial behaviour. In S. A. Mednick, T. E. Moffitt, & S. A. Stack (Eds.), *The causes of crime*. Cambridge: Cambridge University Press, 1987, pp. 92–109.

Cloninger, C. R., Reich, T., & Guze, S. B. The multi-factorial model of disease transmission 2. Sex differences in the familial transmission of sociopathy (anti-social personality). *British Journal of Psychiatry*, 1975, *127*, 11–22.

Cloninger, C. R., Reich, T., & Guze, S. B. Genetic-environment interactions and antisocial behaviour. In R. D. Hare & D. Schalling (Eds.), *Psychopathic behaviour*. New York: Wiley, 1978, pp. 225–237.

Cloninger, C. R., Sigvardsson, S., Bohman, G., & von Knorring, A. L. Predisposition to petty criminality in Swedish adoptees: 2. Cross-fostering analysis of gene-environment interaction. *Archives of General Psychiatry*, 1982, *39*, 1242-1247.

Cockett, R. Borstal training: A follow-up study. *British Journal of Criminology*, 1967, *7*, 150–183.

Cohen, L. E. & Felson, M. Social change and crime rate trends: A routine activity approach. *American Sociological Review*, 1979, *44*, 588–608.

Cohen, S., & Taylor, L. *Psychological survival: The experience of long-term imprisonment*. Harmondsworth: Penguin, 1972.

Coker, J. B., & Martin, J. P. *Licensed to live*. Worcester, England: Billing & Sons, 1985.

Cole, C. F. *The American system of criminal justice*. North Scituate, Mass.: Duxbury, 1975.

Coleman, J. S., Campbell, E. G., Hobsan, C. J., McPartland, J., Mood, A. M., Weinfeld, F. D., & York, R. L. *Equality of educational opportunity*. Washington D. C.: U. S. Government Printing Office, 1966.

Cone, J. D. The Behavioural Assessment Grid (BAG): A conceptual framework and taxonomy. *Behaviour Therapy*, 1978, *9*, 882–888.

Cone, J. D. & Hawkins, R. P. Current status and future directions in behavioural assessment. In J. D. Cone & R. P. Hawkins (Eds.), *Behavioural assessment: New directions in clinical psychology*. New York: Brunn/Mazel, 1977.

Conley, J. J. The hierarchy of consistency: A review and model of longitudinal findings on adult individual differences in intelligence, personality, and self-opinion. *Personality and Individual Differences*, 1984, *5*, 11–26.

Conley, J. J. Longtidunal stability of personality traits: A multitrait-multimethod-multioccasion analysis. *Journal of Personality and Social Psychology*, 1985, *49*, 1266–1282.

Conners, C., & Eisenberg, L. The effects of methylphenidate on symptomatology and learning in disturbed children. *American Journal of Psychiatry*, 1963, *120*, 458–464.

Conners, C., & Rothschild, G. Drugs and learning in children. In J. Hellmuth (Ed.), *Learning disorders* (Vol. 3). Seattle: Special Child Publications, 1968, pp. 191–223.

Copas, J. B., O'Brien, M., Roberts, J., & Whiteley, J. S. Treatment outcome in personality disorder: The effects of social, psychological and behavioural variables. *Personality and Individual Differences*, 1984, *5*, 565–573.

Cornish, D. B., & Clarke, R. V. G. *Residential treatment and its effects on delinquency.* Home Office Research Study No. 32. London: H. M. S. O., 1975.

Cortes, J. B., & Galtti, F. M. *Delinquency and crime: A biopsychosocial approach.* New York: Seminar Press, 1972.

Cote, G., & Leblanc, M. Aspects de personalite et comportement delinquant. *Bulletin de Psychologique*, 1982, *36*, 265–271.

Cox, V. C., Paulus, P. B., & McCain, G. Prison crowding research. *American Psychologist*, 1984, *39*, 1148–1160.

Craft, A., & Craft, M. Treatment of sexual offenders. In M. Craft & A. Craft, (Eds.), *Mentally Abnormal Offenders.* London: Bailliere Tindall, 1984, pp. 403–416.

Craft. A., Craft, M., & Spencer, M. Sexual offences: Intent and characteristics. In M. Craft & A. Craft (Eds.), *Mentally Abnormal Offenders.* London: Bailliere Tindall, 1984.

Craig, M. M., & Glick, S. Ten years experience with the Glueck Prediction Table. *Crime and Delinquency*, 1963, *9*, 249–261.

Crowford, D. A. The HDHQ results of long-terms prisoners: Relationship with criminal and institutional behaviour. *British Journal of Social and Clinical Psychology*, 1977, *16*, 391–354.

Crowford, D. A. Modification of deviant sexual behaviour: The need for a comprehensive approach. *British Journal of Medical Psychology*, 1979, *52*, 151–156.

Crowford, D. A. Treatment approaches with paedophiles. In M. Cook & K. Howells (Eds.), *Adult sexual interest in children.* New York: Academic Press, 1981, pp. 181–217.

Crowford, D. Behaviour Therapy. In M. Craft & A. Craft (Eds.), *Mentally Abnormal Offenders.* London: Bailliere Tindall, 1984, pp. 417–435.

Crowford, D. A., & Allen, J. V. A social skills training programme with sex offenders. In M. Cook & G. W. Wilson (Eds.), *Love and attraction: An international conference.* Oxford: Pergamon Press, 1979.

Crowford, D. A., Howells, K. The effect of sex education with disturbed adolescents. *Behavioural Psychotherapy*, 1982, *10*, 339–345.

Crepault, C., & Couture, M. Men's erotic fantasies. *Archives of Sexual Behaviour*, 1980, *9*, 565–581.

Crowe, R. The adopted offspring of women criminal offenders. *Archives of General Psychiatry*, 1972, *27*, 600–603.

Crowe, R. An adoptive study of psychopathy. In R. Fieve, D. Rosenthal, & H. Brill (Eds.), *Genetic research in psychiatry.* Baltimore: John Hopkins University Press, 1975, pp. 115–134.

Curzon, L. B. *A dictionary of law.* London: Pitman, 1986.

Cusson, M., & Pinsonneault, P. The decision to give up crime. In D. B. Cornish & R. V. Clarke (Eds.), *The reasoning criminal: Rational choice perspectives on offending.* New York: Springer-Verlag, 1986, pp. 72–82.

Dahlberg, G. *Twin births and twins from an hereditary point of view.* Stockholm: Tiden, 1926.

Dahlstrom, W. G., & Dahlstrom, L. (Eds.), *Basic Readings on the MMPI.* Minneapolis: University of Minnesota Press, 1980.

Dalgard, O. S., & Kringlen, E. A Norwegian twin study of criminality. *British Journal of Criminology*, 1976, *16*, 213–232.

Daly, M. & Wilson, M. *Sex, evolution and behaviour.* North Scituate, Mass.: Duxbury, 1978.

Daum, I., & Reitz, E. Personality correlates of delinquent behaviour in juveniles and adolescents: Evidence from German studies. *Personality and Individual Differences*, in press.

Davidson, M. A., McInnes, R. G., & Parnell, R. W. The distribution of personality traits in 7-year old children. *British Journal of Educational Psychology*, 1957, *27*, 48–61.

Davidson, P. O., & McDougal, L. Personality and pain tolerance measures. *Perceptual and Motor Skills*, 1969, *28*, 787–790.

Davidson, W. S., & Seidman, E. Studies of behaviour modification and juvenile delinquency: A review, methodological critique and social perspective. *Psychological Bulletin*, 1974, *81*, 998–1011.

Davies, M. B. *The use of the Jesness Inventory on a sample of British probationers.* London: H. M. S. O., 1967.

Davies, T. S. Collaborative clinical experience with cyproterone acetate. *Journal of International Medical Research*, 1975, *3*, 16–19.

Davis, G. E., & Leitenberg, H. Adolscent sex offenders. *Psychological Bulletin*, 1987, *101*, 417–427.

Davis, H. D., Porter, J. W., Burton, J., & Levine, S. Sex and strain differences in lever press shock escape behaviour. *Physiology and Psychology*, 1976, *4*, 351–356.

Davis, K. R., & Sines, J. O. An antisocial behaiour pattern associated with a specific MMPI profile. *Journal of Consulting and Clinical Psychology*, 1971, *36*, 229–234.

DeFries, J. C., Vanderberg, S. G., & McClean, G. E. Genetics of specific cognitive abilities. *Annual Review in Genetics*, 1976, *10*, 179–207.

Department of Defense. *Profile of american youth: 1980 nationwide administration of the Armed Forces Vocational Aptitude Battery.* Washington, D. C.: Office of the Assistant Secretary of Defense, 1982.

Department of Health, Education and Welfare. *Intellectual development and school achievement of youths 12–17 years.* Washington, D. C.: U. S. Government Printing Office, 1976.

Dettenborn, H. Beziehungen im psychologisch relevanten Determinationskamplex der Jugendkriminalität. *Probleme und Ergebnisse der Psychologie*, 1971, *39*, 27–29.

Diamond, M. C. Age, sex, and environmental influences. In N. Geschwing, & A. M. Galaburda (Eds.), *Cerebral dominance: The biological foundations.* Cambridge, Mass.: Harvard University Press, 1984, pp. 134–146.

Dicken, C. F. Simulated patterns on the Edwards Personal Preference Schedule. *Journal of Applied Psychology*, 1959, *43*, 372–377.

Dickstein, E. B. Biological and cognitive bases of moral functioning. *Human Development*, 1979, *22*, 37–59.

Dietz, P. E. *Sexual deviations: Classification and relation to offences.* Paper presented at the conference "The State of Forensic Psychiatry," held at the Royal Institute of British Architects, London, October, 1986.

Dietz, P. E., Cox, D. J., & Wegener, S. Male genital exhibitionism. In W. J. Curran, A. L. McGarry & S. A. Shah (Eds.), *Forensic psychiatry and psychology.* Philadelphia: F. A. Davis Co., 1986, pp. 363–385.

Dinitz, S., & Conrad J. P. The dangerous two percent. In D. Shichor & D. H. Kelly (Eds.), *Critical issues in juvenile delinquency*, Massachusetts, Toronto: Lexington Books, 1980, pp. 139–155.

Ditchfield, J. A. *Police cautioning in England and Wales.* Home Office Research Study No. 37. London: H. M. S. O., 1976.

Dixon, M. *Juvenile delinquency prevention programs.* Washington, D. C.: National Science Foundation, 1974.

Doering, C. H., Bordie, H., Kraemar, H. C., Noos, R. H. Becker, H. B., & Hamburg,

D. A. Negative effect and plasma testosterone: A longitudinal human study. *Psychosomatic Medicine*, 1975, *37*, 484–491.

Dongerink, H. A., & Bertilson, H. S. Psychopathy and physiological arousal in an aggressive task. *Psychophysiology*, 1975, *12*, 682–684.

Douglas, J. M. B. Premature children at primary school. *British Medical Journal*, 1960, *1*, 1008.

Douglas, J., & Ross, J. M. Characteristics of delinquent boys and their homes. In J. M. Thoday & A. S. Parkes (Eds.), *Genetic and environmental influences on behaviour*. Edinburgh: Oliver & Boyd, 1968, pp. 114–127.

Down, J. L. H. Observations on an ethnic classification of idiots. *London Hospital Clinical Lecture Reports*, 1866, *3*, 259–262.

Downes, D., & Rock, P. *Understanding deviance*. Oxford: Oxford University Press, 1982.

Dubey, D. R. Organic factors in hyperkinesis: A critical evaluation. *American Journal of Orthopsychiatry*, 1976, *46*, 353–366.

Duncan, O. D., Featherman, D. L., & Duncan, B. *Socioeconomic background and achievement*. New York: Seminar Press, 1972.

Dunford, F.D., Osgood, W., & Weichselbaum, H. F. *National evaluation of juvenile diversions projects*. Washington, D.C.: The National Institute of Juvenile Justice and Delinquency Prevention, Office of Juvenile Justice and Delinquency Prevention, U.S. Department of Justice, 1981.

Dunlop, A. B. *The approved school experience*. Home Office Research Study No. 25. London: H.M.S.O., 1974.

Earls, C. M., & Quinsey, V. L. What is to be done? Future research on the assessment and behavioral treatment of sex offenders. *Behavioral Sciences and the Law*, 1985, *3*, 377–390.

East, W. N. *The adolescent criminal*. London: Churchill, 1942.

Easterlin, R. A. Does human fertility adjust to the environment? *American Economic Review*, 1971, *61*, 399–410.

Eaves, L.J., & Eysenck, H. J. The nature of extraversion: A genetical analysis. *Journal of Personality and Social Psychology*, 1975, *32*, 102–112.

Eaves, L. J., & Eysenck, H. J. Genetical and environmental components of inconsistency and unrepeatability in twins' responses to a neuroticism questionnaire. *Behaviour Genetics*, 1976, *6*, 145–160. (a)

Eaves, L. J., & Eysenck, H. J. Genotype × age interaction for neuroticism. *Behaviour Genetics*, 1976, *6*, 359–362. (b)

Eaves. L. J., & Eysenck, H. J. A genotype-environmental model for psychoticism. *Advances in Behaviour Research and Therapy*, 1977, *1*, 5–26.

Eaves, L. J., Eysenck, H. J., & Martin, N. G., *Genes, culture and personality: An empirical approach*. New York: Academic Press, in press.

Eaves, L. J., & Young, P. A. Genetical theory and personality differences. In R. Lynn (Ed.), *Dimensions of personality*. London: Pergamon Press, 1981, pp. 129–179.

Eeg-Olofsson, D. The development of the EEG in normal adolescents from the ages of 16 to 21 years. *Neuro-paediatrie*, 1971, *3*, 11–45.

Ehrenkranz, J., Bliss, E., & Sheard, M. H. Plasma testosterone: Correlation with aggressive behaviour and social dominance in man. *Psychosomatic medicine*, 1974, *36*, 469–475.

Ehrlich, I. The deterrent effects of capital punishment: A question of life and death. *American Economic Review*, 1975, *65*, 397–417.

Ehrlich, I. Capital punishment and deterrence: Some further thoughts and additional evidence. *Journal of Political Economy*, 1977, *85*, 741–788.

Eiben, O. G. *The physique of women athletes.* Budapest: Hungarian Scientific Council for Physical Education, 1972.

Eilenberg, H. D. Remand home boys, 1930–1955. *British Journal of Criminology,* 1961, *2,* 111–131.

Einhorn, H. J., & Hogarth, R. M. Judging probable cause. *Psychological Bulletin,* 1986, *99,* 3–19.

Eisenberg, J. F. *The mammalian radiations: An analysis of trends in evolution, adaptation, and behaviour.* Chicago: University of Chicago Press, 1981.

Eitzen, D. S. The effects of behavior modification on the attitudes of delinquents. In J. S. Stumphauzer (Ed.), *Progress in behaviour therapy with delinquents.* Springfield, Ill.: Charles C Thomas, 1979, pp. 146–155.

Ekman, G. On the number and definition of dimensions in Krestschmer's and Sheldon's constitutional systems. In Kungsgat *Essays in Psychology* (pp. 83–98) Uppsala, 1951. (a)

Ekman, G. On typological and dimensional systems of reference in describing personality. *Acta Psychologica,* 1961, *8,* 1–24. (b)

Elliott, D. S. A repertoire of impact measures. In M. Klein & K. S. Teilmann (Eds.), *Handbook of criminal justice evaluation.* Beverly Hills: Sage, 1980, pp. 507–544.

Ellis, L. Genetics and criminal behaviour. *Criminology,* 1982, *20,* 45–66.

Ellis, L. Evidence of neuroendrogenic etiology of sex roles from a combined analysis of human, nonhuman, primate and nonprimate mammalian studies. *Personality and Individual Differences,* 1987, in press.

Ellis, L. Criminal Behaviour and r-vs. K selection: An extension of gene-based evolutionary theory, *Personality and Individual Differences,* 1988, *9,* 697–708.

Ellis, L. Androgens, brain functioning and criminality. *Social Biology,* in press. (a)

Ellis, L. Criminal behaviour and r- vs. K-selection. *Personality and Individual Differences,* in press. (b)

Ellis, L. The relationship of ciminality and psychopathy with eight other behavioural manifestations of sub-optimal arousal, in press. (d)

Ellis, L. The victimful-victimless crime distinction, and seven universal demographic correlates of victimful behaviour. *Personality and Individual Differences,* 1988, *9,* 525–548.

Empey, L. T. *American delinquency: Its meaning and construction.* Homewood, Ill.: Dorsey, 1978.

Empey, L. T. Field experimentation in criminal justice: Rationale and design. In M. W. Klein & K. S. Teilmann (Eds.), *Handbook of criminal justice evaluation.* London: Sage, 1980, pp. 143–176. (a)

Empey, L. T. Revolution and counterrevolution: Current trends in juvenile justice. In D. Shichor & D. H. Kelly (Eds.), *Critical issues in juvenile delinquency.* Massachusetts, Toranto: Lexington Books, 1980, pp. 157–180. (b)

Empey, L. T., & Erickson, M. L. *The Provo experiment: Evaluating community control of delinquency.* Lexington, Mass. : Heath, 1972.

Empey, L. T., & Lubeck, S. G. *The Silverlake experiment: Testing delinquency theory and community intervention.* Chicago: Aldine, 1971.

Ennis, P. *Criminal victimization in the United States: a report of a national survey* (Field Surveys. Washington, D.C.: President's Commission on Law Enforcement and Administration of Justice, 1967.

Epps, P., & Parnell, R. W. Physique and temperament of women delinquents compared with women undergraduates. *British Journal of Medical Psychology,* 1952, *25,* 249–255.

Epstein, A. W. Fetishism: A comprehensive view. In J. Masserman (Ed.), *Dynamics of deviant sexuality*. New York: Grune & Stratton, 1969.
Erickson, M. L. The changing relation between official and self reported measures of delinquency: An exploratory descriptive study. *Journal of Criminal Law, Criminology and Police Science*, 1972, *63*, 388–395.
Erickson, M. L., & Gibbs, J. P. Punishment, Deterrence, and juvenile justice. In D. Shichor & D. H. Kelly (Eds.) *Critical issues in juvenile delinquency*. Massachusetts, Toronto: Lexington Books, 1980, pp. 183–202.
Evans, D. R. Subjective variables and treatment effects in aversion therapy. *Behaviour Research and Therapy*, 1970, *8*, 147–152.
Evans, P. Most prisoners on remand avoid jail. *The Times*, 19, June 1987, p. 5.
Evil preacher jailed sixteen years for drug rape of virgin. *The Times*, 14 February 1987, p. 3.
Exner, F. *Kriminalbiologie in ihren Grandzugen*. Hamburg: Hanseatische Verlagsaustalt, 1939.
Eysenck, H. J. Symposium: The development of moral values in children. 7. The contribution of learning theory. *British Journal of Educational Psychology*, 1960, *30*, 11–21.
Eysenck, H. J. *Experiments with drugs*. Oxford: Pergamon, 1963.
Eysenck, H. J. *Crime and personality*. London: Routledge & Kegan Paul, 1964.
Eysenck, H. J. *The biological basis of personality*. Springfield, Ill.: Charles C Thomas, 1967.
Eysenck, H. J. *The structure of human personality* (3rd Ed.). London: Mathuen, 1970.
Eysenck, H. J. Personality, learning and "anxiety." In H. J. Eysenck (Ed.), Handbook of abnormal psychology (2nd Ed.). London: Pitman, 1973, pp. 340–419.
Eysenck, H. J. The biology of morality. In T. Lickona (Ed.), *Moral development and behaviour*. New York: Holt, Rinehart Winston, 1976, pp. 108–123. (a)
Eysenck, H. J. *Sex and personality*. London: Open Books, 1976. (b)
Eysenck, H. J. *Crime and personality* (3rd ed.). London: Routledge & Kegan Paul, 1977.
Eysenck, H. J. The biosocial model of man and the unification of psychology. In A. J. Chapman & D. M. Janes (Eds.), *Models of Man*. Leicester: British Psychological Society, 1980, pp. 49–62. (a)
Eysenck, H. J. The biosocial nature of man. *Journal of Social and Biological Structures, 1980*, *3*, 125–134. (b)
Eysenck, H. J. Psychopathie. In U. Baumann, H. Berbalk, & G. Seidenstucker (Eds.), *Klinishe Psychologie: Trends in Forschung and Praxis* (Vol. 3). Wien: H. Huber, 1980, pp. 323-360. (c)
Eysenck, H. J. (Ed.). *A model for personality*. New York: Springer, 1981.
Eysenck, H. J. The sociology of psychological knowledge, the genetic interpretation of the IQ, and Marxish-Leninist ideology. *Bulletin of the British psychological Society*, 1982, *35*, 449–451.
Eysenck, H. J. A biometrical-genetical analysis of impulsive and sensation seeking behaviour. In M. Zuckerman (Ed.), *Biological bases of sensation seeking, impulsivity and anxiety*. Hillsdale, N. J.: Lawrence Erlbaum, 1983, pp. 1–27. (a)
Eysenck, H. J. Drugs as research tools in psychology: Experiments with drugs in personality research. *Neuropsychobiology*, 1983a, *10*, 29–43. (b)
Eysenck, H. J. Psychopharmacology and personality. In W. Janke (Ed.), *Response variability to psychotropic drugs*. Oxford: Pergamon Press, 1983, pp. 127–154. (c)
Eysenck, H. J. Is there a paradigim in personality research? 1983d, *17*, 369–397.
Eysenck, H. J. Meta-analysis: An abuse of research integration. *Journal of Special Education*, 1984, *18*, 41–59.

Eysenck, H. J. The definition of personality disorders and the criteria appropriate for their description. *Journal of Personality Disorders*, 1987, *1*, 211–219. (a)

Eysenck, H. J. Personality theory and the problem of criminality. In B. J. Mc Gurk, D. M. Thornton, & M. Williams (Ed.), *Applying psychology to imprisonment.* 1987, pp. 29–58. London: H.M.S.O.

Eysenck, H. J. Personality and ageing: An exploratory analysis. *Journal of Social Behaviour and Personality*, in press. (a)

Eysenck, H. J. Psychological factors in the perception and toleration of pain, in press. (b)

Eysenck, H. J., Arnold, W., & Meili, R. (Eds.). *Encyclopedia of Psychology.* London: Search Press, 1972.

Eysenck, H. J., & Barrett, P. Psychophysiology and the measurement of intelligence. In C. R. Reynolds & V. Willson (Eds.), *Methodological and statistical advances in the study of individual differences.* New York: Plenum Press, 1985, pp. 1–49.

Eysenck, H. J., & Cookson, D. Personality in primary school children: 1 Ability and achievement. *British Journal of Educational Psychology*, 1969, *39*, 109–112.

Eysenck, H. J., & Eysenck, M. W. *Personality and individual differences.* New York: Plenum Press, 1985.

Eysenck, H. J., & Eysenck, S. B. G. *Manual of the Eysenck Personality Inventory (J).* London: University of London Press, 1965.

Eysenck, H. J., & Eysenck, S. B. G. *Psychoticism as a Dimension of Personality.* London: Hodder & Stoughton, 1976.

Eysenck, H. J., & Eysenck, S. B. G. Psychopathy, personality and genetics. In R. D. Hare & D. Schalling (Eds.), *Psychopathic behaviour.* London: Wiley, 1978, pp. 197–223.

Eysenck, H. J., & Eysenck, S. B. G. Recent advances in the cross-cultural study of personality. In J. N. Butcher & C. D. Spielberger (Eds.) *Advances in personality assessment* (Vol. 2). Hillsdale, N. J.: Erlbaum, 1983, pp. 41–69.

Eysenck, H. J., & Martin, I. (Eds.). *The theoretical foundations of behaviour therapy.* New York: Plenum Press, 1987.

Eysenck, H. J., Nias, D. K. B., & Cox, D. N. Sport and personality. *Advances in Behaviour Research and Therapy*, 1982, *4*, 1056.

Eysenck, H. J., Wakefield, J. A., & Friedman, A. Diagnosis and clinical assessment: The DSM-III. *Annual Review of Psychology*, 1983, *34*, 167–193.

Eysenck, H. J., & Wilson, G. *The psychology of sex.* London: Dent, 1979.

Eysenck, H. J., & Eysenck, H. J. Mischel and the concept of personality. *British Journal of Psychology*, 1980, *71*, 191–209.

Eysenck, S. B. G., & Eysenck, H. J. Crime and personality: An empirical study of the three-factor theory. *British Journal of Criminology*, 1970, *10*, 225–239.

Eysenck, S. B. G., & Eysenck, H. J. A comparative study of criminals and matched controls in three dimensions of personality. *British Journal of Social and Clinical Psychology*, 1971, *10*, 362–366. (a)

Eysenck, S. B. G., & Eysenck, H. J. Crime and personality: Item analysis of questionaire responses. *British Journal of Criminology*, 1971, *11*, 49–62.(b)

Eysenck, S. B. G., & Eysenck, H. J. The personality of female prisoners. *British Journal of Psychiatry*, 1973, *122*, 693–698.

Eysenck, S. B. G., & Eysenck, H. J. Personality and recidivism in Borstal boys. *British Journal of Criminology*, 1974, *14*, 285–287.

Eysenck, S. B. G., & Eysenck, H. J. Personality differences between prisoners and controls. *Psychological Reports*, 1977, *40*, 1023–1028.

Eysenck, S. B. G., & Eysenck, H. J. Impulsiveness and venturesomeness in children. *Personality and Individual Differences*, 1980, *1*, 73–78.

Eysenck, S. B. G., Rust, J., & Eysenck, H. J. Personality and the classification of adult offenders. *British Journal of Criminology*, 1977, *17*, 169–179.

Fahrenberg, J., Selg, H., & Hampel, R. *Das Freiburger Personlichkeits-inventar.* Gottingen: Hogrefe, 1978.

Fairhead, S. *Petty persistent offenders.* Home Office Research Study No.66. London, H.M.S.O., 1981.

Fakouri, E., & Jesse, F. W. Unobtrusive detection of potential juvenile delinquency. *Psychological Reports*, 1976, *39*, 551–558.

Farley, F. H. The big T in personality. *Psychology Today*, 1986, *20*(May), 44–52.

Farley, F. H., & Farley, S. V. Stimulus-seeking motivation and delinquent among institutionalized delinquent girls. *Journal of Consulting and Clinical Psychology*, 1972, *39*, 94–97.

Farley, F. H., & Sewell, T. Test of an arousal theory of delinquency. *Criminal Justice and Behaviour*, 1976, *3*, 315–320.

Farrington, D. P. Self-reports of deviant behaviour: Productive and stable? *Journal of Criminal Law and Criminology*, 1973, *64*, 99–110.

Farrington, D. P. Experiments on deviance with special reference to dishonesty. In L. Berkowitz (Ed.), *Advances in experimental social psychology* (Vol. 12). New York: Academic Press, 1979, pp. 138–152.

Farrington, D. P. Truancy, delinquency, the home and the school. In L. Hersov & I. Berg (Eds), *Out of school.* Chichester: Wiley, 1980, pp. 241–259.

Farrington, D. P. Longitudinal analyses of criminal violence. In M. E. Wolfgang & N. A. Weiner (Eds.), *Criminal violence*, Beverley Hills: Sage, 1982, pp. 171–200.

Farrington, D. P. Offending from 10 to 25 years of age. In K. T. Van Dusen & S. A. Mednick (Eds), *Prospective studies of crime and delinquency.* Boston: Kluwer-Nijhoff, 1983, pp. 17–37. (a)

Farrington, D. P. Randomized experiments in crime and justice. In M. Morris & M. Tenry (Eds.), *Crime and justice* (Vol. 4, pp. 83–98). Chicago: University of Chicago Press, 1983. (b)

Farrington, D. P. Delinquency prevention in the 1980s. *Journal of Adolescence*, 1985, *8*, 3–16.

Farrington, D. P. Stepping stones to adult criminal careers. In D. Olweus, J. Block, & M. Radke-Yarrow (Eds.) *Development of antisocial and prosocial behaviour.* New York: Academic Press, 1986, pp. 359–384.

Farrington, D. P., & Bennett, T. Police cautioning of juveniles in London. *British Journal of Criminology*, 1981, *21*, 123–135.

Farrington, D. P. Biron, L., & LeBlanc, M. Personality and delinquency in London and Montreal. In J. Gunn & D. P. Farrington (Eds.), *Abnormal offenders, delinquency and the criminal justice system* pp. 121–148. New York: Wiley, 1982.

Farrington, D. P., & Kidd, R. F. Is financial dishonesty a rational decision? *British Journal of Social and Clinical Psychology*, 1977, *16*, 139–146.

Farrington, D. P., & Knight, B. J. Stealing from a "lost" letter: Effects of victim characteristics. *Criminal Justice and Behavior*, 1980, *7*, 423–436.

Farrington, D. P., & Nuttall, C. P. Prison size, overcrowding, person violence, and recidivism. *Journal of Criminal Justice*, 1980, *8*, 221–231.

Farrington, D. P., Ohlin, L. E., & Wilson, J. Q. *Understanding and controlling crime: Toward a new research strategy.* New York: Springer-Verlag, 1986.

Federal Bureau of Investigation. *Crime in the United States: Uniform crime reports.* Washington D.C.: U.S. Government Printing Office, 1985.

Feldman, M. P. *Criminal behaviour: A psychological analysis.* Chichester: Wiley, 1977.

Feldman, M. P., & MacCulloch, M. J. *Homosexual behaviour: Therapy and Assessment.* Oxford: Pergamon Press, 1971.

Feldman, R. A., Chaplinger, T. E., & Wodarski, J. S. *The St. Louis conundrum: The effective treatment of antisocial youths*. Englewood Cliffs, N. J.: Prentice-Hall, 1983.

Feshbach, N. D. Empathy, empathy training and the regulation of aggression in elementary school children. In R. M. Kaplan, V. J. Konecni, & R. W. Novaco (Eds.), *Aggression in children and Youths*. The Hague: Martinus Nijhoff, 1984.

Feyerherm, W. Measuring gender differences in delinquency. In M. Q. Warren (Ed.), *Comparing female and male offenders*. Beverly Hills: Sage, 1981, pp. 46–54.

Field, E. Research into detention centres. *British Journal of Criminology*, 1969, *8*, 62–71.

Field, L. H. Benpridoc in the treatment of sexual offenders. *Medicine, Science and the Law*, 1973, *13*, 195–196.

Field, L. H., & Williams, M. A note on the scientific assessment and treatment of the sex offender. *Medicine, Science and the Law*, 1971, *11*, 180–181.

Finckenauer, J. O. *Scared straight! and the panacea phenomenon*. Englewood Cliffs, N.J.: Prentice-Hall, 1982.

Firestone, P., Levy, F., & Douglas, V. I. Hyperactivity and physical anomalies. *Canadian Psychiatric Association Journal*, 1976, *21*, 23–26.

Firestone, P., Peters, S., Rivier, M., & Knights, R. M. Minor physical anomalies in hyperactive, retarded and normal children and their families. *Journal of Children Psychology and Psychiatry*, 1978, *19*, 155–160.

Fiske, D. W. The relation between physique and measures of intelligence, temperament and personality in superior adolescent boys. *Psychological Bulletin*, 1942, *39*, 459–478.

Fiske, D. W. A study of relationships to somatotype. *Journal of Applied Psychology*, 1944, *28*, 504–519.

Fitzgerald, P. J. *Criminal law and punishment*. Oxford: Claredon Press, 1962.

Floderus-Myrhed, B., Pederson, N., & Rasmuson, I. Assessment of heritability for personality based on a short form of the Eysenck Perroanlity Inventory: Studies of 12,898 pairs. *Behaviour Genetics*, 1980, *10*, 153–162.

Flor-Henry, P. Cerebral aspects of sexual deviation. In G. D. Wilson (Ed.), *Variant sexuality: Research and theory*. London & Sydney: Croom Helm, 1987, pp. 49–83.

Florida Division of Corrections. Impact of the Gideon decision upon crime and sentencing in Florida: A study of recidivism and sociocultural change (Research Monograph No. 2). Research and Statistics Division, 1966.

Foggitt, R. *Personality and delinquency*. Unpublished Ph.D. thesis, University of London, 1974.

Folkard, M. S. Second thoughts on IMPACT. In E. M. Goldberg & N. Connelly (Eds.), *Evaluating research in social care*. London: Heinemann, 1981

Folkard, M. S., Fowles, A. J., McWilliams, B. C., McWilliams, W., Smith, D. D., Smith, D. E., & Walmsley, G. R. *Intensive matched probation and after care treatment: Vol. 1. The design of the probation experiment and an interim evaluation*. Home office Research Study No. 24. London: H.M.S.O., 1974.

Fottrell, E. A study of violent behaviour among patients in psychiatric hospitals. *British Journal of Psychiatry*, 1980, *136*, 216–221.

Foulds, G. A., Caine, T. M., & Creasy, M. A. Aspects of extra- and intro-punitive expression in mental illness. *Journal of Mental Science*, 1960, *106*, 599–610.

Fowler, A. J. *Prison Welfare: An account of an experiment at Liverpool*. Home Office Research Study No. 45. London: H.M.S.O., 1978.

Fox, V. *Community-based corrections*. Englewood Cliffs, N.J.: Prentice-Hall, 1977.

Franks, C. M. Recidivism, psychopathy and personality. *British Journal of Delinquency*, 1956, *6*, 192–201.

Freeman, D. G. Sexual dimorphism and the status hierarchy. In D. R. Omark, F. F. Strayer, & D. G. Freedman (Eds.), *Dominance relations.* New York: Garland Press, 1980, pp. 261–271.

Frost, B. Capital punishment and deterrence: Conflicting evidence? *Journal of Criminal Law and Criminology,* 1983, *74,* 927–942.

Fulker, D. W. The genetic and environmental architecture of psychoticism, extraversion and neuroticism. In H. J. Eysenck (Ed.), *A model for personality.* New York: Springer, 1981, 88–122.

Fuller, J. L., & Simmel, E. C. *Behaviour genetics: Principles and applications.* Hillsdale, N.J.: Lawrence Erlbaum, 1983.

Furneaux, W. D., & Gibson, H. B. *Manual of the New Junior Maudsley Inventory.* London: University of London Press, 1966.

Gabrys, J. B., Peters, K., Robertson, G., Utendale, K., Schumph, D., Laye, R., O'Haire, T., Allard, I., & Phillips, N. Personality attributes of children with conduct disorders: The discriminent power of the Junior EPQ. *Personality and Individual Differences,* in press.

Gadgil, M., & Solbrig, O. T. The concept of r- and K-selection: Evidence from wild flowers and some theoretical considerations. *American Naturalist,* 1972, *106,* 14–31.

Gandelman, R. Gonadal hormones and sensory function. *Neuroscience and Behaviour Reviews,* 1983, *7,* 17.

Garrett, C. J. *Efficacy of treatment for adjudicated delinquents: Meta-analysis.* Paper presented at the annual meeting of the American Society of Criminology, Cincinnati, Ohio, November 1984.

Garrett, C. J. Effects of residential treatment on adjudicated delinquents: A meta-analysis. *Journal of Research and Crime and Delinquency,* 1985, *22,* 287–308.

Garrity, D. C. The prison as a rehabilitative agency. In D. R. Cressey (Ed.), *Studies in institutional organization and change.* New York: Holt Rinehard & Winston, 1961.

Gazzaniga, M. S. *The social brain.* New York: Basic Books, 1985.

Gattaz, W. F., & Beckman, H. Platelet MAO activity and personality characteristics: A study in schizophrenic patients and normal individuals. *Acta Psychiatrica Scandinavica,* 1981, *63,* 479–485.

Gayford, J. J. Indecent exposure: A review of the literature. *Medicine, Science and The Law,* 1981, *21,* 233–242.

Gebhard, P. H., Gagnon, J. H., Pomeroy, W. B., & Christenson, C. V. *Sex offenders.* New York: Harper & Row, 1965.

Giallombardo, R. Female delinquency. In D. Shichor & D. H. Kelly (Eds.), *Critical issues in juvenile delinquency.* Massachusetts, Toronto: Lexington Books, 1980, pp. 63–82.

Giallombardo, R. Female delinquency. In R. Giallombardo (Ed.), *Juvenile delinquency, a book of readings.* New York: Wiley, 1982, pp. 37–51.

Giarretto, H. A comprehensive child sexual abuse treatment programme. *Child Abuse and Neglect,* 1982, *6,* 263–278.

Gibb, F. Rapists can seek parole in 3 years. *The Times,* 4 February 1987, p. 3.

Gibbens, T. C. N. *Psychiatric studies of Borstal lads.* New York: Oxford University Press, 1963.

Gibbens, T. C. N. Borstal boys after 25 years. *British Journal of Criminology,* 1984, *24,* 49–62.

Gibbons, D. C. Offender typologies—two decades later. *British Journal of Criminology,* 1975, *15,* 140–156.

Gibson, H. B. An investigation of personality variables associated with susceptibility to hypnosis. University of London, Unpublished Ph.D. dissertation, 1962.

Gibson, H. B. The factorial structure of juvenile delinquency: A study of self-reported acts. *British Journal of Social and Clinical Psychology,* 1971, *10,* 1–9.

Gittelman, R., Mannuzza, S., Shenker, R., & Bonagura, N. Hyperactive boys almost grown up: Psychiatric status. *Archives of General Psychiatry*, 1985, *42*, 937–947.

Gittleson, N. L., Eacott, S. E., & Mehta, B. M. Victims of indecent exposure. *British Journal of Psychiatry*, 1978, *132*, 61–66.

Gladstone, F. J. Vandalism among adolescent schoolboys. In Clarke, R. V. G. (Ed.), *Tackling vandalism.* Home Office Research Study, No. 47, pp. 19–39 London: H.M.S.O., 1978.

Glaser, D. The interplay of theory, issues, policy, and data. In M. W. Klein & K. S. Teilmann (Eds.), *Handbook of criminal justice evaluation.* London: Sage, 1980, pp. 123–142.

Glass, G. V. Integrating findings: The meta-analysis of research. In L. Schulman (Ed.), *Review of research in education.* Itasca, Ill.: Peacock, 1977.

Gledhill, R. Judge Nina shows the way. *The Daily Mail,* 14 February 1987, p. 1.

Glick, R. M., & Neto, V. V. *National study of women's correctional programs.* Washington, D.C.: National Institute of Law Enforcement and Criminal Justice, 1977.

Glueck, S., & Glueck, E. *Unraveling juvenile delinquency.* New York: Commonwealth Fund, 1950.

Glueck, S., & Glueck, E. *Physique and delinquency.* New York: Harper, 1956.

Glueck, S., & Glueck, E. *Predicting delinquency and crime.* Cambridge, Mass.: Harvard University Press, 1959.

Glueck, S., & Glueck, E. (Eds.). *Identification of predelinquent validation studies and some suggested uses of the Glueck Table.* New York: Intercontinental Medical Books Corporation, 1972.

Goldberg, E. M., Gibbons, J., & Sinclair, I. *Problems, tasks and outcomes: The evaluation of task-centered casework in three settings.* London: Allen & Unwin, 1985.

Goldberg, E. M., & Stanley, S. J. Task-centered casework in a probation setting. In E. M. Goldberg, J. Gibbons, & I. Sinclair (Eds.), *Problems, tasks and outcomes: The evaluation of task-centered casework in three settings.* London: Allen & Unwin, 1985, pp. 89–166.

Goldfarb, W., & Batstein, A. Physical stigmata in schizophrenic children. Quoted by Paulhus & Martin, 1986.

Gordon, R. A. An explicit estimation of the prevalence of commitment to a training school, to age 18, by race and sex. *Journal of the American Statistical Association,* 1973, *68*, 547–553.

Gordon, R. A. Prevalence: The rare datum in delinquency measurement and its implications for the theory of delinquency. In M. W. Klein (Ed.), *The juvenile justice system.* Beverley Hills: Sage, 1976, pp. 201–284.

Gordon R. A. *IQ-commensurability of black-white differences in crime delinquency.* Paper presented in the symposium "Crime and Employment" at the annual meeting of the American Psychological Association, Washington, D.C., August 1986. (a)

Gordon, R. A. Scientific justification and the race-IQ-delinquency model. In T. F. Hartnagel & R. A. Silverman (Eds.), *Critique and explanation.* New Brunswick: Transaction Books, 1986, pp. 91–131. (b)

Gordon, R. A. SES versus IQ in the race-IQ-delinquency model. *International Journal of Sociology and Social Policy,* in press.

Gordon, R. A., & Gleser, L. J. The estimation of the prevalence of delinquency: Two appoaches and a correction of the literature. *Journal of Mathematical Sociology,* 1974, *3*, 275–291.

Gorenstein, E. E., & Newman, J. P. Disinhibitory psychopathology: A new perspective and a model for research. *Psychological Review,* 1980, *87*, 301–315.

Goring, C. B. *The english convict.* London: 1913.

Gosselin, C., & Wilson, G. *Sexual variations: Fetishism, transvestism and sado-masochism.* London: Faber & Faber, 1980.

Gossop, M. Drug dependence, crime and personality among female addicts. *Drug and Alcohol Dependence*, 1978, *3*, 359–364.

Gossop, M. R., & Kristjannson, I. Crime and personality. *British Journal of Criminolgy*, 1977, *17*, 264–273.

Gostin, L. *Institutions observed: Towards a new concept of secure provision in mental health care.* London: King Edward's Hospital Fund for London, 1986.

Gottschalk, R., Davidson, W. S., Gensheimer, L. K., II, & Mayer, J. P. Community-based interventions. In H. C. Quay (Ed.) *Handbook of juvenile delinquency.* New York: Wiley, 1987, pp. 266–289.

Gray, J. A. Learning theory, the conceptual nervous system and personality. In V. D. Nebylitsyn & J. A. Gray (Eds.), *The biological basis of individual behaviour.* New York: Academic Press, 1972, pp. 372–399.

Gray, J. A. Causal theories of personality. In J. R. Royce (Ed.), *Multivariate analysis and psychological theories.* New York: Academic Press, 1976.

Gray, J. A. A critique of Eysenck's theory of personality. In H. J. Eysenck (Ed.), *A model for personality.* New York: Springer-Verlag, 1981, pp. 246–276.

Gray, J. A. *The neuropsychology of anxiety: An enquiry into the function of the Septo-Hippocampal system.* Oxford: Oxford University Press, 1982.

Greenberg D. F. Measuring the incapacitive effects of imprisonment: Some estimates. *Law and Society Review*, 1975, *9*, 541–580.

Greenwood, P. W. *Rand research on criminal careers: Progress to date.* Santa Monica: Rand Corporation, 1979.

Greenwood, P. W. Career criminal prosecution. *Journal of Criminal Law and Criminology*, 1980, *71*, 85–88.

Grizzle, G. A., & Witte, A. D. Criminal justice evaluation techniques: Methods other than random assignments. In M. W. Klein & K. S. Teilmann (Eds.), *Handbook of criminal justice evaluation.* London: Sage, 1980, 259–302.

Groth, A. N., Burgess, A. W., & Holmstrom, L. L. Rape: Power, anger and sexuality. *American Journal of Psychiatry*, 1977, *134*, 1239–1243.

Gudjonsson, G. H. Delinquent boys in Reykjavik: A follow-up study of boys sent to an institution. In J. Gunn & D. P. Farrington (Eds.), *Abnormal offenders, delinquency, and the criminal justice system.* Chichester: Wiley, 1982, pp. 203–212. (a)

Gudjonsson, G. H. The nature of shoplifting in Iceland. *Forensic Science International*, 1982, *19*, 209–216. (b)

Gudjonsson, G. H. Sexual variations: Assessment and treatment in clinical practice. *Sex and Marital Therapy*, 1986, *1*, 191–212.

Gudjonsson, G. H. The significance of depression in the mechanism of compulsive shoplifting. *Medicine, Science and the Law*, 1987, *27*, 171–176.

Gudjonsson, G. H., & Drinkwater, J. Intervention techniques for violent behaviour. In C. Hollin & K. Howells (Eds.), *Clinical approaches to criminal behaviour* (Issues in Criminological and Legal Psychology No. 9). Leicester: British Psychological Society, 1986.

Gudjonsson, G. H., & Mackeith, J. A regional secure unit at the Bethlem Royal Hospital—the first fourteen months. *Medicine, Science and the Law*, 1983, *23*, 209–219.

Gudjonsson, G. H., & Singh, K. *The Revised Gudjonsson Blame Attribution Inventory*, in press, Journal of Personality and Individual Differences.

Gunn, J. Sexual offenders. *British Journal of Hospital Medicine*, 1976, *15*, 57–65.

Gunn, J., Robertson, G., Dell, S., & Way, C. *Psychiatric aspects of imprisonment.* London: Academic press, 1978.

Gupta, B. S. Extraversion and reinforcement in verbal operant conditioning. *British Journal of Psychology*, 1976, *67*, 47–52.

Gupta, B. S., & Nappal, M. Impulsivity-sociability and reinforcement in verbal operant conditioning. *British Journal of Psychology*, 1978, *69*, 203–206.

Gustafsson, J. E. A unifying model for the structure of intellectual abilities. *Intelligence*, 1984, *8*, 179–203.

Hafner, H., & Boker, W. *Crimes of violence by mentally abnormal offenders: A psychiatric and epidemiological study in the Federal German Republic*. Cambridge: Cambridge University Press, 1982.

Hagen, R. *The bio-sexual factor*. Garden City, N.Y.: Doubleday, 1979.

Hall, R. E. *Ask any woman: A London inquiry into rape and sexual assault*. London: Falling Wall Press, 1985.

Hallman, R. S., & Rachman, S. Current status of aversion therapy. In M. Hersen, R. M. Eisler, & P. M. Miller (Eds.), *Progress in behavior modification* (Vol. 2). New York: Academic Press, 1976, pp.

Hallock, S. L. Delinquency. In B. B. Wolman (Ed.), *Manual of child psychopathology*. New York: McGraw-Hill, 1972, pp. 541–562.

Halperin, J. M., & Gittleman, R. Do hyperactive children and their silbings differ in IQ and academic achievement? *Psychiatry Research*, 1982, *6*, 253–258.

Halverson, C. F., & Victor, J. B. Minor physical anomalies and problem behaviour in elementary school children. *Child Development* 1976, *47*, 281–285.

Hammond, W. H. *The sentence of the courts: A handbook for courts on the treatment of offenders*. London: H.M.S.O., 1964.

Hammond, W. H., & Chayen, E. *Persistent Criminals*. Home Office Studies in the Causes of Delinquency and the Treatment of Offenders No. 5. London: H.M.S.O., 1963.

Handler, E., & Schuett, L. Are prison inmates really "naked nomads"? *American Journal of Correction*, 1979, *39*, (Nov./Dec.) 16, 18–31.

Hare, R. D. *Psychopathy: Theory and research*. New York: Wiley, 1970.

Hare, R. D. Psychopathy. In P. Venables & M. Christie (Eds.), *Research in psychophysiology*. New York: Wiley, 1975, pp. 325–348.

Hare, R. D. Psychopathy and electrodermal responses to nonsignal stimulation. *Biological Psychology*, 1978, *6*, 237–246.

Hare, R. D. Psychopathy and physiological activity during anticipation of an aversive stimulus in a distraction paradigm. *Psychophysiology*, 1982, *19*, 266–271.

Hare, R. D., & Connolly, J. F. Perceptual asymmetrics and information processing in psychopaths. In S. A. Mednick, T. E. Moffitt, & S. A. Stack (Eds.), *The causes of crime*. 1987, pp. 218–238. New York: Cambridge University Press.

Hare, R. D., & Cox, D. N. Clinical and empirical conceptions of psychopathy, and the selection of subjects for research. In R. D. Hare & D. Schalling (Eds.), *Psychopathic behaviour*. New York: Wiley, 1978, pp. 1–21. (a)

Hare, R. D., & Cox, D. N. Psychophysiological research on psychopathy. In W. H. Reid (Ed.), *The psychopath*. New York: Brunner/Mazel, 1978, pp. 146–168.

Hare, R. D., & Craigen, D. Psychopathy and physiological activity in a mixed-motive game situation. *Psychophysiology*, 1974, *11*, 197–206.

Hare, R. D., & Quinn, M. J. Psychopathy and autonomic conditioning. *Journal of Abnormal Psychology*, 1971, *77*, 223–235.

Hare, R. D., & Schalling, D. (Eds.) *Psychopathic behaviour*. New York: Wiley, 1978.

Hartl, E., Monnelli, E., & Eldeken, R. *Physique and delinquent behaviour*. New York: Academic Press, 1982.

Hartmann, D. P., Roper, B. L., & Bradford, D. C. Some relationships between behavioural and traditional assessment. *Journal of Behavioural Assessment*, 1979, *1*, 3–21.

Hartung, J. Polygyny and inheritance of wealth. *Current Anthropology*, 1982, *23*, 1–12.

Haslam, D. R. Individual differences in pain threshold and level of arousal. *British Journal of Psychology*, 1967, *58*, 139–142.

Hathaway, S. R. & Monachesi, E. D. The personalities of predelinquent boys. *Journal of Criminal Law, Criminology and Police Science*, 1957, *48*, 149–163.

Hawton, K. Behavioural approaches to the management of sexual deviations. *British Journal of Psychiatry*, 1983, *143*, 248–255.

Hayashi, S. A study of juvenile delinquency by twin method. *Acta Criminologica et Medicinae Legalis Japonica*, 1963, *29*, 153–172.

Healy, W. *The individual delinquent: A text-book of diagnosis and prognosis for all concerned in understanding offenders*. Boston: Little, Brown, 1915.

Heath, A. C., Berg, K., Eaves, L. Y., Solaas, M. H., Corey, L. A., Sundet, J., Magnus, P., & Nance, W. E. Education policy and the heritability of educational attainment. *Nature*, 1985, *314*, 734–736.

Heim, N., & Hursch, C. J. Castration for sex offenders: Treatment or punishment? A review and critique of recent European literature. *Archives of Sexual Behavior*, 1979, *8*, 281–304.

Helzel, M. F., & Rice, M. E. (1985) on the validity of social skills assessments: An analysis of nde-play and ward staff ratings of social behavior in a maximum security setting. Canadian Journal of Behavioral Science, *7*, 400–411.

Hills, C. M. & Walter, T. L. (1979). Reducing juvenile delinquency: A behavioral-employment intervention program. In J. S. Stumphauzeh (Ed.) *Progress in behavior therapy with delinquents*. Springfield: Charles C. Thomas, 287–301.

Hindelang, M. (1976). *Criminal Victimization in Eight American Cities*, Cambridge, MA: Ballinger.

Hirschi, T., Hindeling, M. J. & Wais, J. G. (1980). The status of self-reports measures. In M. W. Klein and K. S. Teilman (Eds.), *Handbook of Criminal Justice* Evolution. London: Sage Publications, 473–488.

Hollin, C. R., & Henderson, M. Social skills training with young offenders: False expectations and the "failure of treatment." *Behavioural Psychotherapy*, 1984, *12*, 331–341.

Holcomb, W. R., Adams, N. A., & Ponder, H. M. The development and cross-validation of an MMPI typology of murderers. *Journal of Personality Assessment*, 1985, *49*, 240–244.

Brown, C. W., & Hollender, M. H., Roback, H. B. (1977) Genital exhibitionism in women, *American Journal of Psychiatry, in behavior therapy with delinquents. 134*, 436–438.

Holmstrom, L. L., & Burgess, A. W. Sexual behaviour of assailants during reported rapes. *Archives of Sexual Behaviour*, 1980, *9*, 427–439.

Home Office. *Prison rules* (SI 1964 No. 388). London: H.M.S.O., 1964.

Home Office. *The sentence of the court: A handbook for courts on the treatment of offenders*. London: H.M.S.O., 1966.

Home Office. *The sentencing of the court*. London: H.M.S.O., 1970.

Home Office. *Previous convictions, sentence and reconviction: A statistical study of a sample of 5000 offenders convicted in January 1971*. London: H.M.S.O., 1979.

Home Office. *Probation and after-care statistics, England and Wales 1980*. London: H.M.S.O., 1981.

Home Office. *The British crime survey*. Home Office Research Study No. 76. London: H.M.S.O., 1983.

Home Office. *Adult prisons and prisoners in England and Wales*. Home Office Research Study No. 84. London: H.M.S.O., 1985.

Home Office. *Criminal statistics: England and Wales 1985*. London: H.M.S.O., 1986. (a)

Home Office. *Prison statistics: England and Wales 1985*. London: H.M.S.O., 1986. (b)

Home Office. *The sentence of the court: Handbook for courts on the treatment of offenders*. London: H.M.S.O., 1986. (c)

Hood, R., & Sparks, R. *Key issues in criminology*. London: Word University Library, 1970.

Hooton, E. A. *The American criminal*. Cambridge, Mass.: Harvard University Press, 1939. (a)

Hooton, E. A. *Crime and the man*. Cambridge, Mass.: Harvard University Press, 1939. (b)

Hormuth, S., Lamm, H., Michelitsch, I., Sheuermann, H., Trommsdorf, G., & Vogele, I. Impulskontrolle and einige Persönlichkeits-charakteristica bei delinquenten und nicht delinquenten Jugendlichen. *Psychologische Beiträge*, 1977, *19*, 340–359.

Hough, M., & Mayhew, P. *Taking account of crime: Key findings from the second British Crime Survey*. Home Office Research Study No. 85. London: H.M.S.O., 1985.

Howard League. *Unlawful sex: Offenders, victims and offenders in the criminal justice system of England and Wales*. London: Waterlow, 1985.

Howells, K. Some meanings of children for paedophiles. In M. Cook & G. Wilson (Eds.), *Love and attraction: An international conference*. Oxford: Pergamon Press, 1979.

Howells, K. Mental disorder and violent behaviour. In P. Feldman (Ed.), *Developments in the study of criminal behaviour, violence* (Vol. 2). Chichester: Wiley, 1982, pp. 163–200.

Howells, K. The management of angry aggression: A cognitive-behavioural approach. In W. Dryden & P. Trower (Eds.), *Developments in cognitive psychotherapy*. London: Lawrence Erlbaum, 1987.

Hrdy, S. B. *The woman who never evolved*. Cambridge, Mass: Harvard University Press, 1981.

Hucker, S. J., & Ben-Aron, M. H. Elderly sex offenders. In R. Langevin (Ed.), *Erotic preference, gender identity, and aggression in men: New research studies*. London: Lawrence Erlbaum, 1985, pp. 211–243.

Hullin, R. Sword of Damocles. *Social Work Today*, 1983, *14*, 4.

Hullin, R. The Leeds Truancy Project. *Justice of the Peace*, 1985, *149*, 488–491.

Humphreys, L. G. Characteristics of type concepts with special reference to Sheldon's typology. *Psychological Bulletin*, 1957, *54*, 218–228.

Hunt, E. H. A note on growth, somatotype and temperament. *American Journal of Physiological Anthropology*, 1949, *7*, 79–89.

Hurwitz, S., & Christiansen, K. O. *Criminology*. London: Allen & Unwin, 1983.

Hutchings, B., & Mednick, S. A. Criminality in adoptees and their adoptive and biological parents: A pilot study. In S. Mednick & K. O. Christiansen (Eds.) , *Biosocial bases of criminal behaviour*. New York: Gardner Press, 1977, pp. 127–141.

Hutchings, B., & Mednick S. A. Genetic and psychophysiogical factors in a social behaviour. In R. D. Hare & D. Schalling (Eds.), *Psychopathic Behaviour*, 1978, pp. 239–253. New York: Wiley.

Jaman, D. *Parole outcome and time served by first releases convicted for robbery and burglary 1965 releases*. California Department of Corrections, Measurement Unit, 1968.

James, S. Treatment of homosexuality: superiority of desensitization/arousal as compared with anticipatory avoidance conditioning: Results of a controlled trial. *Behaviour Therapy*, 1978, *9*, 28–36.

Jamison, R. N. Psychoticism, deviancy and perception of risk in normal children. *Personality and Individual Differences*, 1980, *1*, 87–91.

Janes, C. L., Hesselbrock, V., & Stern, J. A. Parental psychopathology, age, and race as related to electrodermal activity of children. *Psychophysiology*, 1978, *15*, 24–33.

Janoff, I. Z., Beck, L. H., & Child, I. C. The relation of somatotype to reaction time, resistance to pain, and expressive movement. *Journal of Personality*, 1950, *18*, 454-460.

Jardine, R., Martin, N. G., & Henderson, A. S. Genetic covariation between neuroticism and the symptoms of anxiety and depression. *Genetic Epidemiology*, 1984, *1*, 89–107.

Jensen, A. R. *Bias in mental testing*. New York: Free Press, 1980.

Jensen, A. R., & Faulstich, M. E. Difference between prisoners and the general population in psychometric *g*. *Personality and Individual Differences*, in press.

Jensen, A. R., & Reynolds, C. R. Race, social class and ability patterns on the WISC-R. *Personality and Individual Differences*, 1982, *3*, 423–438.

Jesness, C. F. *The Fricot Ranch Study* (Research Rep. No. 47). Sacramento, Calif.: California Department of Youth Authority, 1965.

Jesness, C. F. *The Jesness Inventory: Manual*. Palo Alto: Consulting Psychologists Press, 1972.

Jesness, C. F. Comparative effectiveness of behavior modification and transactional analysis programs for delinquents. *Journal of Consulting and Clinical Psychology*, 1975, *43*, 758–779.

Jolly, A. *The evolution of primate behaviour* (2nd ed.). New York: Macmillan, 1985.

Jones, I. H. & Frei, D. Provoked anxiety as a treatment of exhibitionism. *British Journal of Psychiatry*, 1977, *131*, 295–300.

Kafner, F. H. The maintenance of behaviour by self-generated stimuli and reinforcement. In A. Jacobs & L. B. Sachs (Eds.), *The psychology of private events*. New York: Academic Press, 1971.

Kafner, F. H., & Phillips, J. B. *Learning foundations of behaviour therapy*. Chichester: Wiley, 1970.

Kaltsouris, B., & Higdon, G. School conformity and its relation to creativity. *Psychological Reports*, 1977, *40*, 715–718.

Kaplan, H. B. Patterns of juvenile delinquency (Vol. 2, Law and Criminal Justice Series). Beverly Hills: Sage, 1984.

Kaplan, R. M., Konecni, V. J., & Novaco, R. W. (Eds.) *Aggression in children and youths*. The Hague: Martinus Nijhoff, 1984.

Karoly, P. Comparison of "psychological styles" in delinquent and nondelinquent females. *Psychological Reports*, 1975, *36*, 567–570.

Katz, S., & Mazur, M.A. *Understanding rape victims: A synthesis of research findings*. New York: Wiley, 1979.

Kaufman, A. S., & Doppelt, J. E. Analysis of WISC-R standardization data in terms of the stratification process. *Child Development*, 1976, *47*, 165–171.

Kazdin, A. E. Treatment of antisocial behaviour in children: Current status and future directions. *Psychological Bulletin*, 1987, *102*, 187–203.

Keller, D. J., & Goldstein, A. Orgasmic reconditioning reconsidered. *Behaviour Research and Therapy*, 1977, *16*, 299–301.

Kempe, C. H., Silverman, F. N., Steel., B. F., Droegemueller, W., & Silver H. K. The battered-child syndrome. *Journal of the American Medical Association*, 1962, *181*, 17–24.

Kendel, E., Mednick, S., Kirkegaard-Sorensen, L., & Hutchings, B., Rosenberg, R., Schulsinger, F. IQ as a potential factor for subjects at high risk for antisocial behaviour. *Journal of Counselling and Clinical Psychology*, 1988, *56*, 224–226.

Kendler, K. S., Heath, A., Martin, N. G., & Eaves, L. J. Symptoms of anxiety and depression in a volunteer twin population. *Archives of General Psychiatry*, 1986, *43*, 213–221.

Kinsey, A. C., Pomeroy, W. B., & Martin, C. E. *Sexual Behaviour in the human male*. Philadelphia: W. B. Saunders, 1948.

Kirigin, K. A., Braukmann, C. J., Atwater, J. D., & Wolf, M. M. An evaluation of teaching-family (achievement place) group for juvenile offenders. *Journal of Applied Behavioral Analysis*, 1982, *15*, 1–16.

Kirigin, K. A., Wolf, M. M., Braukmann, C. J., Fixsen, D. L., & Phillips, E. L. Achievement place: A preliminary outcome evaluation. In J. S. Stumphauzer (Ed.), *Progress in behaviour therapy with delinquents*. Springfield, Ill.: Charles C Thomas, 1979, pp. 118–145.

Klein, N. C., Alexander, J. F., & Parsons, B. V. Impact of family systems intervention on recidivism and sibling delinquency: A model of primary prevention and program evaluation. *Journal of Consulting and Clinical Psychology*, 1977, *45*, 469–474.

Klein, N. W. Labelling, deterrence, and recidivism: A study of police disposition of juvenile offenders. *Social Problems*, 1979, *22*, 293–303.

Klinteberg, B., Levander, S. E., Oreland, L., Asberg, M., & Schalling, D. Neuropsychological correlates of platelet MAO activity in female and male subjects. *Biological Psychology*, in press.

Knight, B. J., & West, D. J. Temporary and continuing delinquency. *British Journal of Criminology*, 1975, *15*, 43–50.

Knights, R., & Hinton, G. The effects of methylphenidate (Ritalin) on the motor skills and behaviour of children with learning problems. *Journal of Nervous and Mental Diseases*, 1969, *148*, 643–653.

Kobrin, S., Hellum, F. R., & Peterson, J. W. Offense patterns of status offenders. In D. Shichor & D. H. Kelly (Eds), *Critical issues in juvenile delinquency*. Massachusetts, Toronto: Lexington Books, 1980, pp. 203–235.

Kobrin, S., & Klein, M. W. *National evaluation of deinstitutionalization of status offender programs*. Washington, D.C.: National Institute for Juvenile Justice and Delinquency Prevention, Office of Juvenile Justice and Delinquency Prevention, U.S. Department of Justice, 1982.

Kolarsky, A., Freund, K., Machek, J., & Polak, O. Male sexual deviations: Associations with early temporal lobe damage. *Archives of General Psychiatry*, 1967, *17*, 735–743.

Kranz, H. *Lebensschicksale Krimineller Zwillinge*. Berlin: Julius Springer, 1936.

Krauss, S. (Ed.). *Encyclopaedic handbook of medical psychology*. London: Butterworth, 1976.

Kretschmer, E. *Körperbau und Charakter*. Berlin: Springer, 1948.

Kreuz, L. E., & Rose, R. M. Assessment of aggressive behaviour and plasma testosterone in a young criminal population. *Psychosomatic Medicine*, 1972, *34*, 321–332.

Krilov, D. V., Kulakova, T. P., Kantonistova, N. S., & Chamaganova, T. G. Erb-und Umwelteinflüsse auf die physische und psychishe Entwicklung in der Ontogenese. In W. Friedrich & O. Kabat vel Job (Eds.), *Zwillingsforschung International*. Berlin: VEB, 1986, pp. 43–85.

Krisberg, B. Utility of process evaluation: Crime and delinquency programs. In M. W. Klein & K. S. Teilmann (Eds.), *Handbook of criminal justice evaluation*. London: Sage, 1980, pp. 217–236.

Landis, T., Graves, R., & Goodglass, H. Aphasic reading and writing: Possible evidence for right hemisphere participation. *Cortex*, 1982, *18*, 105–112.

Lane, D. *Persistent failure and potential success: A study of failure to respond to therapy in children*. Unpublished M. Phil. thesis, 1977. University of London.

Lane D. A. *Whatever happened to the impossible child?* London: Inner London Education Authority.

Lane, D. A. Personality and antisocial behaviour: A long-term study. *Personality and Individual Differences*, 1987, *8*, 799–806. (a)

Lane, D. A. Psychological evidence in the juvenile courts. In G. Gudjonsson & J. Drinkwater (Eds.), *Psychological evidence in court* (Issues in Criminological and Legal Psychology No. 11). Leicester: British Psychological Society, 1987. (b)

Lane, D., & Hymans, M. The prediction of delinquency: A correlation between a measure of personality and classroom behaviour. *Personality and Individual Differences*, 1982, *3*, 87–88.

Lange, J. *Verbrechen als Schicksal*. Leipzig: Thieme, 1929.

Langevin, R. *Sexual strands: Understanding and treating sexual anomalies in men*. London: Faber & Faber, 1983.

Langevin, R. *Erotic preference, gender identity, and aggression in men: New research studies*. London: Lawrence Erlbaum, 1985.

Langevin, R., Handy, L., Russon, A. E., & Day, D. Are incestuous fathers pedophilic, aggressive, and alcoholic? In R. Langevin (Ed.), *Erotic preference, gender identity, and aggression in men: New research studies*. London: Lawrence Erlbaum, 1985, (pp. 161–179).

Langevin, R., Hucker, S. J., Ben-Aron, M. H., Purins, J. E., & Hook, H. J. Why are pedophiles attracted to children? Further studies of erotic preference in heterosexual pedophilia. In R. Langevin (Ed.), *Erotic preference, gender identity, and aggression in men: New research findings*. London: Lawrence Erlbaum, 1985, (pp. 181–209).

Langevin, R., Hucker, S. J., Handy, L., Purins, J. E., Russon, A. E., & Hook, H. J. Erotic preference and aggression in pedophilia: A comparison of heterosexual, homosexual and bisexual types. In R. Langevin (Ed.), *Erotic preference, gender identity, and aggression in men*. London: Lawrence Erlbaum, 1985, pp. 137–160.

L4ngevin, R., & Lang, R. A. The courtship disorders. In G. D. Wilson (Ed.), *Variant sexuality: Research and theory*. Beckenham, Kent: Croom Helm, 1987, pp. 202–228.

Langevin, R., Paitich, D., & Russon, A. E. Are rapists sexually anomalous, aggressive, or both? In R. Langevin (Ed.), *Erotic preference, gender identity, and aggression in men: New research studies*. London: Lawrence Erlbaum, 1985. pp. 17–38.

Lanyon, R. I. Theory and treatment in child molestation. *Journal of Consulting and Clinical Psychology*, 1986, *54*, 176–182.

Laschet, V. Antiandrogen in the treatment of sex offenders: Mode of action and therapeutic outcome. In J. Zubin & J. Money (Eds.), *Contemporary sexual behaviour: Critical issues in the 1970s*. Baltimore: John Hopkins University Press, 1973.

Laub, J. H. Urbanism, race and crime. *Journal of Research in Crime and Delinquency*, 1983, *20*, 183–198.

Laufer, W. S., Skoog, D. K., & Day, J. M. Personality and criminality: A review of the California Psychological Inventory. *Journal of Clinical Psychology*, 1982, *38*, 562–573.

Law Enforcement Assistance Administration. *Criminal victimization in the United States, 1977*. Washington, D.C.: U.S. Government Printing Office, 1979.

Laws, D. R. The assessment of dangerous sexual behaviour in males. *Medicine and Law*, 1984, *3*, 127–140.

Laws, D. R., & O'Neil, J. A. Variations on masturbatory conditioning. *Behavioural Psychotherapy*, 1981, *9*, 111–136.

Laws, D. R., & Pawlowski, A. V. An automated fading procedure to alter sexual responsiveness in pedophiles. *Journal of Homosexuality* 1974, *1*, 149–163.

Laycock, G., & Tarling, R. Police force cautioning: Policy and practice. In D. Moxon (Ed.), *Managing criminal justice*. London: H.M.S.O., 1985, pp. 54–64.

Le Blanc, R. E., & Tolor, A. Alienation, distancing, externalizing, and sensation seeking in prison inmates. *Journal of Consulting and Clinical Psychology*, 1972, *39*, 514.

Lee-Evans, M. The potential of self control training procedures in the treatment of sex offenders. In J. Gun (Ed.), *Sex offenders—a symposium* (Special Hospitals Research Rep. No. 14). London: DHSS, pp. 31–79.

Lee-Evans, M. The direct assessment of sexual skills in an institutional setting. In P. Pratt (Ed.), *Sexual assessment: Issues and Radical Alternatives* (Issues in Criminological and Legal Psychology No. 8). Leicester: British Psychological Society, 1986.

Legras, A. M. *Psychese en Criminalitet lig Twellingen.* Utrecht: Kemink en Zonn, 1932.

Lenin, W. I. Ein liberaler Professor uber die Gleichheit. In Werke, Bd.20 Berlin: Deutscher Verlag der Wissenschaften, 1965.

Lerman, P. *Community treatment and social control: A critical analysis of juvenile correctional policy.* Chicago: University of Chicago Press, 1975.

Levine, F. M., Tursky, B., & Nichols, D. C. Tolerance for pain, extraversion and neuroticism: Failure to replicate results. *Perceptual and Motor Skills*, 1966, *23*, 847–850.

Levine, J. P. The potential for crime overreporting in criminal victimization surveys. *Criminology*, 1976, *3*, 307–330.

Lewis, D. E. The general deterrent effect of longer sentences. *British Journal of Criminology*, 1986, *26*, 47–62.

Liberman, R. P., & Ferris, C. *Antisocial behavior and school performance: Comparison between Welcome Home and Rancho San Antonio.* Unpublished report to the California Council on Criminal Justice, 1974.

Liberman, R. P., Ferris, C., Salgado, P., & Salgado, J. Replication of the Achievement Place Model in California. *Journal of Applied Behavioural Analysis*, 1975, *8*, 287–299.

Lidberg, L., Modin, I., Oreland, L., Tuck, J.R., & Gillner, A. Platelet monoamine oxidase activity and psychopathy. *Psychiatry Research, 1985, 16*, 339–343.

Lidhoo, M. L. *An attempt to construct a psychodiagnostic tool for the detection of potential delinquents among adolescents aged 14–19 years.* Unpublished Ph. D. thesis, University of Punjab, 1971.

Lipton, D., Martinson, R., & Wilks, J. *The effectiveness of correctional treatment: A survey of treatment evaluation studies.* New York: Praeger, 1975.

Litzelman, D. Sex differences in the amplitudes and latencies of the human auditory brainstem potential. *Electroencephelography and Clinical Neurophysiology*, 1980, *48*, 351–356.

Loeb, J., & Mednick, S. A. Asocial behaviour and electrodermal response patterns. In K. O. Christiansen & S. A. Mednick (Eds.), *Crime, society and biology a new look.* New York: Gardner Press, 1976, pp. 204–222.

Loeb, J., & Mednick, S. A. A prospective study of predictors of criminality: 3. Electrodermal response patterns. In S. A. Mednick & K. O. Christiansen (Eds.), *Biosocial bases of criminal behaviour.* New York: Gardner Press, 1977, pp. 245–254.

Loehlin, J.C., & Nichols, R. C. *Heredity, environment and personality: A study of 850 sets of twins.* Austin, Tex.: University of Texas Press, 1976.

Logan, C. H. Evaluation research in crime and delinquency: A reappraisal. *Journal of Criminal Law, Criminology and Police Science*, 1972, *63*, 378–387.

Lombroso, C. *L'uomo delinquente.* Milan, 1876.

Lombroso, C. *Crime, its causes and remedies.* Boston: Little, Brown, 1917.

Lorion, R. P., Tolan, P. H., & Wahler, R. G. Prevention. In H. C. Quay (Ed.) *Handbook of juvenile delinquency.* New York: Wiley, 1987, pp. 383–416.

Losel, F. *Handlungskontrolle und Jugenddelinquenz.* Stuttgart: Enke, 1975.

Losel, F., & Wustendorfer, W. Personlichkeitskorrelate delinquenten Verhaltens oder offizieller Delinquenz? *Zeitschrift fur Sozialpsychologie*, 1976, *7*, 177–191.

Lubin, A. A note on Sheldon's table of correlations between temperamental traits. *British Journal of Statistical Psychology*, 1950, *3*, 186–189.

Luengo, M. A., & Nunez, M. *Differential patterns of personality and antisocial behaviour: A study of locus of control, extraversion, psychoticism and neuroticism.* Paper read at the 3rd European Conference on Personality, Gdansk, Poland, September 1986.

Lundman, R. J. *Prevention and control of juvenile delinquency.* Oxford: Oxford University Press, 1984.

Lykken, D. T. A study of anxiety in the sociopathic personality. *Journal of Abnormal and Social Psychology,* 1957, *55,* 6–10.

Lykken, D. T. Fearlessness. *Psychology Today, 18,* 16 Sept. 1982, 20-28.

Lykken, D. T., Tellegen, A., & Thorkelson, K. Genetic determination of EEG frequency spectra. *Biological Psychology,* 1974, *1,* 245–259.

Lynn, R., & Eysenck, H. J. Tolerance for pain, extraversion and neuroticism. *Perceptual and Motor Skills,* 1961, *12,* 161–162.

MacArthur, R. H. Some generalised theories of natural selection. *Proceedings of the National Academy of Science,* 1962, *48,* 1893–1897.

MacArthur, R. H., & Wilson, E. O. *The theory of island biography.* Princeton, N.J.: Princeton University Press, 1967.

MacCulloch, M. J., Snowden, P. R., Wood, P. J. W., & Mills, H. E. Sadistic fantasy, sadistic behaviour and offending. *British Journal of Psychiatry,* 1983, *143,* 20–29.

MacDonald, G. J., & Di Furia, G. A guided self-help approach to the treatment of the habitual sex offender. *Hospital and Community Psychiatry,* 1971, *22,* 34–37.

Magnusson, D. Antisocial conduct of boys and autonomic activity/reactivity (Rep. No. 652). Stockholm: University of Stockholm, Department of Psychology, 1986.

Magnusson, D., Klinteberg, B., & Schalling, D. Hyperactive and aggressive behaviour in childhood and adult impulsivity: A follow-up study of male subjects (Rep. No. 656). Stockholm: University of Stockholm, Department of Psychology, 1987.

Maguire, M., & Corbett, C. *The effects of crime and the work of victims support schemes.* London: Gower, 1987.

Maisch, H. *Incest.* New York: Stein & Day, 1972.

Maletzky, B. M. "Assisted" covert sensitization in the treatment of exhibitionism. *Journal of Consulting and Clinical Psychology,* 1974, *42,* 34–40.

Maletzky, B. M. Assisted covert sensitization. In D. J. Cox & R. J. Daitzman (Eds.), *Exhibitionism: Descriptions, assessment, and treatment.* New York: Garland Press, 1980, pp. 187–251. (a)

Maletzky, B. M. Self-referred vs. court-referred sexually deviant patients: Success with assisted covert sensitization. *Behaviour Therapy,* 1980, *11,* 306–314. (b)

Mani, K. A comparative study of murderers and violent criminals using Eysenck's Personality Inventory. *Indian Journal of Criminology,* 1978, *6,* 41–44.

Mannheim, H., & Wilkins, L. T. *Prediction methods in relation to Borstal training.* Home Office Studies in the Causes of Delinquency and the Treatment of Offenders No. 1. London: H.M.S.O., 1955.

Marcus, B. A dimensional study of a prison population. *British Journal of Criminology,* 1960, *1,* 130–153.

Marks, H. E., & Hobbs, S. H. Changes in stimulus reactivity following gonadectomy in male and female rats of different ages. *Physiology and Behaviour,* 1972, *8,* 1113–1119.

Marks, I., Gelder, M., & Bancroft, J. Sexual deviants two years after electric aversion. *British Journal of Psychiatry,* 1970, *117,* 173–185.

Marks, I. M., & Sartorius, N. H. A contribution to the measurement of sexual attitude: The semantic differential as a measure of sexual attitude in sexual deviations. *Journal of Nervous and Mental Disease,* 1968, *145,* 441–451.

Marquis, J. N. Orgasmic reconditioning: Changing sexual object choice through controlling masturbation fantasies. *Journal of Behavior Therapy and Experimental Psychiatry,* 1970, *1,* 263–271.

Marshall, W. L. Satiation therapy: A procedure for reducing deviant sexual arousal. *Journal of Applied Behavior Analysis,* 1979, *12,* 377–389.

Marshall, W. L., & Barbaree, H. E. The reduction of deviant arousal: Satiation treatment for sexual aggressors. *Criminal Justice and Behaviour,* 1978, *5,* 294–303.

Martin, A. L. Values and personality: A survey of their relationship in the case of juvenile delinquence. *Personality and Individual Differences,* 1985, *4,* 519–522.

Martin, J. E., & Inglis, J. Pain tolerance and narcotic addiction. *British Journal of Social and Clinical Psychology,* 1965, *4,* 224–229.

Martin, N. G., Eaves, L. J., Heath, A. C., Jardine, R., Feingold, L. M., & Eysenck, H. J. Transmission of social attitudes. *Proceedings of the National Academy of Sciences, U.S.A.,* 1986, *83,* 4364–4368.

Martin, N. G., Eaves, L. J., Kearsey, M. J., & Davies, P. The power of the classical twin study. *Heredity,* 1978, *40,* 97–116.

Martin, N., & Jardine, R. Eysenck's contribution to behaviour genetics. In S. Modgill & C. Modgill (Eds.), *Hans Eysenck: Consensus and controversy.* Philadelphia: Falmer Press, 1986, pp. 3–47.

Martin, S. E., Sechrest, L. B., & Redner, R. *New Directions in the rehabilitation of criminal offenders.* Washington: National Academy Press, 1981.

Martinson, R. What works? Questions and answers about prison reform. *The Public Interest,* 1974, *35,* 22–54.

Martinson, R. California research at the crossroads. *Crime and Delinquency,* 1976, *22,* 180–191.

Martiny, M. *Essai de Biotypologie.* Paris: Peyronnet, 1948.

Maskin, M. B. The differential impact of work-oriented vs. communication-oriented juvenile correction programs upon recidivism rates in delinquent males. *Journal of Clinical Psychology,* 1976, *32,* 434–433.

Mastellone, M. Aversion therapy: A new use for the old rubberband. *Journal of Behaviour Therapy and Experimental Psychiatry,* 1974, *5,* 311–312.

Masters, F. W., & Greaves, D. C. The Quasimodo Complex. *British Journal of Plastic Surgery,* 1967, *20,* 204–209.

Matarazzo, J. D. *Wechsler's measurement and appraisal of adult intelligence* (5th Ed.). Baltimore: Williams & Wilkins, 1972.

Mather, K., & Jinks J. L. *Biometrical genetics* (2nd Ed.). Ithaca, N. Y.: Cornell University Press, 1971.

Mathias, J. L., & Collins, M. Enforced group treatment of exhibitionists. *Current Psychiatric Therapy,* 1971, *7,* 139–145.

Mathis, H. Emotional responsivity in the antisocial personality. (University Micofilms No.

Matousek, M., & Petersen, I. Frequency analysis of the EEG in normal children and adolescents. In P. Kellaway & I. Petersen (Ed.), *Automation of clinical electroencephelography.* New York: Raven Press, 1973, pp. 351–56.

Mattes, J. A., Boswell, L., & Oliver, H. Methylphenidate in adults with minimal brain dysfunction symptomatology. *Psychopharmacology Bulletin,* 1982, *18,* 114–115.

Max, L. Breaking a homosexual fixation by the conditioned reflex technique. *Psychological Bulletin,* 1935, *32,* 734.

McCall, G. J., *Observing the law.* Rockville, Md.: National Institute of Mental Health, 1975.

McClearn, G. E., & DeFries, J. C. *Introduction to behavioural genetics.* San Francisco: Freeman, 1973.

McCleary, R. A. Response-modulating function of the limbic system: and suppression. In E. Steller & J. M. Sprague (Eds.), *Progress in physiological psychology* (Vol. 1). New York: Academic Press, 1966, pp. 209–271.

McCord, J. A thirty-year follow-up of treatment effects. *American Psychologist,* 1978, *33,* 284–289.

McCord, R. M., & Wakefield, J. A. Arithmetic achievement as a function of introversion-extraversion and teacher-presented reward and punishment. *Personality and Individual Differences*, 1981, *2*, 145–152.

McCord, W., McCord, J., & Zola, D. K. *Origins of crime: A new evaluation of the Cambridge-Somerville youth study*. New York: Columbia University Press, 1959.

McCreary, C. P. Personality profiles of persons convicted of indecent exposure. *Journal of Clinical Psychology*, 1975, *31*, 260–262.

McCue, P., Booth, S., & Root, J. Do young prisoners under-state their extraversion of personality invertories? *British Journal of Criminology*, 1976, *16*, 282–283.

McEwan, A. W. Eysenck's theory of criminality and the personality types and offences of young delinquents. *Personality and Individual Differences*, 1983, *4*, 201–204.

McEwan, A. W., & Knowles, L. Delinquent personality types and the situational contexts of their crimes. *Personality and Individual Differences*, 1984, *5*, 339–344.

McEwan, K. L., & Devins, G. M. Is increased arousal in social anxiety noticed by others? *Journal of Abnormal Psychology*, 1983, *92*, 417–421.

McGarvey, B., Gabrielli, W. F., Bentler, P. M., & Mednick, S. A. Rearing social class, education, and criminality: A multiple indicator model. *Journal of Abnormal Psychology*, 1981, *90*, 354–364.

McGrew, W. C. Evolutionary implications of sex differences. In (Eds.), *The great apes*. Menlo Park, Calif. Benjamin/Cummings, 1979, pp. 440–462.

McGuire, J., & Priestley, P. *Offending behaviour: Skills and stratagems for going straight*. London: Batsford Academic & Educational, 1985.

McGuire, R. J., Carlisle, J. M., & Young B. G. Sexual deviations as conditioned behaviour: A hypothesis. *Behaviour Research and Therapy*, 1965, *2*, 185–190.

McGurk, B. J. Personality types among "normal" homicides. *British Journal of Criminology, 1978, 18*, 146–161.

McGurk, B. J. & McDougall, C. A new approach to Eysenck's theory of criminality. *Personality and Individual Differences*, 1981, *2*, 338–340.

McGurk, B. J., & McEwan, A. W. Personality types and recidivism among Borstal trainees. *Personality and Individual Differences*, 1983, *4*, 165–170.

McGurk, B. J., McEwan, A. W., & Graham, F. Personality types and recidivism among young delinquents. *British Journal of Criminology*, 1981, *21*, 159–165.

McKissack, I. J. Early socialization: The baseline in delinquency research. *International Journal of Criminology and Penology*. 1975, *3*, 43–51.

McNaughton, S. J. r- and K-section in typha. *American Naturalist*, 1975, *109*, 251–261.

Mechanic, D. Response factors in illness: The study of illness behaviour. In T. Millon (Ed.), Medical behavioural science. Philadelphia: W. B. Saunders, 1975, pp. 345–367.

Mednick, S. A. Autonomic nervous system recovery and psychopathy. *Scandinavian Journal of Behaviour Therapy*, 1975, *4*, 55–68.

Mednick, S. A. Preface. In S. A. Mednick & K. O. Christiansen (Eds.), *Biosocial bases of criminal behaviour*. New York: Gardner, 1977, pp. 9–10.

Mednick, S. A., & Christiansen, K. O. *Biosocial bases of criminal behaviour*. New York: Gardner Press, 1977.

Mednick, S. A., Gabrielli, W. F., & Hutchings, B. Genetic factors in the etiology of criminal behaviour. In S. A. Mednick, T. E. Moffitt, & S. A. Stack (Eds.), *The causes of crime*. Cambridge: Cambridge University Press, 1987, pp. 74–91.

Mednick, S. A., Moffitt, T. E., & Stack, S. A. *The causes of crime: New Biological approaches*. Cambridge: Cambridge University Press, 1987.

Megargee, E. I. Undercontrolled and overcontrolled personality types in extreme antisocial aggression. *Psychological Monographs*, 1906, *80* (Whole No. 611).

Meiselman, K. C. *Incest*. San Francisco: Jossey-Bass, 1978.

Mendelson, W., Johnston, N., & Stewart, M. Hyperactive children as teenagers: A follow-up study. *Journal of Nervous and Mental Disorders*, 1971, *153*, 273–279.

Methvin, E. H. The proven key to crime control. *Reader's Digest*, 1986 (May) pp. 83–89.

Meyer, H. J., Borgatta, E. F., & Jones, W. C. *Girls at vocational high*. New York: Russell Sage, 1965.

Meyer-Bahlburg, H., Beam, B. A., Sharma, M., & Edwards, J. A. Aggressiveness and testosterone measures in man. *Psychosomatic Medicine*, 1974, *36*, 269–274.

Michael, C. M. Follow up studies of introverted children: 4. Relative incidence of criminal behaviour. *Journal of Criminal Law and Criminality*, 1956, *47*, 414–422.

Michalewski, H. J., Thompson, L. W., Patterson, J. V., Bowman, T. S., Mitchell, J., Rogers R., Cavenaugh, J., & Wasylier, O. The role of trait anxiety in violent and non-violent delinquent behaviour. *American Journal of Forensic Psychiatry*, 1980, *7*, 241–249.

Michigan Department of Corrections. *A six-month follow-up of juvenile delinquents visiting the Ionia Reformatory*. Michigan: Michigan Department of Corrections, 1967.

Miller, W. B. The impact of a "total community" delinquency control project. *Social Problems*, 1962, *10*, 168–191.

Millham, S., Bullock, R., & Cherrett, P. *After grace—teeth. A comparative study of the residential experience of boys in approved schools*. London: Human Context Books, 1975.

Mills, C. M., & Walter, T. L. Reducing juvenile delinquency: A behavior-employment intervention program. In J. S. Stumphauzer (Ed.), *Progress in behaviour therapy with delinquents*. Springfield, Ill.: Charles C Thomas, 1979, pp. 287–300.

Mitchell, J. F. *The measurement of anxiety in a population of male juvenile delinquents*. Unpublished manuscript, 1987.

Mitchell, S., & Richardson, P. J. *Archbold: Pleading, evidence and practice in criminal cases*. London: Sweet & Maxwell, 1986.

Mochizuki, Y., Go, T., Ohkubo, H., Tatara, T., & Motomura, T. Developmental changes of BAEPs in normal human subjects from infants to young adults. *Brain Developments*, 1982, *4*, 127–136.

Moffitt, T. E., Gabrielli, W. F., Mednick, S., & Schulsinger, F. Socioeconomic status, IQ, and delinquency. *Journal of Abnormal Psychology*, 1981, *90*, 152–156.

Mohr, J. W., Turner, R. E., & Jerry, M. B. *Paedophilia and exhibitionism*. Toronto: University of Toronto Press, 1964.

Monahan, J., & Monahan, B. Police and the mentally disordered. In J. C. Yuille (Ed.), *Police selection and training*. Boston: Martinus Nijhoff, 1986, pp. 175–186.

Monahan, J., & Steadman, H. *Mentally disordered offenders: Perspectives from law and social science*. New York: Plenum Press, 1983.

Monti, P. M., Brown, W. A., & Corriveau, D. P. Testosterone and components of aggressive and sexual behaviour in man. *American Journal of Psychiatry*, 1977, *134*, 692–694.

Moon, P. Crime Stoppers brings 7,500 arrests. *The Globe and Mail*, 22 June 1987, p. 11.

Morash, M. Gender, peer group experiences and seriousness of delinquency. *Journal of Research in Crime and Delinquency*, 1986, *23*, 43–67.

Morgan, P. *Delinquent fantasies*. London: Temple Smith, 1978.

Morrison, J., & Stewart, M. The psychiatric status of the legal families of adopted hyperactive children. *Archives of General Psychiatry*, 1973, *28*, 858–891.

Morrow, L., Vrtunski, P. B., Kim, Y., & Boller, F. Arousal responses to emotional stimuli and laterality of lesion. *Neuropsychologia*, 1981, *19*, 65–71.

Mott, J. *The Jesness Inventory: An application to approved school boys*. London: H.M.S.O, 1969.

Mowrer, O. H. *Learning theory and symbolic process.* New York: Wiley, 1960.

Mrazek, F. J. Sexual abuse of children. In B. Lahey & A. E. Kazdin (Eds.), *Advances in child clinical psychology* (Vol. 6). New York: Plenum Press, 1984, pp. 199–215.

Myers, R. G., & Berah, E. F. Some features of Australian exhibitionists compared with paedophiles. *Archives of Sexual Behavior,* 1983, *12,* 541–547.

Naar, R. A note on the intelligence of delinquents in Richmond, Virginia. *British Journal of Criminology,* 1965, *5,* 82–85.

Nachshom, I., & Denno, D. Violent behaviour and cerebral hemisphere function. In S. A. Mednick, T. E. Moffitt, & S. A. Stack (Eds.), *The causes of crime.* Cambridge: Cambridge University Press, 1987, pp. 185–217.

Nagin, D. General deterrence: A review of the empirical evidence. In A. Blumstein, J. Cohen, & D. Nagin (Eds.), Deterrence and incapacitation: Estimating the effects of criminal sanctions on crime. Washington: National Academy of Science, 1978, pp. 95–139.

Narayanan, S., & Mani, K. Personality and motivation in relation to crime. *Indian Journal of Criminology,* 1977, *5,* 32–36.

Newman, G. *Comparative deviance: Perception and law in six cultures.* New York: Elsevier, 1976.

Newman, H. H., Freeman, F. N., & Holzinger, X. J. *Twins: A study of heredity and environment.* Chicago: University of Chicago Press, 1937.

Newman, J. P., Widom, C. S., & Nathan, S. Passive avoidance in syndromes of disinhibition: Psychopathy and extraversions. *Journal of Personality and Social Psychology,* 1985, *48,* 1316–1327.

Newton, M. Reconviction after treatment at Grendon: Chief Psychologist's Reports (Home Office Series B, No. 1). Unpublished manuscript, 1971.

Nichols, K. A. Severe social anxiety. *British Journal of Medical Psychology,* 1974, *47,* 302–306.

Nichols, S., & Newman, J. P. Effects of punishment on response latency in extraverts. *Journal of Personality and Social Psychology,* 1986, *30,* 624–630.

Nietzel, M. T. *Crime and its modification: A social learning perspective.* New York: Pergamon Press, 1979.

Nietzel, M. T., & Himelein, M. J. Prevention of crime and delinquency. In B. A. Edelstein & L. Michelson (Eds.), *Handbook of prevention.* New York: Plenum Press, 1986, pp. 195–221.

Novaco, R. W. Anger control: the development and evaluation of an experimental treatment. Lexington, Mass.: Heath, 1975.

Novaco, R. W. Anger and coping with stress. In J. P. Foreyt & D. P. Rathjen (Eds.), *Cognitive behaviour therapy.* New York: Penguin, 1978, pp. 135–162.

O'Connor, A. A. Female sex offender. *British Journal of Psychiatry,* 1987, *150,* 615–620.

O'Donnell, J., O'Neill, S. O., & Staley, A. Congenital correlates of distractibility. *Journal of Abnormal Child Psychology,* 1979, *7,* 465–470.

O'Donnell, J. P., & van Tuinan, M. Behaviour problems of preschool children: Dimensions and congenital correlations. *Journal of Abnormal Child Psychology,* 1979, *7,* 61–75.

Olczak, P. V., Parcell, S. R., & Stott, M. W. R. Defining juvenile delinquency: Specificity of the research sample and the right of treatment. *Journal of Clinical Psychology,* 1983, *39,* 1007–1012.

Olweus, D. Stability of aggressive reaction patterns in males: A review. *Psychological Bulletin,* 1979, *86,* 852–975.

Olweus, D. Testosterone and adrenaline: Aggressive antisocial behaviour in normal adolescent males. In S. A. Mednick, T. E. Moffitt., & S. A. Stack (Eds.), *The causes of crime.* Cambridge: Cambridge University Press, 1987, pp. 203–282.

Orchowsky, S., & Taylor, K. *The Insiders Juvenile Crime Prevention Program: An as-*

sessment of a juvenile awareness program. Richmond, Va.: Virginia Department of Corrections, 1981.

Oreland, L., van Knorring, L., & Schalling, D. Connections between monoamine oxidase, temperament and disease. In W. Patton, J. Mitchell, & D. Turner, (Eds.): *Proceedings of the 9th International Congress of Pharmacology* (Vol. 2). London: Macmillan, 1984, pp. 105–109.

Ortmann, J. The treatment of sexual offenders: Castration and antihormone therapy. *International Journal of Law and Psychiatry*, 1980, 3, 443–451.

Ostapiuk, E. Strategies for community intervention in offender rehabilitation: An overview. In P. Feldman (Ed.), *Developments in the study of criminal behaviour: Vol. 1. The prevention and control of offending*. Chichester: Wiley, 1982, pp. 135–166.

Owens, R. G. The relationship between sexual arousal and sexual behaviour. In P. Pratt (Ed.), *Sexual assessment: Issues and radical alternatives*. (Issues in Criminological and Legal Psychology No. 8. Leicester: British Psychological Society, 1986, pp. 18–23.

Palmer, T. Martison revisited. *Journal of Research in Crime and Delinquency*, 1975, *12*, 133–152.

Palmer, T. *Correctional intervention and research*. Massachusetts, Toronto: Lexington Books, 1978.

Palmer, T. The effectiveness issue today: An overview. *Federal Probation*, 1983, *47*, 3–10.

Palmer, T. Treatment and the role of classification: A review of basics. *Crime and Delinquency*, 1984, *30*, 245–267.

Parliamentary All-Party Penal Affairs Group. *Life-sentence prisoners*. Chichester: Barry Rose, 1985.

Parnell, R. W. Physique and mental break down in young adults. *British Medical Journal*, 1957, *1*, 1484–1490.

Parsonage, W. *Perspectives on victimology*. Beverly Hills & London: Sage, 1979.

Passingham, R. E. Crime and personality: A review of Eysenck's theory. In V. D. Nebylitsyn & J. A. Gray (Eds.), *Biological bases of individual behaviour*. London: Academic Press, 1972, pp. 342–371.

Patterson, C. M., Kosson, D. S., & Newman, J. P. Reaction to punishment, reflectivity, and passive avoidance learning in extraverts. *Journal of Personality and Social Psychology*, 1987, *52*, 565–575.

Patterson, G. R. *Coercive family process*. Eugene, Ore.: Castolia, 1982.

Patterson, G. R. Performance models for antisocial boys. *American Psychologist*, 1986, *41*, 432–444.

Paulhus, D. L., & Martin, C. L. Predicting adult temperament from minor physical anomalies. *Journal of Personality and Social Psychology*, 1986, *50*, 1235–1239.

Pearce-McCall, D., & Newman, J. P. Expectations and success following noncontingent punishment in introverts and extraverts. *Journal of Personality and Social Psychology*, 1986, *50*, 439–446.

Pearson, G. *Hooligan: A history of respective fears*. London: Macmillan, 1984.

Pease, K. Community service and prison: Are they alternatives? In K. Pease & W. McWilliams (Eds.), *Community service by order*. Edinburgh: Scottish Academic Press, 1980.

Pease, K. *Community service orders: A first decade of promise*. London: Howard League for Penal Reform, 1981.

Pease, K., Billingham, S., & Earnshaw, I. *Community service assessed in 1976*. Home Office Research Study No. 39. London: H.M.S.O., 1977.

Pease, K., Durkin, P., Earnshaw, I., Payne, D., & Thorpe, J. *Community service orders*. Home Office Research Study, No. 29. London: H.M.S.O., 1975.

Perez, J., & Torrubia, R. Sensation seeking and antisocial behaviour in a student sample. *Personality and Individual Differences*, 1985, *6*, 401–403.

Perkins, D. The treatment of sex offenders. In P. Feldman (Ed.), *Developments in the study of criminal behaviour* (Vol. 1). Chichester: Wiley, 1982, pp. 191–214.

Perkins, D. Psychological treatment of offenders in prison and the community. In T. Williams, E. Alves & J. Shapland (Eds.), *Options for the mentally abnormal offender.* (Issues in Criminological and Legal Psychology No. 6). Leicester: British Psychological Society, 1984, pp. 36–46.

Perkins, D. Sex offending: A psychological approach. In C. Hollin & K. Howells (Eds.), *Clinical approaches to criminal behaviour.* (Issues in Criminological and Legal Psychology No. 9). Leicester: British Psychological Society, 1986, pp. 56–66.

Perkins, D. Psychological treatment programmes for sex offenders. In B. J. McGurk, D. M. Thomton, & M. Williams (Eds.), *Applying psychology to imprisonment.* London: H.M.S.O., 1987, pp. 191–215.

Persky, H., O'Brien, C. P., Fine, E., Howard, W. J., Khan, M. A., & Beck, R. W. The effects of alcohol and smoking on testosterone function and aggression in chronic alcoholics. *American Journal of Psychiatry*, 1977, *134*, 621–625.

Persky, H., Smith, K. D., & Basu, G. K. Relation of psychological measures of aggression and hostility to testosterone production in man. *Psychosomatic Medicine*, 1971, *32*, 265–277.

Petrie, A., Collins, W., & Solomon, P. The tolerance for pain and for sensory deprivation. *American Journal of Psychology*, 1960, *73*, 80–90.

Petursson, H., & Gudjonsson, G. H. Psychiatric aspects of homicide. *Acta Psychiatrica Scandinavica*, 1981, *64*, 363–372.

Phillips, D. P. The deterrent effect of capital punishment: New evidence on the old controversy. *American Journal of Sociology*, 1980, *86*, 139–148.

Phillips, E. L. Achievement place: Token reinforcement procedures in a home-style rehabilitation setting for pre-delinquent boys. *Journal of Applied Behavior Analysis*, 1968, *1*, 213–223.

Phillpotts, G. J. O., & Lancucki, L. B. *Previous convictions, sentence and reconviction.* Home Office Research Study No. 53. London: H.M.S.O., 1979.

Pierson, G. R. The role of the HSPQ in the Greenhill Program. In R. B. Cattell & M. D. C. Cattell (Eds.), *Handbook for the H.S.P.Q.* Illinois: IPAT, 1969.

Pierson, G. R., & Kelly, R. F. Anxiety, extraversion, and personal idiosyncracy in delinquents. *Journal of Psychology*, 1963, 56, 441–445.(a)

Pierson, G. R., & Kelly, R. F. HSPQ norms in a state-wide delinquent population. *Journal of Psychology*, 1963, *56*, 185–192. (b)

Pierson, G. R., Moseley, J., & Olsen, M. The personality and character structure of the delinquent: Some social psychological implications. *Journal of Genetic Psychology*, 1967, *110*, 139–147.

Pitkanen-Pulkkinen, L. Long-term studies on the characteristics of aggressive and non-aggressive juveniles. In D. F. Brain & D. Benton (Eds.), *Multi-disciplinary approaches to aggression research.* Amsterdam: Elsevier-North Holland, 1981, pp. 225–243.

Plattner, W. Das Körperbauspektrum. *Zeitschrift fur die gesamte Neurologie und Psychiatrie*, 1938, *160*, 703–712.

Plomin, R., & DeFries, J. C. *Origins of individual differences in infancy.* London: Academic Press, 1985.

Plomin, R., DeFries, J. C., & McClearn, G. E. *Behavioural genetics: A primer.* San Francisco: Freeman, 1980.

Porges, S. W. Peripheral and neurochemical parallels of psychopathology: A psychophysiological model relating autonomic imbalance to hyperactivity, psychopathy and autism. In H. W. Reese (Ed.), Advances in child development and behaviour. New York: Academic Press, 1977, pp. 213–228.

Porteus, S. D. *Porteus Maze Test: Fifty years of application*. Palo Alto: Pacific Books, 1965.

Powell, G. E. Psychoticism and social deviancy in children. *Advances in Behaviour Research and Therapy*, 1977, *1*, 27–56.

Powell, G. E., & Stewart, R. A. The relationship of personality to antisocial and neurotic behaviours as observed by teachers. *Personality and Individual Differences*, 1983, *4*, 97–100.

Power, D. J. *Criminal law and psychiatry*. London: Kluwer Law, 1987.

Powers, E., & Witmer, H. *An experiment in the prevention of juvenile delinquency: The Cambridge-Somerville Youth Study*. New York: Columbia University Press, 1951.

Pratt, J. Diversion from the juvenile court. *British Journal of Criminology*, 1986, *26*, 212–233.

Preston, M. A. Intermediate treatment: A new approach to community care. In P. Feldman (Ed.), *Developments in the study of criminal behaviour: Vol. 1. The prevention and control of offending*. Chichester: Wiley, 1982, pp. 167–190.

Prins, H. *Offenders, deviants or patients? An introduction to the study of socio-forensic problems*. London: Tavistock, 1980.

Prins, H. *Dangerous behaviour, the law, and mental disorder*. London: Tavistock, 1986.

Prinz, R. J., Connor, P. A., & Wilson, C. C. Hyperactive and aggressive behaviour in childhood: Intertwined dimensions. *Journal of Abnormal Child Psychology*, 1981, *9*, 191–202.

Pulkkinen, L. Self-control and continuity from childhood to late adolescence. In P. B. Baltes & O. G. Brim (Eds.), *Life-span development and behaviour* (Vol. 4). New York: Academic Press, 1982, pp. 63–103.

Pulkkinen, L. The search for alternatives to aggression. In A. P. Goldstein & M. H. Segall (Eds.), *Aggression in global perspective*. New York: Pergamon Press, 1983, pp. 104–144.

Pulkkinen, L. A two-dimensional model as a framework for interindividual differences in social behaviour. In D. Saklofske & S. B. G. Eysenck (Eds.), *Individual differences in children and adolescents: International perspectives*. London: Hodder & Stoughton, 1988.

Pulkkinen, L. Delinquent development: Theoretical and empirical considerations. In M. Rutter (Ed.), *Risks and protective factors in psychosocial development*. In press.

Puser, E. Figural aftereffect as a personality correlate. *Proceedings of the 16th International Congress of Psychology*. Amsterdam: North Holland, 1960.

Qualls, C. B. *The prevention of sexual disorders*. New York: Plenum Press, 1978.

Quay, H. C. Psychopathic personality as pathological stimulation-seeking. *American Journal of Psychiatry*, 1965, *122*, 180–183.

Quay, H. C., & Parsons, L. *The differential behavioural classification of the juvenile offender*. Washington, D.C.: U.S. Bureau of Prisons, 1971.

Quinn, J. T., Harbison, J. J. M., & McAllister, H. An attempt to shape human penile responses. *Behaviour Research and Therapy*, 1970, *8*, 213–216.

Quinn, P. O., & Rapaport, J. L. Minor physical anomalies and neurologic status sin hyperactive boys. *Pediatrics*, 1974, *53*, 742–747.

Quinsey, V. L. The behavioral treatment of rapists and child molesters: An example of an institutional program. *Penetangishene Mental Health Center Research Report*, 1984, *1*, 1–40. (a)

Quinsey, V. L. Sexual aggression: Studies of offenders against women. In D. N. Weisstub

(Ed.), *Law and mental health: International Perspectives* (Vol. 1). Oxford: Pergamon Press, 1984 (b), pp. 84–121.

Quinsey, V. L. Men who have sex with children. In D. Weisstub (Ed.), *Law and mental health: International perspectives* (Vol. 2). New York: Pergamon Press, 1986, pp. 140–172.

Quinsey, V. L., Chaplin, T. C., & Upfold, D. Sexual arousal to nonsexual violence and sadomasochistic themes among rapists and non–sex-offenders. *Journal of Consulting and Clinical Psychology,* 1984, *52,* 651–657.

Rabkin, J. G. Criminal behaviour of discharged mental patients: A critical appraisal of the research. *Psychological Bulletin,* 1979, *86,* 1–27.

Rachman, S. Sexual fetishism: An experimental analog. *Psychological Record,* 1966, *16,* 293–296.

Rachman, S., & Hodgson, R. *Obsessions and compulsions.* Englewood Cliffs, N. J.: Prentice-Hall, 1980.

Rachman, S., & Teasedale, J. *Aversion therapy and behaviour disorder: An analysis.* London: Routledge, 1969.

Rachman, S. J., & Wilson, G. T. *The effects of psychological therapy.* London: Pergamon Press, 1980.

Rada, R. T. Alcoholism and the child molester. *Annals of the New York Academy of Sciences,* 1976, *273,* 492–496.

Rada, R. T., Laws, D. R., & Kellner, R. Plasma testosterone levels in the rapist. *Psychosomatic Medicine,* 1976, *38,* 257–268.

Rahman, A., & Husain, A. Personality and female criminals in Bangladesh. *Personality and Individual Differences,* 1984, *5,* 473–374.

Rahman, M. A., & Eysenck, S. B. G. Psychoticism and response to treatment in neurotic patients. *Behaviour Research and Therapy,* 1978, *16,* 183–189.

Raine, A., & Venables, P. Classical conditioning and socialization: A biosocial interaction. *Personality and Individual Differences,* 1981, *2,* 273–283.

Ramachandran, V. *An experimental study of the behaviour patterns of criminals and neurotics.* Unpublished Ph.D. thesis, University of Kerala, 1970.

Rapaport, J. L., & Quinn, P. O. Minor physical anomalies (stigmata) and early developmental deviation: A major biologic subgroup of hyperactive children. *International Journal of Mental Health,* 1975, *4,* 29–44.

Rapoport, R. *The community as doctor.* London: Tavistock, 1960.

Razinowicz, L. *Sexual offences.* London: Macmillan, 1957.

Razinowicz, L. The criminal in society. *Journal of the Royal Society of Arts,* 1964, *112,* 916–929.

Reckless, W. C., & Dinitz, S. *The prevention of juvenile delinquency: An experiment.* Columbus, Ohio: Ohio State University Press, 1972.

Redmond, D. E., Baulu, J., Murphy, D. L., Loriaux, D. L., & Zeigler, M. G. The effects of testosterone on plasma and platelet monoamine oxidas (MAO). *Psychosomatic Medicine,* 1976, *38,* 315–326.

Rees, L. Constitutional factors and abnormal behaviour. In H. J. Eysenck (Ed.), *Handbook of abnormal psychology.* London: Pitman, 1973, pp. 487–539.

Rees, L., & Eysenck, H. J. A factorial study of some morphological and psychological aspects of human constitution. *Journal of Mental Science,* 1945, *91,* 8–21.

Reichard, C. C., & Elder, T. S. The effects of caffeine on reaction time in hyperkinetic and normal children. *American Journal of Psychiatry,* 1977, *134,* 144–148.

Reichel, H. The intelligence–criminality relationship: A critical review (Suppl. 66). Stockholm: University of Stockholm, Department of Psychology, August 1987, pp. 5–47.

Reid, I. The development and maintenance of a behavioural regime in a secure youth treatment centre. In P. Feldman (Ed.), *Developments in the study of criminal be-*

haviour: Vol. 1. The prevention and control of offending. Chichester: Wiley, 1982, pp. 79–106.

Report of the Canadian Sentencing Commission. *Sentencing reform: A Canadian approach.* Ottawa, Canada: Canadian Government Publishing Centre, February, 1987.

Riley, D., & Shaw, M. *Parental supervision and juvenile delinquency.* Home Office Research Study No. 83. London: H.M.S.O., 1985.

Robertson, G., & Gunn, J. A ten-year follow-up of men discharged from Grendon Prison. *British Journal of Psychiatry*, 1987, *151*, pp. 674–678.

Robins, L. N. *Deviant children grown up.* Baltimore: Williams & Wilkins, 1966.

Robins, L. N. Follow-up studies of behaviour disorders in children. In H. C. Quay & J. S. Werry (Eds.), *Psychopathological disorders of childhood.* New York: Wiley, 1972, pp. 118–134.

Robins, L. Sturdy childhood predictors of adult antisocial behaviour: Replications from longitudinal studies. *Psychological Medicine*, 1978, *8*, 611–622.

Robins, L. N., & Ratcliff, K. S. Childhood conduct disorders and later arrest. In L. N. Robins, P. J. Clayton, & J. K. Wing (Eds.), *The social consequences of psychiatric illness.* New York: Brunner/Mazel, 1980, pp. 214–232.

Roff, J. D., & Wint, R. D. Childhood aggression and social adjustment as antecedents of delinquency. *Journal of Abnormal Child Psychology*, 1984, *12*, 111–126.

Romig, D. A. *Justice for our children.* Lexington, Mass: Heath, 1978.

Rooth, F. G. Indecent exposure and exhibitionism. *British Journal of Hospital Medicine*, *5*, 1971, 521–533.

Rooth, G. Exhibitionism—outside Europe and America. *Archives of Sexual Behaviour*, 1973, *2*, 351–362. (a)

Rooth, G. Exhibitionism, sexual violence and paedophilia. *British Journal of Psychiatry*, 1973, *122*, 705–710. (a)

Rosanoff, A. J., Handy, L. M., & Rosanoff, F. A. Criminality and delinquency in twins. *Journal of Criminal Law and Criminology*, 1934, *24*, 923–934. (b)

Rose, G., & Marshall, T. F. *Counselling and school social work: An experimental study.* London: Wiley, 1974.

Rose, R. J., & Ditto, W. B. A developmental-genetic analysis of common fears from early adolescence to early childhood. *Child Development*, 1983, *54*, 361–368.

Rose, R. M. Testosterone aggression and homosexuality: A review of the literature and implications for future research. In E. J. Sachar (Ed.), *Topics in psycho-criminology.* New York: Stratton, 1975, pp. 83–103.

Rosen, A., & Schalling, D. Probability learning in psychopathic and non-psychopathic criminals. *Journal of Experimental Research in Personality*, 1971, *5*, 191–198.

Rosen, G. D., Berrebi, A. S., Yutzey, D. A., & Denenberg, V. H. Prenatal testosterone causes shift of asymmetry in neonatal tail posture of the rat. *Developmental Brain Research*, 1983, *9*, 99–101.

Rosenberg, J. B., & Weller, G. M. Minor physical anomalies and academic performance in young school children. *Developmental Medicine and Child Neurology*, 1973, *15*, 131–135.

Ross, R. R., & Fabiano, E. A. *Time to think: A cognitive model of delinquency prevention and offender rehabilitation.* 1985. Johnson City, N.J.: Institute of Social Sciences and Arts, 1985.

Ross, R. R., & McKay, H. B. A study of institutional treatment programs. *International Journal of Offender Therapy and Comparative Criminology*, 1976, *20*, 167–173.

Ross, R. R., & Price, M. J. Behaviour modification in corrections: Autopsy before mortification. *International Journal of Criminology and Penology*, 1976, *4*, 305–315.

Rostan, L. *Cours elementaire d'hygiene.* Paris: 1828.

Rotenberg, M., & Nackshon, I. Impulsiveness and aggression among Israeli delinquents. *British Journal of Social and Clinical Psychology*, 1979, *18*, 59–63.

Rowe, D. C. Biometrical genetic models of self-reported delinquent behaviour: A twin study. *Behaviour Genetics*, 1983, *13*, 473–489.

Rowe, D. C., & Osgood, D. W. Heredity and sociological theories of delinquency: A reconsideration. *American Sociological Review*, 1984, *49*, 526–540.

Royce, J. R., & Powell, A. *Theory of personality and individual differences: Factors, systems, and processes*. Englewood Cliffs, N.J.: Prentice-Hall, 1983.

Rubin, R. T. The neuroendocrinology and neurochemistry of antisocial behaviour. In S. A. Mednick, T. E. Moffitt, & S. A. Stack (Eds.), *The causes of crime*. Cambridge: Cambridge University Press, 1987, pp. 239–262.

Rushton, J. P. Socialization and the altruistic behaviour of children. *Psychological Bulletin*, 1976, *83*, 898–913.

Rushton, J. P. *Altruism, socialization and society*. Englewood Cliffs, N.J.: Prentice-Hall, 1980.

Rushton, J. P. Differential K theory and race differences in E and N. *Personality and Individual Differences*, 1985, *6*, 769–770. (a)

Rushton, J. P. Differential K theory: The sociobiology of individual and group differences. *Personality and Individual Differences*, 1985, *56*, 441–452. (b)

Rushton, P., & Bogaert, A. Race differences in sexual behaviour: Testing an evolutionary hypothesis. *Journal of Research in Personality*, in press.

Rushton, J. F., & Chrisjohn, R. D. Extraversion, neuroticism, psychoticism and self-reported delinquency: Evidence from eight separate samples. *Personality and Individual Differences*, 1981, *2*, 11–20.

Rushton, J. P., Fulker, D. W., Neale, M. C., Blizard, R. A., & Eysenck, H. J. Altruism and genetics. *Acta Genetica Medicae et Gamellologiae* 1984, *33*, 265–271.

Rushton, J. P., Fulker, D. W., Neale, M. C., Nias, D., & Eysenck, H. J. Altruism and aggression: The heritability of individual differences. *Journal of Personality and Social Psychology*, 1986, *50*, 1192–1198.

Russell, D. E. H. The prevalence and incidence of forcible rape and attempted rape of females. *Victimology*, 1982, *7*, 81–93.

Rutter, M., & Giller, H. *Juvenile delinquency: Trends and perspectives*. Penguin, Middlesex 1983.

Rutter, M., & Madge, N. *Cycles of disadvantage: A review of research*. London: Heinemann, 1976.

Saklofske, D. H., McKerracher, D. W., & Eysenck, S. B. G. Eysenck's Theory of Criminality: The C scale as a measure of antisocial behaviour. *Psychological Reports*, 1978, *43*, 683–686.

Sanocki, W. The use of Eysenck's inventory for testing young prisoners. *Przeglad Penitencjarny* (Warszawa), 1969, *7*, 53–68.

Sapsford, R. *Life sentence prisoners: Reaction, response and change*. Milton Keynes: Open University Press, 1983.

Sapstead, D. Leader of gang raid on vicarage receives a 14-year jail term. *The Times*, 4 February 1987, p. 3.

Sarri, R., & Bradley, P. W. Juvenile aid panels: An alternative to juvenile court processing in South Australia. *Crime and Delinquency*, 1980 *26*, 42–62.

Satinder, K. P. Arousal explains difference in avoidance learning of genetically selected rat strains. *Journal of Comparative and Physiological Psychology*, 1977, *91*, 1326–1336.

Satterfield, J. H. The hyperactive child syndrome: A precursor of adult psychopathy? In R. D. Hare & D. Schalling (Eds.), *Psychopathic behaviour: Approaches to research*. Chichester: Wiley, 1978, pp. 329–346.

Satterfield, J. H. Childhood diagnostic and neurophysiological predictors of teenage arrest rates:‘ An eight-year prospective study. In S. A. Mednick, T. E., Moffitt, & S. A. Stack (Eds.), *The causes of crime*. Cambridge: Cambridge University Press, 1987, pp. 146–167.

Satterfield, J. H., & Dawson, M. E. Electrodermal correlates of hyperactivity in children. *Psychophysiology*, 1971, *8*, 191–197.

Saunders, G. R., & Davies, M. B. The validity of the Jesness Inventory with British delinquents. *British Journal of Social and Clinical Psychology*, 1976, *15*, 33–39.

Sayed, Z. A., Lewis, S. A., & Brittain, R. P. An electroencephalographic and psychiatric study of thirty-two insane murderers. *British Journal of Psychiatry*, 1969, *115*, 1115–1124.

Schalling, D. Tolerance for experimentally induced pain as related to personality. *Scandinavian Journal of Psychology*, 1971, *12*, 271–281.

Schalling, D. Psychopathy-related personality variables and the psychophysiology of socialization. In R. D. Hare & D. Schalling (Eds.), *Psychopathic behaviour: Approaches to research*. Chichester: Wiley, 1978, pp. 85–106.

Schalling, D. Personality correlates of plasma testosterone levels in young delinquents: An example of person-situation interaction? In S. A. Mednick, T. E. Moffitt, & S. A. Stack (Eds.), *The causes of crime*. Cambridge: Cambridge University Press, 1987, pp. 283–291.

Schalling, D., Edman, G., Asberg, M., & Oreland, L. Platelet MAO activity associated with extraversion-related traits. *Personality and Individual Differences*, in press.

Schalling, D., & Levander, S. Ratings of anxiety-proneness and responses to electrical pain stimulation. *Scandinavian Journal of Psychology*, 1964, *5*, 1–19.

Schalling, D., Lidberg, L., Levander, S. E., & Dahlin, Y. Spontaneous autonomic activity as related to psychopathy. *Biological Psychology*, 1973, *1*, 83–97.

Schalling, D., & Rosen, A. S. A note on Porteus Q-score and the construct of psychopathy. Stockholm: Report from the Psychological Laboratories No. 307, 1970.

Schlegel, W. S. Genetic foundations of social behaviour. *Personality and Individual Differences*, 1983, *4*, 483–490.

Schmid, N. *Banken zwischen Legalitat und Kriminalitat*. Heidelberg: Kriminalistik Verlag, 1980.

Schmidt, G. Foreword. In J. Bancroft, *Human sexuality and its problems*. London: Churchill Livingstone, 1983.

Schnackenberg, R. C. Caffeine therapy for hyperkinetic children. *Current Psychiatric Therapies*, 1975, 39,

Schulsinger, F. Psychopathy, heredity and environment. *International Journal of Mental Health*, 1972, *1*, 190–206.

Schulsinger, F. Psychopathy: Heredity and environment. In S. Mednick & K. O. Christiansen (Eds.), *Biosocial bases of criminal behaviour*. New York: Gardner Press, 1977, pp. 109–125.

Schwab, G. Über die Beziehungen der Körperlichen Konstitution zum Verbrechertyp. Quoted by Hurwitz and Christiansen, 1983.

Schweinhart, L. J., & Weikart, D. P. Young children grow up: The effects of the preschool programme on youths through age 15 (Monogr. High/Scope Educ. Res. Found. No. 7). Ypsilanti, Mich. High/Scope Press, 1980.

Schwenkmezger, P. *Risikoverhalten und Risikobereitschaft*. Weinheim: Beltz, 1977.

Schwenkmetzger, P. Risikoverhalten, Risikobereitschaft und Delinquenz: Theoretische Grundlagen und Differentialdiagnostische Untersuchungen. *Zeitschrift fur Differentielle und Diagnostische Psychologie*, 1983, *4*, 223–239.

Scott, J. P., & Fuller, J. L. *Genetics and the social behaviour of the dog*. Chicago: University of Chicago Press, 1965.

Sechrest, L., & Rosenblatt, A. Research methods. In H. C. Quay (Ed.), *Handbook of juvenile delinquency*. New York: Wiley, 1987, pp. 417–450.

Sechrest, L., White, S. O., & Brown, E. D. *The rehabilitation of criminal offenders: Problems and prospects*. Washington: National Academy of Sciences, 1979.

Seltzer, C. C. The relationship between the masculine component and personality. *American Journal of Physical Anthropology*, 1945, *3*, 33–38.

Seltzer, C. C. Body disproportions and dominant personality traits. *Psychosomatic Medicine*, 1946, *8*, 75–97.

Seltzer, C. C. A comparative study of the morphological characteristics of delinquents and non-delinquents. In S. Glueck & E. Glueck (Eds.), *Unraveling juvenile delinquency*. New York: Commonwealth Fund, 1950, pp. 307–350.

Seltzer, C. C. Constitutional aspects of juvenile delinquency. In *Cold Spring Harbor Symposia on Quantitative Biology*, 1951, *15*, 361–372.

Sendi, I. B., & Blomgren, P. G. A comparative study of predictive criteria in the predisposition of homicidal adolescents. *American Journal of Psychiatry*, 1975, *132*, 423–433.

Serber, M. Shame and aversion therapy. *Journal of Behaviour Therapy and Experimental Psychology*, 1970, *1*, 213–215.

Sethna, E. R., & Harrington, J. A. Evaluation of group psychotherapy. *British Journal of Psychotherapy*, 1971, *118*, 641–658.

Shanmugan, T. E. A study of personality patterns among delinquents. *Indian Journal of Criminology*, 1975, *3*, 7–10.

Shanmugan, T. E. Personality factors underlying drug abuse among college students. *Psychological Studies*, 1979, *24*, 24–35.

Shannon, L. W. *Assessing the relationship of adult criminal careers to juvenile careers*. Iowa City, Iowa: Iowa Urban Community Research Center, 1981.

Shapland, J. M. Self-reported delinquency in boys aged 11 to 14. *British Journal of Criminology*, 1978, *18*, 255–266.

Shaw, C. R., & McKay, H. D. *Juvenile delinquency and urban areas*. Chicago: University of Chicago Press, 1942.

Shaw, C. R., Zorbaugh, F. M., McKay, H. D., & Cottrell, L. S. *Delinquency areas: A study of the geographic distribution of school truants, juvenile delinquents, and adult offenders in Chicago*. Chicago: University of Chicago Press, 1929.

Shaw, M. J. *Social work in prison*. Home Office Research Study No. 22. London: H.M.S.O., 1974.

Shekin, W. O., Davis, L. G., Byland, D. B., Brunngraber, E., Fikes, A., & Lanham, F. Platelet MAO in children with attention deficit disorder and hyperactivity: A pilot study. *American Journal of Psychiatry*, 1982, *139*, 936–938.

Sheldon, W. H., Hartl, E. M., & McDermott, E. *Varieties of delinquent youth*. New York: Harper, 1949.

Sheldon, W. H., & Stevens, S. S. *The varieties of human physique*. New York: Harper, 1940.

Sheldon, W. H., & Stevens, S. S. *The varieties of temperament*. New York: Harper, 1942.

Shinnar, S., & Shinnar, R. The effect of the criminal justice system on the control of crime: A quantitative approach. *Law and Society Review*, 1975, *9*, 581–612.

Short, J. F., & Nye, F. I. Extent of unrecorded juvenile delinquency: Tentative conclusions. *Journal of Criminal Law and Criminology*, 1958, *49*, 296–302.

Shouse, M. W., & Lubar, J. F. Physiological basis of hyperkinesis treated with methylphenidate. *Pediatrics*, 1978, *62*, 343–351.

Shuey, A. M. *The testing of Negro intelligence* (2nd Ed.). New York: Social Science Press, 1966.

Siddle, D. A. Electrodermal activity and psychopathy. In S. A. Mednick & K. O. Christiansen (Eds.), *Biological bases of criminal behaviour.* New York: Gardner, 1977, pp. 199–211.

Siddle, D. A., Mednick, S. A., Nicol, A. R., & Foggitt, R. H. Skin conductance recovery in antisocial adolescents. *British Journal of Social and Clinical Psychology*, 1976, *15*, 425–428.

Sigal, J. J., & Weinfeld, M. Control of aggression in adult children of survivors of the Nazi persecution. *Journal of Abnormal Psychology*, 1985, *94*, 556–564.

Silverman, G. Recent advances in evaluation methods. In M. W. Klein & K. S. Teilmann (Eds.), *Handbook of criminal justice evaluation.* London: Sage, 1980, pp. 53–62.

Sills, F. D. A factor analysis of somatotypes and their relationship to achievements in motor skills. *Research Quarterly*, 1950, *21*, 424–437.

Silva, F., Martorell, C., & Clemente, A. Socialization and personality: Study through questionnaires in a preadult Spanish population. *Personality and Individual Differences*, 1986, *7*, 355–372.

Silva, F., Martorell, C., & Salvador, A. Assessment of antisocial behaviour in children and adolescents: New data with the ASB scale. *Personality and Individual Differences*, 1987, *8*, 977–978.

Silver, L. B., Dublin, C. C., & Lourie, R. S. Does violence breed violence? Contributions from a study of the child abuse syndrome. *American Journal of Psychiatry*, 1969, *126*, 404–407.

Simon, R. J., & Benson, M. Evaluating changes in female criminality. In M. W. Klein & K. S. Teilmann (Eds.), *Handbook of criminal justice evaluation.* London: Sage, 1980, pp. 549–571.

Sinclair, I.A.C. *Hostels for probationers.* Home Office Research Study No. 6. London: H.M.S.O., 1971.

Sinclair, I.A.C. The influence of wardens and matrons on probation hostels: A study of a quasi-family institution. In J. Tizard, I. A. C. Sinclair & R. V. G. Clarke (Eds.), *Varieties of residential experience.* London: Routledge & Kegan Paul, 1975.

Sinclair, I., & Chapman, B. A typological and dimensional study of a sample of prisoners. *British Journal of Criminology*, 1973, *13*, 341–353.

Sinclair, I. A. C., & Clark, R. V. G. Acting-out behaviour and its significance for the residential treatment of delinquents. *Journal of Child Psychology and Psychiatry*, 1973, *14*, 283–291.

Sinclair, I. & Clarke, R. Predicting, treating, and explaining delinquency: The lessons from research on institutions. In P. Feldman (Ed), *Developments in the studies of criminal behaviour: Vol. 1. The prevention and control of offending.* Chichester: Wiley, 1982, pp. 51–78.

Sinclair, I. A. C., Shaw, M. J., & Troop, J. The relationship between introversion and response to casework in a prison setting. *British Journal of Social and Clinical Psychology*, 1974, *13*, 57–60.

Singh, A. Reliability and validity of self-reported delinquency studies: A review. *Psychological Reports*, 1979, *44*, 987–993.

Singh, A. Personality of female truants. *Child Psychiatry Quarterly*, 1980, *19*, 60–66. (a)

Singh, A. A study of the personality and adjustment of female juvenile delinquents. *Child Psychiatry Quarterly*, 1980, *19*, 52–59. (b)

Singh, U. P., & Aktar, S. N. Criminals and non-criminals: A comparative study of their personality. *Indian Journal of Psychology*, 1971, *46*, 257–263.

Skinner, W. F. Delinquency, crime, and development: A case study of Iceland. *Journal of Research in Crime and Delinquency*, 1986, *23*, 268–294.

Smith, C. Concordance in twins: Methods and interpretation. *American Journal of Human Genetics*, 1974, *26*, 454–466.

Smith, C. S., Farrant, M. R., & Merchant, H. J. *The Wincroft Youth Project: A social work programme in a slum area.* London: Tavistock, 1972.

Smith, D. E. Relationships between the Eysenck and Jesness Personality Inventories. *British Journal of Criminology*, 1974, *14*, 376–384.

Smith, D. E., & Smith, D. D. Eysenck's psychoticism scale and reconviction. *British Journal of Criminology*, 1977, *17*, 387–388.

Smith, D. W. The relation between ratio indices of physique and selected scales of the Minnesota Multiphasic Personality Inventory. *Journal of Psychology*, 1957, *43*, 325–331.

Smith, D. W. *Recognizable patterns of human malformation.* Philadelphia: W. B. Saunders, 1970.

Smith, H. C. Psychometric checks on hypotheses derived from Sheldon's work on physique and temperament. *Journal of Personality*, 1949, *17*, 310–320.

Smith, J. C., & Hogan, B. *Criminal law* (5th Ed.). London: Butterworth, 1986.

Smith, S. R. Voyeurism: A review of the literature. *Archives of Sexual Behaviour*, 1976, *5*, 585–608.

Smukler, A. J., & Schiebel, D. Personality characteristics of exhibitionists. *Diseases of the Nervous System*, 1975, *36*, 600–603.

Snow, R. E., Kyllonen, P. C., & Marshalek, B. The typography of ability and learning correlations. In R. J. Sternberg (Ed.), *Advances in the psychology of human intelligence* (Vol. 2). London: Erlbaum, 1984, pp. 47–103.

Soloff, P. H. Seclusion and restraint. In J. R. Lion & W. H. Reid (Eds.), *Assaults within psychiatric facilities.* New York: Grune & Stratton, 1983.

Solomon, R. L., Turner, L. H., & Lessac, M. S. Some effects of delay of punishment on resistance to temptation in dogs. *Journal of Personality and Social Psychology*, 1968, *8*, 233–236.

Soothill, K. Is treatment necessary? The analysis of long-term change without specific intervention. In P. Pratt (Ed.), *Sexual assessment: Issues and radical alternatives* (Issues in Criminological and Legal Psychology, No. 8). Leicester: British Psychological Society, 1986, pp. 39–47.

Soothill, K. L., & Gibbens, T. C. N. Recidivism of sexual offenders: A re-appraisal. *British Journal of Criminology*, 1978, *18*, 267–276.

Soothill, K. L., Way, C. K., & Gibbens, T. C. N. Rape acquittals. *Modern Law Review*, 1980, *43*, 159–172.

Sorrentino, A. *Organizing against crime.* New York: Human Sciences Press, 1977.

Spengler, A. Manifest sadomasochism of males: Results of an empirical study. *Archives of Sexual Behavior*, 1977, *6*, 441–456.

Sperry, R. Some effects of disconnecting the cerebral hemispheres. *Science*, 1982, *217*, 1223–1226.

Spring, C., Greenberg, L., Scott, J., & Hopwood, J. Electrodermal activity in hyperactive boys who are methylphenidate responders. *Psychophysiology*, 1974, *11*, 436–442.

Stanley, S., & Baginsky, M. *Alternatives to prison: An examination of non-custodial sentencing of offenders.* London: Peter Owen, 1984.

Stanton, A. M. *When mothers go to jail.* Massachusetts, Toronto: Lexington Books, 1980.

Steg, J. P., & Rapaport, J. L. Minor physical anomalies in normal, neurotic, learning-disabled and severely disturbed children. *Journal of Autism and Childhood Schizophrenia*, 1975, *5*, 299–307.

Steiner, B. W. (Ed.). *Transsexualism and gender identity.* Springfield: Charles C Thomas, 1984.

Steiner, B. W., Langevin, R., & Sanders, R. M. Crosschecking, erotic preference, and aggression: A comparison of male transvestites and transsexuals. In R. Langevin

(Ed.), *Erotic preference, gender identity, and aggression in men: New research studies*. London: Lawrence Erlbaum, 1985, pp. 261–275.

Steller, M., & Hunze, D. Zur Selbstbeschreibung von Delinquenten im Freiburger Persönlichkeitsinventar (FPI)–Eine Sekundäranalyse empirischer Untersuchunge. *Zeitschrift fur Differentielle und Diagnostische Psychologie*, 1984, *5*, 87–110.

Stelmack, R. M. The psychophysiology of extraversion and neuroticism. In J. J. Eysenck (Ed.), *A model for personality*. New York: Springer, 1981, pp. 38–64.

Stevenson, I., & Wolpe, J. Recovery from sexual deviation through overcoming non-sexual neurotic responses. *American Journal of Psychiatry*, 1960, *116*, 737–742.

Stewart, M. A. Hyperactive children. *Scientific American*, 1970, *223*, 94–98.

Still, G. F. Some abnormal conditions in children. *Lancet*, 1902, *1*, 1008–1012, 1077–1082, 1163–1168.

Stott, D. H. *The social attitudes of children*. London: University of London Press, 1971.

Stott, D. H., Marston, N.C., & Neill, S. J. *Taxonomy of behaviour disturbance*. London: University of London Press, 1975.

Strelau, S., & Eysenck, H. J. *Personality dimensions and arousal*. London: Plenum Press, 1987.

Stumpfl, F. *Die Ursprünge des Verbrechens: Dargestellt am Lebenslauf von Zwillingen*. Leipzig: Georg Thieme, 1936.

Stumphauzer, J. S. *Behaviour therapy with delinquents*. Springfield, Ill.: Charles C Thomas, 1973.

Stumphauzer, J. S. *Behaviour modification principles: An introduction and training manual*. Venice, Calif.: Behaviormetrics, 1977.

Stumphauzer, J. S. *Progress in behaviour therapy with delinquents*. Springfield, Ill.: Charles C Thomas, 1979.

Stumphauzer, J. S. *Helping delinquents change: A treatment manual of social learning approaches*. New York: Haworth Press, 1986.

Stumphauzer, J. S., Aiken, T. W., & Veloz, E. V. East side story: Behavioural analysis of a high juvenile crime community. *Behavioral Disorders*, 1977, *2*, 76–84.

Sturup, G. K. Castration: The total treatment. In H. L. Resnik & M. E. Wolfgang (Eds.), *Sexual behaviour: Social, clinical and legal aspects*. Boston: Little, Brown, 1972.

Sugmati, S. *Psychiatric studies of the criminal by the twin method: Twin studies I*. Japanese Society for the Promotion of Scientific Research, 1954, 137.

Sutherland, E. H. Mental efficiency and crime. In K. Young (Ed.), *Social attitudes*. New York: Holt, 1931, pp. 357–375.

Sutherland, E. H., & Cressey, D. R. *Criminology*. New York: Harcourt Brace Jovanovich, 1978.

Sutker, F. Vicarious conditioning and sociopathy. *Journal of Abnormal Psychology*, 1970, *76*, 380–386.

Sykes, G. The pains of imprisonment. In N. Johnston, L. Savitz, & M. E. Wolfgang (Eds.), *The sociology of punishment and correction* (2nd ed.). New York: Wiley, 1962, pp. 131–137.

Symposium on Current Death Penalty Issues. *Journal of Criminal Law and Criminology*, 1983, *74*, 659–1101.

Tanner, J. M. *The physique of the olympic athlete*. London: Allen & Unwin, 1964.

Tarter, R. E., Alterman, A. I., & Edwards, K. L. Alcoholic denial: A biophysiological interpretation. *Journal of Studies on Alcohol*, 1984, *45*, 214–218.

Taylor, I., Walton, P., & Young, J. *The new criminology*. London: Routledge & Kegan Paul, 1973.

Taylor, P., & Gunn, J. Risk of violence among psychotic men. *British Medical Journal*, 1984, *288*, 1945–1949.

Taylor, T., & Watt, D. C. The relation of deviant symptoms and behaviour in a normal population to subsequent delinquency and maladjustment. *Psychological Medicine*, 1977, *7*, 163–169.

Tennent, G., Bancroft, J., & Cass, J. The control of deviant sexual behaviour by drugs: A double-blind controlled study of benpeidol, chlorpromazine and placebo. *Archives of Sexual Behaviour*, 1974, *3*, 261–271.

Teplin, L. The criminalization of the mentally ill: Speculation in search of data. *Psychological Bulletin*, 1983, *94*, 54–67.

Teplin, L. Criminalizing mental disorder: The comparative arrest rate of the mentally ill. *American Psychologist*, 1984, *39*, 794–803.

Teplin, L. A. (Ed.). *Mental health and criminal justice*. Beverley Hills: Sage, 1984.

Thorne, G. L. Sensation seeking scale with deviant population. *Journal of Consulting and Clinical Psychology*, 1971, *37*, 106–110.

Thornhill, R., & Thornhill, N. W. Human rape: An evolutionary analysis. *Ethology and Sociobiology*, 1983, *4*, 137–173.

Thornton, D. Treatment effects on recidivism: A reappraisal of the "nothing works" doctrine. In B. J. McGurk, D. M. Thornton, & M. Williams (Eds.), *Applying psychology to imprisonment*. London: H.M.S.O., 1987, pp. 181–189.

Thorpe, J. G., Schmidt, E., Brown, P., & Castell, D. Aversion-relief therapy: A new method for general application. *Behaviour Research and Therapy*, 1964, *2*, 71–82.

Tienari, P. *Psychiatric illnesses in identical twins*. Copenhagen: Munksgaard, 1963.

Tjaden, P. G., & Tjaden, C. D. Differential treatment of the female felon: Myth or reality. In M. Q. Warren (Ed.), *Comparing female and male offenders*. Beverly Hills: Sage, 1981, pp. 73–88.

Toby, J. An evaluation of early identification and intensive treatment programs for predelinquents. *Social Problems*, 1965, *13*, 160–175.

Toch, H., & Adams, K. Pathology and disruptiveness among prison inmates. *Journal of Research in Crime and Delinquency*, 1986, *23*, 7–21.

Torgersen, S. The nature and origin of common phobic fears. *British Journal of Psychiatry*, 1979, *134*, 343–351.

Torpy, D., & Tomison, A. Sex offenders and cyproterone acetate—a review of clinical care. *Medicine, Science and the Law*, 1986, *26*, 279–282.

Tucker, D. M., Stensile, C. E., Roth, R. S., & Shearer, S. L. Right frontal lobe activation and right hemisphere performance. *Archives of General Psychiatry*, 1981, *38*, 2–9.

Tutt, N. *Care or custody: Community homes and the treatment of delinquency*. London: Darton, Longman & Todd, 1974.

Tutt, N., & Giller, H. Police cautioning of juveniles: The practice of diversity. *Criminal Law Review*, September, 1983, 587–595.

Vando, A. *A personality dimension related to pain tolerance*. Unpublished Ph.D. dissertation, Columbia University, 1969.

van Knorring, L., Oreland, L., Haggendal, H., Magnusson, T., Almay, B., & Johansson, F. Relationship between platelet MAO activity and concentrations of 5-HIAA and HVA in cerebrospinal fluid in chronic pain patients. *Journal of Neural Transmitters*, 1984, *66*, 37–46.

Venables, D. Progress in psychophysiology: Some applications in a field of abnormal psychology. In P. Venables & M. J. Christie (Eds.), *Research in psychophysiology*. London: Wiley, 1975, pp. 94–116.

Venables, P. H. Autonomic nervous system factors in criminal behaviour. In S. A. Mednick, T. E. Moffitt, & S. A. Stack (Eds.), *The causes of crime*. Cambridge: Cambridge University Press, 1987, pp. 110–136.

Venables, P. H., & Raine, A. Biological theory. In B. McGurk, D. Thornton, & M. William (Eds.), *Applying psychology to imprisonment.* London: H.M.S.O., 1987, pp. 3–23.

Vetter, H. J., & Silverman, I. J. *The nature of crime.* Philadelphia: W. B. Saunders, 1978.

Virkkunen, M. Metabolic dysfunctions among habitually violent offenders: Reactive hypoglycemia and cholesterol levels. In S. A. Mednick, T. E. Moffitt, & S. A. Stack (Eds.), *The causes of crime.* Cambridge: Cambridge University Press, 1987, pp. 292–311.

Volavka, J. Electroencephalogram among criminals. In S. A. Mednick, T. E. Moffitt, & S. A. Stack (Eds.), *The causes of crime.* Cambridge: Cambridge University Press, 1987, pp. 137–145.

Voss, H. Differential association and reported delinquent behaviour: A replication. *Social Problems,* 1964, *12,* 78–85.

Waldrop, M. F., Bell, R. Q., & Goering, J. D. Minor physical anomalies and inhibited behaviour in elementary school girls. *Journal of Child Psychology and Psychiatry,* 1976, *17,* 113–122.

Waldrop, M. F., Bell, R. Q., McLaughlin, B., & Halverson, C. F. Newborn minor physical anomalies predict short attention span, peer aggression, and impulsivity at age 3. *Science,* 1978, *199,* 563–564.

Waldrop, M. F., & Goering, J. D. Hyperactivity and minor anomalies in elementary school children. *American Journal of Orthopsychiatry,* 1971, *41,* 602–607.

Waldrop, M. F., & Halverson, C. F. Minor physical anomalies and hyperactive behaviour in young children. In J. Hellmuth (Ed.), *Exceptional infant: Studies in abnormalities* (Vol. 2). New York: Brunner/Mazel, 1971, pp. 343–380.

Waldrop, M. F., Pederson, F. A., & Bell, R. Q. Minor physical anomalies and behaviour in preschool children. *Child Development,* 1968, *39,* 391–400.

Walker, N. *Punishment, danger and stigma.* Oxford: Blackwell, 1980.

Walker, N., Farrington, D. P., & Tucker, G. Reconviction rates of adult males after different sentences. *British Journal of Criminology,* 1981, *21,* 357–360.

Walmsley, R. Recorded incidence and sentencing practices for sexual offences. In M. Craft & A. Craft (Eds.), *Mentally abnormal offenders.* London: Bailliere Tindall, 1984.

Walmsley, R. *Criminology of sex offending.* Paper presented at the conference "The State of Forensic Psychiatry," held at the Royal Institute of British Architects, London, October, 1986.

Walmsley, R., & White, K. *Sexual offences, consent and sentencing.* Home Office Research Study No. 54. London: H.M.S.O., 1979.

Walters, G. C., & Grusec, J. E. *Punishment.* San Francisco: Freeman, 1977.

Wankowski, J. A. *Temperament, motivation and academic achievement.* Birmingham Educational Survey and Counselling Unit, 1973.

Wanlass, R. L., Kilmann, P. R., Bella, B. S., & Tarnowski, K. J. Effects of sex education on sexual guilt, anxiety, and attitudes: A comparison of instruction formats. *Archives of Sexual Behaviour,* 1983, *12,* 487–502.

Wardell, D., & Yeudall, L. T. A multidimensional approach to criminal disorders: The assessment of impulsivity and its relation to crime. *Advances in Behaviour Research and Therapy,* 1980, *2,* 159–177.

Warr, M. The accuracy of public beliefs about crime. *Criminology,* 1982, *20,* 185–204.

Wassan, A. S. Stimulus-seeking, perceived school environment and school misbehaviour. *Adolescence,* 1980, *59,* 603–608.

Watts, F. N., Powell, G. E., & Austin, S. V. The modification of abnormal beliefs. *British Journal of Medical Psychology,* 1973, *46,* 359–363.

Weeks, H. A. *Youthful offenders at Highfields*. Ann Arbor, Mich.: University of Michigan Press, 1958.

Weiner, I. B. On incest: A survey. *Exerpta Criminologica*, 1964, *4*, 137–155.

Weis, J. (1980) *The status of self-report measures*. In M. Klein & K. S. Teillmann (Eds.). *Handbook of Criminal Justice Evaluation*. London: Sage Publications, pp. 473–488.

Weiss, B., Minde, K., Werry, J. S., Douglas, V., & Nemeth, R. Studies on the hyperactive child, *Archives of General Psychiatry*, 1971, *24*, 409–414.

Weiss, G., & Hechtman, L. T. *Hyperactive children grown up: Empirical findings and theoretical considerations*. New York: Guilford Press, 1986.

Weiss, G., Hechtman, L., & Perlman, T. Hyperactives as young adults: Schools, employer, and self-rating scales obtained during 10-year follow-up evaluation. *American Journal of Orthopsychiatry*, 1978, *48*, 438–445.

Weller, M. P., & Weller, B. Crime and psychopathology. *British Medical Journal*, 1986, *292*, 55–56.

Werff, C., van der. Recidivism and special deterrence. *British Journal of Criminology*, 1981, *21*, 136–147.

West, D. J. *The habitual prisoner*. London: Macmillan, 1963.

West, D. J. *The young offender*. New York: International Universities Press, 1967.

West, D. J. *Delinquency: Its roots, careers and prospects*. London: Heinemann, 1982.

West, D. J. Homosexuality and lesbianism. *British Journal of Psychiatry*, 1983, *143*, 221–226.

West, D. J. *Sexual crimes and confrontations: A study of victims and offenders*. Brookfield, Gower, 1987.

West, D. J., & Farrington, D. P. *Who becomes delinquent*. London: Heinemann, 1973.

West, D. J., & Farrington, D. P. *The delinquent way of life*. London: Heinemann, 1977.

West, D. J., Roy, C., & Nicholas, F. L. *Understanding sexual attacks*. London: Heinemann, 1978.

Whelen, R. An experiment in predicting delinquency. *Journal of Criminal Law, Criminology and Police Science*, 1954, *45*, 432–441.

White, H. R., Labonvie, E. W., & Bates, M. E. The relationship between sensation seeking and delinquency: A longitudinal analysis. *Journal of Research in Crime and Delinquency*, 1985, *22*, 197–211.

Whitehill, M., DeMyer-Gapin, S., & Scott, T. J. Stimulation seeking in antisocial preadolescent children. *Journal of Abnormal Psychology*, 1976, *85*, 101–104.

Wiberg, A., Gottfries, C., & Oreland, L. Low platelet monoamine oxidase activity in human alcoholics. *Medical Biology*, 1977, *55*, 181–186.

Wickramasekera, I. A technique for controlling a certain type of sexual exhibitionism. *Psychotherapy, Theory, Research and Practice*, 1972, *9*, 207.

Widom, C. S. Juvenile delinquency. In W. J. Curran, A. L. McGarry, & S. A. Shah (Eds.), *Forensic psychiatry and psychology*. Philadelphia: F. A. Davis Co., 1986, pp. 263–283.

Williams, M. Aspects of the psychology of imprisonment. In S. McConville (Ed.), *The use of imprisonment*. London: Routledge & Kegan Paul, 1975.

Williams, M. Aspects of the psychology of imprisonment. In S. McConville (Ed.), *The use of imprisonment: Essays in the changing state of English penal policy*. London & Boston: Routledge & Kegan Paul, 1976, pp. 32–42.

Wilson, G. D. *The secrets of sexual fantasy*. London: Dent, 1978.

Wilson, G. D. & Cox, D. N. Personality of paedophile club members. *Personality and Individual Differences*, 1983, *4*, 323–329.

Wilson, G. D., & McLean, A. Personality, attitudes and humor preference of prisoners and controls. *Psychological Reports*, 1974, *34*, 847–854.

Wilson, J. Q., & Herrnstein, R. J. *Crime and human nature*. New York: Simon & Schuster, 1985.

Witmer, H. L., & Tufts, E. *The effectiveness of delinquency prevention programs*. Washington, D.C.: U.S. Government Printing Office, 1954.

Wittman, P. M. A proposed classification of fundamental psychotic behaviour reactions. *American Psychologist*, 1947, *2*, 420.

Wittman, P. M. The Elgin check list of fundamental psychotic behaviour reactions. *American Psychologist*, 1948, *3*, 280.

Wolfgang, M. E. Cesare Lombroso. In H. Mannheim (Ed.), *Pioneers in criminology*. London: Stevens, 1960, pp. 287–319.

Wolfgang, M. E., Figlio, R. M., & Sellin, T. *Delinquency in a birth cohort*. Chicago: University of Chicago Press, 1972.

Wolfgang, M. E., & Tracy, P. E. *The 1945 and 1958 birth cohorts: A comparison of the prevalence, incidence, and severity of delinquent behaviour*. Paper presented at the Harvard University conference on "Public Danger, Dangerous Offenders and the Criminal Justice System," Cambridge, Mass., 1982.

Wolman, B. B. *Dictionary of behavioral science*. New York: Van Nostrand Reinhold, 1973.

Woodman, D. Biochemistry of psychopathy. *Journal of Psychosomatic Research*, 1979, *23*, 342–360.

Woodrow, K. M., Friedman, G. D., Seigelaub, A. B., & Collen, M. F. Pain tolerance: Differences according to age, sex and race. *Psychosomatic Medicine*, 1977, *34*, 548–556.

Woodward, M. *Low intelligence and delinquency*. London: Institute for the Study and Treatment of Delinquency, 1955.

Wright, M. *Making good: Prisons, punishment and beyond*. London: Burnett Books, 1982.

Wright, N. *Understanding human behaviour* (Vol. 1). New York: Columbia House, 1974.

Wright, S. The interpretation of multivariate systems. In O. Kempthorne, T. A. Bancroft, J. W. Gowen., & J. L. Lisk (Eds.), Iowa: Iowa State College Press, 1954, pp. 11–33.

Wright, W. E., & Dixon, M. C. Community prevention and treatment of juvenile delinquency: A review of evaluation studies. *Journal of Research in Crime and Delinquency*, 1977, *14*, 35–67.

Wundt, W. M. *Grundzuge der Physiologischen Psychologie*. Leipzig: Englemann, 1874.

Yaffe, M. The assessment and treatment of paedophilia. In B. Taylor (Ed.), *Perspectives on paedophilia*. London: Batsford Academic & Educational Press, 1981, pp. 77–91.

Yarborough, J. C. *Evaluation of JOLT as a deterrence program*. Michigan: Michigan Department of Corrections, 1979.

Yochelson, S., & Samenow, S. E. *The criminal personality* (Vols. 1–3). New York: Aronson, 1976.

Yoshimasu, S. The criminological significance of the family in the light of the studies of criminal twins. *Acta Criminologicae et Medicinae Legalis Japonica*, 1961, *27*, pp. 114–123.

Yoshimasu, S. Psychopathie und Kriminalitat. *Acta Criminologicae et Medicinae Legalis Japonica*, 1941. Quoted by Mednick & Christiansen, 1977.

Zentall, S. S., Gohs, D. E., & Culatta, B. Language and activity of hyperactive and comparison children during listening tasks. *Exceptional Children*, 1983, *50*, 255–263.

Zuck, C. H. The plasticity of the physique from early adolescence through adulthood. *Journal of Genetic Psychology*, 1958, *92*, 205–214.

Zuckerman, M. Psychological measures of sexual arousal in the human. *Psychological Bulletin*, 1971, *75*, 297–329.

Zuckerman, M. *Sensation seeking: Beyond the optimal level of arousal*. Hillsdale, N.J.: Lawrence Erlbaum, 1979.

Zuckerman, M. (Ed.). *Biological bases of sensation seeking, impulsivity and anxiety.* Hillsdale, N.J.: Lawrence Erlbaum, 1983.

Zuckerman, M., Ballenger, J. C., & Post, R. M. The neurobiology of some dimensions of personality. *International Review of Neurobiology*, 1984 *25*, 391–436.

Zuckerman, M., Eysenck, S. B. G., & Eysenck, H. J. Sensation seeking in England and America: Cross-cultural, age and sex comparisons. *Journal of Consulting and Clinical Psychology*, 1978, *1*, 139–149.

Index